Sh Ch Hillpark Hamlet Photo: Robert Smith

Photo: Robert Smith

Contents

Introduction and Acknowledgements

Whilst browsing in a secondhand bookshop in the north of England, I came across one of the late H S Lloyd's books on Cocker Spaniels, in which was a section on judging the breed with explanatory photographs. This kindled an idea in my mind that, as I had taken part in Welsh Springer Spaniel seminars on judging, I could perhaps produce something similar in the form of a booklet.

After discussion with Robert Smith, my canine photographer friend of many years, the seed was sown, and with encouragement from him and my publishers, with some trepidation I accepted the challenge of writing a book on the breed.

I am indebted to Robert for his set of photographs on my method of judging, and to Christine Knowles and her beautiful bitch, Sh.Ch. Northoaks Sea Mist of Menstonia, who acted as 'models'. I am grateful to Donald and Zoe Short for their diagrams which complement this section.

Thanks also go to The Kennel Club for their help and co-operation during my visits to the Library. Further encouragement came from our veterinary surgeon and friend, Mike Dale, whose contribution on health is comprehensive, and yet makes easy reading, and he was happy for me to supplement his work with our own hints and experiences. Thanks are also due to Mike Stockman, MRCVS, Chairman of the Welsh Springer Spaniel Joint Health Group, for his contribution. I attended a seminar, where Geoff Skerritt, a specialist in Veterinary Neurology, was speaking on epilepsy and, as a result, I was delighted when he very kindly agreed to write an article on the subject for me.

The list of new Champions in the breed since 1992 was kindly compiled by Dave and Babs Harding.

Over the years, we have made many friends overseas, and their help with information and photographs is greatly appreciated. Wendy and Alan Gillespie of K9 Kards have been a great help to me in finding memorabilia and then dating it for me.

As we have a dual-purpose breed, I needed help on the working side, and I am grateful to Gordon Pattinson, Eileen Falconer and Julie Revill (boosted as always with a hot cup of tea), one from each decade of our Welsh Springer lives, who have given freely of their experience and knowledge to this section.

Without the tolerance, encouragement and help of my family and many friends, this venture would not have come to fruition. In particular, my husband, John, has had to listen endlessly as the book has progressed, has spurred me on when doubts were creeping in, and taken the photographs of trimming and whelping,(with the help of 'Sophie').

My son Robert's computer, on very lengthy and generous loan, had to become a friend rather than an enemy, and my frequent cries for help to my daughter and son-in-law, Gillian and Martin, were answered with speed and patience. Robert's technical knowledge of nutrition also helped me. Thankfully, they are all owners of our Hillpark Welsh Springers!

We retired from the general Championship Show circuit in 1992, and now go to the shows when we have the time and energy, for a day out, and to enjoy meeting our many friends. Writing this book has been a wonderful experience for me, and it has been fascinating to piece together the history and development of our beautiful breed. If I have helped readers by sharing our experiences with them, and widening the interest and enthusiasm for devotees of the breed, new and old, then I shall have achieved what I set out to do. A quick plea, however; I have tried to gather as many photographs as possible to show the Welsh Springer in all its different roles. Naturally, some of them, especially those in the chapters on history and development, are rather ancient and difficult to reproduce. Some of them are rather dark and grainy but, I hope, interesting for all that.

Forewords

As a young girl, Anne Walton was an enthusiastic member of the Pony Club, where she rode competitively, eventually going on to the Riding Club. Her time was also taken up as a Young Farmer, where she learned about stock judging which came in handy when she married a farmer, and showed Jersey cattle, pigs and Hampshire Down sheep. Her canine interests could have been initiated by the family pet cocker spaniel, which came from the famous 'Of Ware' kennels, but when she and her husband, John, had their first pedigree dog in 1965, it was a Welsh Springer Spaniel, and two years later, she joined the Parent Club of the breed – the Welsh Springer Spaniel Club.

Four years after joining, she became Secretary, a position which she held for 12 years, and for a number of those years she was Treasurer as well. She retired as Secretary in 1986 to take on the mantle of Chairman of the Club, a post she held until 1994. Anne was elected a Vice President in 1993 and President in 1996. In 1990, very deservedly she was elected an Honorary Life Member of the Club.

To date, Anne has served this Club in every possible capacity, and richly deserves her present position. She is also an Honorary Member of the Welsh Springer Spaniel Club of America. Since 1976, she has been a Kennel Club Breed Council Representative, and was elected as a member of The Kennel Club in 1986.

Anne's judging career shows how highly her opinion is sought. She judged at Crufts in 1994, the Welsh Springer Spaniel Club in 1980 and again in 1988. Her overseas appointments have included Finland, Sweden, the Netherlands and the USA Specialty. At Open show level, she has judged all the gundogs, as well as the Gundog Group and Best in Show.

Finally, Anne has bred some fine Welsh Springer Spaniels, making up eight Show Champions, which is an enviable record in anyone's book. She has exported puppies to Scandinavia, Germany, France, Switzerland, Canada, USA and Australia, where they have been shown with great success. Few people in dogs can claim recognition as an administrator, breeder, judge and now author. The breed is indeed fortunate to have Anne Walton as a lover of Welsh Springer Spaniels.

A E ('Ed') Simpson
Member of the Kennel Club General Committee
President of the South Eastern Welsh Springer Spaniel Club

The steady growth in the popularity of the Welsh Springer Spaniel during the first century of its official existence gives great satisfaction to those of us who are devoted to this endearing, useful and attractive breed. The existence of a world-wide circle of enthusiasts gives added pleasure. Strong links have been forged over the years, and there is great interest in the production of a variety of breed materials.

In over 30 years of ownership, Anne Walton's breed experience has been both wide and deep, encompassing four fields of expertise – as a caring breeder of quality dual-purpose stock, a highly successful show exhibitor, an efficient breed club administrator and a popular international championship show judge. No one is better suited to make a major contribution to the literature of our breed.

John Phillips
Chairman, Welsh Springer Spaniel Club

Dedication

The book is dedicated to Polly Garter of Doonebridge,
the start of it all.

chapter 1
History

Welsh Springers are the oldest spaniels in the group. True or false? Some will expect me to try to prove that our beautiful red and white spaniels have been here longer than any other breed of spaniel. I am not attempting to do this: merely to offer historical evidence, and to leave it to readers to come to their own conclusions.

Spaniels appear to have been in existence in Europe for centuries, some would say even back to the Stone Age, and there is speculation that they may have originated in Spain. In *Chambers' Encyclopaedia* Vol 1X SOU–VIT (1874) is this description:

Spa'niel, *a kind of dog, of which there are many breeds, differing considerably in size and other characters. None of the spaniels are large; some are amongst the smallest of dogs. Some are used for sporting purposes, others are merely kept as pets and companions. All of them are lively, playful, docile and affectionate to a high degree. The S. is ever petitioning for regard, and shews boundless joy on receiving marks of kind attention. The name S. is said to indicate the introduction of this kind of dog into England from Spain. In the days of falconry, spaniels were much used for starting the game.*

Springer, *a kind of dog, regarded as a variety of the Spaniel (q.v.). It is small, elegant, usually white, with red spots, black nose and palate, long pendant ears, and small head. Its aspect is very lively and its manners equally so. It is used by sportsmen for raising game in thick and thorny coverts. There are several breeds or sub-varieties.*

From a painting in the Van Dyck Gallery in the The Hermitage Museum, St Petersburg.

There is a suggestion that red and white spaniels were in Wales in the 6th century, and in his prologue to the Wife of Bath's Tale in *The Canterbury Tales*, Chaucer (born in 1328) wrote, 'For as a Spaynel she wol on him lepe' – familiar to owners of Welsh Springers!

Shakespeare and Edmund Spencer in the 16th century mentioned spaniels; red and white dogs of spaniel type can be seen in many old paintings, and are referred to in literature over many centuries. On a visit to The Hermitage Museum in Leningrad (now St Petersburg) in 1988, there was great excitement when I came across a Van Dyck painting of 1680, with two little girls, and a dog which portrayed all the characteristics of a Welsh Springer – similar markings, the expression on the face, and the paw lifted to give a gentle pat. Who could mistake it?

In the Picture Gallery in Buckingham Palace, now open to the public in the summer, there were the unmistakable red and white spaniels in Barent Graat's painting of *A Family Group* (1658), and Melchior de Hondecoeter's *Birds and a Spaniel* (1665).

Clifford Hubbard has given me permission to quote from Richard Thornhill's book *The Shooting Directory* (1804), one of the finest treasures in his collection of rare and beautiful books. Thornhill is bemoaning the paucity of Welsh Springers, remarking that 'some still remain about London' but that they are rarely found in any other part of England; and adds that they were red-and-white, with rather short ears, and the tail somewhat 'bushy, and seldom cut'.

C A Phillips, in his article about the Welsh Springer in J Sidney Turner's *Kennel Encyclopaedia* (1907) states:

We have an authentic record of red and white spaniels having existed in these isles for at least 350 years, or, to be quite correct, since 1570, but for how long previous to this date it is impossible to state with any accuracy.

In the year 1570, at the request of Conrad Gesner, the German naturalist, Dr Caius compiled his work on 'English Dogges', and in his reference to English or British Spaniels he commences in these words 'The Spaniell is so named from Spain whence they came. The most part of their skynnes are white, and if they be marcked with any spottes they are commonly red'.

It would appear from this description that Dr Caius has gone out of his way to give the most prevalent colour of the Spaniels which were in existence in this country at the time he wrote his book.

Still, it would be a somewhat bold statement to say that this is the same dog from which the Welsh Spaniel originated. There can be little doubt but that the red and white Spaniel was well distributed throughout this country at one time, but their place seems to have been entirely usurped by the liver and white coloured one in England itself; nevertheless, there is no reason why the breed should not have been fostered in some remote locality such as South Wales. It is contended by those interested in the breed that such was the case, and certainly there seems to be more reason in their claim than in the bare assertion that they were an offshoot from the Clumber, to which breed they were certainly antecedent so far as this country was concerned. The Neath Valley seems to have been the principal home of the breed for many years, and Mr A T Williams of Ynisygerwn, Neath, tells us that these Spaniels have been used for sporting purposes by his family for upwards of a century. In addition to this strain, which was kept entirely for sporting purposes, are the dogs of Sir John Talbot Llewelyn of Penllergare; Colonel Lewis of Green Meadow; and Colonel J Blandy Jenkins of Llanharan, Glamorgan, although he believes his strain to have come originally from the same stock as that of Mr Williams.

Col Blandy-Jenkins says that red Welsh Spaniels were kept at Llanharan, as they were also in the Vale of Neath and at Pentyrch by the Rev Horatio Thomas, the Rector. He crossed a bitch bred by Rev Thomas with a dog belonging to Mr William Morgan of Triensaran, near Bridgend, that came from the Neath Valley. The strain thus established was the best he had, and he believes that most of the best Spaniels now about the country came from this strain.

Another well-known Spaniel authority in South Wales, whilst admitting that there is no documentary evidence, states that his information on the origin of the breed amounts to this: that the Spaniels referred to were called the Llanharan strain and were kept by Colonel Blandy-Jenkins at Llanharan House, and that he heard through a friend who got his information from the old huntsman of the Llanharan Hounds (who only died lately, aged 90). This old huntsman said that when he was a boy at Llanharan a couple of these Spaniels were brought there by some gipsies, and that the then owner of the place (father or grandfather of the present owner) took a fancy to them and bought them from the gipsies. This strain has been at Llanharan ever since and has, of course, spread about Glamorgan.

There is no question as to the uniform type of these Spaniels, although they may vary somewhat in their shade of colour, and some would appear to be different in the colour of the nose, the flesh coloured nose being considered more correct than the black; but if we take into consideration the fact that it is only of late years that the breed has been introduced to the Show Bench, and no very great attention given to particular points except for Sporting purposes, their great inclination to breed to type cannot help but point to the fact of their antiquity.

Two positions of Corrin. Born: 25 June 1893.

So far as the Show Bench is concerned, the breed is young, and the numbers of exhibitors few, but it is slowly gaining fresh adherents, and may in time blossom out as strong as any other variety of Spaniel. In the writer's opinion, Ch Corrin was by far the best specimen of the variety that has been seen on the bench; he was from the tip of his nose to the end of his tail a beautiful Spaniel throughout, and even by those who were not particularly enchanted with the breed he was always admired.

The strongest kennels at the present time are those of Mr A T Williams and Mrs H D Green [sic], the best specimens being Ch Rover of Gerwn, Ch Rock, Tramp of Gerwn, Ch Longmynd Megan, Longmynd Myfanwy and Gypsy of Gerwn. The late Mr W H David, of Neath, was one of the earliest exhibitors and supporters of the breed.

Drury and others in *British Dogs* (1903) state:

No Welshman would deny that, in former days, breeds of red-and white Spaniels were existent in several parts of England as well as in Wales. Symonds, for example, mentions them in Suffolk in the eighteenth century; and the picture of the Spaniels belonging to a gentleman (a dweller, however, on the Welsh border) who died in the middle of the eighteenth century, bears eloquent testimony that the red-and-white Spaniels of that period were of the same type as those of today, and gives them an authentic record in antecedence of the Clumber.

Ch Rock, bred by A T Williams. Sire: Corrin.
Born: 9 June 1903.

But the English red-and-white breeds have died out long ago; and South Wales seems to be the only region that has cherished and preserved them to the present day, which fact goes far to justify the claim of their fellow-countrymen that these Spaniels shall be for the future called Welsh, and that all red-and-white Springers shall appear at trials and exhibitions under this title. Anyhow, the antiquity of the Welsh Spaniels is proved by 'A Quartogenarian' in his letter (Nov. 1833) to the Sporting Magazine, in which, referring to a 'yellow-and-white' Spaniel, that had

Photograph of spaniels in the *Kennel Gazette*, July 1900.

been given to Mr Prowse Jones by an Officer, he adds 'who got it somewhere about Brecon of what was then there termed the old Welsh breed'.

The enemies of this most sporting gundog seem to think it an almost conclusive argument against him that, till lately, he was unknown in the show-ring, and, indeed, outside his own 'sphere of influence'; whereas the preservation of his type is due to his having thus escaped the attention of 'fanciers'.

As workers these Spaniels have no superiors; and the methodical quartering, so merrily and so steadily executed by a team of four at the 1901 trials, delighted every one.

Much of their sport is dependent upon this excellent worker. The ground to be worked includes some of the roughest character, with dense cover, which necessitates an active, perservering, strong, high couraged dog that will face anything. He must also be able to work all day, and day after day. When this Spaniel was brought out at the field trials of the Sporting Spaniel Society, his working qualities immediately placed him in a high position.

The speculation amongst experts must have been taking place at the turn of the century, as can be seen in the *Kennel Gazette* of July 1900, where there is a photograph of a picture (see above) 'the subject of which is spaniels':

Although we are not permitted to give the history of the picture, we can vouch for its origin, and we are able to assure those into whose hands it may fall that the picture is at least 150 years old. The owner of the dogs represented died in the year 1755, and the picture has hung in the same house ever since. We are informed that the surrounding scenery is that of an ancient deer park, and that the identical spot is well-known to the descendants of the original owner of the dogs.

The spaniels are of a type which no doubt will be of interest to those experts who may have agreed to differ on the subject of what a spaniel should be in these latter days. That they are well-bred is perhaps self-evident from the picture itself; that the owner would have been possessed of anything but well-bred spaniels is hardly probable, seeing that he was the master of a pack of harriers in the days when the fox was still esteemed a 'striking beast of the chase'.

As to the qualities of the spaniels herein depicted, it is not for us to express an opinion. 'Where doctors differ,' etc. At all events, the photograph may help the doctors to decide what is the true and original type of the working spaniel, for the game shown in the picture, although perhaps a trifle out of drawing, shows that these spaniels were kept for work, not for show; and so far as sporting dogs go, it is undoubtedly the object of the judges and others connected with the show bench to emphasise those points which have been found to have been of real value in the field.

No doubt it is often difficult even for experts to say what are the points that have the most value in the field, but we think that by presenting to them the type of a spaniel that was in use for actual work at such a long distance of time, it may help them to decide how far and in what right or wrong directions we have departed from the ideals of our forefathers. It must be remembered in this connection that 150 years ago the spaniel had to find his game in all sorts of rough places. In those days land was practically undrained. Furze bushes and other exceedingly rough places abounded, and the spaniel had therefore not only to be a dog of considerable range, but also to be possessed of unflinching courage to face the ordeal of bramble et hoc genus omne that might come is his way. Moreover, it was absolutely necessary that he should be a water dog, and capable of paddling, or even swimming, if need be, through flooded places.

Again, it was absolutely necessary with the ancient weapons that he should be well broken and hunt under the eye of his master. The reasons for this are so obvious that it is hardly necessary to recapitulate them, and it is equally obvious that he should 'down charge' during the lengthy process of re-loading.

Anyhow, we must leave it to the experts to decide what manner of spaniel this is. Suffice it for us to say that this is undoubtedly one of the types in existence a century and a half ago, and that in those days shows were unknown, and strains in the kennels of country gentlemen were jealously guarded, were kept as pure as possible, and that it is from these prototypes that the strains of the present day have been evolved.

Welsh Springers were first introduced into the showring as Welsh Cockers, and were entered in the *Kennel Club Stud Book* under different names, first as Cockers and later as Welsh Springers, inevitably causing some confusion. In *The Twentieth Century Dog* (1904), Herbert Compton states:

In the Spaniel Club's Annual Report for 1902 it is announced: 'The first committee meeting of the year was specially called on February 3rd to consider the decision of the Kennel Club to place on the register classes for "English springers, other than Clumber and Sussex", and "Welsh springers, red and white", which the committee unanimously decided to protest against'.

Compton admitted that he 'cannot but harbour qualms and doubts', but was 'fortified by the decision of The Kennel Club, and the opinions of Welsh spaniel experts, who can speak of and vouch for the purity and antiquity of the breed from long personal and family experience'. He enquired of Sir John Talbot Dillwyn Llewelyn, Bart, of Penllergaer, who wrote:

Mr Williams, of Ynisygerwn, has now got the best spaniels – Welsh springers – which I know of, of our old breed. They are red and white, medium size, and in my younger days we had a very good team. I have a fair team now, but was unlucky a year or two ago. They are good workers. I believe my father had them many years; they were natives of the Vale of Neath, and tradition says we had the best then. Certainly I consider, when I was a young man in the 'Fifties, mine were the best anywhere.

Compton also sought information from Mr Williams and received the following reply:

This dog is of very ancient origin; he is probably the oldest of all the spaniel breeds now in Great Britain. With comparatively little care or breeding he has preserved his type and valuable working qualities. These spaniels have never been kept for the show-bench, but have been bred and kept purely for work by sportsmen – principally in South Wales – and notably by such old shooting families as those of Colonel J Blandy-Jenkins of Penllergaer, Colonel Henry Lewis of Greenmeadow, and others. These families have possessed these dogs for upwards of a hundred years. The Welsh spaniel is a distinct variety, and differs from all other breeds in type and other respects; writings and pictures, dating back some hundreds of years, describe and depict this spaniel. When field trials for spaniels were established the Welsh springer very speedily came to the front, and proved himself a most excellent worker and a great winner at the trials. The Kennel Club has placed the variety in the Stud Book as a distinct breed, and classes are provided for them at their show, and also at many others. The colour is red (of varying shades) and white, and a standard of points has been adopted for the variety by The Kennel Club. In Wales the ground to be worked comprises some of the very roughest and densest character, and necessitates a very high-courage, active, and perservering dog; not only must he be able to work ground of this description, but he must be able to do so all day, and day after day. I work a team of ten or twelve of these spaniels at one time, and without them should not find half of my game. They are fast, merry workers, will face the thickest covert, have rare noses, and the most extraordinary powers of endurance in work. In short, there is no doubt the breed are the best working spaniels, and at the same time very handsome. The Kennel Club went deeply into the matter, and decided the Welsh spaniel was a distinct breed of the most valuable description.

Mr Williams was the prime mover for their recognition, and was the owner of the highly acclaimed first registered Welsh Springer, Corrin (see photograph on page 8), originally listed as a Welsh Cocker. Corrin was born on 25 June 1893, was sired by Dash out of a bitch called Busy; he was bred by Colonel K J Blandy-Jenkins, JP of Llanharran. Mr Williams describes Corrin in Compton's book:

He is of medium height, weighs 42lb, and of the correct red and white colour. His eyes are dark hazel, not prominent, and without haw; ears small and set fairly low; tail, low carriage and very lively motion; coat dense and straight; excellent bone; moderately feathered; strong body and well-sprung ribs, with length of body proportionate to that of leg; loin muscular and very strong, slightly arched and well coupled up; feet round, with thick pads; general appearance symmetrical, compact, strong, and active; built for endurance and activity. Is beyond doubt the most typical Welsh spaniel living, and the sire of all the best spaniels now being exhibited. Won championship at Birmingham and Crystal Palace, and other prizes too numerous to mention.

There is also a description of a bitch called Fanny of Gerwn, owned by Mrs H D Greene, bred by a Mr A Treherne, sired by Dash again, out of Fan, and born in September 1899:

She has won various prizes, and is described by her former owner, Mr Williams, as 'perfect in head, legs, body, coat, and colour'.

In Compton's opinion, Corrin and Fanny of Gerwn were

...to my eyes a pair of as beautiful working spaniels as any one could wish to see, looking at them from an artistic point of view.

Mr Williams gives his definition of his ideal Welsh Spaniel.

The old Welsh breed is not affected by shows, but has been bred and kept by shooting sportsmen for its working properties. A spaniel full of intelligence, and that, with the

Fanny of Gerwn.

mere sight of a gun, instantly brims over with delight. His greatest pleasure is to set to work immediately, and force out for the gun whatever there may be in the shape of game or rabbits.

The ideal Welsh spaniel must be exceedingly active and strong, able to negotiate the most difficult as well as the thickest places, and to last out the longest day. His colour must always be red and white, the red deepening with age. His head fairly long and strong, but not settery type. Ears should be small, offering a minimum of resistance and opportunity to gorse and briars; eyes dark and full of spaniel expression; body very muscular, not long on any account, with thick coat, not curly; stern down, never above the line of his back, with plenty of movement; legs of medium length, with plenty of bone and good round feet. And for disposition he must possess utter devotion to his master, high courage, and not afraid of a fight if imposed upon him, but not quarrelsome. If whipped, never sulky, but ready to start off working again instantly. Always a pleasure to the master to have the dog with him, whether in actual work or at home.

An extract from an article by Baron Jaubert that appeared in the *Illustrated Kennel News* is also quoted by Compton:

There are many valuable strains of dogs in England which never appear at shows, and are consequently ignored. Their owners – true sportsmen – preserve their dogs with care, and despise perpetual changes and fashions. Welsh spaniels, dogs intended for sport, and not prepared like modern dogs, would not have the least chance at a show of beating the inordinately long and low new type of spaniel which has been in favour for some time. Therefore the Welsh owners did not show them.

The Sporting Spaniel Society (which was founded to bring back spaniels from the 'dogs of fancy', into which dog shows had gradually transformed them, to a type more suitable to a working dog) succeeded in obtaining at exhibitions a special class for 'working type spaniels'. And then a Welsh dog was brought out at Birmingham in December 1899, which made a sensation. This was Corrin, belonging to Mr A T Williams, a magnificent red and white dog. Mr Purcell-Llewellin gave him a first in a class of twenty-four: the dog afterwards won at many other of the very first shows, including a championship at Crystal Palace.

All this time ink was flowing freely. The pillars of the ordinary breeds of spaniels would not admit the Welsh; the dog could not, ought not, to exist. Endless letters appeared in the newspapers, but the last word has been said by the Kennel Club, which has recognised the Welsh spaniel as a separate breed. He comes victorious out of the struggle; not only does he exist, but he is of perfectly pure blood and more ancient breed than certain other spaniel strains.

There are a few kennels that have kept the pure strain of Welsh spaniels for over a hundred and fifty years; I will mention those of Mr Jones of Pontneath, Sir John Llewellyn of Penllergaer. Colonel Lewis of Greenmeadow, and Mr A T Williams of Ynisygerwn. The breed of spaniels has existed at the latter kennels since 1750. The grandfather of Mr Williams used to go shooting in the years from 1805 to 1850 with a team of twelve to fourteen dogs trained by himself. Now Mr Williams uses teams of from three to eight dogs, trained by a keeper. Two guns walk about 32 yards to the right and left of the keeper, who directs the dogs.

Colonel Lewis and Mr David of Neath also keep these dogs, and their kennels confirmed my impression that they were a distinct variety, very consistent in type, very uniform, and sharply defined by shape and coat. The latter is of a warm brick-red colour, though orange is allowable, sometimes inclining to wine-colour, a specially distinctive shade. The ear is rather small, though quite long enough for sporting dog; the body well off the ground, but not so much that the dog can be called 'leggy'. It is obvious that a dog built like this could gallop and jump as could none of the 'long and low' show dogs, wittily defined, in the course of the recent polemics, as 'living drain-pipes', for whom 'vast halls and long corridors' are necessary. The Welsh 'starters' – a term more frequently employed in Wales than 'springers' – show amongst themselves similar differences of height and weight to those seen amongst pointers, where members of the same litter may be classed, some as large and others as small pointers. The scale of points indicates a sufficiently wide margin, ranging from 30–43lb. Below 30lb we find the Welsh cocker, which is entered in the ordinary cocker class at dog shows, but proves its Welsh origin by its red markings.

We had an opportunity of seeing these spaniels hunt the steep slopes of the Neath valley. The ground was a bed of matted bracken, which hid completely the fallen stones, and made walking very difficult. Large rocks rose, isolated, from this gilded covert, in which there were sometimes strong brambles and interwoven dead branches; at any time one may find one's self entangled in invisible ruins. These are just the places where one or two cockers are invaluable to dislodge the rabbits that double into them as if in a stack of faggots. In a country like this the two teams we saw at the field trials worked for six consecutive hours. The dogs swarmed round their men as lightly and gaily as if in a stubble-field; they showed as much energy at the close of the day as they had done at the beginning. They proved themselves to possess excellent noses and great keenness. They reconciled – a necessary point in teams – the greatest activity with perfect immobility at the flushing of game or the sound of a gun. The sixty-six head of game to four guns certainly gave us more pleasure than 400 head would at a battue. We began the day with the before-mentioned prize-winner, Corrin, who, despite his ten years showed an energy and a dash as great as those of the puppies – a proof that the breed is sound.

With all the information that he had gleaned, Compton ends by saying: 'The reader will be able to form his own opinion as to whether to agree with the decision of the Kennel Club [to register Welsh Springers] or that of the Spaniel Club [to protest against it]'.

All these quotations put the very strong case for the Welsh Springer, and A T Williams, with W Arkwright and W H David, succeeded in persuading The Kennel Club to classify it as a new variety, backed up by the old writings and pictures, where spaniels were invariably red and white. But it had not been achieved without considerable opposition from other spaniel enthusiasts of the time, with heated correspondence in journals on the subject. To explain the red or orange markings and the ear shaped like a vine leaf it was freely asserted that Welsh Springers were nothing but cross-breds between the ordinary English Springer and probably a Clumber.

For me, the Welsh Springer is a 'very ancient and distinct breed of pure origin', as the Breed Standard states today just as it did when it was first composed, on the breed's recognition in 1902. It is of interest that it was not until 1967 that the section describing the Welsh Springer as 'a distinct variety, which has been bred and preserved purely for working purposes' was deleted from the original characteristics in the Standard.

From *The Sleeping Sportsman* by Gabriel Metzu (1630–1667), showing a typical Springer of the 17th century.
Photo: J Caswell-Smith

chapter 2
Development of the Breed

After Recognition

Initially, exhibitors were few, and they differed from most other dogs on the show bench because the majority were trained to the gun. It was accepted that Mr Williams' Corrin was the best Welsh Springer that had ever been seen. W H David exhibited Kimla Dash, which he sold to Mrs H D Greene (Longmynd), a very successful breeder at Craven Arms. At one time, she had eight show bench champions, some of the best being Ch Calon Fach, Ch Longmynd Myfanwy and Ch Longmynd Megan.

In January 1903, A Williams wrote an article about Welsh Springers:

Ch Longmynd Megan.

Ch Longmynd Calon Fach. Photo: Thomas Fall

Since the Kennel Club gave this Spaniel a place, as a distinct breed, in their 'List of Breeds', comparatively few months have elapsed, but it is not too much to say that during that time greater interest has been taken, outside of Wales, in this splendid working Spaniel than has ever been the case before. More studious care also has already been taken in mating and breeding, and, although it is yet a good deal too soon to see the results, it may be taken for granted that in future we shall see a more uniform type than has been the case hitherto.

The standard of points having been settled, breeders have an authoritative guide before them, and it is to be hoped judges will have due regard to that standard and not encourage such exaggerations as have been permitted in other breeds, so that shows may not have the effect of spoiling this dog for work. The highest and first object should be to protect and preserve his working qualities and abilities. Up to the present time, and for hundreds of years past, he has been bred purely and exclusively for work, and it would be the greatest disaster to the dog and to sport if he were to be allowed to sink into a creature that cannot work.

A Maud Earl painting of two Longmynd champions (probably Megan and Myfanwy).
Reproduced by kind permission of The Kennel Club.

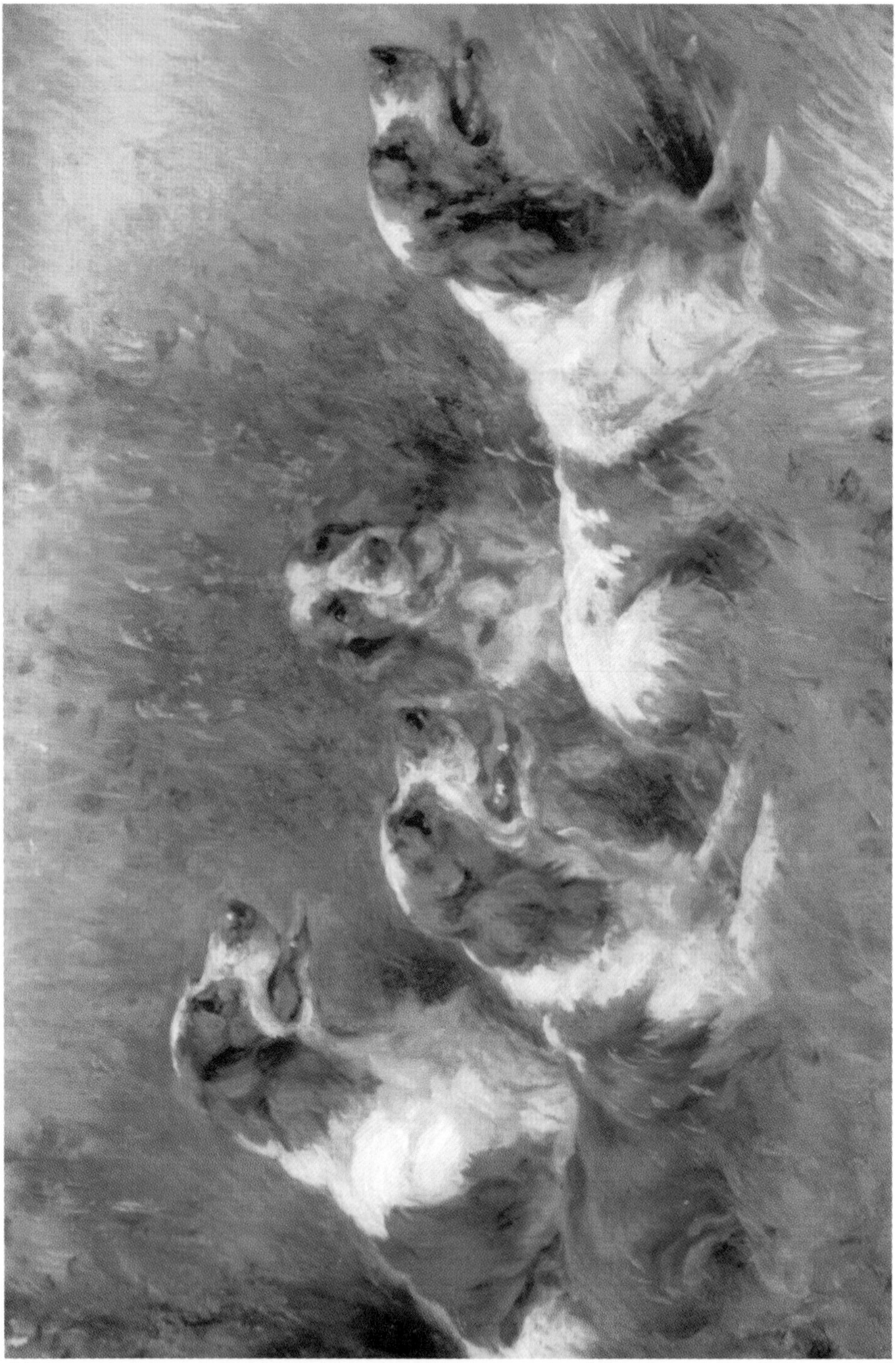

English Setters [sic] *at Rest*, by Maud Earl.
Reproduced by kind permission of Richard Omel.

As he is, there is no better, nor more amiable, and trustworthy, companion and friend, so that there can be no excuse, on that score, for altering his disposition. At the same time, he stands out as a pre eminent worker, and all that is required is to breed in accordance with the Kennel Club's standard of points for this dog, without exaggerating it in any respect. Of course, uniformity is desirable, and this is the thing to be attained.

Present owners of this Spaniel are in some cases gentlemen, who have never exhibited, and who do not attend dog shows, and it can be understood that it is more difficult to induce them to do so. There are others, however, who are now taking up the breed, and it is to be hoped they will exhibit a little more public spirit, in the interest of sport generally. At the same time, the latter gentlemen must be allowed time, because in some cases they owned other Spaniels. They are, gradually, giving the others up, so that they may replace them with the Welsh Springer. This is so, not only in Wales, but also in England. This should lead to one result, viz., – that in future we shall have a larger number of beautiful Welsh Spaniels than we have ever had before. Some owners, from past experience of the influence of the bench upon other breeds, are anxious, and perhaps nervous, as to the influence it may exercise upon the working properties of this dog, and it will be for the show judges to maintain the position, and to satisfy owners that the effect of the bench will be to preserve one breed, and not to spoil it.

Now that Field Trials for Spaniels have been started, and it is to be hoped established, this should assist the judges in maintaining a hard working type, with all the necessary sporting qualities, and Field Trial Winners should be encouraged, in every shape and form, on the bench. With a sporting dog, 'handsome is as handsome does', but in saying this, there should be no desire to disparage appearances and good looks, but, on the contrary, to encourage them. At the same time, the standard of beauty should be the structure and make that can best accomplish the object for which the dog exists.

This Spaniel will undoubtedly assist breeders in producing dogs that can stand any amount of work, and he is now being freely used at stud for this purpose.

The official recognition of the breed by the Kennel Club has given the liveliest satisfaction to many sportsmen.

During the past year, Miss Maud Earl included representatives of this breed in her group of oil paintings of Hounds and Gundogs, and during their exhibition at Messrs Graves' Gallery, there was no picture which attracted more attention than that of the Welsh Springers. This picture was most opportune, and will be of great value in the future in assisting to represent what these Spaniels were like in the year 1902, when they were first admitted as a distinct breed into the Stud Book, and which is therefore perhaps the most memorable year in their history.

Maud Earl's paintings of dogs are world renowned, and a number of them are to be found hanging at The Kennel Club in London. Her most famous painting of Welsh Springers is of two of Mrs H D Greene's Longmynd champions (see page 15). It hangs in the Ladies' Room and is often reproduced. For many years, it was understood that the two dogs were Megan and Calon Fach. However, doubt has now been cast on this assumption, and it is probable that they are Megan and her sister, Myfanwy.

Another, not so well known, has come to my notice recently; this is in card form, and has the title *English Setters at Rest* beneath it and is reproduced on the opposite page.

Four English Setters? Welsh Springer enthusiasts would cast some doubt on that! I can see my own dogs there, as I am sure many others can – the heads, the expressions, the positions in which they are resting and, of course, the markings. They present a beautiful picture, as do all Maud Earl's masterpieces. Perhaps these dogs also came from the Longmynd kennel, and the hills in the background could be the Longmynd Hills.

A Croxton Smith, in his *Everyman's Book of the Dog* (1909), quotes:

[Mrs H D Greene] who has a large kennel, says: 'I am sure Welsh Springers only need to be known more; they are so intelligent, so affectionate, and so picturesque, and are as active as a terrier'.

Soon after the recognition of the breed, The Welsh Spaniel Club was formed, with Mrs Greene as secretary, but it was disbanded at the outbreak of the First World War when Mrs Greene decided to put all her dogs down, as she thought that there would be insufficient food available to feed them. This was a great loss, as her dogs were typical of the breed. However, there is at least one legacy from those times: Cliff and Mary Payne of the Tregwillym kennels – one of the greatest of our Welsh Springer kennels – became the proud owners of a medal (see opposite), which has a small figure of a Welsh Springer on one side and an inscription on the back: *1909 – Shrewsbury won by Mrs H D Greene's Ch Longmynd Morgan.*

On one of my many visits to Tregwillym House, I learned that it had been found when some tram lines in Cardiff were being dug up, and had been presented to the Paynes by the Borough Surveyor.

C A Phillips, one of the great gundog experts, wrote in the *Kennel Encyclopaedia* (1907) of the Welsh Springer's uniform type:

...although they may vary somewhat in their shade of colour, and some would appear to be different in the colour of the nose, the flesh-coloured nose being considered more correct than the black; but if we take into consideration the fact that it is only of late years that the breed has been introduced to the Show Bench, and no very great attention given to particular points except for Sporting purposes, their great inclination to breed type cannot help but point to the fact of their antiquity.

After the First World War

There was still considerable interest in the breed, particularly in the South Wales area, on the bench as well as in the field. Under the leadership of Col Downes Powell of the O'Matherne kennel, the Welsh Springer Spaniel Club was formed, and received recognition by The Kennel Club in 1923. It emphasised the dual-purpose nature of the breed which is still maintained today. The balance sheet for the first year showed £8.18s.10d. (approximately £8.94) to be carried forward, which was considered very satisfactory, and by the end of 1923, Club membership was 110.

In the 1920s, considerable pressure appears to have been applied to maintain the type of Welsh Springer first described by A T Williams. He judged the breed at The Kennel Club's 62nd show in 1923, and wrote:

I suggest a good deal can still be done to produce better heads, straighter fronts, darker eyes, and the avoidance of the gay tail carriage.

He decried the pale colour, and commented on the expression not being 'quite pleasing' on one exhibit; another 'too fine and long in muzzle for me, wide in front and loaded in shoulder', and 'might be a little finer in skull, and would more taking if more broken in colour', 'looks a worker', and 'if squarer in muzzle, would take some beating'.

Col Downes Powell was the judge of the 19 Welsh Springers entered at Crufts in 1924, the first time that they had been scheduled there since 1914 when just five Welsh Springers entered. He commented on the need for good body and colour, and again, the heads. On another occasion, his critique noted 'few dogs rather small and too Cocker-like, and breeders should remember these dogs are "Springers".' Again mention was made of colour of coats, and comments about movement, balance – and, of course, heads.

One cannot help wondering what these two experts would say about the dogs being exhibited today. Some of our judges would no doubt agree with them, particularly with the danger of losing the beautiful head and soft expression, together with, perhaps, poor hind movement and lack of muscling.

The two sides of a medal, with wording:
(left) *Welsh Spaniel Club* (right) *1909 Shrewsbury won by Mrs H D Green's Ch Longmynd Morgan.*

Considerable correspondence was carried out in the canine press on Welsh Springer type as well. One writer expressed the opinion that 'dark eyes and black noses would inevitably hold the field eventually, although they are foreign to the Welsh Springer. No one could wish for a more beautiful combination than clear white balanced with bright red and contrasted with dark eyes and black nose. This delightful effect will undoubtedly raise the breed in popularity'.

It was admitted that crossing was taking place. Apparently, a Cocker cross was 'resorted to accidentally, – that is, accidentally in so much that the breeder simply chose a sire with consideration only for type and colour, without regard to breeding'. The writer was of the opinion that this choice was amply justified, proved by the numerous successes of the strain, with the colour being 'distinctly good', with 'a definite red, bright and solid'. There was also a suggestion for an English Springer cross to improve size, type and stamina, but another correspondent did not approve of doing this simply to obtain the casual black nose or black eye at the expense of the whole character of the Welsh Springer. He stated that the late A T Williams

...crossed them both ways, using the dam of the one breed and the sire of the other, or say, English sire and Welsh dam and vice versa; but he at that time told me that it was not intended to improve the outward appearance of the Welsh Spaniel, but to see what change would take place in the character of the progeny as field dogs; and if my memory serves me well enough, the cross-bred dogs were entered at field trials, and registered at the KC as such. I wonder how many of our present breeders would care to register their dogs as crossbreeds? Re colour, I believe we are in for some trouble unless the Club judges will take courage, and stop awarding prizes to the very dark semi-liver coloured dogs now on the bench. I believe it would well repay to revert back to the old colour of the Welsh Spaniel, viz., a bright reddish orange.

Others were adamant in advocating that they 'should leave well alone'.

When Mrs Greene's very successful kennel was dominating the show ring, her dogs 'took on still brighter red markings', and 'lemons' were taboo. There was then a suggestion that the Irish Setter may have something to do with the development of the Welsh Springer. That correspondent did, however, still claim that 'before the time of record, the Welsh Springer has been a pure and distinct breed, clearly defined in its type and characteristics'.

One of our contemporaries, Bryan Kidd, has some information on what happened in the 1920s. He had an uncle, Ernest Garrett, who died recently. He was an under-keeper in Sussex where his father was farm bailiff. He and his elder brother (also a keeper)

The second field trial organised by the Welsh Springer Spaniel Club.
Reported in *South Wales News*, 11 December 1924

acquired their first Welsh Springer Spaniel bitch at that time, and bred several litters from then until the late 1940s, but did not register any of the puppies. The dogs appeared under the family name of Garrett, the best known being Nell Garrett, Shot Garrett and Druid O'Garrett, and these are to be found in the pedigrees of many famous dogs of the time.

The first Field Trial was held in 1923 by the Welsh Springer Spaniel Club, which had Lord Swansea as President, A T Williams as Chairman, and Col Downes Powell as Secretary. The Trial was held at Raperra Park and was reported to be a great success, with four Welsh Springer entries in each of the Puppy and Open classes and a further five in an Open stake, four Welsh Springers and a Cocker entered by Col Downes Powell.

The following year, Captain Talbot Fletcher (subsequently President) hosted the Trial at his home, Margam Park, Port Talbot, where it was held for many years. The *South Wales News* reported on the two day Trial, the first of which was devoted entirely to Welsh Springers, with four entries in the puppy class, six in the non-winners' stake, and six in the open class. On the second day, there were classes for Any Variety Spaniel, with Brace and Team stakes.

Some of the most successful winners at Field Trials were Col Downes Powell, Mr W Rickards, Mrs Horsfield, and Mrs Marjorie Mayall, well known for her dual-purpose Rockhill Welsh Springers. Captain and Mrs Talbot Fletcher entertained all to lunch at the Castle, and the events always ended with the Club's Annual Dinner at Porthcawl.

In 1927, Col Downes Powell described the Welsh Springer in *Pedigree Dogs*:

In temperament, Welsh Springers are most docile and easily broken if well handled, but owing to their keenness can easily be spoiled by ill-treatment. They are rather inclined to be headstrong, and perhaps take a little more preliminary breaking than any other breed. Welsh Springers are particularly brainy dogs and there is no better and gamer gun dog when properly handled, and au contraire, no wilder dog living if ill-treated. As companions and pets they are delightful and as house-dogs and guards cannot be excelled.

This is so similar to the description which I myself like to give to prospective owners – the breed has not changed!

Now the breed was becoming more widespread, not only in Wales where Welsh Springers had been for so many years. Col Downes Powell recorded that they were known in Herefordshire, Shropshire, Devon, Somerset and Cornwall, 'and of late years,

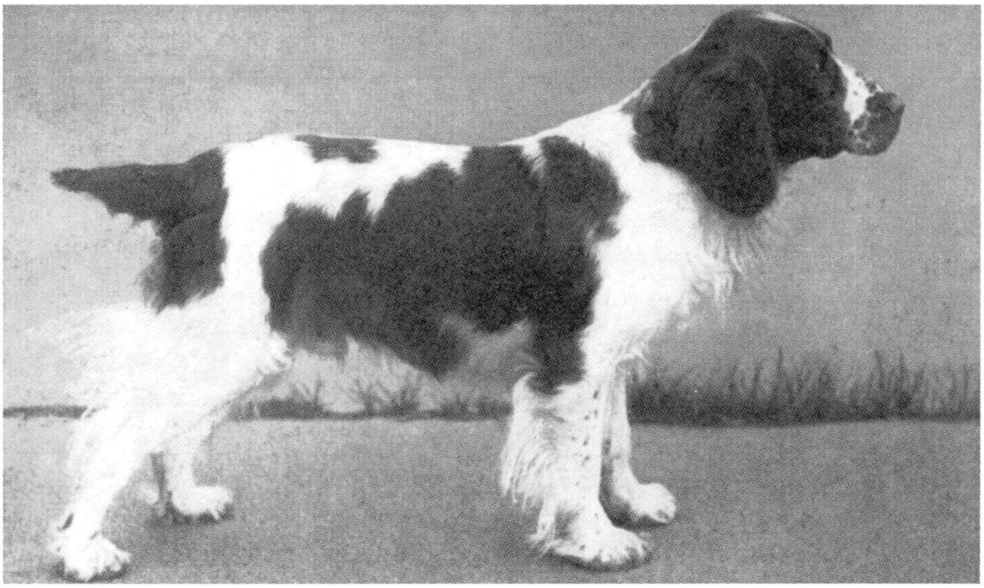

Ch Musketeer O'Matherne. Photo: R Robinson

they are being bred in Lancashire and throughout the Midlands and South of England'. He named the most successful show exhibitors of the time as Mrs L Morgan, Messrs F Morris, J Jones, R Lewis and himself.

For the first 20 years after recognition, registrations of Welsh Springers varied in numbers. There were no registrations in 1918, the last year of the Great War, but in 1925 they topped the 100 mark for the first time with 127, and remained fairly constant until the outbreak of the Second World War. They were down to 21 in 1942, but by 1945 they were up again to 107.

At Crufts Show, the breed was scheduled again in 1924, the first time since 1914, and it was scheduled annually until the.outbreak of the Second World War. The Show was not held again until 1948, when there was an entry of 22 Welsh Springers.

In the 1930s, competition was keen in the showring, despite the industrial depression which inevitably meant that there was predominantly local interest in the South Wales area. Col Downes Powell's O'Matherne dogs, notably Ch Marksman and Ch Musketeer, and his Ch Felcourt Flapper, A J Dyke's Ch Marglam Marquis, F Morris' Ch Barglam Bang, J Turford's Chief of Mons, J Jones' Ch Merglam Bang and Ch Shot O'R Baili, Dr H B Jones' Lad and Lass of Tolworth, Mrs Marjorie Mayall's Ch Mair O'R Cwm, and the Rev D Stewart's Ch Serenade o'Silian were among the most successful. A new name entered the arena: Harold Newman, later to become one of our all-time greats in the breed, with his Pencelli kennel. Harold started with a bitch called Barmaid, and from her mating with Ch Marksman O'Matherne, he found his first big winner, Dere Mhlaen. Col Downes Powell wrote, after judging him in 1937:

Dere Mhlaen, born 24 September 1932.

The best dog in the Show was Dere Mhlaen, a five-year old in good bloom and coat; he is a good mover and very sound; good head, feet and legs, and an excellent body; a shade more lip would improve and he might be just a shade bigger.

The stud fee was £2 2s 0d prepaid (£2.20) plus return carriage!

In 1938, in Edward Ash's *The New Book of the Dog*, Col Downes Powell expressed his opinion on the Welsh Springers which he considered were the best of the day:

Three I liked best in last10 years	**I consider them excellent in:**	**In my opinion their faults were:**
	Dogs	
Ch Marksman O'Matherne	Type, substance, movement	As a dog, might be a shade shorter coupled.
Ch Musketeer O'Matherne	Type, movement, colour and symmetry. (I think him the best of his breed I have ever seen.) His balance. is wonderful.	A mere fraction short of foreface.
Ch Shot O'R Baili	Type, substance and expression, a great spaniel.	His ears are too pendulous. Rather a sluggish mover, but a great dog.
	Bitches	
Ch Felcourt Flapper	Substance, type and movement, a very great bitch, her colour was perfect.	Always a trifle short in coat and feather.
Ch Mair O'R Cwm	Substance, type and colouring.	Rather sluggish in movement, and a shade short in neck.
Marigold O'Matherne	Type, colour, movement and substance. Won her 3 challenge certs before she was 18 months old. Unfortunately she died before she obtained her working certificate.	As a bitch, she might have been a shade longer in body. Her expression, too, was affected by nerves – apt to frown.

There was always a steady demand for the working Welsh Springer, well known for its excellent nose and the ability to go through anything, however dense the cover. Field Trials continued to be held but entries were never very high, and classes were always provided for other spaniel breeds to make up numbers.

Those pre-War years were of some significance for me as well. My father used to say of my mother: 'it is all right as long as it is the best'. Consequently, when it came to buying a puppy, they chose a Cocker Spaniel, and it had to be the best, one from H S Lloyd's Of Ware kennel. Bert Lloyd had won Best in Show with Luckystar of Ware in 1930 and 1931, and then went on to repeat these successes with Exquisite Model of Ware in

Ch Mair O'R Cwm. Photo: Thomas Fall

Ch Shot O'R Baili.

Ch Fellcourt Flapper.

1938 and 1939, and yet again with Tracy Witch of Ware in 1948 and 1950. We had Blackin' Topper of Ware, a well-built black dog, purely as a pet, and a very well-loved one. That was when my love of spaniels began – and perhaps a candle was lit, and I started assessing their virtues?

The author and Topper.

The Second World War

Sh Ch Dewi Saint, born 12 July 1943.

During the Second World War, all activities of the Welsh Springer Spaniel Club ceased. The routine matters necessary to keep the Club alive were performed by Col Downes Powell. Sadly, all the Club's records, apart from the cash book, together with those of the previous Welsh Spaniel Club, were destroyed by enemy action. The breed survived, largely thanks to the Colonel, who nominated Harold Newman to continue breeding. Harold was always very proud of the honour; his great dog Dewi Sant was the sire of many of the top Welsh Springers of the time, and most of the dogs today have him in their pedigrees. Dewi Sant was descended from Harold's first Welsh Springer, Barmaid.

Harold's interest was in the showring, and his Pencelli kennel continued with outstanding success until his death in 1980. Mrs Mayall (Rockhill), and Mr Hal Leopard (Rushbrooke) who had been Assistant Secretary of the Welsh Springer Spaniel Club in 1932, were the chief dual-purpose enthusiasts. Cliff Payne, another of our great and influential breeders, purchased his first Welsh Springer in 1938 purely for work, and labelled the dog as the best worker he has ever owned. Initially, Cliff was only concerned with the working side but, during the War, he purchased several Welsh Springers for breeding, resulting in the establishment of one of the great dual-purpose post-war kennels in the breed – the Tregwillym kennel.

After the Second World War

In April 1946, six members of the Welsh Springer Spaniel Club met in Cardiff to re-assess the situation of the Club. Several officers and members had died, but it was resolved that those present, together with three other members, under the chairmanship of Mrs Mayall, should form the Committee until a General Meeting could be called. Col Downes Powell was appointed Secretary, but resigned because of ill health a year later, and became Chairman. He was succeeded as Secretary by Mr Hal Leopard, who remained in that office until he became President in 1963. Field Trials were left in abeyance, as 'there was no ground, no game, and nobody knew of any dogs'. However, in November 1946, a one day Field Trial with Any Variety Spaniel and Any Variety Spaniel Novice Stakes was held at the last minute at Margam Park, for members only.

Sh Ch Dere Damsel, born 4 April 1947.

Sh Ch Rushbrooke Ruadh

Shows were offering several classes for the breed, all guaranteed by the Club, and the first post-war Championship Show for the breed was held jointly with some other breeds at Cardiff in 1947. Mr D Hazzleby was the judge of the 26 dogs entered, the top awards going to Harold Newman's Dewi Sant, and A J Dyke's Marglam Marchioness. T H Morgan's Sh Ch Dere Damsel (see the lower picture on the opposite page) was another big winner just after the War.

By now, Cliff Payne had entered the show scene, and another new name appeared: Miss D H Ellis. Harold Newman had started her off with two dogs, Jester of Downland and Philosopher of Downland, both sired by Dewi Sant, and usually handled in the showring by Harold. He often used to tell how he drove up to Miss Ellis' home in Sussex, prepare the dogs and show them for her. Hal Leopard's dual-purpose Rushbrooke dogs were also coming to the fore.

In 1947, the 10 members attending the General Meeting of the Welsh Springer Spaniel Club heard that there was a cash balance of £25 1s 8d (£25.7½) carried forward from 1946. In the second Club Year Book after the War, the Committee Report on 1947 stated that a One Day Field Trial was held at Garth in Breconshire in November, but entries were poor, 'owing to the fact that other clubs were holding trials during that month, before the removal of the basic petrol ration.' Shows were almost back to pre-war and 'membership is rapidly increasing, and the breed is gaining greatly in popularity.' As the Club had lost all its records, Col Downes Powell, with his usual foresight, gave a résumé of the Club's history, thus filling in the somewhat hazy past:

In the summer of 1922 I met Dr T W Risely in Cardiff and he suggested to me that a Welsh Springer Spaniel Club should be formed. I reminded him there was prior to the War (1914–18) a Welsh Spaniel Club, but it had seemingly ceased to exist. He told me he could get several members and I agreed to talk the matter over with some people I knew and let him know the result. Risely was a young man just recently qualified and full of energy and go. Unfortunately he was killed in a motor accident within two years. I saw several men keen on sporting dogs and the result was I was asked to call a meeting of those interested at Cardiff to discuss the matter. I also wrote to the late Mrs Greene, the late Secretary of the Welsh Spaniel Club and she not only promised her help, but sent me all sorts of literature, Minute Books, Register of Members, etc. of the old Spaniel Club.

The meeting was a success. Among those present were Messrs T Williams, F Morris, L Morgan, G W Herne, D Neale, D Hazzleby, Major H Gunn, Dr. T W Risely and myself. We decided to form the Club and those present with one or two others were appointed as a working committee. I promised to write to several prominent men I knew and get their assistance and the following promised not only their assistance, but some sent cheques: the late Lord Kenyon, Sir H W Williams Wynn, Lord Tredegar, Lord Swansea, Col H Lewis, Mrs Greene, of course, and some other I cannot quite remember now.

It should be noted I am writing this article from memory as all records and documents I had belonging to the Club were destroyed by enemy action in 1942.

Further meetings of the Committee were held and in January 1923, the Kennel Club gave us their blessing and registered the Welsh Springer Spaniel Club, which has continued to function ever since, except between the years 1939 (September) and 1946, when we lay dormant – but during the war years we kept up our registration and occasionally assisted at a show here and there. Our first year (1923) was a great success and we had before the end of the year nearly a hundred members. We had KC certificates at two or three shows and in the autumn, thanks to the help of the then Lord Tredegar and Sir L Foster Stedman, we held our first Field Trials at Ruperra Park. It was a one day affair and we had three stakes, one for Welsh Springers, which brought out six entries and one for cockers with eight entries, and a mixed stake, AV, which I think had five or six entries. These trials made a great impression and the following year we were invited by our new President, Capt Talbot Fletcher, to go to Margam. We expanded to two days and had eight stakes. These trials were as successful as any held that season and our name was made as a very successful field trials organisation. Our membership increased to nearly 150 and so we went on.

In the meantime we had KC Certificates at all leading shows and demands were coming in from all over the world for Welsh Springers. Dogs were sent to India, America, Europe, Assam, Australia and Canada, and so this grand and keen working dog has become known around the world.

It is quite impossible to show how the activities of the Club have gone on from strength to strength in the short space placed at my disposal, but I should like to pay tribute to so many of my old friends who have passed on for all the work they put in on behalf of the Club, viz. T Williams, Mrs Greene, J Jones, Lord Swansea, Sir H Williams Wynn, Lord Kenyon, Lord Tredegar, D E R Griffiths, Dr T W Risely, J S Davies, G W Herne, F W Morris, H C Hargreaves and Sir L Foster Stedman. At the same time I am glad to think we have a few of the pioneers still left in Douglas Neale, D Hazzleby, G C Williams and Mrs Mayall, with our present secretary, H J H Leopard. In conclusion I should like to say that the twenty-five years during which I acted as Honorary Secretary and Treasurer have been among the happiest years of my life. I am sure with the new blood coming in, this Club will prosper and increase its importance.

Ch Branksome Beauty and Ch Brancourt Bang.

It appears that there was still an emphasis on Field Trials, and in 1948 there was a two-day Trial in Wales, arrangements being made jointly with The Spaniel Club, whose two-day Trial would be run the following two days. They were reported to be among the most successful Trials that the Club had held.

Although more shows were classifying Welsh Springers, and membership of the Breed Club had increased from 79 to 118 in 1948, 55% of those were solely interested in Field Trials, and of the remainder only 24 showed

Welsh Springers at Championship Shows.

In 1949, Mrs M I Morgan's bitch, Branksome Beauty (see opposite), obtained a Qualifying Certificate, and became the first post-war Champion in the breed.

Ch Rushbrooke Racer, born 7 February 1946.

The 1950s and 1960s

In February 1950, Miss Ellis made history by flying to the United States with a team of five Welsh Springers, which she exhibited at American shows. After a short tour, all the dogs were sold to Americans. This received much publicity, and it was hoped that this unique venture would help to popularise the breed. Her tale is told in the section on the United States in chapter 12.

Hal Leopard's Ch Rushbrooke Racer was the Welsh Springer Spaniel of the Year 1950, with many Field Trial awards.

The year 1951 marked the end of an era in the life of the Welsh Springer Spaniel Club. It was reported in the Club's Year Book that

...early in 1951 the Club suffered a heavy blow in the death of our President, Captain A Talbot Fletcher, a man whose generosity has meant so much to the Club ever since its inception. A great sportsman has passed from us, his memory leaving a nostalgia for those great days before the War when the Club held its Annual Field Trials at Margam and Captain Talbot Fletcher entertained all-comers, officials, competitors and spectators alike, at Margam Castle.

Concern was expressed that very few Welsh Springers were running at Field Trials and, if the breed were to gain in popularity, it was essential that they should compete successfully at Trials. No Field Trial was held in 1954, due to myxamotosis, and the 1956 Trial was abandoned.

Meanwhile, interest in showing was increasing. The big winners in the 1950s included Miss Ellis' Jester of Downland, D F Hughes' Ch Snowdonian Lad (bred by Miss Ellis), L Hughes' Ch Lassie of Menai, Mary King's Sh Chs Kim and Kestrel of Kenswick, Dr Rickards' Sh Ch Mikado of Broomleaf (bred by Mrs K Doxford), Hal Leopard's Ch Rushbrooke Runner, Mrs Dorothy Morriss' Sh Ch Stokecourt Jonathan and Sh Ch Stokecourt Gillian, Frank Hart's Sh Ch Denethorp Dido and Ch Denethorp Danny, and Mrs Mayall's Ch Rockhill Rhiwderin.

Sh Ch Mikado of Broomleaf. Photo: F W Simms

Ch Brancourt Bushranger (left) and Sh Ch Stokecourt Gillian, Cardiff 1956.
Judge: Mrs Judy de Casembroot. Photo: C M Cooke

Mrs Morriss and Frank Hart were great dual-purpose enthusiasts of the breed for many years. Hubert Arthur's Sh Ch Brancourt Belinda was an all-time great, both in the showring and as a brood bitch. In 1955, Mr and Mrs T H Morgan's Brancourt Bushranger won Best in Show at South Wales Kennel Association's Championship Show at Cardiff, a feat never before achieved by a Welsh Springer.

Cliff Payne's Tregwillym kennel had started with working dogs but, in the 1950s, he began to take top honours in the showring as well with Sh Chs Token, Top Score, Trigger and Tulita, all big winners, and there were more to come. At the same time, Miss Ann West, another who was to become one of the breed's most successful exhibitors, hit the headlines with her bitches, Sh Chs Belinda of Linkton and Arabella of Linkhill.

Soon there came another milestone: 1953 was noted for the number of registrations falling below 100 for the first time since 1944, and this was repeated in 1955, but that was the last time in the history of the breed. By 1957, they had risen to 143, but there was poor support in the Welsh Springer Stakes at the Club's 27th Field Trial, and entries at the shows were also on the decline. According to the 'Annual Report' in the Welsh Springer Spaniel Club Year Book 1957–1958:

The breed is popular amongst the one-dog owner class of shooters and dog lovers but curiously support from Exhibitors and Field Trial people is lacking.

Having mourned the loss of Col Talbot Fletcher in 1951, another page was turned in the history of the Welsh Springer Spaniel Club with the passing of 'our beloved President and Chairman, Colonel Downes Powell'. Brigadier C P G Wills had succeeded him as Chairman, with Cliff Payne as Vice Chairman, and their personal message to the membership was:

We feel that the most fitting tribute we can pay to his work and memory is for each and everyone of us to do all in our power to further the well-being of the Welsh Springer. We can only do this by halting the decline in Show entries, and by putting dogs under training and running them in Trials; encouraging our friends to do likewise. Those who, quite frankly, find this impossible can contribute materially by interesting shooting men in the breed and exploring the possibility of their allowing field trials over their land.

I quote from the tribute to Col Downes Powell, written in the Welsh Springer Spaniel Club's Year Book of 1958 by the Secretary of the Club, Mr Hal Leopard:

Early this year, our late President, Colonel Downes Powell, was taken ill suddenly at his home, and passed away at the age of 84. He was, of course, known to very many people up and down the country for his great love of dogs, a love which he had had during the whole of his life. He was born in Breconshire, the son of a well-known 'Sporting Parson', the Reverend Canon J T Powell of Pantyscallog, from whom his love for dogs and horses was inherited.

Colonel Downes Powell was a man of many parts. He was firstly a great sportsman in every sense. He was an unusually good shot, and once or twice was invited to shoot at Sandringham; a great horseman, he rode in the Grand National in 1903 and, it is believed, finished the course; as a boy, he owned a greyhound, bred by his father, which subsequently twice won the Waterloo Cup.

Although so greatly interested in all breeds of gundogs, Spaniels were his favourites, and at one time or another, he had shown and run at Field Trials some of all the varieties. His first love was, however, the Welsh Springer Spaniel, and in the '20's and early '30's, he owned many good ones, perhaps the most notable being the great Ch Marksman O'Matherne, a dog which he rightly considered to be the best Welsh Springer ever bred. Although he sold several of his dogs to the United States, he actually refused an offer of no less than £2,500 for Marksman.

Colonel Downes Powell had at one time or another occupied every office of the Welsh Springer Spaniel Club. He was a man of unflagging energy, and through his efforts, the Club became one of the leading Field Trial Societies in the country. He did much to foster the Welsh Springer both at Shows and Trials. As a Judge of all breeds of dogs, either at Trials or Shows, he was absolutely fearless in his placings. As a raconteur, he was without peer, and his stories, usually with a doggy flavour, were always enjoyed by his audience with the greatest relish.

Our late President was laid to rest next to his parents in the little churchyard of Dyfynog in Breconshire. It is curious that as your Secretary arrived at the lychgate to pass through into the church for the funeral service, a very fine Welsh Springer dog came up the road and stood outside the gate. One of the breed he loved so much was there for the last farewell.

This is indeed a very touching tribute to someone to whom all Welsh Springer owners of today owe so much, a man who was a barrister, a civic dignitary and a Justice of the Peace, as well as a true devotee of our breed.

The Welsh Springer Spaniel Club remained without a President until Hal Leopard's election in 1963.

Cliff Payne's Tregwillym kennel was one of the most successful in the breed, with dogs like Ch Statesman and Sh Ch Golden Tint (see overleaf). The latter broke the breed record with 33 Challenge Certificates to her credit.

Statesman was behind so many of the big winners, and was undoubtedly one of the most influential dogs in the breed. Harold Newman was there, too, with Sh Ch Easter Parade, another dog which was to continue to influence the breed. Between them, Harold Newman and Cliff Payne (see overleaf) were without question the two most outstanding and influential breeders of post-war years. They were highly respected by all, and were generous in their advice and help to other breeders, new and old. I was fortunate in being among the receivers of their generosity, advice and encouragement, and have always looked upon them as friends and mentors.

Lt Col J H R Downes Powell.

Sh Ch Golden Tint of Tregwillym. Photo: C M Cooke

Harold Newman and Cliff Payne.

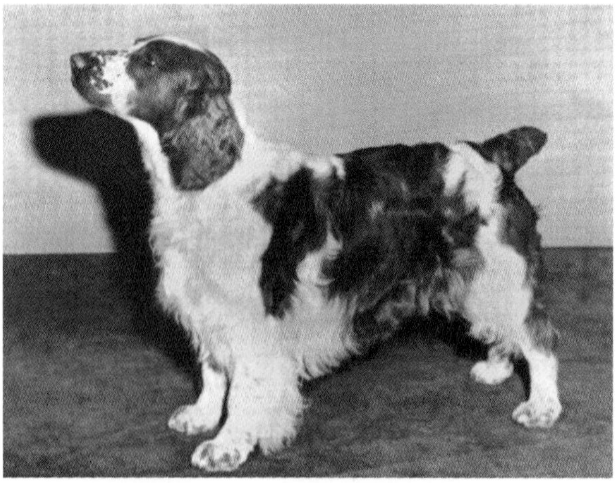

Sh Ch Deri Darrell of Linkhill.

Ch Rockhill Rhiwderin, now owned by Frank Hart, returned to the showring in the 1960s with great success, and Hubert Arthur's Sh Ch Brancourt Belinda continued to take many top honours, with his Sh Ch Fashion Plate, and Sh Ch Diplomat of Hearts, a son of Belinda, also coming to the fore. Ann West's Sh Ch Deri Darrell of Linkhill, son of Ch Statesman of Tregwillym, and another of her big winners, Sh Ch Arabella of Linkhill, entered the arena, followed by her daughter, Sh Ch Liza of Linkhill. Deri Darrell went on to be an all-time great, with the distinction of winning 26 Challenge Certificates, including those at Crufts for six successive years, five of them with Best of Breed, and in 1964, he was Best in Show at the West of England Ladies' Kennel Society's Championship Show.

Mrs D M Perkins' Sh Ch Bruce of Brent had a similar distinction at the Ladies' Kennel Association's Championship Show in 1970, having held the position of Leading Dog of the Year in 1969 and 1970.

Also in the 1960s, Ken Burgess started to bring the Plattburn kennel into the limelight. Based on Frank Hart's Denethorp lines, he made up two big winners, Sh Chs Paramount and Penny. George Couzens' bitch Krackton Surprise Packet had the distinction of becoming a full Champion.

While the show bench was going from strength to strength in the 1960s, the Field was experiencing a difficult time. The separate Field Trial for Welsh Springers in 1962 had to be cancelled due to lack of entries, and in 1963 the General Committee of the Breed Club split into Shows and Field Trials sub-committees. In July 1965, a Special General Meeting was held when it was agreed to sponsor the formation of a new Club (later called The Welsh & English Counties Spaniel Club), to conduct Field Trials for Any Variety Spaniel, and the Field Trial Sub-committee was to serve as Committee to the new Club. The working side had been dominated by three kennels, Hal Leopard's Rushbrooke, Mrs Dorothy Morriss' Stokecourt, and Cliff Payne's Tregwillym kennels.

Sh Ch Bruce of Brent.

Registrations rose steadily during the 1960s, reaching 385 in 1969, and in the same year Crufts entries reached an all-time high of 47. In 1963, Hal Leopard became Chairman, handing the post over to Dr Esther Rickards in 1966, when he became President. Dr Rickards was a powerful and formidable character, well known and loved throughout the gundog world, and owner of the world-famous Tarbay Cocker, Irish Water and Sussex Spaniels, before showing Welsh Springers with considerable success.

This decade was also notable for us. We bought our first Welsh Springer, Polly Garter of Doonebridge, purely as a pet and without guidance as to which lines we should aim for. How impressive it was to see all the red names on her pedigree when we went to choose her. It was even more exciting when Pete Painter, a neighbour (and, coincidentally, a breed expert and championship show judge of many years' standing), pointed out that Polly had all the top bloodlines and many of the big winners behind her: Sh Ch Denethorp Dihewyd, Ch Rockhill Rhiwderin, Sh Ch Diplomat of Hearts, Sh Ch Deri Darrell of Linkhill and, of course, Sh Ch Dewi Sant and Ch Statesman of Tregwillym. Inevitably, Polly entered the showring. After winning the Reserve Challenge Certificate at Windsor in 1968 in the capable hands of Jane Painter, we had our first litter by Red Chief of Tregwillym, and the puppies were registered with our new Hillpark affix in 1969. We kept a bitch, but tragedy struck when she was run over at eight months of age. We tried again, this time going to Sportsman of Tregwillym, a son of the famous Ch Statesman. As a result, we kept Pollyanna, who went on to be our first Show Champion, and one our best brood bitches.

Sh Ch Hillpark Pollyanna. Photo: C M Cooke

The 1970s to the 1990s

With ever increasing support at shows, the Welsh Springer Spaniel Club held its first Open Show in 1970, and attracted an entry of 111 dogs for judge Jack Griffiths. It was held at Witney in Oxfordshire and, now that I was handling our Polly at local shows, Pete Painter and his daughter, Jane, who was Secretary of the Club, persuaded us to enter. We did not go: it was too far, I thought, to travel 100 miles, just to a dog show. Ten months later, I was showing in Manchester, 200 miles away!

The first Welsh Springer Spaniel Club Championship Show was due to take place two months later, to be judged by the Chairman, Dr Esther Rickards. Tragedy had struck. Jane Painter was shortly to be married and, whilst making the preparations, her mother had collapsed and died. Several of us discussed the situation at Manchester and, somehow, this resulted in Gordon Pattinson and myself volunteering to run the Show. Fortunately, we had Dr Rickards to steer us through with her great experience and expertise in Kennel Club procedure and, despite breaking a number of KC rules and regulations, it all went smoothly and we survived. Eighty-five dogs were entered.

The Club Annual General Meeting was to take place after the show, something which would not even be contemplated today. Jane Painter was not able to continue as Club Secretary and, with a great deal of persuasion, I was elected to the position – and remained there for 15 years!

This was a significant time for the development of the breed. In 1971, 409 Welsh Springers were registered, and this trend continued right through the following decades. More and more new faces came into the showring and, in 1976, 20 sets of Challenge Certificates were on offer. This meant that there was an increase in big winners, too. Ken Burgess' Sh Ch Plattburn Progressor was a star of the time and also was used extensively at stud. Ken Burgess had a string of other very successful dogs, notably Sh Chs Plattburn Perchance, Pinetree and Probability, and Kaliengo Flash (see opposite).

Progressor was the sire of Harold Newman's great winner, Sh Ch Progress of Pencelli. Harold also had Sh Ch Roger of Pencelli, a son of Sh Ch Bruce of Brent, and both these outstanding dogs had a great influence on the breed, with their offspring meeting with great success abroad as well as in this country.

Cliff Payne had yet another top-class bitch, Sh Ch Contessa of Tregwillym (see opposite), bred by Dr Anne Christie from Tregwillym stock. Contessa had the distinction of winning 30 Challenge Certificates, and was awarded Best in Show at the Ladies' Kennel Association's Championship Show in 1976. Maggie Mullins judged the breed, Maurice Gilliat the Group, and Dr Rickards awarded Best in Show.

Yet another full champion, George Courzens' Ch Krackton Surprise Packet, had a Tregwillym sire, this time Nobleman of Tregwillym.

One of the most successful kennels of Welsh Springers of all time is Noel and Dodo Hunton Morgans' Dalati kennel. They started their long line of Dalati title holders in 1971, and new stars have emerged continuously ever since. Among the biggest winners at that time were Del, Fflur, Delwen, Rhian, Helwr (owned by L Rees), and Gwawr (owned by Denis Phillips – see opposite). Del and Dalati Fflur also qualified in the Field, joining the very few Welsh Springers to hold the title of Champion.

There were several smaller, but nonetheless successful, kennels. Gordon Pattinson's dual purpose Champion Tidemarsh dogs, Rip and Tidemark (page 34), were there. The Mullins' Sh Ch Athelwood Sweet Rosalie (who won the bitch Challenge Certificate at Crufts in 1980 and 1981), John Thirlwell's Sh Ch Dalati Gwent and Peter Ravenhill's Sh Ch Derosse Lucky Sovereign, both sired by Sh Ch Progress of Pencelli (page 34), were amongst the big winners.

Barbara Ordish had success with her Goldsprings kennel, using Harold Newman's Progress and Roger (and with our own Hillpark line behind it). Our kennel was also meeting with some success; our Sh Ch Mr Polly (overleaf) was awarded Best of Breed at Crufts in 1975 with Harold Newman judging, and the Dog Challenge Certificate the following year.

We also had two other title holders, Sea Esther (sired by Progress) and Reverie (page 35), both daughters of Sh Ch Hillpark Pollyanna. As it has always been our policy not to campaign our dogs once they have gained their titles, they stayed at home, while we brought out a new youngster.

The Welsh Springer Spaniel Club lost two great and influential personalities during this period. Harold Newman was elected President in 1975, and continued to give of his great knowledge and experience to all who sought it. Five years later, as he was preparing for Crufts, he died suddenly, having suffered from angina for some time. I had spent another happy and educational visit to the Rhondda Valley, and had just written to Harold to confirm that my Reverie was in whelp to Pencelli Mwyn (Monty). We kept a dog puppy, and called him Monty; he was not a show dog, but lived to a great age, and was one of the greatest characters that we have ever had. After Harold's death, his Monty went to Sweden, where he also had a very long life, and a successful show career.

The other great loss to the Club was the passing of Dr Rickards, who was Chairman

(Left) BIS: Sh Ch Kaliengo Flash,
(right) BOS: Sh Ch Goldsprings Guillemot.

Sh Ch Contessa of Tregwillym winning BIS.

Sh Ch Dalati Gwawr.

Ch Tidemarsh Tidemark.

Progeny Class. Winner: Sh Ch Progress of Pencelli.

Sh Ch Hillpark Mr Polly.

from 1966 to 1977. She had been invaluable to the Club during its rapid expansion, and a great friend and confidence builder to me, particularly during my early years in office. Dr Rickards was succeeded by Noel Hunton Morgans, who became President of the Club in 1984, a position he held for 10 years.

In the 1970s, the Welsh Springer, with its distinctive red and white colouring, began to appear in advertisements on television, cards, calendars and cans of food. Further publicity came when the Post Office featured a Welsh Springer on a 10½p stamp (below), one of a series which was launched to coincide with Crufts in 1979.

The stamp caused considerable opposition from Welsh Springer people, as the dog appeared to be a very poor specimen. It materialised that the artist, Peter Barrett, had originally selected four regional breeds, English Setter, Welsh Corgi, Irish Wolfhound and Collie. The Post Office was not happy with the Corgi because of its Royal connections, and the artist had had to produce a different Welsh breed at short notice. That was the Welsh Springer, and he used a Welsh Springer cross as a model! There was a special launch of the stamp by the Post Office in Cardiff, with an

British Dogs (Welsh Springer Spaniel). Reproduced from a stamp designed by Peter Barrett.

exhibition of photographs, paintings and trophies, covering all aspects of the breed, and a beautiful perpetual challenge cup was presented by Wales and Marches Postal Board for the best Welsh Springer at the South Wales Kennel Association's Championship Show.

Welsh Springer Spaniel Club Championship Show 1979. (Left) BIS: Sh Ch Hillpark Reverie, (right) Reserve BIS: Sh Ch Derossé Lucky Sovereign.

Until 1978, when William Pferd from the United States produced his book *The Welsh Springer Spaniel*, there was little literature devoted solely to the breed. This was a welcome volume. John Phillips broadened the spectrum with his comprehensive historical masterpiece, *The Essential Welsh Springer Spaniel*, published in 1984. Both books are currently out of print, but are definite collectors' items.

The Welsh Springer Spaniel Club and the breed continued to flourish in the 1980s, and in 1989 registrations reached 800, having risen steadily throughout the decade. Membership stood at 930 at the end of 1986. The Club Championship Shows were held annually. In 1983, 192 dogs entered, and two judges officiated for the first time. Apart from 1984 when there was again one judge for both dogs and bitches, this practice has continued ever since. This show has become the highlight of the year, with spectators coming from all over the world. Some regard the prestigious Best in Show award at this show to be a greater achievement than Best of Breed at Crufts.

In the 1980s, the Hunton Morgans' Dalatis were still to the fore with new stars, and their stock was behind many of the big winners. It was during this decade that a new and outstanding star emerged: Sh Ch Dalati Sioni. This dog was not only a great winner himself, but has proved to be the most influential sire of his time, achieving the status of Britain's Top Stud Dog All Breeds in 1992. During this time, John Thirlwell's Sh Chs Ferndel Stroller and Paperlace, John and Joy Hartley's Sh Ch Weslave Winter Mist, Roy and Mavis Harrison's Sh Ch Fiveacres Frivolity, Christine McDonald's Ch Northey Woodpecker, and Tricia Hylton's Ch Melladomina Jessie Meade (they both gained their Working Certificates, too) were all big winners, and all had Dalati behind them. Christine McDonald had another very big winner, and another full Champion, Ch Northey Stormcloud. Trudy Short's Ch Parkmist Jade also gained his title at the age of 12 years.

Sh Ch Golden Boy of Tregwillym.

Cliff Payne's powerful Tregwillym line continued to provide the breed with soundness and type, and still he was able to bring out yet another good one, Sh Ch Golden Boy of Tregwillym. This

Sh Ch Wainfelin Barley Mo, BOB at Leeds Championship Show 1987, judged by the author.

dog was used quite extensively at stud, and amongst his progeny were the Pickerings' Sh Ch Twiggy of Freewheelin' and our own Sh Ch Hillpark Moonlight. Margaret Powell's Sh Ch Blorenge Megan, bred by John Kenefick, and of Tregwillym breeding, was a very big winner, and then another record breaker, Mansel and Avril Young's Sh Ch Wainfelin Barley Mo, joined the truly elite.

He was my real favourite, the one that I consider was the nearest thing to a perfect Welsh Springer that I have had my hands on. I used him as a model when I was asked to make a video about judging the breed for some Finnish judges who were at Leeds Championship Show in 1987; he went on to win the Gundog Group later in the day, which was a great thrill for me. He was sired by Tregwillym Royal Mint, as was Len and Kath Morgan's Sh Ch Cwrt Afon Poeth Goch, and another record breaker, Sh Ch Dalati Sarian, who won the Gundog Group at Crufts in 1990, a great occasion for all Welsh Springer enthusiasts.

Noel Hunton Morgans with Sh Ch Dalati Sarian.
Photo: Marinus Nijhoff

Other new names were coming forward in the 1980s. Ken and Del Spate had several title holders with their Delkens kennel, the star being Sh Ch Delkens Teralea. Sh Ch Menstonia Misty Morn and Sh Ch Menstonia Moonraker came from Christine Knowles' kennel. And there was the dog, unpronounceable for many of us, Sh Ch Ymynwy Cymreig Swynwr, bred by Lyn Bowen and owned by Graham Holder.

While Sh Ch Dalati Sarian was collecting the Bitch Challenge Certificates, there was another very big winner in dogs, John Perry's Sh Ch Russethill Ringmaster of Sierry, son of Sh Ch Dalati Sioni and bred by Doreen Gately, who has based her breeding on Dalati bloodlines with tremendous success. Ringmaster won the Contest of Champions in 1989, and I had given his mother, Sh Ch Delkens

Toneia at Russethill, the Bitch Challenge Certificate at the Breed Club Show in 1988 when she was a Veteran. Sh Ch Russethill Ringleader, Ringmaster's litter brother, also collected six Challenge Certificates for owner Hazel Leary. Another Russethill star is Sh Ch Russethill Royal Tan, again sired by Sh Ch Dalati Sioni, and out of Russethill Reverie.

Interest was growing on the working side, largely due to the enthusiasm of Mrs Dorothy Morriss (Stokecourt). Gordon Pattinson's dogs were great workers, and with Angie Lewis (Riscoris), Eileen Falconer (Hackwood) and Ray Plunkett (Clankerry), the dual-purpose Welsh Springer was proving that it was still a reality.

Sh Ch Russethill Royal Tan. Photo: Bill Gately

Although only a relatively small section of the Welsh Springer Spaniel Club was involved in the competitive working side, working tests were held in various parts of the country, and several Certificates of Merit were awarded. Then, in 1983, the Diamond Jubilee year of the Club, the Field Trial was revived after a break of 23 years. Eileen Falconer's Hackwood Kingfisher (see overleaf) had the distinction of winning the event that year, and again in 1984.

Clankerry Taffy.

John Phillips has nurtured the working side for many years now, and his efforts have been rewarded with a small but strong contingent of enthusiasts, particularly in Essex. Christine McDonald (Northey), Derek and Pat Dean (Pasondela), Julie Revill (Julita) and Gill Tully (Highclare), all are demonstrating that the Welsh Springer is a true dual purpose breed. In South Wales, John and Jayne Derrick (Mynyddmaen) lead another very successful and enthusiastic team.

Welsh Springers have always been well represented at the Show Spaniels' Field Day (see overleaf), an annual event held by the Midland English Springer Spaniel Society specifically for show spaniels, giving them the opportunity to qualify in the field as well. Many Welsh Springers have gained their qualifying certificates, and on most occasions they have taken the top awards in the other tests on the day.

Hackwood Kingfisher: winner of Welsh Springer Spaniel Club Field Trial 1983 and 1984.

With the large explosion in popularity of Welsh Springers in the 1980s, some health problems were inevitably coming to light and causing concern amongst owners and breeders.

In the past, if a dog had any health problem, it was quietly put to sleep and buried. It was considered that if a dog could jump a five-bar gate and do a day's work, there could not be much wrong with it physically. If a dog had a fit, this was nothing new: it was something which has always been common in all dogs, pedigree and otherwise, and many old books about dogs will tell you how to deal with the problem. In my collection, I have a wonderful handbook by 'Stonehenge' (J H Walsh), *The Dog: Its Varieties and Management in Health and Disease*, price one shilling (5p), published in 1893. There it is: 'Epilepsy, with the inconvenience of it':

...coming on without notice, and in the setter and pointer is peculiarly annoying, because it generally shows itself at the time when their services are most wanted, namely, during the middle of a day's shooting. Very often this happens during the excitement of the 'point', but the fit is scarcely remarked till the birds are sprung, when the dog generally falls, and is seized with struggles and foaming at the mouth. Generally this lasts for a few minutes, extending sometimes to half an hour, after which he recovers himself, and will even continue his work without loss of nose. With regard to the causes of epilepsy nothing is known, but its attacks are aggravated by improper food, and by the addition of flesh without due preparation, as is often heedlessly done just before the shooting season. The treatment consists in attention to the general health, and in the administration twice a day of a dose of bromide of potass in a pill, which varies from one to three grains, according to the size of the dog. Aperients, or even emetics, will be more likely to do good than any other medicine, and the use of the former is by far the most likely palliative measure.

Times have changed, and we are more health conscious, for ourselves as well as for our dogs. The Welsh Springer Spaniel Club adopted a policy of naming any dog or bitch which had produced fitting offspring, initially without verifying the cause – and there are many causes, as can be seen in the article by Geoff Skerritt in chapter 7 on health. As a result, some well established and very successful bloodlines were lost forever, both in the field and in the showring. Inevitably the gene pool was weakened, and breeders have found it very difficult to plan a breeding programme, as the emphasis has tended to be on health rather than on maintaining a type and improving the stock. Hips and eyes also came into the equation. Dogs' hips began to be X-rayed and scored regularly. This provided an indication of the state of hips in the breed and acted as a guideline for breeders in their choice of breeding stock, together with testing for eye defects.

It is vitally important that everything should be done to minimise, if not eliminate, any disease in our dogs. Sometimes, though, we may have to take a few calculated risks if we are to preserve the true Welsh Springer, with the true Welsh Springer temperament, that we have always known.

In the early days of the breed's development, it was accepted that some outcrossing with other breeds took place. During the 1970s, the Welsh Springer Spaniel Club had some correspondence with overseas breeders, who suggested that the introduction of some English Springer blood might enhance the performance of the Welsh Springer in the field. This met with total disapproval by the Breed Club in this country. However, I have my suspicions that some Cocker Spaniel blood was introduced at this time: some larger, pendulous and curly ears began to appear. In more recent years, there has been a change in coat colour: still red, but nearer liver than the beautiful, rich red that is so typical of the Welsh Springer. This raises the question as to whether or not some English Springer blood may have been introduced. I take heart from Eric Fitch Daglish's assurance, in his *Dog Breeder's Manual*, that when there are occasional outcrosses, usually the effects are temporary, being overwhelmed in due course by breeding back to the original stock and using the old lines.

For some years, the Welsh Springer Spaniel Club had been expanding rapidly in membership, both at home and overseas. At the end of 1980, membership stood at 619, and the time had come for a second Breed Club to be formed. In 1981, the Welsh Springer Spaniel Club of South Wales received the blessing of The Kennel Club, achieved Championship status in 1985, and is a thriving and well-supported Club in every aspect of the breed. This was followed in 1986 by an equally successful regional Club: The South Eastern Welsh Springer Spaniel Club. They achieved Championship status in 1992, and Dodo Hunton Morgans and I had the honour of judging at their first Championship Show. In 1991, the North of England Welsh Springer Spaniel Club was recognised, with an expanding membership, and many enthusiasts are members of more than one, if not all, of the four Clubs.

The last decade of the century is confirming the popularity and strength of the breed. Entries at shows have continued to be buoyant, with up to 200 dogs being entered at the Breed Club Championship Shows.

It is also proving to be an era for breaking records in the showring. In the dogs, it is being dominated by the Wainfelin and Russethill kennels. Sh Ch Wainfelin Barley Mo was the first star, retiring from the showring in 1991 with 41 Challenge Certificates and many group wins and other successes to his credit, and several other big winners have come from this kennel during this period.

A South Eastern Welsh Springer Spaniel Club training group with trainer Julie Revill.

Sh Ch Russethill Royal Salute Over Nyliram.
Photo: Ruth Dalrymple

The new record holder is Tom Graham's Sh Ch Russethill Royal Salute over Nyrilam (Sh Ch Dalati Sioni ex Russethill Reverie), bred by Doreen Gately. Nearly 60 Challenge Certificates have been awarded to him and he has many big wins behind him, including Top Gundog of the Year, Reserve in the Group at Crufts and Best in Show at the Southern Counties Championship Show in 1993, the first Welsh Springer for 17 years to take this award at an all-breeds Championship Show.

Not to be outdone by the dogs, Sh Ch Northoaks Sea Mist of Menstonia (Sh Ch Dalati Sibrwd ex Menstonia Moonlight Mist), bred by Chris Anderson, broke the record for bitches with 33 Challenge Certificates, and again had some very big wins at the higher level. She is owned by Christine Knowles, another notable breeder and exhibitor with her Menstonia kennel.

Behind these record-breakers, and others who have met with notable success, are still Cliff Payne's Tregwillym and the Hunton Morgans' Dalati bloodlines, proving their continual influence on the breed. Although Dalati Welsh Springers do not appear so often in the ring now, they still continue to take top awards in the breed.

Other very successful kennels of the decade so far include Aranwr (Letch), Cwrt Afon (Morgan), Ferndel (Thirlwell), Highclare (Tully), Northey (McDonald), Northoaks (Anderson), Solva (Luckett Roynon), Taimere's (Tain), Tarendes (Jones) and Weslave (Hartley).

In the latter years, we have seen some others coming to the fore, and these include Dalville (Dalrymple), Kazval (Whyte), Mapleby (Bye), and Mynyddmaen (Derrick). No doubt others will emerge to join them as the new millennium begins.

The working side of the breed continues to thrive, particularly in the south east of England and South Wales, with Field Trials, Working Tests and training classes being enjoyed by Welsh Springers from enthusiastic supporters.

Club Fun Days are always very popular days out for dogs and families. With the emphasis on **fun**, they also provide an opportunity for pet owners to meet other Welsh Springer owners, and to learn about the different aspects of our breed. They may include a match or exemption show (described in Chapter 8 on Showing), demonstrations on trimming, handling, gundog training, and, most popular of all, competitions – timed scurries, fancy dress and obstacle races.

Sh Ch Taimere's Tempest, BOB Crufts 1994.

Fun Day: timed scurry.

Fun Day: fancy dress.

Docking became the subject of conversation, culminating in the banning of docking by lay people in this country in 1993. Breeders give support to the Council of Docked Breeds that works hard to maintain the option of docking puppies, and there are veterinary surgeons who continue to provide this service. Even today, it is relatively rare to see an undocked Welsh Springer in the showring in the United Kingdom.

Welsh Springer Spaniel Field Trial 1992.

Registrations in the 1990s have fluctuated somewhat. In 1991, 718 were registered, only 491 in 1992; in 1997, 465 Welsh Springers were registered compared with 13869 English Springers!

The Welsh Springer Spaniel Club had a new President in 1994, Mrs Vi Buchanan, but sadly she passed away the following year, and I had the great honour of succeeding her.

The year 1997 ended with a great triumph for the breed. John Thirlwell and Ruth Dalrymple's Sh Ch Dalville Dancing Water, the top-winning Welsh Springer of the year, repeated Sh Ch Bruce of Brent's success in 1964 by going Best in Show at the Ladies' Kennel Association Championship Show.

Far from being just a dual-purpose breed, Welsh Springers should perhaps be called multi-purpose. They are on display at the Game Fairs and The Kennel Club Discover Dogs event; they take part in obedience, agility and junior handling, hold diplomas for passing The Kennel Club Good Citizen Dog Scheme, and are used to sniff out drugs. They are, of course, very photogenic and are in great demand by the media and advertising world. But I still maintain that they are at their best living as part of the family, a loyal companion and friend.

chapter 3
Why Choose a Welsh Springer?

Is a Welsh Springer for Me?

If you are considering whether a Welsh Springer is the right dog for you, you are looking at an animal which customarily has a docked tail, is not too big and yet is big enough to be a real dog, not a toy. The male will be about 48cm (19in) at the withers, and the female about 46cm (18in) when fully grown, weighing 17–22kg (35–40lb). Probably the Welsh Springer's most appealing characteristic is his disposition. He loves life. He loves to be with the family, a member of your family, a child. He will follow you around the house, wherever you go, and will love to be included in whatever you and your family are doing. He is most affectionate, and this makes him a wonderful companion, not only for adults, but children as well.

Good companions.

The Welsh Springer is very energetic and expressive, and is always eager to demonstrate his affection for you when you come home. For this reason, we generally do not recommend families with very young children and toddlers to start with a Welsh Springer. It is far better to wait until the children are able to cope, and not be knocked over too easily by the loving friend. Our grandchildren have had Welsh Springers with them ever since they were born, with parents who knew the breed, and this is rather different. Our own children were aged six and four when we bought our first Welsh Springer, which we feel is ideal.

Welsh Springers are very sensitive dogs, and seem to be aware of what is required of them, tolerating being crawled over and having their hair pulled, and being generally manhandled. They are very intelligent, and are quick to sum up a situation. Once the suitcase appears, you will find it very hard to leave the house without your dog, and if you are out and leave him behind, he will know that he is not accompanying you this time, and will probably keep vigil on the windowsill until he hears you return. He will recognise the sound of your car and, if you are talking on the telephone with the dog apparently asleep at your feet, he has an uncanny sense and will get up just before you reach the end of your conversation.

Welsh Springers are not good kennel dogs on the whole, as they tend to bark when left. What they really want is to be with you. They cannot be regarded as guard dogs, but most will bark when there is someone at the door, some will try to 'answer' the telephone for you. With their unfailing loyalty, I would always feel safe in any untoward situation. If I am alone in the house when it is dark and someone calls, I always answer the door with a Welsh Springer at my side. They do not appreciate scruffy-looking individuals, and will give them a noisy warning.

Helping in the garden.

When it comes to the evening, sitting watching television, the Welsh Springer's resting place is on his back on your lap, with legs in the air, and the bottom jaw dropping. This is his seventh heaven, and the cat must take second place. If a Welsh Springer grows up with a cat, they will probably become the best of friends, curling up together, but the Welshman does tend to chase cats, and he will need to be disciplined, just like a child, right from the beginning, right from Day One. If there is a fire burning in the hearth, you will have to expect to take a seat behind him – or, in our case, behind them!

The Welsh Springer puppy will, like any other puppy, do a certain amount of damage: dig holes in your lawn, remove your newly-planted flowers and shrubs, and generally 'help' you in the garden. It is all part of his life.

He is not a patient dog: if he wants to come in, he will probably make his presence known by scratching the door and, on a wet day, his muddy paws will cross your newly washed kitchen floor. He will delight in chewing children's plastic toys, flower pots and socks if they are left available for him and, if you arrive home with tired feet after a day in your new high heels and slip them off while you have a cup of tea, don't be surprised if the puppy picks one up and lies watching you with his big honest eyes as he quietly chews the back! His eyes say it all.

When considering a Welsh Springer, you must bear in mind that the dog, after the puppy stage, will need to be taken for a walk every day, whatever the weather. He will not exercise himself just by being let loose in the garden. His walk should include an opportunity for running free, off the lead, for at least half an hour, and the minimum time you should expect to devote to the daily walk would be an hour, with a further short walk at another time in the day.

Dogs are not always welcome in town parks, and often there are restrictions, so they have to be kept on a lead. It must never be forgotten that the Welsh Springer is a gundog, a country-loving dog, and a town flat is not a suitable environment for him. A confined, bored Welsh Springer will create havoc. You must have a well-fenced garden, the fence ideally at least 1.5m (5ft) high, with a secure gate.

The coat will need brushing and combing daily, and it is advisable to keep the feet trimmed, and also to cut away the hair under the ears to allow air to circulate, as the Welsh Springer has a pendulous ear that provides an excellent place for bacteria to thrive and cause an infection. This trimming should be done about every six weeks. It is quite easy to do yourself as you will see in Chapter 6.

As a general rule, Welsh Springers are good eaters and enjoy their meals, but just a few start off well as puppies but become fussy, and it is then difficult to tempt them to eat a good meal. This can be worrying for the new owner and, indeed, the experienced breeder. The dog remains full of life and, if you consult the vet, you will probably be told that there is nothing wrong with him. So be patient, and remember that the Welsh

Running free. Photo: John Curtis

Springer remains a puppy longer than most breeds; in fact, they tend not to settle down until they are about 18 months old, perhaps not reaching maturity until four or five years of age.

For a general daily maintenance diet, we find that approximately 300g (9oz) of a good complete food is right for our adult dogs, and I always add a tablespoonful of meat and a little gravy to the meal, just to make it more interesting. The meat can be fresh or tinned, tripe or chicken – in fact, anything that is available, and the dogs do well on it.

You may choose to feed meat and a mixer meal; the daily requirement of meat (or other protein) for an adult Welsh Springer is approximately 340g (12oz).

Many owners like to take their dogs on holiday with them, and there are hotels and self-catering holiday cottages where dogs are welcomed. For good relations, make sure that your dog is well behaved, is kept off the furniture, and is under control at all times, especially in the countryside – and, of course, clean up behind him, straight into a plastic bag, which is easily carried in your pocket.

Some say that dogs cannot recognise colour but I disagree. Without doubt, Welsh Springers spot one of their own kind at a distance, and are able to distinguish them from

any other breed. I believe that they are pack dogs, and like to be with others of their breed. In our household, we have a pack leader and, as in nature, this position has to be established, creating a pecking order. This has to be re-established every time one of the dogs has been away from the others. One of the 'pack' will look after the others: wash their faces and ears, and tend any wound that there might be. It is not always appreciated that dogs wash themselves like cats. One of our bitches only washes her own offspring, from different litters, one a dog much bigger than herself, and she will hold the heads down with her paw as she performs her duties.

A bitch will teach her puppies to play by lowering her front legs and chest, with the hindquarters left in the standing position, challenging the pups to come forward. You will find that your puppy will want to play with you in the same way.

Welsh Springers have a very unfortunate trait, which may cause owners some distress. When out for a walk, they love to roll in evil-smelling dirt: cow pats, dead and decaying animals or birds and, worst of all, the very pungent fox excrement. They revel in sliding their necks along the dirt, both sides, and even down their backs, requiring immediate washing down on their return, with a sweet-smelling shampoo or, as suggested recently on television, by rubbing tomato sauce on it!

It is accepted that dogs are not loyal to their partners. However, on a recent trip to Egypt, we were fascinated to notice that, wherever we went, dogs were roaming the streets

Playing in the snow.

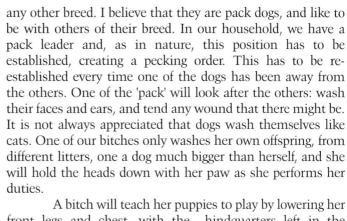

and temples or lying asleep in pairs, dog and bitch apparently living together. This certainly posed a question.

Conclusion

I quote from "Stonehenge" (J H Walsh) in his book *The Dog: Its Varieties and Management in Health and Disease*, dated 1893, where the canine species is summed up admirably:

The dog possesses all the qualities of intelligence and spirit. Where can we find a more certain, more constant, or more devoted friendship, a more faithful memory, a stronger attachment, more sincere abnegation, a mind more loyal and frank? The dog does not know what ingratitude is. He does not abandon his benefactor in danger or adversity. With joy he offers to sacrifice his life for those who feed him. He pushes his devotion so far as to forget himself. He does not recall the corrections, the unkind treatment, to which he has been subjected; he thirsts for caresses, while the indifference of those who are dear to him plunges into deep distress. Noble creature! the favourite of the rich, consolation of the poor, inseparable companion of the unfortunate; thanks to thee, the miserable individual who dies alone in the midst of society, counts at least one friend at his melancholy funeral; he does not descend alone into the cold grave, for thou comest to shed on his tomb the sincere tears of affection and regret, and such is the excess of thy grief, that no one can tear thee from that spot where sleeps the corpse of him thou lovest!

A Welsh Springer wearing 'snowboots'.

And what intelligence! what penetration! what finesse is there in this admirable companion of our gladness and sorrow! How well he can read countenances; how skillfully he knows how to interpret the sentiments conveyed in gestures and words! In vain you may threaten, in vain try to frighten him. Your eye betrays you; that smile, which scarcely appears upon your lips, has unmasked your feelings; and so far from fearing and avoiding you, he comes to solicit your attention.

The Welsh Springer has so much to give and if, after considering all the aspects of the breed, you feel that his attributes and characteristics can fit into your lifestyle, he is definitely for you. You either hate them or are obsessed with them, and then no other breed will ever suffice!

chapter 4

Making Your Choice

Having decided that a Welsh Springer is for you, where do you go from there? When we made that decision in 1965, we thought that you could go out and buy one, there and then. How wrong can you be? We had reached our decision by studying *The Observer's Book of Dogs*, and finding that every time we finished on page 158 – The Welsh Springer Spaniel. It fitted the bill for an active, country-loving family: Mum, Dad, and two small children aged four and six years. We had never actually seen one, so at the local agricultural show our first port of call was the Exemption Dog Show – no Welsh Springers, and no one seemed able to tell us where we could find one.

Quite by chance, a litter was advertised in the local paper, four dogs and two bitches. An appointment was made, and the outcome was the purchase of the only bitch still for sale, the 'pick of the litter', at a cost of 14 guineas (£14.70), which my husband thought was far too much to pay for a puppy. I had to work hard to persuade him! That was Polly Garter of Doonebridge, bought as a pet and, unbeknown to us, carrying the top bloodlines in her pedigree. This was eventually to be our introduction to showing and breeding (with a lot of help from those already in the breed), and Polly became the foundation bitch of our Hillpark kennel.

Choosing a Puppy as a Pet

You can start by looking at the advertisements in your local paper: you may be lucky, but Welsh Springers are not easy to find. Make sure that you can see the puppies with their mother. Puppy farmers send puppies off to dealers or pet stores, probably at the age of five weeks, and possibly without pedigrees and registration certificates. It is *always* best to go direct to a breeder. The Kennel Club (see **Useful Addresses**) will give you the names of the secretaries of the Breed Clubs, who will have lists of breeders with puppies available, or that are expecting a litter. They can also give you some idea of the price that you will have to pay for a puppy. You can go to a Dog Show – Crufts, perhaps – buy a catalogue, look at the dogs, talk to the owners, and make a note of the dogs that appeal to you. Most exhibitors are very happy to talk to and help anyone interested in the breed. Puppies may not be available at that time, but you can put your name on a waiting list. The breeders will want to know all about you, just as you will want to know all about them. It is a two-way process of 'vetting' each other: the breeders will be as anxious as the purchasers that the right puppy is supplied to the right home.

While you are at Crufts, you can visit the 'Discover Dogs' section, where all the recognised breeds are on show with experts on hand to advise and answer your questions. This is now also staged annually in London in the autumn.

If you cannot make it to Crufts, dog shows are held all over the country throughout the year and are advertised in the canine papers every week. It is always a good idea to arrange to visit the breeders so that you can see the dogs in their own environment and have a chance for a general discussion with their owners. If possible, visit more than one kennel and, once you have decided that you like what you see, ask to put your name on the waiting list and enquire about the price of a puppy. The breeders will then contact you once they have something to offer, or maybe one of their stud dogs has sired a litter, often to a pet bitch, which they can recommend.

We do not usually allow interested parties to view our puppies until they are at least three weeks old, when they are just starting to move around their bed. When you visit at that time, the mother will be with the pups and, although our bitches are always proud and happy to show off their young, some bitches can be protective. It is really far better to go when the puppies are five weeks old, and are active and responsive. You may not be able to choose the one you want, especially if the breeders are thinking of keeping one or two themselves as, although they may have a good idea of their final choice, they will not be making their decision until the last minute. What you will decide is whether or not you like the look of the litter, and we find that prospective owners do not mind which puppy they have – they love them all! Neither the breeder nor the interested party is under any obligation at this stage but, if an agreement is made, it is wise from all points of view to pay a deposit and obtain a receipt.

Playing with seven-week-old puppies.

If you are choosing a puppy as a pet, you will be looking for one that most appeals to you, the one, perhaps, that comes to you first, the one with the cheekiest expression, or the one with more red or white on it. The choice is entirely yours but, as breeders, we find that new owners often choose the puppy which we have already thought might be the one for them, although we never tell them until they have made their own decision.

A good Welsh Springer should look healthy, with bright eyes, and have an outgoing temperament. Markings do not matter; as a pet owner, you will be looking for a dog that is going to fit into your lifestyle.

Make a list of the questions that you want to ask the breeder, and find out before you collect the puppy what sort of diet it will be on, so that you can get some of the same food to start with. You can always change the diet to something else once the puppy has settled in. Many breeders will have small packs of puppy food to give you, and you should be given full details of the diet, the dates of worming, the puppy's pedigree, The Kennel Club Registration Certificate, (this is not always available until later, but make sure that it is in hand), and details of the Breed Clubs. The puppy's registration certificate should be signed on the reverse side by the breeder, transferring the puppy to you, as the new owner. If you wish to register the puppy at The Kennel Club under your name, you should complete the transfer form, and return it with the required fee to The Kennel Club. You should also check whether or not the puppy has been vaccinated. This is usually done at the 10-week stage, but you need to check this with your veterinary surgeon. Many breeders insure their puppies for a few weeks after they leave them, so check up on that. We are now having our puppies tattooed before they leave us, and this certificate will also be enclosed in our puppy's folder.

For a first bed, we recommend a cardboard box with the front cut out, and a small blanket. It is easy to replace at no cost, and it is bound to be chewed in the early days and months. A 70cm (27in) plastic bed, readily available from pet stores, is ideal later on, again lined with a blanket. You can use a bean bag, but wicker baskets and soft 'edible' beds are best left until well after puppyhood.

You can also use a collapsible cage. These are becoming popular with dog owners: not only can a cage be used when house-training a puppy and when you want to leave it safely at home when you go out, but it can be used in the car instead of a dog guard; if you go to a hotel where they welcome dogs, both you and the management will feel happy that there will be no accidents if you have a cage. The ideal size for a Welsh Springer is 78cm (31in) long x 53cm (21in) wide x 61cms (24in) high. Your breeder will probably be able to tell you where they can be obtained; they are also advertised in the weekly canine press.

When you arrive to collect your puppy, it will probably be about eight weeks old. The journey home may be its first time in a car, so bring a towel and some newspaper with you to deal with any mishap. Usually, if someone nurses the puppy for the journey, it sleeps all the way but if it is travelling in a box or cage, it is best to line the container well with newspaper, just in case.

Choosing a Puppy for Showing

No breeder can ever guarantee that a puppy will turn out to be a top winner in the showring, Much thought will have been given to the pairing of the dog and the bitch which, on paper, should produce a good show prospect. However, it is never a certainty, and you should bear this in mind when purchasing a puppy for showing.

If this is your first show puppy, you will need some help. Go to a number of shows, and decide on the type of Welsh Springer that you like. Talk to exhibitors and breeders, and have a good look at the dogs on the benches at the Championship shows. Breed Club shows provide an excellent opportunity to see dogs from most of the breeders' kennels.

Once you have come to a decision, you should approach the breeders, letting them know what you are looking for. They should then let you know when they have something which they feel would be suitable for you. Selecting a show specimen is always a bit of a gamble, and we have all found that the best one from a litter is the one sold as a pet!

The breeder will probably want you to select your puppy when it is eight weeks old. Study the Breed Standard (see chapter 9) before you arrive at the kennels. When you see the litter, one might catch your eye straight away, not just because of the markings, but the puppy's general presence. Pick the pup up and put it on the table – with the breeder's agreement, of course. Then try and get an overall picture of the pup – do you like its head, has it got a straight front, is its general conformation and angulation good and, above all, is its temperament out-going? Look and see if it has a scissor bite (that is, whether the lower incisors touch the inside of the upper incisiors) and, if you are choosing a male, you should be able to feel two small testicles. These are not always apparent at this age but, personally, I would not take the risk that they might descend later.

Assessing eight-week-old puppies.

The pigment of the nose might still have a small pink fleck, but our experience is that this fills in and is not a problem. The red coat may be fluffy and could be light in colour. This also will change as the puppy grows, and the red patches on the body seem to spread. The Breed Standard says that the colour of the Welsh Springer is red and white. If one looks at the old pictures of the breed, most show patches of red on a white background rather than solid reds that appear to be the tendency at the moment. The red certainly is striking, especially with the sun on the dogs' backs, but the true pearly white sparkles and can be very eye-catching. A good shoulder can be accentuated by the markings, and vice versa.

At eight weeks old, the pup's tail can be carried rather high, particularly when it is excited. The pup is still learning to co ordinate, and as long as the tail is set correctly, the carriage should come right in due course. The majority of breeders are still having their puppies' tails docked and, as Welsh Springers are working dogs, personally I hope that this will always be the case.

During your assessment, ask the breeder to show you what he considers to be the puppy's good points, and whether or not he would recommend that puppy rather than another one. In the end, the choice is yours, but he will know his stock and have a pretty good idea of how they might finish. You have to remember that you are a novice, and you and the puppy will be learning together. You may be lucky with your first show puppy, but what you are really looking for is the basis of your kennel for the future. From this point of view, it is better to start with a bitch rather than a dog. Then you have the chance of using the top stud dogs when you want to breed your own litter.

As with any purchase of a puppy, you will need all the documentation already referred to when you collect the puppy. You may have to pay more for a show puppy, but this is not always the case.

Choosing a Puppy from your own Litter

Here you have the advantage of seeing the puppies from the moment that they are born, and right through their early development. Some people say that they see what they are looking for as the puppy drops out and is still wet. I tend to agree with that, always bearing in mind that it is easy to be blind to the other puppies' virtues, which could be greater than those of your original eye-catcher.

An eight-week-old puppy.
Note that the tail is carried high.

You will notice the puppy that climbs out of bed first, and the first out of the kennel, and that is often the boldest all the way through. As their characters develop, you will be drawn to the one with the outgoing temperament. At about five or six weeks of age, you will be anxious to get the pups up on to a table to see how balanced they are, their angulation and shoulder placement – if you can get them to stand still long enough!

Look for bone and substance, a straight front even at this age, with only a very small gap between the tops of the shoulder blades. Heads will change and eyes will go darker, but you should still look for an honest expression, with a good stop (see page 108) and the scissor bite. In fact, you are really looking for the puppy that comes nearest to fulfilling your interpretation of the breed. In some breeds, such as the Cocker Spaniel, the eight week old puppy is a miniature adult of the breed. In Welsh Springers, this is not necessarily so – they can finish longer in body, or long or short in the leg, and this makes it harder to select your potential winner.

When we are looking for a show puppy, we spend hours just watching them – at play, at meal times or in the nest, and then we try to see the movement, which is not easy at this stage! We assess and re-assess each puppy as they play together. We may change our minds as the days go by but, in the majority of cases, the one what we picked out first is the one that stays.

It is a big responsibility when we send a puppy overseas, as the choice is ours. As it is carrying the Hillpark flag, naturally we want it to be a good representative of our kennel. The puppy will not be going until it is 12 weeks old, so we leave it as long as we can before making our final selection. On occasions, we have given the various tests and vaccinations required by the overseas buyer to more than one puppy so that we have the best chance of selecting the right one.

Choosing an Older Dog

The same puppy as the one on the opposite page at eight months.

If breeders have a promising litter, and are looking for a future show prospect, they will often run on more than one puppy and make their final decision later. An older puppy might be more suitable for you, as you will avoid the demanding early training stage of puppyhood, and you may have an opportunity of obtaining one that has not quite lived up to its early potential. You may still have to house-train the puppy if it is kennel-reared, but this should not be a problem. You are, of course, not being offered the runt of the litter: rather one of the best, and one that the breeder felt was worth running on.

There is also the possibility of obtaining a dog that needs re-homing. There is a Welsh Springer Spaniel Rescue and Re-housing scheme and, from time to time, dogs and bitches do have to be re-homed. This can be for a variety of reasons – the previous owner may have died, or there are changed domestic circumstances and, sadly, sometimes a Welsh Springer may have been sold to an unsuitable home in the first place. Before a Welsh Springer is re-homed, full investigations will be made, both on the dog's past and on its future. It is vital that the right home is found, to suit both dog and new owner so that a happy conclusion is reached. Care of the older dog will obviously be different, both in feeding and exercise, but dogs are very adaptable and will settle into a new environment quite quickly.

Dog or Bitch?

The choice is really yours. There are advantages and disadvantages for both. With the dog, you will have the problem of neighbouring bitches coming into season, when he will tend to roam if he is not kept under strict control. He may lift a leg on your furniture, or demonstrate his sexual desires on your leg or on a cushion. He will need to be disciplined, and made to realise that this behaviour is not acceptable.

With the bitch, you have to deal with the season every six or eight months, not only with attention from neighbouring males, but the inconvenience of bloodstains on your floor and carpets. She will have to be kept strictly under control, too, as it is surprising how agile an interested male can be. What used to be a sufficiently high fence is no longer an obstacle, and even an open downstairs window can be inviting – we have experienced it in our early days of dog ownership! The bitch appears to lose her sense of hearing when you call her, and will be very independent.

When asked the question, I generally advise new owners to choose a puppy of the same sex as the majority of the dogs in their neighbourhood. They will then have fewer problems themselves, and will not be upsetting their neighbours.

We are often asked about the difference in temperament between dogs and bitches. On the whole, dogs are more consistent with their affection and devotion, as bitches can be obstinate and independent when they are in season, but either sex will give you all the love that you ever ask for – and more.

Buying Two Puppies of the Same Age

This is not something that we encourage first-time owners to do. It can be easier to rear two puppies together, as they will probably settle and play happily with each other rather than chew your valuable possessions; but it can be harder to house-train them, as both will need to be put out at the same time, and probably one will dominate the other. Some prospective owners think that they would like two puppies, a dog and a bitch, but there will be difficulties when the bitch comes into season, however vigilant everyone is in keeping them apart.

Owners of an older dog sometimes want another puppy 'before it is too late'. In this case, a new puppy will probably settle in quickly, provided that the older dog is willing to accept it. With careful introduction, he usually does, and often gets a second lease of life as a result.

Neutering

This is called castration for the dog, and spaying for the bitch. Many owners have their dogs or bitches neutered for convenience, and many vets encourage it. It makes for a far easier life but, of course, it does have its disadvantages. A neutered Welsh Springer tends to put on weight, and any titbits should definitely be cut out. Manufacturers of total foods now have low calorie diets available, and these are ideal for both neutered and older dogs. An overweight Welsh Springer is highly undesirable, and the condition is as unhealthy as for the human race.

Anther disadvantage is that the coat of a neutered Welsh Springer becomes very profuse on the legs and the lower part of the body. This will need continuous trimming and thinning, and the dog or bitch will no longer have the sleek coat that appeals to so many.

Rearing Your Puppy

Settling In

You will have made your preparations for the new member of your family but, for the puppy, moving to a new family can be a very traumatic experience. He will have been used to his happy surroundings, playing with his brothers and sisters. Now you are subjecting him to a different lifestyle – yours.

As soon as you arrive home, put the pup down on the grass to relieve himself. Then carry him into the part of the house which is going to be his own and show him his bed. The pup will need lots of love and encouragement at this stage. Give him a chance to settle in before all the friends and neighbours come to admire him. You can offer him a small meal: something tempting such as a little chicken or rabbit with puppy meal and gravy, or some warm milk, but don't worry if he will not eat. This is probably the biggest worry for new puppy owners, especially when it goes on for several days and you begin to think that the pup is fading away. You can try tripe, pilchards, or even the cat's tinned food but, above all, have confidence that the pup will soon settle down to the diet that he has been used to. You may have one of the rare Welsh Springers that decide not be interested in food at all, and this is a big worry for the new owner, experienced or not. Seeing everything rejected is very dispiriting. Some people try hand feeding, something which I have never had to do, and I would try to avoid this if at all possible. We have had one or two fussy eaters but, by the time that they are adults, they have decided that food is a necessity of life. Choosy bitches seem to come right after having a litter.

Introducing the New Puppy

If you have other dogs, introduce the puppy carefully, and do not leave them together unsupervised until you are confident that the puppy has been accepted.

A cat will be very superior, and sit well out of reach but, very soon, you will probably find pup and cat together, and they will become good friends, even washing each other.

Dylan being introduced to Rupert.

Puppies love children, but do not overwhelm the puppy. Introduce them to each other quietly, and make sure that children know how to pick up the puppy. Puppies wriggle, and are easy to drop and injure. Lift the puppy, and hold his body so that he is lying along your arm. with his front legs in your hand. You can then hold the front legs with your fingers, and the pup will feel safe and not try to jump down.

Puppies need plenty of sleep, and should be given the opportunity to curl up on their own, undisturbed.

Probably the first few nights will be noisy. The puppy no longer has his

'Well, I know where *I'm* going to sleep – how about you?'

siblings to snuggle into, and he is lonely. You can leave the radio on very quietly, or have a clock ticking, and put a hot water bottle, wrapped in a small blanket, in his bed. You will probably have some disturbed nights, but be firm, telling the pup to go to bed. Whatever happens, unless you intend to have him in your bedroom, do not be tempted to take him upstairs, 'just for the first few nights'. Before you know where you are, he will be sharing your bed with you!

Alternatively, you can use the collapsible cage, to which I have already referred, and this will also help in house training. A pup will be very reluctant to soil his bed and, once he gets used to being in the cage, you can shut him in when you go out, knowing that he is happy and will not be chewing your furniture. To get the pup used to a cage, put his meals in it and leave the door open. Encourage the pup to sleep in there when you are in the room with him. Before long, probably you will find that the pup will choose to go into the cage and regard it as his own.

You will have to get up as soon as you hear the first murmur in the morning, as the pup will be desperate to go outside. Give lots of praise whenever he does what is required, and a firm 'no' when he misbehaves. Welsh Springers are strong-willed, and you must be emphatic with your commands, right from the start.

Every time the pup wakes up, and after every feed, put him out in the garden to relieve himself. When he is sniffing and wandering about, that probably means that he needs to go out, so put him out every time. We try to have our puppies at least newspaper-trained before they leave us at eight weeks. Put plenty of newspaper on the floor and, as the days go by, gradually confine the paper to the area near the door until the puppy realises that that is where he makes for when he needs to go out to relieve himself. There will no longer be any need for newspaper once the message is understood.

Feeding

Essential Nutrients

A dog needs to have a balanced diet, made up of six essential nutrients. Each of these plays a crucial part in maintaining a healthy animal.

Proteins

Proteins are present in every organ of the body, and are used for the building of muscle, hair, skin, enzymes and hormones.

Carbohydrates

These are present in many forms: sugars, starch and cellulose. Carbohydrates are a useful source of energy, and provide the 'bulk' which helps to keep the gut open.

Oils and fats
Oils and fats provide the dog with his major source of energy, but are also important in the production of hormones, and as a body insulator when laid down as fat.

Minerals
Dogs have a requirement for some 20 minerals, such as calcium for bones and teeth, potassium, magnesium and sodium for balancing fluid levels. Mineral balances are crucial, and excess quantities can be toxic.

Vitamins
Dogs require about 12 different vitamins in small quantities. Their main role is as part of the body's enzymes and immune system. An imbalance of vitamins can have a toxic effect.

Water
Water accounts for some 60% of the dog's weight. It is the most vital nutrient, performing such tasks as being the transport medium in blood, removing poisonous waste and regulating body temperature.

The Feeding Routine
From the time that you collect your eight-week-old puppy, he will need four meals a day. The rule is 'little and often', as he is growing fast and his activity level is high. You can continue the diet that the breeder will have given you, or you can change to another diet, but this should be done over a period of a few days, not suddenly, or you may find that the puppy has a tummy upset.

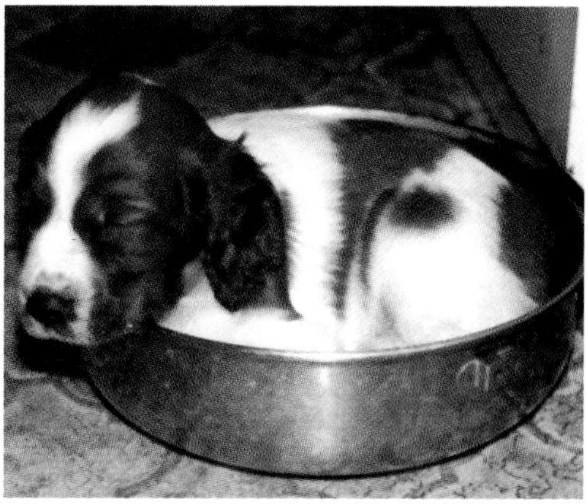
'Dinner time!'

There are a number of different ways of feeding, and it is really your choice as to what you give. The traditional diet is two milky meals, made with specially formulated powdered milk, with wholewheat biscuits, or rice pudding or egg custard, and two meals consisting of puppy biscuit meal mixed with protein – minced meat, tripe, chicken or scrambled egg (we usually cook the meat and chicken) – fed in the ratio of two-thirds protein to one-third biscuit meal. Quantities will vary, but your breeder will have told you how much the puppy has been having at each meal, and this should be increased as the puppy grows, and according to appetite. As a guideline, 75g (3oz) of meat mixed with 50g (2oz) biscuit meal could be what your puppy was having at each solid meal at eight weeks of age. You will need to add extra calcium in the form of tablets or powder, according to the manufacturers' instructions.

An alternative diet would be canned puppy food with a complementary mixer, used as directed. Some canned foods contain meat but are not complete; others have a mixture of meat and cereal. Some are fortified with additional ingredients to make them complete and balanced.

You can also use complete foods, which are becoming very popular, and this is the method which we are using at present. These are balanced foods, and **no additives such as calcium or vitamins are required**, as the foods have been manufactured specially to include everything that is needed to rear strong, healthy puppies. The dry food can be fed as it is, or mixed with gravy or warm water. I now have to make an admission: when we feed total food, we also add a little meat (tripe, which they love, but the smell is offensive to some people; scrambled egg; or good quality cooked or tinned meat), as I put the human element into it, and feel sure that the dogs like variety! At this stage, our puppy would be on a meat-based complete puppy food (32% protein), which he would stay on until approximately 12 weeks of age, when he is looking for something with a larger bite size.

We then gradually change to a meat-based junior food (approximately 30% protein), and feed this until the pup is about 12 months old. Another gradual change then takes place, to a standard cereal-based complete food (approximately 28% protein).

All foods we use are extruded and wheat gluten free, as these are gentler on the stomach, and aid digestion. I continue to 'humanise' my dogs' diets a little, adding a spoonful of meat with gravy or stock to each meal. Stock is made easily by adding water to any chicken carcass or meat bones left over from our own meal, which is then simmered for several hours, after which all bones are disposed of – never fed to the dogs. The only bones they ever get are cooked marrow bones, and these they get regularly as they are good for their teeth as well as providing them with hours of pleasure.

We have tried all these methods, and found them satisfactory, so which to use is really your decision.

We also give milk to our dogs, but not all dogs can assimilate it, and it can result in very loose faeces.

Make sure that fresh, clean water is always available. This is particularly important if you are feeding dry food.

When the puppy reaches six months, the number of meals can be cut down to three a day. Cut out one of the milky meals if you are still feeding them. Then, by nine months, another meal can be dropped and, at a year old, most puppies will require only one main meal a day. Some youngsters continue to need two meals a day after 12 months. Once they show a lack of interest in the second meal, it is a good indication that it can be dropped. If we still want a youngster to put on more weight, we will continue to feed the extra meal, perhaps for several months. Our principle is that if the ribs and spine are clearly visible, the dog is probably too thin; if the body 'rolls' when the dog trots, he is too fat! Each dog is watched daily, and some changes may be made to their diets depending on circumstances, for instance, for dogs on the show circuit, or pregnant bitches. The dogs never have titbits during the day; any household scraps go into their evening meal. They all have their own bowl, named (for my benefit, so that I can vary the quantity and contents for each dog if I need to, and for other people should someone else be feeding the dogs for me), and each is fed in the same place every time. They know which is their own meal, and this avoids arguments. Once the fast eaters have finished, they have to leave the room while the others finish, and then they all go out to relieve themselves. This is our routine, and I feel it is good for new owners and their dogs to establish their own routine.

We feed our adult dogs at 6pm, and they seem to have in-built clocks, as they are all sitting waiting for their meal at the appointed time, even when the clocks change at the beginning and end of summer. Last thing at night, when they have been out to relieve themselves and are ready for bed, they all have to sit around us before receiving a 'goodnight' hard biscuit each.

Light or senior diets are available if weight becomes a problem in older age, particularly with neutered dogs, but weight can usually be controlled by varying the quantity of standard food, and being very strict on just one meal a day and no titbits.

Old literature is always worth exploring, and again I quote from 'Stonehenge', this time on his *Management of Pet Dogs* (1893):

The food of pet dogs is almost too heating in its nature, considering that they are generally deprived of a proper amount of exercise.

I am sometimes induced for the sake of brevity to recommend correspondents to diet their dogs as they do their children. But unfortunately the latter are also often crammed with all sorts of improper articles of food; and I should perhaps be less liable to mislead my readers if I advised them to give their dogs the same kind of food which they would think right for the children of their acquaintances. Theory and practice are often widely separated, and many a mother is so weak as to allow her own child to tease her into giving creams and pastry, which she would, 'on principle', refuse to another not holding the same power over her maternal feelings. We all know how well bachelors' wives and old maids' children are managed, and therefore I would in a few words wind up the general principles of managing pet dogs by suggesting that, if the plans so often recommended by the wise virgins of this world for feeding their nephews and nieces are carried out in favour of pet dogs, a great improvement will be effected in their health and appearance.

Wise words indeed. Times have not changed, and 'Stonehenge's' principles are equally applicable today.

The Developing Puppy

Puppies grow at different rates. Some have reached their mature height by six months, others not until perhaps 10 months. Those that look mature at an early age can be finished by the time they are three years old, where others may take four years to mature, and still look young by the time they are seven or eight. If you have a slow developer, you just have to be patient! If a puppy has knobbly knees, this is an indication that a considerable amount of growing is still to be done. Sometimes the front half of the puppy appears to be taller than the back and later, perhaps, vice versa, and then some go through the leggy stage. This is all part of growing up.

While puppies are growing, they do not need much exercise. We do not take ours on long walks until they are least five months old. There is a theory that over-exercising can contribute to hip dysplasia. It is equally important that a puppy should not be too heavy, so that its body 'rolls' when he moves. A solid, well-covered puppy should be aimed for.

To begin with, the puppy's teeth are very sharp, and the pup should be disciplined whenever he uses them when playing with you with a firm 'no'. By four months of age, the incisors (those in the front, between the canines) will be dropping out. Nature requires the puppy not to be without teeth for long, and very soon the permanent teeth come through. Then you can see whether or not the puppy will have the correct scissor bite, (the lower incisors touch the inside of the upper incisors). The sharp canine teeth usually start falling out at about four months; sometimes these new teeth are through before the milk teeth have dropped out. This does not usually cause a problem and, next time you look, they will have gone, but, if they are retained, it may require the vet's attention. Teething will go on until the pup is about six months old.

The adult teeth will need to be kept clean. Products are on the market now for this, but one of the best ways is to give your dog a large marrow bone to chew, which will give him a lot of pleasure, and will act as a deterrent to chewing furniture. The puppy must never be allowed to get bored. To protect your furniture, you can try smearing it with a lot of hot chilli sauce or cayenne pepper, mixed with petroleum jelly.

The puppy must become used to discipline. He should have his own toys to play with, and be made to understand what is permissible and what definitely is not. There are bound to be disasters, but precautions can be taken. We always recommend to our new puppy owners that they and their puppy will benefit from attending obedience classes, and details of these are often advertised in vets' surgeries, or are obtainable from The Kennel Club. Make sure that the puppy knows his name from the outset and, with a little patience on your part, the pup should come when called, and sit and stay. He should also understand the word 'No', right from the start. You need to be kind as well as firm, and praise heavily every time the pup does as you ask. Do not be cross when he comes after he has done something wrong: go to him to correct him. You can transmit your fear to a dog. If you are not nervous, he will soon realise that he should not be either, and vice versa.

If you treat your puppy like a well disciplined child, you will probably not go far wrong. Do not leave loose electric wires; do not put down slug pellets; be very careful with weedkillers as some are lethal, and the instructions should be read very carefully before use; plastic is attractive to puppies and, if eaten, can cause problems, as can pairs of tights and foam cushions.

Puppies will not need a lot of grooming for thc first few months, other than a regular brush and some light trimming of the hair on the feet. Your pup will need to be accustomed to being handled and brushed, so that it is not upset when further trimming is necessary later on. Not all coats grow as quickly as others, or are of the same texture. Some Welsh Springers grow profuse feathering on their legs, others hardly any. Ears need to be examined regularly and any signs of canker or wax attended to (see Chapter 6 on Health).

Lead training will be necessary, once the puppy's vaccinations have been completed. A number of different types of collar are available. You can use one made of soft nylon while the pup gets used to wearing one. Leather collars, with identity discs, are suitable for general use. You should be able to get two fingers between the collar and the dog's neck, so that it will not slip over its head. If you are intending to show your puppy, it is best to use a soft fabric collar, so that the natural flow of the neck is not spoilt. Choke chains are dangerous, and should not be used unless the dog is on a lead for training or obedience classes. You will also need an identity disc for the puppy, obtainable from pet stores.

Start taking the pup round your garden on the lead, talking to him and encouraging him all the time, until he will trot easily beside you without pulling. He will soon realise that it is easier and more comfortable if he does not resist. When you take the pup out, gradually introduce him to cars and traffic, and be careful when meeting other dogs. He will be naturally inquisitive, but keep a tight lead and allow him to socialise and meet other people so that he gains confidence. He will probably stop frequently, to sniff at everything; firmly jerk him back on the lead, and teach him the word ' Leave', but always give lots of praise when he does as you ask. Do not forget to take a supply of plastic bags to clean up behind your pup, particularly in public places, and do not take him into recreation areas or children's playgrounds.

You will probably wonder when it is safe to take off the lead. Practise in the garden first by taking off the lead as you walk the pup round. Once he realises that he is loose and runs away, call him back, encouraging him to come to you with open arms, with lots of praise. When you are out for a walk in a suitable place, where there are no other dogs, use the same routine; he will probably rush off at first, but will soon come back to you, and you can gradually progress to more open country. Welsh Springers are renowned for looking up when you call, and continuing with what they were doing after you have called, so you will have to be really firm and demanding, giving an abundance of praise when you get the required result. This is when obedience classes will help both you and your puppy.

The earlier you can train your puppy to travel in the car, the better. It is essential to have either a dog guard or a travelling cage, not only for your safety, but for the dog's comfort and security as well. Most Welsh Springers travel well in cars, but we have found that if a puppy suffers from car sickness, he usually grows out of it or the problem is overcome by doing a long journey. It is advisable not to feed a dog before a journey. You can give travel sickness pills, using the same dosage as for a child, and several products are obtainable from pet stores or advertised in the canine press. Other suggestions are to give a ball of cornflour moistened with water before a journey, or ginger biscuits. This old-fashioned recipe given to me by breeder Doreen Gately certainly is worth a try:

- grate half an inch of fresh ginger into a small breakfast cup
- half fill with boiled water
- strain and add half a teaspoonful of honey
- give two tablespoonfuls two hours before travel.

It is imperative to socialise the puppy at an early age. A well-reared puppy should be outgoing and happy to meet people. Introduce your pup to children as soon as you can if you do not have them in your household, but remember that puppies need a lot of sleep between their play times. Welsh Springer puppies are very exuberant, and are really too much for most toddlers. As I have indicated, we do not advise families with very young children to have one as their first dog.

You can expect a bitch puppy to come into season at any time from six months of age. We find that ours are usually between eight and nine months old. Dog puppies' maturity will also vary; some will be fully mature by eight months, and others later. He may not cock a leg when urinating until he is a year old.

If you are rearing a Welsh Springer puppy with the intention of showing, it is not advisable to let him run up and down stairs, and the same applies to jumping off the grooming table. It could have a drastic effect on maintaining a good front. The puppy should be handled regularly, in a show position, and if you can get friends to 'go over' him, as in the showring, so much the better.

Ringcraft classes are good, but they can be rather overwhelming for a young puppy if the classes are very full, and particularly if there are a lot of big breeds taking part. Puppy socialising classes are the best but are not, as yet, held in all parts of the country. A puppy can get very bored with ringcraft classes if he is there for too long and too often. If you can find a full length mirror in a junk shop or car boot sale, it is very useful to erect it in the garden, so that you can practise standing and moving your puppy in front of it.

At the end of this period, your puppy will be a year old, and no longer a puppy in name but probably very much so in nature for perhaps a further six months. This is quite usual for Welsh Springers, and they will continue to love life and enthuse about everything with which they are confronted. You should be able now to look forward to many years of enjoyment together.

chapter *6*

Grooming and Trimming

Tango: a suitable case for treatment!

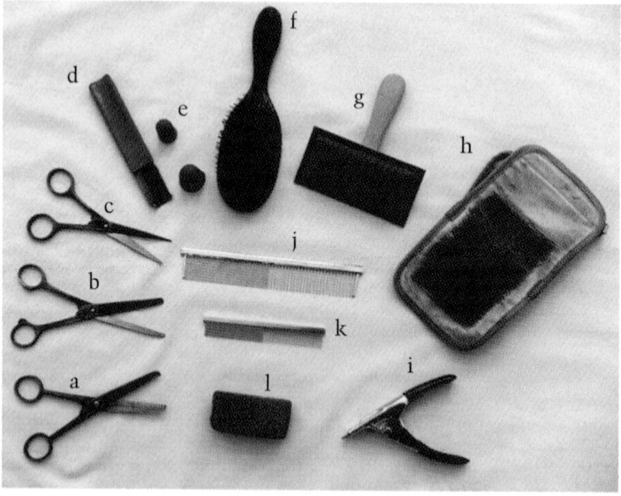

a: 30 tooth thinning scissors, both blades serrated;
b: 46 tooth thinning scissors, both blades serrated;
c: 6in hairdressing scissors; d: stripper; e: finger stalls; f: bristle brush;
g: slicker brush h: grooming glove; i: guillotine nail clippers;
j: large, coarse and medium toothed comb;
k: small, medium and fine toothed comb; l: stripping stone.

Grooming

A healthy and happy Welsh Springer is a well-groomed one, and ideally he should be brushed and combed every day. Puppies will change their coats when they are about eight or nine months old. Bitches lose their coats about two months before they come into season, and dogs seem to change theirs once a year. The Welsh Springer's coat has one feature that must be the envy of many. You can come home from a long walk on a wet day with a very dirty dog. You can spray him down with the garden hose and dry him with a towel, or you can dry his feet with a towel and then leave him to dry naturally. In the morning, all the dirt will have dropped off, leaving a clean, sparkling Welsh Springer ready to greet you. All you then have to do is get out the vacuum cleaner!

Many types of brushes are used for grooming. I find the ideal brush for general use is a rubber-backed bristle one, the type which many of us use on our own hair. It is kind to the dog's skin, yet fulfils its purpose. You can also use a special glove brush, with small wire teeth on one side, and a velour-type back, which will give the coat that extra gloss. Some brushes are two-sided, with wire teeth on one side and bristles on the other. The wire brush can be very harsh if not used carefully, but is useful for brushing out the feathering. A very useful grooming tool is a 'slicker', which is a curved, rubber-backed brush with metal teeth, ideal for brushing out dead hair and mud, and for the feathering.

A variety of combs is also available, the most practical of which is divided into sections, fine and coarse. The fine comb is ideal for use on the ears and for combing out dead hair, particularly when coats are being shed. I also use one regularly in the summer, as I find that this is the best means of disposing of fleas should we be unlucky enough to find them. The coarse comb can be used for general grooming.

Trimming

I have two grades of trimming: the maintenance trim, and the show trim, and what you read is just what I do, not necessarily what others do.

My Maintenance Trim

Equipment: thinning scissors with 46 teeth and single serration; 15cm (6in) hairdressing scissors.

The maintenance trim takes place about every six weeks, and involves feet, ears and tail. It is basically the same as the show trim, but a much quicker version. I often do my first plucking on a puppy's ears while he is lying asleep on the hearthrug in front of the fire in the evening. You are only taking off the dead hair and, as it is not painful, the pup gets used to it at an early age.

Feet

The feet need regular attention. All our dogs live in the house and, at present, I have to live with 28 feet, belonging to seven Welsh Springers. After a period of wet weather and exercising around the farm, all those dirty feet, untrimmed, would be out of the question! I do have kennels for 'drying off' but the prospect is still daunting.

There appear to be two schools of thought on trimming a Welsh Springer's feet. Some trim away the hair that grows up between the toes, and the hair is trimmed level with the pads on the underside of the foot. I trim out all the hair between the toes and pads as not only does it give a neater appearance, remaining so for longer, but also I find that the feet can become sore and smelly if the hair is left. The reason I have been given for leaving hair on the feet is that it protects them, and this may be so, but in over 30 years of exercising Welsh Springers over farmland and on the moors in the north of England, we have never had any problem with damage to their feet due to lack of hair. A shooting Welsh Springer friend used to tell me of the troubles that he had with grass seed penetrating his dogs' feet, ultimately resulting in surgery. Since he has adopted my practice of trimming the feet out fully, he has not had any further problems.

Ears

It is very important that the hair is cut away from the entrance to the ear. Welsh Springer's ears, although smaller than the English Springer's and Cocker's, hang closely over the orifice which, if not kept clear, results in poor air circulation and provides an ideal situation for bacteria to thrive. It is normal for a little wax to be present in the ear, but you can always tell if a dog has bad ears: there will be a dark wax with a very unpleasant smell, and the dog is constantly scratching his ears, rubbing them against the furniture or on the carpet, and shaking his ahead. If your dog has these symptoms, he will need veterinary treatment. If you are vigilant, and clean the dog's ears gently with warm water and cotton wool, you should not have any problems. Be careful that you only clean the parts of the ear that you can see. Never use cotton wool buds, or poke your finger into the ear.

The feathering on the outside of the ear is usually trimmed lightly on alternate Maintenance Trims.

To avoid mats forming behind the ears, and also behind the elbows, I trim away the hair there as well. Grass seeds can get entangled in the mats, and they provide very good accommodation for fleas in the summer.

The tail

The hair is trimmed away from the end and the underside of the tail, and also around the anus.

For the pet owner, it is not absolutely essential to embark on any further trimming than this, as long as the coat is brushed and combed regularly. If you take your Welsh Springer to a Poodle Parlour, make sure to tell them that the coat does not need stripping or clipping all over. Once this has been done, your dog will never have a good coat again.

The toe nails will need attention periodically, and should not be allowed to grow too long. Nail-cutting is not the easiest of tasks; you have to be very careful not to cut too far down into the 'quick', which will then bleed, similar to our own nail. Special guillotine nail clippers are needed, and it is best for the novice to seek help with this.

My Show Trim

Equipment needed (see lower picture on page 60):

- thinning scissors, with 46 teeth and single serration
- thinning scissors, with 30 teeth and double serration
- 15cm (6in) hairdressing scissors
- rubber finger stalls to fit (or a pair of rubber gloves)
- fine ear stripper
- fine comb
- guillotine nail clippers
- stripping stone

My show trim is much more time consuming. It is done between two and five days before the show, and will take me up to three hours if the dog comes to me completely untrimmed. It is a way of trimming that I have adopted from experience over many years, collecting tips from others, both in this country and abroad. No two people will trim their dogs in exactly the same way, but we all have the same goal, of presenting the dog to the judge to its best advantage.

I am not one for over-trimming, as I believe that the Welsh Springer should maintain its appearance of being a working dog and, therefore, should not look too streamlined. When we first started showing in the 1960s, the dogs had far less trimming than they have today. I remember the late Frank Hart of the Denethorp kennel telling me that he expected his dogs to be out shooting one day and straight out of the kennel and into the ring the next. His dogs always looked smart, and it leads one to wonder whether or not today's presentation is really a great improvement.

For the novice gaining experience in trimming for the show ring, there is one great salvation. If you trim off too much hair to begin with, it is always going to grow again. As the saying goes, 'practice makes perfect'. Leave yourself plenty of time, and do not try to do it all in one go. The dog will get bored and you will start to make mistakes.

Trimming Step by Step

Standing the dog on the grooming table, I start by brushing him thoroughly with the soft rubber-backed bristle brush, and combing out the feathers. He then knows that I mean business and it is not a time for play, so that by the time I am ready for the next stage – trimming the feet – he will lie down quietly for me. I do most of my trimming with the dog lying on his side and, as my dogs become used to this from an early age, usually they go to sleep and let me get on with it, without any fuss.

The feet

I lift the front foot and from the top, I draw my index finger up towards me, lifting the hair. Then, using the 46-teeth thinning scissors, I cut away the excess hair, working towards the toes.

I then use the hairdressing scissors to cut out all the hair between the toes and the pads to the shape of the foot. I also trim up the back of the foot to just below the dew claw pad, but this is a matter of preference, and it is not everyone's method. This will then be neatened with the thinning scissors.The hind foot is done in a similar way, shaping to the edge of the pad at the back.

The dog is then turned over, and the procedure repeated on the other side.

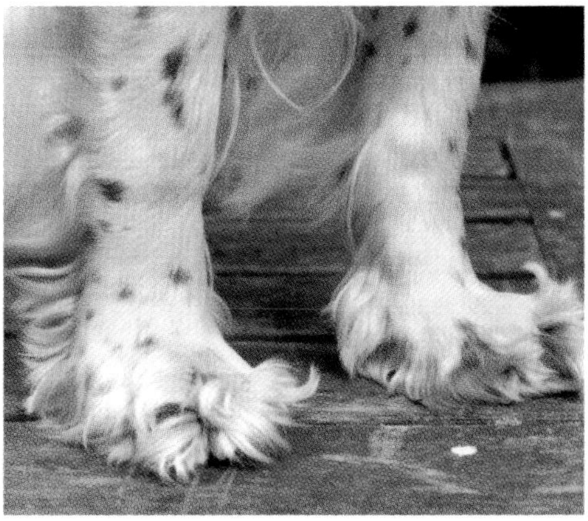

Untrimmed feet (top view).

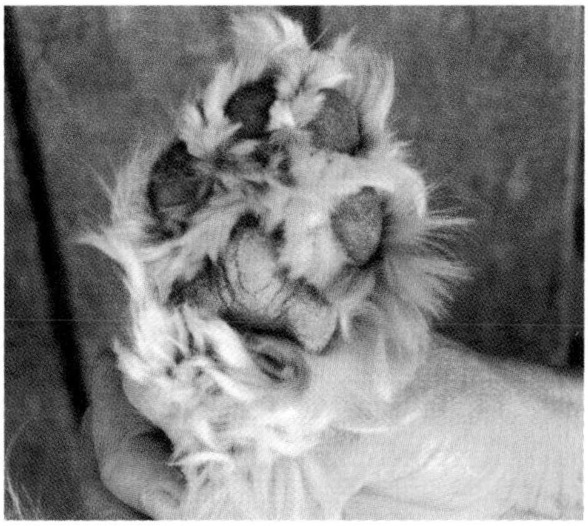

Untrimmed feet (showing the pads).

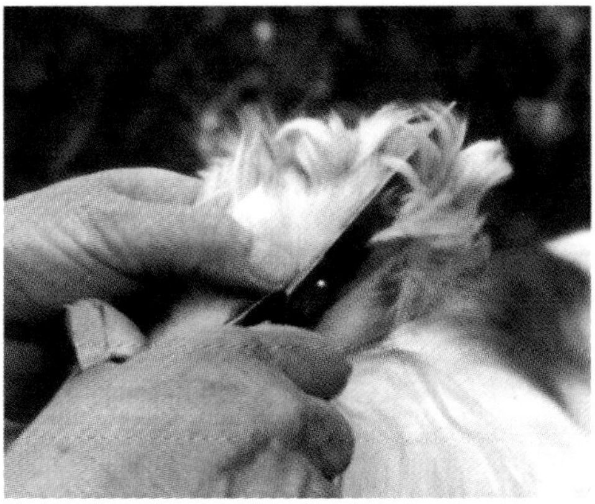

Trimming the top of the foot.

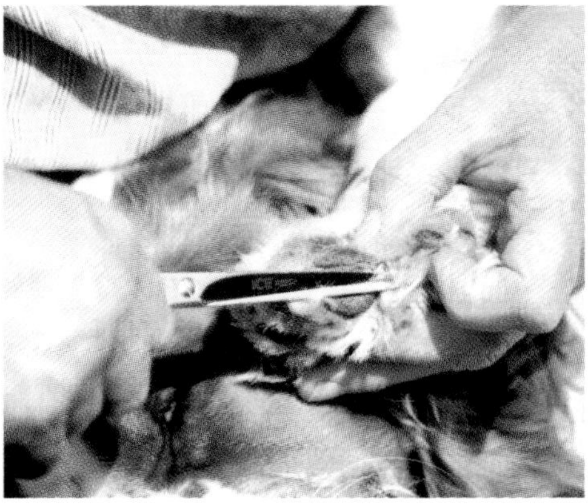

Trimming the underside of the foot.

Trimmed and untrimmed feet, showing the pads (left) and the tops of the feet (right).

The ears

I begin by trimming away the excess hair inside the ear with the 46-teeth thinning scissors. This is, as explained before, for hygienic reasons, but it also enables the ear to lie flat against the cheek.

It is my experience that there are a number of different hair textures in the Welsh Springer, and this is reflected in the ear feathering as well. Some have hair which can be easily plucked, using rubber finger stalls or rubber gloves. Others do not seem to respond so well to this, and have to be thinned with a stripping knife.

Puppies' ears are easy to do using the hand-plucking method. Lift the ear and push the dead hair upwards. Then pluck it off with a downward movement, a little at a time, and pluck the hair away round the edge so that you can see the shape of the ear. You can also use the thinning scissors for this, but for preference, I like to hand-pluck the edges.

I use a stripping knife.to trim thicker feathering, A number of different knives are available, and we all have our favourite one. I use mine in conjunction with the rubber finger stalls, lifting the excess feathering and dead hair and pushing it away from me, and working downwards in the direction of the hair growth, using the stripping knife approximately parallel, for maximum efficiency.

The hair is stripped off a little at a time until I have the neat outline of the ear, which should be shaped 'somewhat like a vine leaf', and still showing some light feathering. It may also be necessary to use the 46-teeth thinning scissors, particularly with the older

The untrimmed ear.

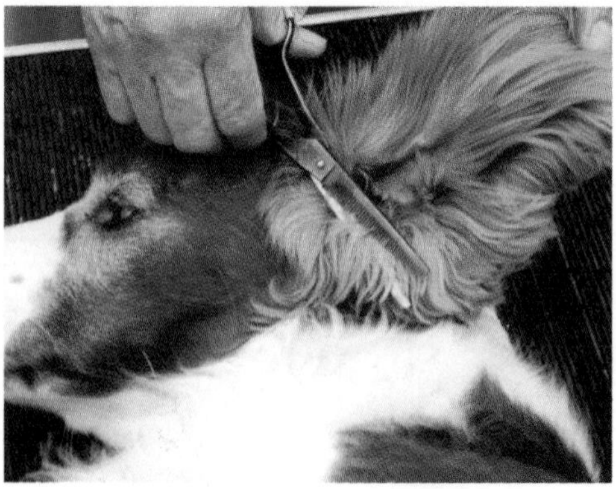

Trimming the inside of the ear.

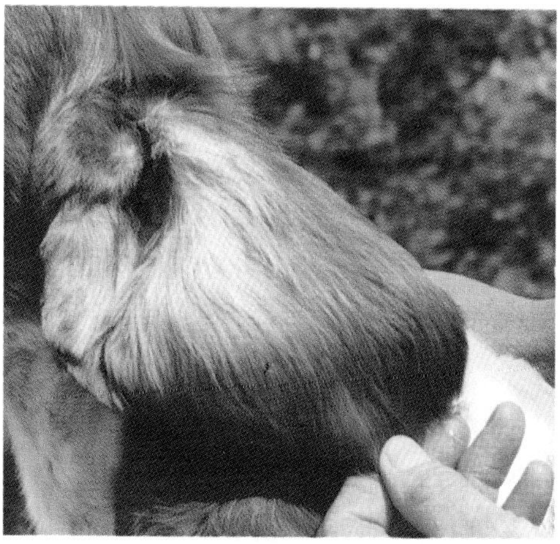

The trimmed inside of the ear.

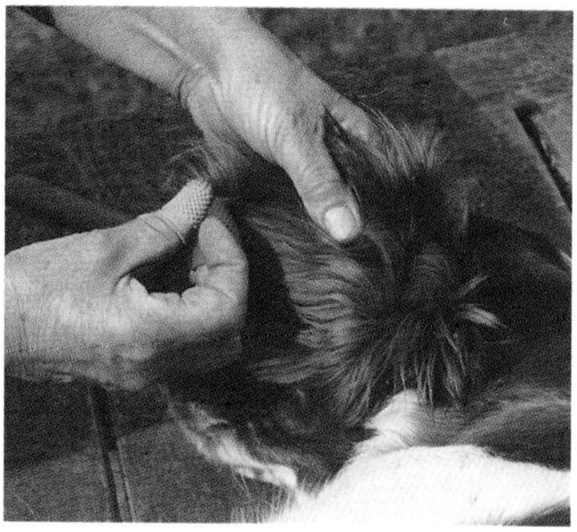

Plucking the ear.

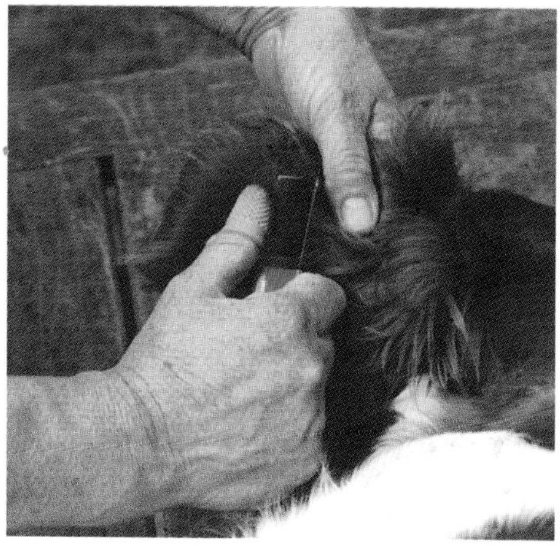

Sripping the ear.

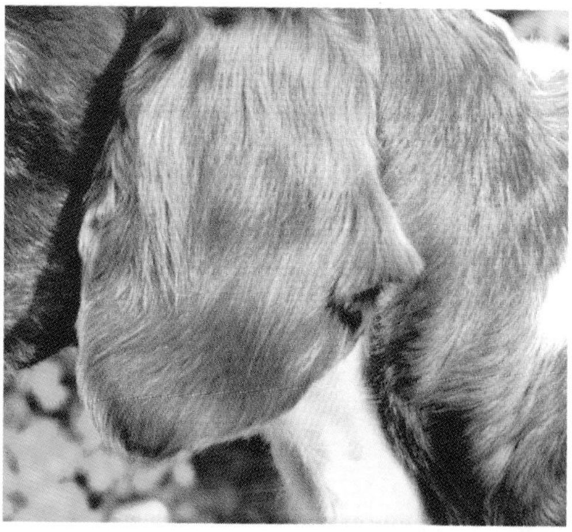

The trimmed ear.

dog and those that have very profuse ear feathering. This will require practice to avoid a jagged appearance, and is done with the dog in a sitting position on the table.

The tail

With the dog standing, and using the 46-teeth thinning scissors, remove the hair to the shape of the tail, at the end and underneath, and around the anus (see adjoining picture and 'before and after' overleaf).

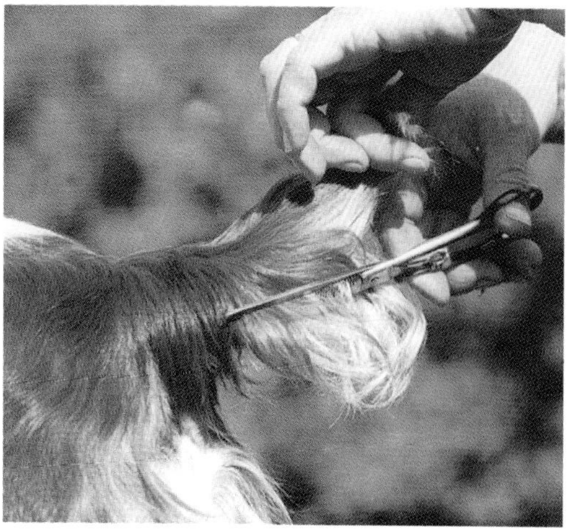

Trimming the tail.

Neck and chest

Using the 46-teeth thinning scissors, the

Before and after: the untrimmed (left) and trimmed (right) tail.

hair is removed below the chin, down the neck and chest to just above the breast bone, tapering it off as I go. The hair grows in different directions, so sometimes I will be working down the neck and sometimes towards the head with the scissors. How much is trimmed depends a little on the conformation of the dog, and this does need experience to obtain the best result to suit the particular dog.

Feathering

Like the texture of the coat, the feathering varies from dog to dog. Some will need constant attention to look tidy, while others never seem to need much at all. If it needs thinning, I use the 30-teeth double serrated scissors, a little at a time, and any too-long wispy ends are thinned out.

On the hind legs (see opposite page), the hair from the hock to the foot is trimmed off by means of the 46-teeth thinning scissors. The excess hair is pushed gently upwards, and trimmed carefully down to the foot so that it blends in neatly.

Trimming the neck

Whiskers

I have mixed feelings about trimming the whiskers. In the natural state, the dog would use his whiskers to judge whether or not he could get through a gap, that is, if his head and whiskers can get through, so can the rest of him! If you wish to remove the whiskers, this should be done with the hairdressing scissors, always cutting away from the eyes. It can depend a little on the dog's face, too. A thin face can look less so if the whiskers are retained, and vice versa with the rather heavier head.

Toe nails

This is done with guillotine nail scissors, and great care must be taken not to cut too far down into the 'quick'.

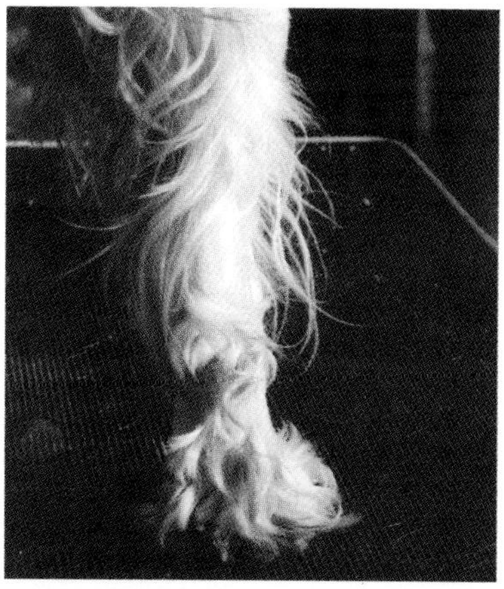

The untrimmed hind leg from the side (left) and from the back.

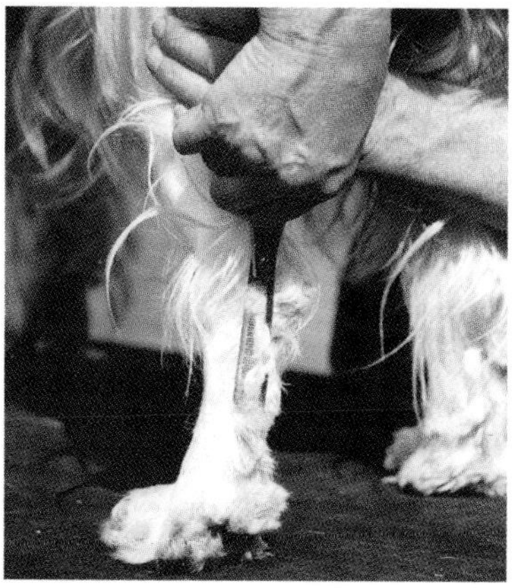

Trimming the hind leg.

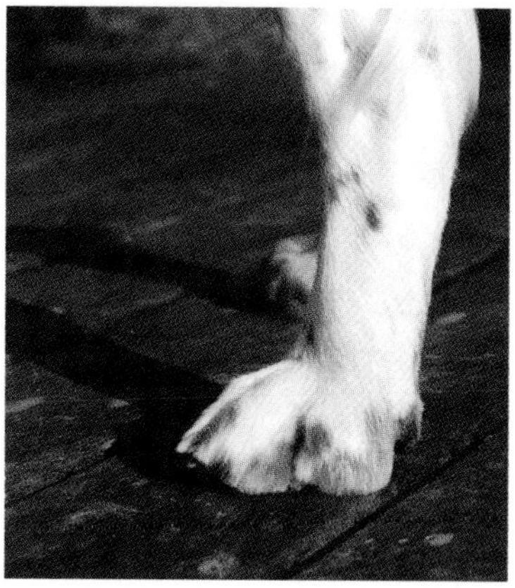

The trimmed hindleg.

Teeth

These will be examined, and any necessary cleaning or scraping will be done. Special toothpaste for cleaning the dog's teeth is now available from pet stores or your veterinary surgeon. You can also try rubbing with a piece of elastoplast wrapped round your forefinger, and dipped in bicarbonate of soda. A calm dog will let you scrape the teeth with the rounded end of a nail file.

To finish

To complete my show trim, I stand the dog on the grooming table, and brush and comb the coat again. Any dead hair on the top of the head is removed with the stripping stone. I found this wonderful grooming aid in the United States some years ago, and it is now available over here as well. If you need to thin the coat anywhere, or any dead hair on the body needs removing, this is the gadget to do it. It has a very unpleasant smell of sulphur, but deserves its place in my grooming box.

A final polish with the velour-backed hand glove, and my show trim is completed.

Electric clippers can be very useful for trimming. I sometimes use them for my maintenance trim, but prefer to hand trim my dogs for the showring. It takes time, but gives me a feeling of satisfaction when I look at the finished dog (see overleaf).

Two trimmed dogs, ready for the show: (top) Robin and (below) Lucy.

chapter 7

Health

One of the most common questions that a dog owner asks himself is when to seek veterinary advice. Like so many girls, I was pony-mad, and when I became the proud owner of a shaggy pony, my father, who was in the Cavalry in the First World War, instilled into me that I must learn not only to ride the pony, but how to look after it. I spent hours reading and re-reading his Army manual *Animal Management*, and then a wonderful book by William Fawcett, *The Young Horseman*, in which there was a chapter called 'Every Horseman his own Vet'. I have always borne this in mind in my life, with our farm animals and with the dogs. When we had a large pig-breeding unit, I was called upon to deal with difficult farrowings, as my hand was more suited to the task than that of our very masculine and well-built vet, Mike Dale. He was always happy that I should take over, and many a costly call-out fee was avoided as a result. It has also stood me in very good stead when it comes to whelpings, where the principle is the same, but on a smaller scale. We all need to consult the vet from time to time, preferably one who will take a real interest in our dogs, and gives sound advice and treatment where necessary. However, there are many ways in which we can help ourselves before it reaches that point, and apply our own first aid.You know your dog better than anyone else, and you can tell when he is not his usual self. Your vet only sees the dog on his table, and sometimes has to rely on your 'gut' feelings when there are no apparent symptoms. Hence the necessity of establishing a good relationship with your vet.

Welsh Springers are a naturally hardy breed, and their average lifespan is 12–13 years. Good health is normal, and the Welsh Springer does not need to be pampered. The healthy dog should be alert, with bright eyes, a cold, wet nose and a shiny coat. When the coat is shed and a new coat is growing, it will not have the same gloss, and may even feel coarse and dry. This is normal, and is not a cause for concern. Moulting will take place twice a year. With the bitch, it is about two months before she comes into season. We find that dogs tend not to drop their coats fully, as the bitch does.

As with all breeds, there are a few inheritable health problems of which one has to be aware, and various screening examinations are available to breeders to try to minimise the incidence. When purchasing a puppy, check that **both** parents have certificates confirming freedom from inheritable eye disease, and that their hip scores are better than the breed average (usually around 20 – see page 85). Fact sheets about diseases affecting the breed are available from the Breed Clubs, produced by the Welsh Springer Spaniel Joint Health Group.

A Welsh Springer in a natural setting.
Photo: Robert Smith

If you are buying a puppy from a breeder in your area, you will probably be told which veterinary practice is used. It would be to your advantage to consult a vet who already knows the kennel from which your puppy came. Many new owners will have to start from scratch, and recommendations may be offered from friends with dogs, or you may decide to contact practices which you have found in Yellow Pages. We advise our puppy owners to contact their veterinary surgeon before the puppy is taken home, and make an appointment for a check-up and first vaccination soon after the puppy is settled. We do not have our puppies vaccinated before they leave us, as they will have received immunity from their mothers that lasts to 8–10 weeks of age.

I have been very fortunate in having had a wonderful vet for many years. Farmers get to know their vets on a personal basis, and I knew Mike Dale first in that capacity, before he became Senior Partner in the practice and in charge of the Small Animal Department. He has always taken a great interest in our Welsh Springers: he has dined in their presence, and even had photographs of them in his consulting room before, sadly, he moved to another area. He knows the breed well, and is a regular contributor to veterinary journals. He has given of his great knowledge to this chapter on health.

Vaccinations

The following sections (Vaccinations, First Aid, Common Health Problems, Medicine Cupboard, Insuring Your Dog and Final Consultation) have been contributed by **Mike Dale, MA, Vet., MB, MRCVS**. *He has permitted me to intersperse his text with our own experiences. As elsewhere in the book, where there is a reference to both dog and vet as 'he', this is for convenience, and applies to both sexes!*

The vaccination programme recommended by your vet will depend on the vaccine type that he uses, and his experience of disease incidence in the area. Protection is offered against the following major diseases:

Distemper

Sometimes called Hardpad, this presents as a cough, high temperature with depression, thick nasal discharge, and progresses to vomiting, diarrhoea, and eventually fitting and death. Even with intensive care, it is difficult to treat successfully, and recovery is rare. Dogs that do recover sometimes have thickened pads and discoloured teeth, and may suffer from fits or twitches later in life. Distemper is extremely infectious.

Parvovirus

In young puppies, this virus causes heart failure; in older dogs, severe vomiting and distinctively foul-smelling haemorrhagic diarrhoea, like strawberry jam. It is usually fatal in very young and very old dogs.

Hepatitis

A virus infection that damages the liver, causing depression, vomiting and thirst. Jaundice (yellow appearance of skin and membranes) is common. Again, even with intensive supportive therapy, death is common.

Leptospirosis

This is a bacterial disease that attacks the liver and kidneys. Signs are depression, high temperature, vomiting, diarrhoea and dramatic jaundice. By the time the dog is showing symptoms, it is often too late to effect a cure. The germs are associated with rodents, and the disease is picked up by contact with stagnant or sewage-contaminated water.

Kennel Cough

Also known as Infectious Bronchitis, this is a severe cough that can last for several weeks. It is very contagious, and readily spreads through groups of dogs that are in contact or within sneezing distance of each other. It is not necessarily fatal but, if not treated promptly, can lead to permanent lung damage. Several viruses and bacteria are implicated. Two types of vaccine are available. One is injectable, often included with those mentioned above, and is aimed at Parainfluenza virus. An intra-nasal vaccine against the organism Bordatella lasts for six months, and is probably best used before a period of risk, such as going into boarding kennels or the commencement of the show season.

First Aid

First aid is about taking immediate action to save life, alleviate pain, or to prevent an injury or illness becoming more serious before professional help can be obtained. Remember that there is precious little that your vet can do 'by the roadside' that will be of any major value. Do not waste time calling the vet to you. Get your dog to the surgery as swiftly as you can, having first warned them of your predicament.

Taking a Temperature

You can take your dog's temperature by using an ordinary clinical glass thermometer. Keep a separate one for the children! Lubricate the bulb with a little vaseline, and push it gently into the rectum, to two thirds of its length. Angle the thermometer so that the bulb presses firmly but gently against the wall of the bowel, and hold it there for a full minute. Normal temperature of a dog is 101.5°F (38.7°C) with an acceptable range of 100.4°–102°F (38–38.9°C)

Pills and Liquid Medicine

Welsh Springers have been specially designed to make this procedure a doddle. To give liquids, tip the muzzle gently upwards. Without opening the jaws, introduce the syringe or spoon into the pouch made by the generous amount of lip at the angle of the mouth. Pour into the side of the mouth at a rate that gives the dog time to swallow. To give a pill, open the mouth by gently pushing your thumb into the side of the mouth, keeping the upper lip fold between the teeth and your finger. Place your thumb on the roof of his mouth, which will make him keep his jaws open. Pop the tablet over the back of his tongue and gently close the mouth. If he has swallowed, he will lick his lips afterwards! Coating the pill in chocolate, butter, marmite or cream cheese, according to his taste, are all ways of sweetening the event. Sometimes a 'back stop' is necessary to keep the dog out of reverse gear. Rarely, with a very boisterous individual, you will require a 'third man' or 'fine leg'.

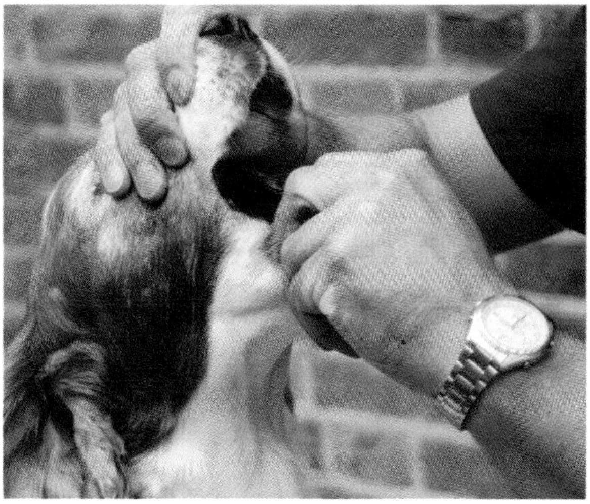

Giving a pill.

Eye Drops and Ointment

Do not use anything in the eye except plain water without veterinary advice. Especially do not be persuaded that cold tea has any therapeutic effect whatsoever. It is very astringent, and potentially damaging.

To give veterinary medications, lift the dog's chin upwards with your left hand (right handed operator). Holding the dropper or tube with the thumb and first two fingers of your right hand, use the knuckle of your little finger to gently raise the dog's eyebrow to expose the eye further. With this technique, medicine and target are all united, and if the dog moves its head during the procedure, you are less likely to squirt anything on the carpet. Drop drops directly onto the eyeball. Squeeze out a length of ointment to allow it to drape onto the eyeball in one movement. Again, you may need a friend or the corner of a room to stop the dog going backwards.

Ear Drops

Never use powder in a dog's ear. It clogs and causes more irritation. Ear cleaners should be introduced into the ear and massaged gently from the outside. Let the dog shake its head (so do not wear your best cream linen suit, or do this in the lounge). Then wipe any loose debris from the outside of the ear canal. You can use cotton buds to clean round the knobbly bits of the outer ear, but do not be tempted to go 'gardening' deeper down the canal. You will only impact wax further down.

Instilling eye drops.

Spaniels' ears provide an ideal environment for bacterial infections and ear mites to thrive, where air circulation is limited, and it is warm and damp. It is essential that the hair growing around the ear orifice is kept trimmed away to allow air circulation – see chapter 5 on trimming. I recommend that this should be done every six weeks. If the dog scratches his ears, shakes his head, or rubs his head along the carpet or a hedge, you should suspect trouble. On inspection, you will probably find that the inside of the ear is very inflamed, with a strong and unpleasant smell. Various drops can be obtained from pet shops but, if the problem persists, a visit to the vet is necessary to ascertain the real cause and the receive the proper treatment – AW.

Sudden frantic rubbing of the side of the face, scratching the ear, or crying or whimpering, usually indicates the entry of a grass seed into an ear. Get veterinary attention as soon as you can. Sometimes the seed can be removed in the consulting room before it is too far down the canal. If there is much damage, or if the seed is too close to the ear drum (or even through it), it must be removed under general anaesthetic. Heroic wrestling matches with a dog in pain are pointless.

Moving an Injured Dog

A dog in distress needs reassurance. The sound of its owner's voice speaking calmly can have a wonderful calming effect. Shrill cries of panic and remorse simply transmit more fear.

Even a Welsh Springer may bite when terrified, in pain or disorientated. If there are no breathing problems or facial injuries, be prepared to place an emergency muzzle of bandage, tie or scarf. Make a loop with a half hitch and, approaching from behind, drop the loop over the dog's muzzle with the ends uppermost. Tighten the scarf and loop the ends under the chin to cross over and come back behind the neck. Tie a quick release knot or a single bow behind the ears.

The proper way to lift a dog is with one arm round the back of his thighs, and the other arm under the chest in front of the front legs. Remember to keep your own back straight, bend your knees, and keep your head, so you lift with your legs, not your spine. Vets cannot treat people for slipped discs! This lift will do for most injuries. If you think a leg is broken high up, try to let it dangle on the side of the dog away from your body. For example, if the left thigh is fractured, have the dog's right side towards you, and bring the arm supporting his back end between his hind legs, rather than around both of them.

A makeshift stretcher can be simply a blanket or coat carried by two or more people. With the dog lying on its side, worst injuries uppermost, endeavour to keep the spine as level as possible.

The right way to lift a dog.

Bleeding

Any wound should be covered with a clean, non-stick dry dressing, and firmly, not tightly, bandaged. If blood is spurting, apply firmer pressure over that point. This can be achieved on a limb by twisting the bandage at each throw over the bleeding point. As a rule, more harm than good is done by tourniquets. If one is applied, it must be slackened every 15 minutes, timed by a watch, not guessed. Blood is like milk. When spilt, there often seems to be much more than there really is.

The most common cause of bleeding in my dogs is from a cut pad, when the tell-tale bloodstains are left on the kitchen floor after a walk. I always bathe a wound first with dilute Dettol or TCP, and then see if I can find the cause. If there is obvious dirt or grit in the wound, a strong solution of salt water helps to cleanse it. I also have a veterinary spray which contains a bactericide, which is excellent. An antiseptic cream can then be applied and the seriousness of the wound gauged. If it is not bad enough to consult the vet, I may cover it with gauze and a small bandage secured with elastic tape. Should there be profuse bleeding, or the wound is deep, immediate veterinary attention must be sought. We have had several cases where a dog has caught a squirrel or a rat, and has then been bitten on the ear. The ear bleeds heavily; I wash the wound with running cold water, and then hold it up above the head, applying pressure to it, until the bleeding stops.

If your dog gets bitten by another dog, immediately wash the wound and, if it is deep, seek veterinary advice. It can develop into an abscess – AW.

Fractures

Fractured means broken. The break will be simple (nothing showing) or compound (ends of bone sticking through the skin). Obviously a compound fracture will quickly become infected. Try to cover the area with a clean dressing or cloth. If there is time, pour warm salt water over the site to wash off any obvious debris. The best way to immobilise a broken leg is with a Robert Jones bandage. After the initial non-stick dressing, apply as much cotton wool as you can practically get round the leg. If the bandage looks absurdly enormous, you have done it right! Cover the cotton wool with an ordinary bandage or crepe.

Concussion

This is most commonly witnessed in road traffic victims. First ensure that there is an airway by clearing the mouth and pulling the tongue forwards. Remove any blood clots from the mouth. Beware of involuntary gnashing movements that might take your finger off! When moving the dog, try to keep his head and neck in a straight line and be aware of loud noises, like a car door slamming, which may stimulate him to come round without warning. Paying due regard to other injuries, get him to the vet's as soon as possible.

Burns

As with children, cool the area rapidly but gently with tepid water. **Do not** plunge the dog in water, as the shock could be lethal. **Do not** smear on butter or any other fat. If the dog will let you, clip away hair from the edges of the burn but, ideally, get to the vet at once. Burns are very painful, and need urgent attention.

Eyes

I am surprised that more Welsh Springers do not suffer from eye injuries, given their talent for forging through prickly undergrowth! Scratches on the cornea (clear part of the eye) can quickly develop into ulcers, and are very painful. The dog will blink the eye furiously, and rub or paw at it. It will look red and water copiously. Have a good look for foreign bodies, especially grass orms. Irrigate the eye with plain warm water. If you do see a grass seed, try to grip it with tweezers. If it does not come easily, or if discomfort is still evident 24 hours after removal, seek veterinary attention.

Poisons

Many people believe their dog has been poisoned when usually there is a far simpler explanation for illness. Poisoning is rare. However, of those genuine cases, the commonest causes are rodenticides and slug bait. Modern rat poisons are anticoagulants, and signs are due to uncontrolled bleeding taking place somewhere in the dog's body. Clinical signs depend on the site of haemorrhage, coughing if in the lungs, for example, or abdominal pain if in the stomach.

Slug poison (metaldehyde) causes tremors, hyperexcitability, high temperature and sometimes fitting.

As a general rule, if poisoning is suspected, present the vet with:

- the poison container;
- a sample of the poison;
- a sample of any material vomited up by the dog;

- a contact telephone number of any professional known to have been using poisonous substances on your premises;
- information about where the dog had been, that is, what type of crop or orchard.

Seek veterinary attention immediately, and do not attempt to make the dog vomit.

Planting bulbs. Photo: John Curtis

Some of the most dangerous poisons are in your garden and on footpaths, in the form of slug pellets and weedkillers. Always read the label on the container before spraying your garden, and be particularly careful on dog walks if there is any sign of weedkilling having been done. Slug pellets must always be well hidden from dogs, and always destroy the container when empty. We had one experience when a puppy had to be rushed to the vet to be stomach pumped after we had found the chewed remains of a slug pellet container – AW.

Stings

A bee sting can sometimes be found at the site of pain, and you may be able to scrape it off with a knife without popping the poison sac. Soak the area in Sodium Bicarbonate solution to neutralise the acid of the sting. Wasps do not leave a sting, and the poison can be neutralised with a weak acid, such as vinegar or fruit juice. If the mouth or throat is involved, see veterinary attention as a precaution, as sometimes quite dramatic swelling can cause obstruction to breathing or swallowing.

Recently we had a terrifying experience. I was out on a walk with my seven Welsh Springers and we came across an enormous swarm of bees, hanging from a branch of a tree just above the ground. Six of the dogs had up to 10 stings on their bodies, one with a sting in her throat, and the eight-month-old puppy was stung all over her body, as well as swallowing some of the bees. Fortunately, I had some Piriton antihistamine tablets, and gave the puppy one before rushing to the vet, which probably saved her life. They all received treatment, which included Piriton, but the puppy had been poisoned, and we spent many anxious hours while she was on a drip. All were in shock, as I was myself. Abscesses developed where the stings had penetrated the skin. We took nearly 70 stings from the puppy's body, and it was a week before her bloodstream started to recover. With expert attention from our caring vet, and lots of tender, loving care from us, miraculously she pulled through. Now Piriton is a 'definite' in my medicine cupboard – AW.

Removal of Foreign Body from Back of Mouth

It is best to do this with two people, one to restrain the dog and hold his mouth open. It can help to pull the tongue forwards out of the way. The assistant then tries to grasp the object with fingers or, more safely, a pair of pliers. Do not try for more than a few minutes before getting veterinary help if you have no success. Two common items are:

- A length of rib bone wedged between the upper teeth arcades. The 'V' shape of these arcades gets narrower towards the front of the mouth. Therefore, to remove the bone, it must be first pushed further back into the mouth, into the wider part of the 'V', before twisting and pulling it out.

- A rubber ball stuck in the back of the mouth can be too slippery to grip, due to saliva. I have solved this one by screwing a corkscrew into the ball and withdrawing it, with the same care that would be applied to a vintage wine!

Snake Bite

Before I worked in the West Country for a short spell, I had never seen an adder bite, and believed that recovery would be most unlikely. However, bites are common there, and all the dogs I saw recovered with suitable symptomatic treatment that was not particularly promptly administered, as victims were usually miles away along a coastal path. Keep the dog calm and limit activity. Carry him to assistance if possible, and don't apply tourniquets, as these invariably cause more trouble. The site of the wound will swell alarmingly, change colour and be painful. Most risk comes from bites to the head or neck, or in puppies or very old dogs.

Do not kill the adder as, apart from being a protected species, it was only defending itself!

Heat Stroke

It takes less than 20 minutes for the interior of a car to reach a fatally high temperature on even an average summer's day. Similarly, any confined space such as a conservatory can result in heat stress. The dog will be distressed and panting frantically. Get him into the coolest place possible, and cool his limbs with cold water. Use ice packs if you have them, concentrating on the limbs and head and neck. If you have a thermometer, you may find his temperature is very high indeed. Anything over 40.5°C (105°F) – and I have seen temperatures as high as 42.7°C (109°F) – should be checked by a vet.

Bloat

The stomach appears abnormally distended. The dog cannot rest, may be salivating profusely, and making futile efforts to vomit. This is a serious emergency. Telephone the vet, tell him the signs, and say that you are on your way. Gastric dilatation seems to occur when a dog takes exercise soon after having had a large meal. It is particularly associated with individuals who wolf their food down in microseconds, taking large amounts of air as they eat. Gas becomes trapped in the stomach which, in its inflated state, becomes highly unstable and liable to twist over, trapping circulating blood in parts of the bowel. This, combined with pressure on the diaphragm restricting breathing, and the leakage of toxins from the damaged bowel into the bloodstream, quickly leads to a life-threatening situation, called toxic shock.

Fortunately, the condition is rather more common in large breeds with deep chests. I have seen it in two Welsh Springers, both of which recovered, thanks to the prompt action of their owners in getting the dogs to the surgery.

Convulsions (Fits)

These are characterised by rapid, regular, jerky movements of the dog's limbs, often involuntary defecation and urination, and lack of response to any efforts by the owner to offer comfort. Convulsions last from a few seconds to a few minutes. On recovery, the dog is disorientated and often frightened for a while.

Do not attempt to restrain a dog during a fit. If necessary, drop cushions near any part of it likely to be banged against furniture or walls. **Do not** stuff gags into the dog's mouth. If possible, darken the room and, as the dog recovers, speak softly and steadily in your normal voice. Hearing is the first sense to return. Any attempt to touch or restrain may precipitate a bite that you will both regret later. If the convulsion lasts for more than five minutes, or if several episodes occur within minutes of each other, telephone the vet at once for advice.

If recovery occurs in a few minutes, and the dog returns to normal, make a note of the duration, what the dog was doing immediately before the fit started, and how frequently they occur if there have been others. Make an appointment for your dog to have a full examination as soon as possible. (See page 87–89: Seizures and Epilepsy.)

Common Health Problems

Worms

All dogs are susceptible to worm infestation. Severe burdens can cause a dull, scurfy coat, swelling of the abdomen, weight loss and diarrhoea. This often leaves the dog more likely to contract other diseases, a state often seen in rescued stray dogs. Most importantly, the roundworm, *Toxocara canis*, can be transmitted to children and cause permanent eye damage although, thankfully, such cases are rare.

Roundworms

Roundworms can grow to nearly 200mm (7in) long, and live in the dog's intestine. Occasionally, great tangles of the beasts can cause a bowel obstruction.

The hormonal changes in a pregnant bitch tend to lower her natural resistance, and permit a build-up of adult worms in anticipation of infecting her offspring. Young worms (larvae) can be transmitted through the womb to unborn puppies, or from the bitch's skin as they are suckled. The bitch is re-infected when she cleans the pups. Roundworms can be picked up accidentally by dogs in their environment, especially where contamination with faeces is heavy. Larvae may also be present in earthworms, birds or rodents eaten by adult dogs.

In ideal conditions, roundworm eggs can remain infective in the environment for several years, acting as an ever-present reservoir to infect both dogs and children. Hence the importance of a strict worming programme for puppies and adults, and the need to make children aware of basic hygiene when handling pets or playing in parks. All responsible dog owners must get into the routine of using 'poop scoopers' when exercising their dogs in public places.

We worm all our puppies three times before they leave us at eight weeks of age, and advise new owners that they should seek advice from their own vet. on worming when they take the puppy for its vaccinations. We do ours again at l2 weeks, then six months and 12 months, and thereafter twice a year. Roundworms appear in the faeces as thin white worms, about 7.5cm (3in) long. When you take your dog out for a walk, slip some plastic bags in your pocket and, when the dog performs, invert the bag over the faeces, tie it up, and drop the bag into a bin. In this way, you are protecting your environment. If every dog owner would do likewise, the anti-dog sector of the general public would have far less to complain about. Many dog walking areas have been lost in recent years, just because owners have failed to act as responsible citizens.

When a dog sits and shuffles along the floor on its rump, this does not signify the presence of roundworms, as is commonly believed, but that the anal glands need emptying (see page 82) – AW.

Tapeworms

Many species of tapeworm can infect a dog. All are tape-like in appearance, segmented, and attach to the lining of the small intestine. Some can grow to several metres long.

Unlike roundworms, tapeworms require another animal in which to develop before they can transmit to another dog. For example, with *Dipylidium caninum*, the Flea Tapeworm, the larvae are carried in fleas. The dog swallows fleas and/or their droppings, and the larvae develop into adults in the dog's intestine. The mature worm sheds individual segments which are passed in the faeces or individually out of the dog's rectum. You may spot them looking like tiny mobile rice grains. Once in the dog's environment, the microscopic eggs are released from the segment, and are consumed by wandering flea larvae. The worm larva becomes infective inside the adult flea, and off we go again when the next dog comes along.

Other hosts used by tapeworms include rodents, birds and even farm animals.

Thus for puppies and breeding bitches the focus is on roundworms, and on tapeworms for adult dogs that are hunting or generally exploring the world. Fortunately, most wormers available through your veterinary surgeon kill both groups of parasite pretty efficiently, and the vet will advise you on the best programme to adopt for your dog's lifestyle.

External Parasites

Fleas

These are particularly prevalent in the summer months, but because of our centrally heated homes, they can now be a problem throughout the year.

The dog will scratch persistently, and the skin becomes sore and red. The most common areas affected are over the lower back, rump and base of tail, where you may well see fleas moving about. A good number of dogs become hypersensitive to the flea saliva which is injected to slow blood clotting when the flea feeds. This 'Flea Allergic Dermatitis' is the reason why some dogs in a household are dramatically more itchy than others. Remember, too, that fleas frequently carry tapeworm larvae that are swallowed by the dog during grooming.

The swiftest way to detect the presence of fleas is to look at combings dropped on to wet, white kitchen roll, using a fine comb. The small black dots that are flea droppings quickly turn red, as they are, in essence, digested blood.

Fleas are picked up outside, particularly in spring and late summer. Eggs laid on the dog fall off on to bedding or carpets, where within 10 days they hatch into larvae. The larvae live off organic debris at the base of the carpet pile before turning into pupae. The pupae can remain dormant for many months, waiting for a passing furry host. They may even be attracted temporarily to people, especially if the house has been empty for a week or so. Your movements when you return home may stimulate the eruption of hundreds of hungry youngsters, happy to settle for a bite of your ankles! Adult fleas remain on the dog for weeks, laying up to 30 eggs a day.

You can see that very quickly the house becomes the main source of re-infestation of the dog. This highly prolific life-cycle can be controlled in two ways. Regular use of a spray, or 'spot on' preparation will keep your dog free of adult fleas, killing them before they have time to bite or lay eggs. Other products render the fleas infertile, preventing the eggs from hatching in the carpet. Your vet will advise you on the best and most economic control strategy to suit your circumstances. At the start of an eradication programme, the carpets should be treated with an ovicidal spray recommended by the vet. Place no faith whatsoever in regular combing, ultra sound devices or herbal remedies to effect eradication, which is an essential goal where flea allergy exists. Avoid frequent use of flea shampoos as, eventually, the skin will become dry and unhealthy.

We find that if we do get flea infestation, it is usually behind the ears or under the elbows, as well as along the spine. I do use a flea comb regularly, as it goes through a Welsh Springer's coat very easily, and I wash the bedding frequently with non-biological washing powder. I also use proprietary brands of flea sprays all round the house and in the dogs' beds, which is usually very effective – AW.

Ticks

Ticks are common in certain areas, and are usually associated with sheep or hedgehogs. A tick is usually spotted on the dog as a solitary grey blob, about the size of a pea. You can kill it with a short burst of flea spray. Alternatively, it will let go if soaked in surgical or methylated spirit. You must be sure that the mouthparts are not left behind, or a suppurating sore will occur. Sometimes it is best just to leave it to finish feeding and drop off, especially if it is too close to an eye to deal with safely. Recently, a special tick-removing hook has been marketed, and it appears to be most efficient at removing ticks, complete with mouthpiece.

Lice

Louse infestation causes scratching, rubbing and biting, very similar to that caused by fleas and mites. Severe infestations can result in sufficient blood loss to cause anaemia. Infestations are easy to diagnose with the aid of good eyesight or a hand lens. The lice are visible throughout the coat as slow-moving, greyish beasts about 1–2mm long. The eggs or 'nits' may be seen glued to the hair shafts. Treatment with an antiparasitic spray or shampoo is effective, but remember that the dog's bed will remain a source of reinfestation, and it should be thoroughly treated or, at best, thrown away. Usual sources of infestation are hedgehogs and poultry. Recently, I have only seen lice on puppies from disreputable puppy farms.

Harvest mites

These are tiny golden spiders, just visible to the naked eye that, not surprisingly from their name, occur around harvest time in late summer/early autumn. They are not parasites as such, but during their visit on a dog can cause intense irritation, especially around the ears and between toes. They can be dispatched with a good flea spray or shampoo.

Mange mites

Sarcoptic mange: This is a true parasite, whose entire life cycle from egg to adult occurs in the layers of the skin. It is spread by close contact with other infected dogs, their lying areas or their faeces that contain infective eggs swallowed by the original host during grooming. In Britain, the urbanisation of the fox has been largely responsible for a dramatic increase in the incidence of mange among domestic dogs.

This condition drives a dog to distraction, with constant scratching. Areas of self trauma quickly develop, and secondary skin infection can make diagnosis of the presence of the mite more difficult. People can be affected by the mite but, being species specific, it will not live for long on us. Human irritations usually disappear once the pet has been treated successfully, but it is always sensible to get advice from your doctor.

Long-standing mange that has not been treated can result in almost total hair loss, with thickened, elephant-like grey skin, and large areas of red weeping sores. Diagnosis can be difficult. Skin scrapes deep enough to draw blood must be taken and examined under a microscope. A big problem is that, in about a fifth of sarcoptic mange cases, it will be impossible to find any mites. This may be the result of just a few parasites causing a generalised hypersensitivity itching. Occasionally, the vet may decide to treat for mange on clinical grounds, even though he cannot find any mites on scrapes. Treatment involves the use of strong washes that must be used repeatedly and with care.

Demodectic mange: This is caused by a cigar-shaped mite that under the microscope looks like an ice cream cone, with all its legs near the top! It is more common in the very young, very old, or in animals whose immune system is damaged. It is not very infectious by contact as such, but is passed from the bitch to her puppies in the first few days of nursing. The localised form occurs as discrete areas of hair loss around the eyes, muzzle and toes, and is not particularly itchy. The generalised, purulent form is characterised by pustules and extensive reddening of the skin, with secondary bacterial infection which does cause a good deal of irritation.

Diagnosis is by skin scraping or biopsy. Pus from an infected pustule may contain thousands of the mites. Treatment is by special antiparasitic washes. The generalised form can be extremely difficult to treat successfully, due to underlying immunity problems, and the presence of certain bacteria that may be very resistant to antibiotics.

Other Skin Troubles

Ringworm

Ringworm is a fungal infection, and presents as discrete areas of hair loss, especially around the head and shoulders. On close inspection, the hairs are seen to be broken off close to the skin surface. There may be itching and redness. A percentage of cases will show green fluorescence under ultra-violet light, and diagnosis is thus swift. However, it is usual to take samples of hair to be cultured, and this can take up to three weeks.

Ringworm is usually picked up in farm areas, or by contact with infected wildlife, especially hedgehogs. The infective, fungal spores may survive for many years in old wooden buildings or fences. It is not a common infection in dogs, but is a potential zoonosis. That means that you may catch it, especially if you handle an infected dog when you have unprotected cuts or scratches.

The dog is treated with a four to six week course of tables and a topical wash to limit spread of infection.

Warts

These are common in the older dog, and are generally harmless. If they threaten to grow into an eye, or are a nuisance by constantly bleeding, then surgical removal should be considered.

Allergies

A large number of dogs of all breeds suffer from allergies that result in constant scratching. At first, there may be no obvious skin lesions, but the self trauma quickly results in inflamed and subsequently infected skin. Many such allergies are seasonal, often related to specific tree or grass pollens, but those due to antigens, such as house dust mites, will occur all year round. Diagnosis is difficult, and is usually achieved by eliminating the other causes of scratching, such as mange, flea infestation, skin infections, and so on. Specific allergy testing can be carried out by a dermatological specialist in order to try to identify the exact cause. Sometimes this can be followed up by a course of desensitising injections over a period of weeks or months. These procedures are expensive, and by no means guaranteed to succeed.

Sensitivity to certain foods may also be involved; for example, to particular types of meat or wheat products. This is investigated by putting the dog on a diet consisting of very limited food type for a period of up to eight weeks. We generally choose a protein source that the dog is least likely to have experienced before, and therefore not had the chance to become sensitive to. Lamb or venison and rice are examples. As you may imagine, this requires considerable discipline on the part of the owner and family. When, as often happens, the source of allergy cannot be identified or eliminated from the dog's environment, treatment has to be symptomatic.

Antihistamines do not seem to work very well, and corticosteroids are usually administered to control severe, damaging itching. Secondary skin infection must be controlled with an antibiotic course, often for several weeks. Certain shampoos are helpful, and some homeopathic remedies can be extremely effective. The inclusion of significant doses of Evening Primrose and Fish Oils in the diet has proved beneficial.

Allergic skin disease is a frustrating condition to treat for dog owner and vet. Considerable trust and patience is required between all three to achieve satisfactory results.

Interdigital Cysts

These are very painful fluid-filled swellings between the toes, usually caused by a penetrating foreign body such as a grass seed. Several times a day, bathe the whole foot for five minutes in warm salt water. The cyst will eventually burst to release a flood of pus or blood-stained fluid. With luck, the grass seed will come out on the tide. If the swelling persists or recurs, it will need thorough investigation under a general anaesthetic.

One of our Hillpark owners told me that he had several cases of interdigital cysts. I suggested that he tried to keep the dog's feet well trimmed, particularly in the summer when the grasses are in seed. Since doing that, he has had no more problems, so that is worth a try – AW.

Thorns

The Welsh Springer has a natural curious instinct to work in all the hedgerows on a country walk and, in these days of mechanical hedge cutting, there is an increased chance of picking up thorns, particularly blackthorns, in the pads. The dog comes back holding up his paw and on inspection, with luck, you can spot the thorn and pull it out. Sometimes, however, the lameness is not noticeable until some hours later, and the thorn is well embedded in a pad. Gently squeezing each pad in two directions at right angles to each other will soon show which toe is hurt. Soak the foot in salt water for about 10 minutes, and see if you can squeeze the thorn out. Repeat every two hours for a few attempts, and the thorn will often pop out. If you have no luck, a deeper investigation under general anaesthetic by the vet will be necessary.

The Welsh Springer's love of hedgerows makes him particularly likely to pick up thorns.
Photo: Robert Smith

Eye Problems

As mentioned in the first aid notes, any abnormality in the eye should receive veterinary attention promptly. In particular, signs of pain, swelling or excessive redness, watering or change of colour of the corner (clear part of the eye) should be regarded as urgent.

There are some inherited eye diseases whose presence can be identified by a routine eye examination under the joint Kennel Club and British Veterinary Association Scheme.

Diarrhoea and Vomiting

All dogs are scavengers by nature and, more than once in their lifetime, will eat something outrageously disgusting. A sudden change in diet, such as a new dog food or a special treat, can have the same effect. Diarrhoea with or without vomiting will follow, such a 'dietary indiscretion', which is the most common cause of these symptoms.

Starve the dog for 24 hours, and allow only boiled water. If he is being sick, allow only small amounts of water to be drunk at a time. If there is no more sickness after the first day, feed a bland diet such as chicken or fish and rice, little and often until stools are a normal consistency again. Only then should you very gradually reintroduce the dog's normal food, taking at least three to four days to make the transition. If vomiting persists, or is at the rate of five or six times a day, take him to the vet. A dog can become dehydrated and collapse with excessive vomiting. Persistent vomiting may indicate the presence of a foreign body in the stomach or intestine. Nothing is impossible – I have removed rubber balls, children's toys, champagne corks, walnuts, tights, stones, condoms and even the dog's own nametag.

Any sign of blood from either end should also be treated with concern, and advice sought. Diarrhoea that resembles strawberry jam indicates life-threatening haemorrhagic enteritis, and requires intensive care as soon as possible.

Dogs with mild stomach upsets will often eat grass, and this is fine. They are usually sick shortly afterwards, and feel a lot better.

I have a slightly different theory on dogs eating grass. I have found that whenever I am working in the garden when the grass is new and lush, the dogs tend to eat it. Soon afterwards, I hear the tell tale sound of vomiting, and later see the faeces containing grass. I have always felt that rather than the dogs having a mild stomach upset, it is nature's way of cleansing the digestive system – a homeopathic remedy, perhaps – AW.

Anal Glands

Anal glands are a pair of ducted scent glands that produce an unpleasant smelling secretion. Situated at 5 and 7 o'clock to the anus, they are usually expressed when the dog defecates. They are rather more forcibly emptied when the dog is very frightened, as in a road accident or dog fight.

If the glands are infected or blocked, your dog may shuffle along on his backside, or constantly bite and lick under his tail. You may be able to express the glands if you have been shown how, or you may need to consult the vet. If they are not attended to, a painful abscess may develop.

Mammary Tumours

Any growth within a mammary gland that appears to increase in size should be checked by a vet as soon as it is discovered. About 40% of mammary tumours are malignant, which means that they spread to other parts of the body. Early surgical removal and laboratory testing give the best chance of survival. It may be necessary to remove the entire line of mammary glands on one or both sides. Before any mammary tumour surgery, it is customary to take an X-ray of the lungs to make sure that there are no secondary tumours that would compromise the anaesthetic.

Mammary tumours can be prevented by spaying. The incidence in bitches spayed before their first season is less than one in a hundred. This increases to one in ten for bitches spayed between the first and second heat. However, early spaying should be discussed in depth with your vet, as potential complications include juvenile vulva, poor coat development, or urinary incontinence.

Pyometra

Pyometra is the abnormal accumulation of fluid in the uterus. The fluid often contains bacteria that produce poisons, which in turn are absorbed into the bloodstream. As a result, the bitch becomes toxaemic, with characteristic signs of excessive thirst, frequent urination, loss of appetite, distended abdomen, and sometimes collapse. In open cases, an abnormal foul discharge drips from the vulva. In closed cases, the fluid is retained, and usually the bitch is more seriously ill.

The condition is extremely common, and most typically occurs four to six weeks after a season in maiden bitches over five years old. However, it has been known in younger dogs, and some that have previously whelped.

Treatment is by ovariohysterectomy (removal of the ovaries and uterus – spaying). A bitch with pyometra can be very ill, and supportive intravenous fluids and anti-toxicity drugs may well be necessary. Hence spaying for this condition is more complicated than the routine procedure of neutering.

Note the profuse coat on the flanks and down the legs of this spayed bitch, 'Ceri'. Usually you also lose the gorgeous, rich red coat that is so attractive in the Welsh Springer Spaniel – AW.

Lameness

Lameness is common in dogs, and there are a number of causes.

If your dog is limping, try to sort out which leg hurts. Get a friend to trot him up and down in a straight line in front of you. At the trot, head movement is pretty well locked to leg movement. Coming towards you, the dog's head will lift higher when the lame front leg hits the ground, and appear to nod when the good leg strikes. Thus, if he nods on his left leg, he is lame in the right foreleg. For the hind legs, watch him going away, and the sore leg will rise and fall through a greater range. The net result is that the hip of the lame leg appears to drop lower than the sound one.

When reporting lameness to your vet, do not forget that your dog's left and right are defined from the dog's point of view, that is, facing forwards! It is amazing how many people get in a muddle. First of all, examine the foot of a lame dog. Look for unusual swelling or redness. Especially examine the pads for thorns or other foreign bodies. Gently compress each pad in two directions at right angles to each other. A pain response will tell you if something is in there. Work up the leg systematically, feeling for abnormal swelling or painful points. Gently flex and extend each joint in turn, to see if you get a wince or cry of pain.

A common hunting injury occurs when a hind foot goes down a pothole, or gets temporarily left behind on a wire fence. The resultant twist can cause a rupture of a cruciate ligament inside the stifle (knee) joint. Typically the dog shrieks in pain, but may gallop on for the rest of the day. Fairly soon, however, he will be seen holding the hind foot right off the ground, with the stifle joint slightly turned inwards. Your vet will discover an instability in the joint. A repair can be performed, using the dog's own tendon tissues to form an artificial ligament.

Less serious strains and twists are common in active dogs worth their salt, and most recover rapidly with adequate rest, and sometimes regular massage. Any lameness that shows no sign of getting better after three days should be referred to your vet.

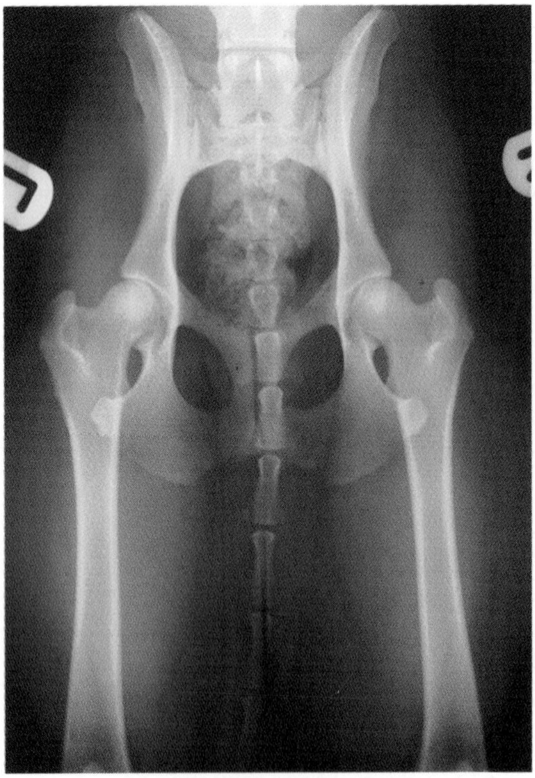

Hip X-ray:
These are excellent hips with a score of 0 + 2.

Hip Dysplasia

Hip dysplasia is abnormal development of the hip joints in young dogs. It is an inherited disease, but its progression may be influenced by other factors, such as rapid growth, over-exercise and unbalanced nutrition. Varying degrees of deformity away from a normal, snug-fitting, ball and socket joint are seen, ranging from barely measurable disparity to total dislocation. Clinical problems may be seen in the young dog due to mechanical instability, or in the older dog due to arthritic wear and tear.

A very large number of breeds are affected, and there exists a national scheme run by The Kennel Club and the British Veterinary Association (BVA), whereby X-rays of potential breeding dogs' hips may be scored. This is best done after the age of 15 months, when bone growth and development has matured. Under general anaesthesia, the dog is placed in a standard position, so that specific measurements of each hip joint can be made and compared with breed standards. One hopes that responsible breeders will breed only from dogs whose score is closest to perfection (see picture on opposite page), and at least better than the breed average.

Genetic selection is about averages, and occasionally (though rarely) a badly scoring dog will be produced from well scoring parents. This can lead to some cynicism as to the value of the scheme, but there is no doubt that if discipline is maintained, an overall improvement in genetic quality in the breed will be achieved.

Each hip is scored out of a possible 53, making a total of 106; the lower the score, the better the hips. The average hip score for the Welsh Springer is around 20.

Medicine Cupboard

Dispose of all out-of-date medicines safely. If in doubt, ask your vet to do it for you. Ointments that your vet gave you last year for an ear or eye problem may have become contaminated with airborne fungal spores or, at best, simply lost their potency. A basic kit will contain:

- digital or glass thermometer
- mild antiseptic solution
- cotton wool
- linen bandages
- antiseptic powder
- magnifying glass
- round-ended, curved on flat scissors
- Vaseline
- cotton wool buds
- non-stick dressing pads
- crepe bandages
- pair of tweezers
- antihistamine tablets (Piriton)
- guillotine-style nail clippers

Insuring Your Dog

There are few situations more upsetting than having to euthanase a dog to alleviate suffering because the owner cannot afford investigation or treatment. Veterinary science has become highly sophisticated in many fields, particularly cancer therapy, ophthalmology and surgery. Individual procedures such as hip replacement or MRI scans (Magnetic Resonance Imaging) can cost well over £1000. Even common ailments such as chronic skin disease can notch up fairly hefty fees when months of daily antibiotic therapy are necessary. Veterinary practices have very high overheads. A number of companies now offer a range of insurance schemes by which the high costs can be met. Insurance cover means that you and your vet can usually offer your dog the very best treatment possible, without the anguish of limiting economics. Remember that routine vaccinations, neutering and certain congenital (present at birth) conditions will not be covered.

Final Consultation

Dogs do not live as long as we do and, sadly, they rarely pass away peacefully in their sleep. Unfortunately, at some time you are likely to have to make a decision to ease your dog's suffering by having him put to sleep. This is a painful time, and you will have to handle powerful emotions of grief and, possibly, guilt.

I find it helps for owners to have advance understanding of what is involved. An overdose of anaesthetic is given by intravenous injection, usually into the front of a foreleg. The dog will normally be held by a nurse, but owners are always welcome to be present, talking and stroking. The dog dozes off, just as with a normal anaesthetic, but obviously much deeper. I tell owners that their dog is already eating T-bone steaks, or chasing rabbits in heaven, even before the needle has been withdrawn.

There should be no guilt. Your dog has given years of unconditional love and enjoyment, and you repay him by sparing any unnecessary suffering at the end. Many practices now offer bereavement counselling. It can be valuable simply to talk about shared experiences or, more specifically, to re-examine the course of a terminal illness, to ensure that owners have fully understood why it went the way it did.

If it should be...

If it should be that I grow frail and weak,
And pain should keep me from my sleep,
Then you must do what must be done,
For this last battle can't be won.

You will be sad, I understand,
Don't let your grief then stay your hand,
For this day, more than all the rest,
Your love and friendship stands the test.

We've had so many happy years,
What is to come can hold no fears.
Would you want me to suffer? So
When the time comes, please let me go.

Take me where my needs they'll tend,
Only stay with me to the end,
And hold me firm and speak to me,
Until my eyes no longer see.

I know in time that you will see
It is a kindness that you do to me,
Although my tail its last has waved,
From pain and suffering I have been saved.

Do not grieve it should be you
Who must decide this thing to do –
We've been so close, we two these years,
Don't let your heart hold any tears.

Anonymous (submitted by three contributors)

Sh Ch Hillpark Reverie at 12 years: a happy old dog.

Seizures and Epilepsy

This section was kindly contributed by **Geoff Skerritt, BVSc, Dip.ECVN, C.Biol, MIBiol, FRCVS**, *Royal College of Veterinary Surgeons Specialist in Veterinary Neurology.*

The incidence of seizures, or fits, is higher in dogs than in human beings, and some breeds of dog are affected much more than others. The Welsh Springer Spaniel is a breed that shows a high incidence and it is known that there is an inherited predisposition to epilepsy in the breed.

Strictly speaking, epilepsy is a condition of recurrent seizures due to non-progressive brain disease. There are many other possible causes of seizures in dogs, some of which are progressive and some where the actual cause is located outside the brain, such as hypoglycaemia or low blood sugar.

It is important to diagnose accurately the cause of seizures in an individual because of the significance for future breeding, treatment regimes and assessment of prognosis. The occurrence of an inherited form of epilepsy in the Welsh Springer Spaniel dictates that an affected individual should not be used for breeding unless an alternative diagnosis is proven.

Types of Seizures

Everyone's image of a seizure, or fit, is of a dramatic episode of collapse accompanied by convulsive activity of the whole body, including defecation, urination and salivation. This is known as a typical generalised, or grand mal, seizure. However, some seizures affect only one region of the body and reflect the specific location of a lesion in the brain. Sometimes the lesion is located in a part of the brain that is responsible for behavioural activity, in which case the episodic abnormality is behavioural rather than muscular. Even abnormal behavioural traits such as intermittent licking of one paw, tail chasing or imaginary fly catching have been classified as psychomotor seizures.

When the seizure activity is restricted to one region of the body, the episodes are called partial seizures. In the dog it is common for partial seizures to develop, within seconds, into generalised seizures.

There are differences between breeds in the nature and progression of seizures. The onset of seizure activity in idiopathic epilepsy is from one to three years of age, although larger breeds of dog may start earlier and small breeds up to six years of age. There is also a tendency for individuals of the larger breeds to suffer from clusters of seizures, that is, episodes of several seizures in quick succession. Affected Welsh Springer Spaniels generally commence seizuring at one to two years of age and do not usually progress to clusters.

Causes of Seizures

There are very many possible reasons for seizures occurring in the dog. Possible extracranial (outside the head) causes range from head trauma, with onset as long as two years after the accident, to idiopathic (or inherited) epilepsy.

The intracranial causes present the greater diagnostic challenge, since a routine clinical examination should alert the veterinarian to the existence of disease in another organ. Lesions in the brain, however, can be extraordinarily difficult to identify. The commonest cause of seizures in pedigree dogs appears to be idiopathic epilepsy in which the only clinical sign, whatever sophisticated diagnostic technique is used, is the occurrence of generalised seizures.

Another important cause of seizures in young dogs is the loss of brain cells through a period of hypoxia (poor oxygenation of the blood) at the time of birth. If a puppy is slow during its passage through the birth canal, there may be too long a time between the separation of the placenta and the start of breathing. It can be very difficult to differentiate seizures with this type of origin from those of inherited epilepsy. It is clearly important to make this distinction before drawing any conclusion concerning the inheritance of epilepsy in an individual.

Seizure Investigation

Seizures are always dramatic in whatever species or breed they occur. For owners it is an alarming experience to see a pet suffer its first seizure. In fact, it is worth remembering that dogs very rarely die during a fit but may become injured if the seizure occurs whilst the dog is in a hazardous location, for example, at the top of a flight of stairs.

Most owners of epileptic pets become very observant and often keep detailed records of their pet's seizure episodes. This is most helpful to the veterinary surgeon since it may reveal a correlation between the occurrence of the fits and normal routines, for example, exercise and feeding, thereby contributing useful diagnostic information.

Because it is so important to establish an accurate diagnosis in a dog suffering from fits, a detailed history needs to be taken; any medical condition, injury or surgical procedure, however long ago, may be significant. A routine physical examination is followed by some selective neurological tests, all with the aim of detecting any evidence of an underlying disease that may be responsible for the fits.

An analysis of a blood sample may give further diagnostic clues, since the blood cells change in number in certain disease states. Similarly, the blood sample will give information on kidney and liver function. Sometimes a sample of cerebrospinal fluid (csf) is taken; this is obtained by inserting a needle into a space adjacent to the spinal cord. Csf can give valuable information about intracranial disease.

Radiography is rarely very helpful in the investigation of seizures. However, magnetic resonance imaging (MRI) scans are a superior way of visualising the brain and almost obligatory if a focal lesion is suspected. In North America this procedure is widely available but, in the United Kingdom, there are currently only two centres that regularly carry out MRI scans.

Electroencephalography (EEG) is a procedure that has less application since modern imaging techniques have been introduced. EEGs are difficult to interpret because of the prevalence of artefacts.

Treatment of Seizures

It is a common misconception that a seizuring dog should be confined in a darkened, quiet room. In fact, the opposite is true; the brain is less likely to show seizure activity if it is being bombarded by environmental stimuli. It is better to arouse a dog that shows the early signs of a seizure with noises and attention.

When it is determined that the cause of seizures is some underlying disease, then treatment is directed towards that disease, although anticonvulsant drugs may be needed in addition.

If non-intracranial cause of the seizures is identified then anticonvulsant drugs are likely to provide the principal therapy. When anticonvulsant drugs are prescribed for a dog suffering from seizures, the intention is to gain the best control possible with the least side effects. Sometimes, a combination of two drugs is necessary to benefit from the complementary different modes of action of the drugs. Control means a reduction in both frequency and intensity of the seizures; complete abolition may not be possible. It is most important that owners understand the need for a steady blood level of the anticonvulsant drugs. Missed or irregular doses may cause such a fluctuation in blood levels that seizures are induced; it is worth remembering that both diarrhoea and vomiting may affect the absorption of drugs. Regular monitoring of the blood levels of the drug ensure that the dose can be adjusted to promote the optimum therapeutic effect.

Outcome for the Seizure Case

Most dogs suffering from seizures show a good response to therapy and in some cases it may be possible eventually to stop drug therapy. However, control is not achieved in all cases, and there can be a number of possible reasons for this. The most frequent reason for failure of therapy is irregular dosing. A small percentage of dogs do not respond to therapy however well-managed and monitored.

Seizures remain a frequent occurrence in dogs, with the Welsh Springer Spaniel as one of the notably affected breeds. As a rule, breeding should be avoided if seizures have occurred in any individual dog, or its immediate ancestors, although no conclusions should be drawn about a dog's probability of carrying inherited epilepsy without an accurate diagnosis.

Welsh Springer Spaniels: Hereditary Problems?

The four Welsh Springer Spaniel Clubs in Great Britain have formed a Joint Health Group, under the Chairmanship of **Mike Stockman, MRCVS**, *member of The Kennel Club General Committee. He has very kindly sent me the following contribution – AW.*

Every breed of 'pure-bred' dog which is restricted to using as its sires and dams only those whose registration appear on a Pedigree Register thereby creates problems for itself! The breed's gene-pool will never, under the conditions presently operated by all the acknowledged Kennel Clubs of the world, allow the introduction of new genes from any other breed of dog to assist in the dilution or eradication of any breed-associated problem.

That paragraph, by way of introduction, may seem a somewhat solemn statement, but it is necessary initially to assure all devotees of the Welsh Springer Spaniel that they are not alone. Whatever apparently inheritable defect is found in any breed of pure-bred dog is a cross that the breeders of that breed have to endure and attempt if possible to eradicate or, at least, to lessen in incidence.

The Welsh Springer can only be described as very unfortunate in falling foul of three separate problems at one time: epilepsy, glaucoma and hip dysplasia.

Those three are not listed in any order or significance; merely in alphabetic order.

The Health Committee set up by the four British Breed Clubs has produced information leaflets on the three conditions, so I will not expand on any of them here. My purpose in making a contribution to Mrs Walton's book is to help those who read it to balance the concept of a breed which is apparently affected by what looks, on the face of it, three defects, against the fact that the breed produces year by year several hundred pups which live eventually to a ripe old age, giving their human companions a lifetime of service and fellowship, and only a small modicum of hassle.

Idiopathic epilepsy (IE) occurs in many breeds; the average human-being has a 'fear' of fits or, for that matter, any form of mental abnormality; folk tend to lower their tones of speaking when discussing such things; it is generally accepted these days that both parents of what is referred to as a 'fitter' are at least carriers of the abnormal gene; the blame cannot be laid at the door of the sire alone; the dam is as much to 'blame'.

IE can be selected against by a careful study of pedigrees if **all** breeders are honest in reporting genuine cases of the facts, backed up by accurate diagnosis.

Glaucoma is another condition which requires diagnosis after a thorough examination of a dog or bitch by a recognised expert.

Finally, hip dysplasia is a multi-factorial condition but, essentially requires high-quality radiography by an experienced veterinary surgeon in order that hip-radiographs may be sent for examination by accepted experts.

It is obviously essential to obtain expert advice, but the decision as to whether a dog or bitch should be used as a member of a breeder's individual gene-pool is, in the last resort, the breeder's. It would be all too easy to consider that the Welsh Springer as a breed was under dire threat from this trio of defects. The facts are not such as to encourage complacency, but sensible and constructive assessment of each potential breeding animal should be the order of the day.

In the words of Corporal Jones of BBC's *Dad's Army*: **'Don't panic!'**

On top of the world: a Welsh Springer in peak condition.

chapter 8

Shows and Showing

When you are the owner of a Welsh Springer, you are joining a 'clan'. You are out for a walk with your dog, or are on holiday in the Lake District, when a stranger stops and greets you with hilarity: 'You have got a Welsh Springer!' They have one sitting in the car, or their parents or friends have them. It is an instant talking point, and the question soon comes: 'Where did you get yours? How is he bred? Do you show or work him?', and experiences are shared. So then you begin to wonder whether, perhaps, your beautiful puppy (or adult dog), the best in the world, of course, should be shown? He is certainly better than the one on the beach! But how do you go about it?

Shows

You may already have been to a dog show, Crufts, perhaps, when you were trying to decide which breed was for you. You may have watched a programme on television. If not, it is a good idea to look in your local paper, to see if an Exemption Dog Show is being held near you, not with the idea of possibly entering at this stage but to give you some idea of what happens. If you bought your puppy from a breeder who shows, as soon as you mention that you might like to try yourself, you are sure to get plenty of advice.

All shows are licensed by The Kennel Club, and are subject to Kennel Club Rules and Regulations. They are subject to inspection by a Kennel Club Field Officer, who ensures that these Rules and Regulations are being adhered to. The most coveted letter for a Club or Society is one from The Kennel Club, congratulating them for the way in which its show was organised! All dogs entered in shows (apart from Exemption Shows) must be registered at The Kennel Club, or have their registration applied for, and they must either be owned by the exhibitor at the time of entry, or the ownership must have been applied for. No puppy under six months of age is eligible to enter a show.

As in other competitive sports, dog showing is divided into 'degrees of difficulty', starting on the bottom rung with the local Exemption Show and going up to the top of the ladder – Crufts. Primary and Sanction Shows are expected to be discontinued on 1 January 1999 (KC Working Party Report, 24 November 1997).

Dapper dog: fancy dress winner.

Exemption Shows

These are run in aid of charities, and any dog can take part, registered or not. There are a number of classes for pedigree dogs, and a variety of fun classes: the dog with the waggiest tail, the dog in the best condition, the dog that the judge would most like to take home, and so on. They are meant to be fun, and provide an ideal opportunity for the dog to get used to shows. They are often used by breeders to introduce their young stock to the showing world. At this stage, it should be immaterial to them whether they win. The shows provide experience for puppies in being handled and shown, and for mixing with other dogs.

Match Shows

These are small shows, held by Clubs or Societies, and confined to their members. It is a form of competition where judging is done by a process of elimination, like a tennis tournament. A Club or Society may hold up to 12 Matches a year, and not more than 64 dogs can compete. If entries warrant it, puppies can be judged separately. They can be held at any suitable venue, inside or out, and no wet weather accommodation has to be provided. The Welsh Springer Breed Clubs hold them periodically as money-raising events, and they are very well supported, being run as social fun days with many other attractions, covering all aspects of the breed, with the emphasis on **fun**. These gatherings provide an excellent opportunity for owners to join in and learn more about their chosen breed, and, as experience is not a pre-requisite, can be the start of further participation; some of our regular show-goers today were encouraged to go further at these events.

No dogs that have won a Challenge Certificate (CC) may take part in Matches.

Limited Shows

These are shows which are run by Clubs and Societies for their own members. There must be a minimum of 12 classes scheduled, one of which must be open to all, and no winners of CCs may take part.

Open Shows

General Open Shows, run by Canine Societies, are held all over the country, and classes for Welsh Springers can be found on nearly every weekend throughout the year. They are, as the title suggests, open to all. There will only be a few classes scheduled for Welsh Springers, usually with dogs and bitches being shown in the same classes.

Breed Clubs also hold Open Shows during the year, and the judges will be chosen with regard to their experience and possible potential for judging at a higher level. Sometimes a breed specialist will have been selected to judge but, on other occasions, judges from other breeds will be given the experience to widen their repertoire. This is very important if we are to have all-rounders in the future. They may not know the breed in quite the detail of the breed specialist, but they should be looking for a good, sound and well-made dog that moves correctly.

Judge and winners at a Club Open Show.

Many more classes are available than at a General Open Show, and dogs and bitches will be scheduled separately, with classes for all ages and stages in a dog's showing career (see appendix G). These shows are always very well supported, and you can expect to find about 100 Welsh Springers entered at the present time. Some new exhibitors find the classification bewildering, and are uncertain which classes they should enter. For example, the Novice class is not always what one might expect. Often very experienced handlers are in this class, with youngsters which have just come out of Puppy classes, and are still technically novices. You may decide that the Maiden class, if there is one, would be more suitable for you as a beginner, and towards the end of the show, there could be a Special New Members class. A Special Beginners class is another slightly misleading class, I feel, as it is not really for true beginners but for those who have never won a CC at a Championship Show – and, remember, that includes some very experienced and long-standing exhibitors!

Championship Shows

These are the most important of our shows, and at present there are 25 Championship Shows held all over the country, where Challenge Certificates are on offer for Welsh Springers. The dogs are judged first, starting with puppies, through to the Open class which, as it says, is open to all. The first prize winners in each class compete against each other, from which the best dog is selected, and he is awarded the CC (known as the 'ticket'), with the judge's second choice receiving the Reserve CC. The same procedure is then followed for the bitches, culminating in the two CC winners competing against each other for Best of Breed (BOB). This winner will then go on to represent the breed in the Gundog Group, under a different judge. The winner from that will meet the other Group winners, and the Best in Show (BIS) will be chosen by another very experienced and all-round judge

Top dogs at a Championship Show:
(left) Ch Ch Russethill Royal Salute over Wyrilam;
(right) Sh Ch Russethill Royal Tan (litter brothers).

Exhibitors will also be seeking to qualify their dogs for Crufts, (which is itself a Championship Show), and they will be aiming to become recognised in the breed by making their dogs into Show Champions (Sh Ch). This title can only be achieved at Championship Shows. Once a dog or bitch has won three CCs under three different judges, it gains the title of Show Champion. There is no limit to the number of CCs. that a dog or bitch can win. Many exhibitors are satisfied with just the three; some like to get four, just to confirm it; others seek to break the breed record. To obtain the title of Champion, a Show Champion must win a prize in the field to show that he has hunting instincts. A Show Spaniels' Field Day is held each year for this.

There is much to be said for retiring a dog or bitch once it has gained its title and completed outstanding entries. We have always done this with ours, and then you can bring them out in due course for a Veteran class, giving newcomers to the breed an opportunity of seeing them in the flesh, not just a name on a pedigree form. We did just that with our Sh Ch Hillpark Hamlet, who gained his title in 1985. He was then retired, but came out again at the Crufts Centenary Show in 1993, when the President of the Welsh Springer Spaniel Club, at that time Mr Noel Hunton Morgans (Dalati), judged our breed and proved to all that our Hamlet was still worthy of his title by awarding him the Reserve CC to the then Breed Record Holder, Mr and Mrs Mansel Young's Sh Ch Wainfelin Barley Mo. Welsh Springers are renowned for being slow developers, and many will look far better in their later years than they did in their heyday on the show circuit.

The classes are laid down by The Kennel Club, with dogs and bitches scheduled separately. The Kennel Club has recently produced an advisory list of criteria for the Breed Clubs' Judges' Lists, which are compiled annually by the Breed Clubs, and judges need to comply with these lists to be able to judge at various levels. All nominations for awarding CCs at Championship Shows are selected by the various societies staging the shows, and the names have to be sent to The Kennel Club, where they will be considered for approval. Even if a judge has been passed by The Kennel Club to award CCs in the breed, each nomination has to be approved every time his or her name is proposed for an appointment. Before being nominated to award CCs, it is important that the candidate should have judged at least one Breed Club Open Show. It is one thing to judge three or four dogs in four classes at an ordinary Open Show, but quite another at a Breed Club Open Show, where there is always a large entry, and very different again at Championship Show level.

At some Championship Shows, CCs are not on offer for Welsh Springers, but the breed is still classified. The requirements for judges of these classes are not so great as for those awarding CCs.

At all the Championship Shows, the dogs will have their own numbered benches, which they should occupy for the duration of their time at the show apart from when they are being judged and exercised. Most of the Shows will take place over two or three days, apart from the one-day Gundog Group Shows.

Then there are the Club Championship Shows. These are the highlight of the year for the Clubs. Challenge Certificates are, of course, on offer, and two judges (chosen by the Club members) officiate, one for dogs, and the other for bitches. To be invited to judge at a Breed Club Show is regarded as a great honour. The classification is very comprehensive, and often includes junior handling. About 200 dogs will take part, with beautiful trophies for the winners of every class. It is a great social occasion, with a packed ringside of enthusiastic spectators and, particularly at the Welsh Springer Spaniel

Progeny Class at a Club Championship Show.

Club's show, many from overseas – the Dutch bring their own coachload, just to watch the show! Winning Best in Show at a Club Championship Show is always a highly coveted achievement.

Crufts

If you mention dog showing, most people think of Crufts, and programmes that they have seen on TV.

Charles Cruft was responsible for running the first all-breeds show in 1891, at the Agricultural Hall in Islington, London. There were 2 437 dogs entered, and the show was advertised as 'The largest and finest collection of dogs ever brought together.' Charles Cruft continued to run the Show until he died in 1938, when it was taken over by his wife. After the Second World War (1939–1945),Crufts Dog Show started again in 1948, when The Kennel Club took over. It has run the Show ever since, moving from Islington to Olympia, and then Earl's Court. In 1990, Crufts moved out of London to The National Exhibition Centre in Birmingham. Many regretted the move, but with ever-increasing entries it had become a necessity. At the Centenary Show in 1991, there was a record entry of over 22 991 dogs, 175 of them Welsh Springers.

Welsh Springers at Crufts

With the recognition of the breed in 1902, their first classification at Crufts, in that year, was as Welsh Spaniels. The Show was held on 12–14 February, and entries closed on 27 January – rather different from today, when entries close about eight weeks before the Show. Entry fees were 10s (50p) per dog, a Brace or Team was also 10s, and entries for Auction were 5s (25p) per dog. Six owners and nine dogs entered. One of the Rules stated that: 'Dogs may be exercised in the appointed places before 10am, or between 5.30 and 6.30pm, and at no other time'. There were two classes: Open Dog with four entries [**Corrin** (1st and Sp), owned by Mr A T Williams, bred by Col J Blandy Jenkins (Dash ex Busy); **Corrin of Gerwn** (2nd), owned and bred by Mr A T Williams (Corin ex Belle); **Kimla Dash** (3rd), owned by Mrs H D Greene, bred by Mr T Jenkins (Crack ex Rose); **Beechgrove Bramble** (HC), owned by Mr F Winton Smith, breeder and pedigree unknown] and Open Bitch with five entries [**Mena of Gerwn** (1st), owned by Mr A T Williams, bred by Mr W Davies (Dash ex Belle); **Fernbank Nellie** (2nd), owned and bred by Mr D H Jones (Dash ex Frolic); **Kimla Lorrie** (3rd), owned by Mr W H David, bred by Mr R M Davies (Dash ex Busy); **Kimla Doll** (HC), owned by Mrs H D Greene, bred by Dr Ivor Lewis (Carlo ex Flora); **Woodside Gambler**, owned by Mr Thomas Harrington, bred by Mrs King (Rotherwood Lad ex Bess)]. Prize money was paid: lst – £2, 2nd – £l and 3rd – 10s. Corrin, our first registered Welsh Springer, was for sale at £1000! Mr W Arkwright was the judge, and here is his report:

Welsh Spaniels were fair. Corrin lst, is too well known to require description. Corrin of Gerwn, 2nd, is a good-looking little dog, and very well-made, but he lacks the spaniel action and style, which so distinguish his sire. Kimla Dash, 3rd, is of a different type; personally, I like neither his expression nor the style of his coat, but he is the reddest of the red in colour, and, except for a slight weakness behind, is a really well-made dog.

The bitches were not so good. Mena of Gerwn lst, though by far the most typical, is very out at elbows. Fernbank Nellie, 2nd, has a good head, but a bad colour. Kimla Lorrie, 3rd, wants lip and an improved tail.

Corrin also appeared in 'Land Spaniels', and won a First easily in the medium-sized dogs, exceeding 25lb, not exceeding 50lb (11–23kg) as did Mena of Gerwn in the medium-sized bitches.

In the small size, not over 25lb (11kg) and over 12 months, second was Williams' Glory (offered at £500), 'a charming miniature Welsh, with a beautiful head, and nice everywhere but in her tail and its movement'.

In 1903, Crufts scheduled 'Springer Spaniels', and there were Open classes for Welsh Springers, exceeding 25lb, not exceeding 50lb. Once again Corrin was offered at £1000, his son for £50. The bitch winner, Forrester Topsy, was offered at £52.10s. The judge was Mr S Smale who wrote:

The Welsh section was well filled, and most of the entries were a typical workmanlike looking lot. Mr A T Williams, the modern father of the breed, again showed his old dog, Corrin, which won in the Open class for dogs. He ought to be allowed to retire now. He very nearly lost lst prize to his son, Corrin of Gerwn, for he is falling off in his hindquarters, and his eye is glazing and assuming that vacant expression characteristic of old age. [Corrin was nearly ten years old.] The bitches were a very good show too, and Forrester Topsy won. The 2nd prize fell to Famous Floss, not quite so typical as most of them, and rather light in eye, but her excellent body, legs, feet, and spaniel like character, and her pink of condition, could not be denied. An old, heavily-marked bitch, exhibited by Mr Williams,was probably as good in type as anything in the class, but she was so far gone in a condition of expectant maternity that it was most difficult to form a correct opinion, so 3rd honours fell to Fernbank Nellie.

It is of interest that Mr Arkwright had judged Corrin in 1900, when he was shown in a class for Working Type Spaniels, the second year in which they had been classified. He wrote:

In the medium sized dogs, a very good class, Corrin, lst, just won. He is a beautiful red and white Welsh Spaniel, strong and active, well balanced, and brimming over with Spaniel action and character, but he shows age a little.

By 1913, only two owners and five dogs entered and, in 1915, there was none. However, at The Kennel Club's 62nd Show, held at Crystal Palace in October 1923, Mr Williams had an entry of 50, and said: 'I suggest a good deal can still be done to produce better heads, straighter fronts, darker eyes, and the avoidance of the gay tail carriage.' He decried the pale colour. His further comments are also of interest: in the Novice class '...the expression not quite pleasing'; in Graduate '...too fine and long in muzzle for me, wide in front and loaded in shoulder'; in Special Limit '...might be a little finer in skull, and would be more taking if more broken in colour'; Open Dog '...expression not pleasing, but looks a worker'; and Open Bitch '... if squarer in muzzle, would take some beating'.

Col Downes Powell had 18 dogs at Crufts in 1924, when they were scheduled as 'Springers (Welsh)'. He emphasised the necessity of a good body and coat colour. In the same year, he judged the breed again at the Crystal Palace show, when he wrote: 'Few dogs rather small and too cocker-like, and breeders should remember these dogs are "Springers".' He also noted movement, balance, heads, and colour of coats again.

Mr Ernest Trimble wrote of his 1933 Crufts entry: 'Disappointing in numbers and quality ... in place of compact little workmanlike dogs I remember Mrs H D Greene and others showing 25 years ago, they are getting a red and white English Springer Spaniel. Not surprising, as they are so often judged by English Springer Spaniel judges.' His notes included comments: 'coat rough; scores in colour, but fails in eye; nice head and colour, but failed in bad shoulders.' He withheld the Bitch CC. Mr Trimble was again the judge at Crufts in 1948, with an entry of 21 dogs. Entries remained fairly static until the late 1960s, when there was a gradual increase, and Miss C M Francis was the first to reach the half century, with 56 dogs in 1970. Mrs Maggie Mullins got the first century in 1986, when 101 dogs were entered. Club President Mr Noel Hunton Morgans judged the

Crufts Centenary Show in 1991, and drew a record entry of 175 Welsh Springers, and it was my turn in 1994, when my entry was 187 dogs, a great honour for me.

Our first experience of Crufts was in 1967. The Show ran over three days, and was held at Olympia in London. Dogs did not have to qualify to take part, and as our first Welsh Springer, Polly Garter of Doonebridge, had met with some success at Open Shows, in the capable hands of Jane Painter, she was duly entered, and came away with a first prize. That was the beginning of our involvement in dog showing, and from that day, I was in charge. Showing animals was not entirely new to me. I started stock judging at school, as a member of the Young Farmers' Club, when I was 10 years old, and all the activities of the Pony Club, and then Riding Clubs, always took up a lot of my leisure time. Showing Jersey cattle and pigs followed when I became a farmer's wife, so that the competitive spirit with dogs was already there, waiting to be discovered.

As entries at Crufts increased, so it became necessary for a qualifier to be introduced. Qualifications have varied over the years, but it is now established that a dog has to win a certain award in specific classes at Championship Shows, which are held all over the country during the preceding year. Any dog who holds the title of Champion or Show Champion, or who has gained a Kennel Club Stud Book Number as a result of winning a certain award, is also eligible. There is also a qualification for dogs which have been successful with certain Irish awards.

Nowadays, it has become the goal post for all Championship Show-goers to 'qualify for Crufts', almost to the extent of becoming an obsession. It is the only Show for which qualification is required to enter. Restricting entries to the very best is an ideal which, however, is not always attained. It can be relatively easy sometimes to qualify a puppy in a small class, and very difficult for a good dog to do so in the well-filled adult classes. Any dog over the age of 12 years is not permitted to enter.

Crufts, our premier Dog Show, is the show-case of British dogdom. Visitors from all over the world gather there, and many are to be found around the Welsh Springer ring every year. Nowadays, it is a four-day Show, with different Groups of dogs being judged each day. The Welsh Springer is a member of the Gundog Group. In recent years, Welsh Springers have been much in evidence in the final stages. In 1990, Mr Noel Hunton-Morgans' Sh Ch Dalati Sarian was the first Welsh Springer to win the Gundog Group. Mr Tom Graham, with Sh Ch Russethill Royal Salute over Nyrilam, bred by Mrs D Gately, was runner-up in the Group in 1993. Maybe one day we shall see one of our beautiful breed taking the top spot at Crufts.

The atmosphere is unique, the Show being as much for the spectator as the exhibitor. Every breed is allocated a special area, and each dog is provided with an open-fronted compartment (known as a bench), with its number above, where it is on view to the public, and is under the close supervision of owners, friends and admirers. Nearby is the ring for that breed, large and carpeted in green, which is particularly advantageous to our red and white breed.

The judge is selected by The Kennel Club, and is someone who is very experienced in the breed which he or she is to judge. It is the top spot in the judge's career – very much an occasion for a new outfit.

Crufts is a social occasion as well, the focal point being the Breed Club stand, stationed near the breed ring, and a meeting place for friends, with an opportunity to purchase the wide variety of Club supplies – badges, ties, notelets and pens – ever-changing tempters.

The ring will be surrounded with chairs, and the knowledgeable and the not-so-knowledgeable will be settling down to study the judging, and choosing their winners.

All around are trade stands, selling every conceivable article relating to dogs and their owners, from car stickers to valuable paintings.

Showing

Training your Puppy for the Showring

One of the best things to have happened in the last 20 years is the proliferation of Ringcraft Classes, which are now held in most parts of the country, and run by Training Clubs, with the object of helping novices and experienced owners in all aspects of showing. They are often held in village halls on one evening in the week, with divided groups for puppies and adults. Some have time devoted to puppy socialising, which is ideal. The Kennel Club will supply you with a list of Training Clubs, or you can probably find details on your vet's notice board.

Ringcraft Classes provide an excellent opportunity for training both you and your puppy for the showring, getting the puppy used to being handled, and receiving help and advice yourself. Generally, puppies are accepted at the classes as soon as they have completed their vaccinations, but it is a good idea to take a pup along to watch for the first evening. It can be quite traumatic for a youngster in a strange and sometimes noisy environment, meeting puppies of all shapes and sizes for the first time. Imagine what it must be like to find yourself looking up between the bean pole legs of a Great Dane!

Clubs will organise their training classes in different ways, but all will follow much the same routine. A Committee member will probably welcome you and your puppy, and there will be a chance to meet others over a cup of coffee. This is a good opportunity to learn from others, as many very experienced owners will be introducing their potential show stock at the classes, and should be only too happy to help and advise you as well.

The emphasis on puppy training should be socialising, but be careful with your puppy. Whilst every encouragement should be given to make friends with other dogs, there is always the odd one that is not blessed with the right temperament. A puppy's show career could be ruined by an unhappy ringcraft experience, and for this reason, I recommend these classes with some reservations. I once took a happy and promising youngster to our local classes, and carried her from the car to the door. There I made the mistake of putting her down while I opened the door, and she was greeted by a thoughtless owner and his threatening Rhodesian Ridgeback, who snapped and barked at my puppy. Although I persevered for some time, she lost all confidence, resulting in her having to be taken out of the ring. We kept her out for a year but, unfortunately, she had another unpleasant experience when she did return, and it was only after she had raised a litter that she regained her ring confidence and established herself as a successful mature adult, and then as a Veteran.

You will need a soft collar and lead, or a slip lead, obtainable from a pet shop, so that the coat on the puppy's neck is not ruffled – no choke chains: leave those for the obedience classes. The class instructors will examine each dog individually. You will be taught how to stand your puppy, usually facing to the right, but by no means always, particularly with our breed, where it could be that the marking is such that one side gives a better impression than the other. The dog needs to be shown to its best advantage, and some exhibitors feel happier themselves with the dog facing to the left. The puppy will then be examined in detail, starting with the head and the examination of the teeth. This procedure is called 'going over' a dog. There may be strips of rubber matting on the floor, and after the going over, you will be asked to move your puppy on the matting, either away from the instructor and back again, or in the form of a triangle: away, across the top, and back again. This is when movement is assessed. You will finish by standing your puppy facing the trainer for his final look. Each dog will go through the same procedure, exactly as he will in the showring itself. Perhaps once a month the class will take the form of a competition, known as a Match Night; there will be a visiting judge, and rosettes will be awarded, all in preparation for a big show.

Entering a Show

We will assume that you are entering a General Open Show. You will have obtained a schedule from your ringcraft class, or seen the show advertised in the canine press and asked for a copy to be sent to you. The schedule will give full details of date and place of the show, with the time of the commencement of judging, and a list of the classes which the Society provides, the names of the judges, and all the rules and regulations and definitions of classes, together with a separate entry form. This can be baffling to the newcomer. Which classes should he enter? If you have a puppy, it would be advisable just to enter the puppy classes for the breed if they are scheduled, and any general Puppy Classes for any breed can also be entered. These general classes will be judged by a different judge, so you will get an opinion from two people on your puppy. If Welsh Springers are not scheduled, there is usually an Any Variety Not Separately Classified class, and sometimes an Any Variety Gundog class, and you would enter just the puppy class. If your dog is over 12 months of age, and there is a class scheduled other than Open, it would be best to enter that. The Open class is for any age of dog, and usually experienced dogs and handlers take part, so competition could be strong.

See appendix G for Definitions of Classes.

The Entry Form

This has a series of columns across the page. The first is left blank, and is for the Show Secretary's use. In the next column, you write the registered name of your dog. If by any chance your dog was not registered when you bought him, and you have applied to The Kennel Club to register him but have not yet received the registration certificate, you must put the letters NAF (Name Applied For) next to your dog's proposed name. If the dog is registered and you are not the registered owner, but have sent the transfer of ownership form to The Kennel Club, you must write TAF (Transfer Applied For) next to the dog's name.

Then follow the details of the breed, the date of your dog's birth, and the name of the dog's breeder. Details of the dog's sire and dam have to be given and, finally, the numbers of the classes which you wish to enter, all on one line. You must sign and date the declaration at the bottom of the form, and make sure that you have entered your name and address. You should complete the details of the number of classes which you have entered, and the cost. The entry fee will be a certain amount for the first class, and a smaller amount for each subsequent class. You may be able to purchase a car park ticket in advance, and order a pre-paid catalogue (which you will collect on arrival). You then send the completed entry form, with full payment, to the secretary of the society in question, whose name and address will also appear on the form. You will see that cntrics close on a certain date and this means that it is the last chance for you to post the entry. No entry can be accepted with a Royal Mail postmark later than that date. As a novice, you will probably post your entry well in advance. At the height of the Championship Show season, when entries are closing every week (often six weeks before a show), many of us who are seasoned exhibitors will probably be leaving it to the closing date, knowing that should we miss the post, the entries will be returned. It is a good idea to get a free certificate of posting from the Post Office, just in case your entry should go astray, and always put on a first class stamp.

Preparing for the Show

No more than a week before the show, you will have to trim your dog (see chapter 6).

Whereas up to then you just did a 'maintenance trim', now there is more to be done. Some people bath their dogs two days before a show. Personally I find this impractical, as I exercise my dogs on our farm every day, and they will not let me miss a day just to keep them clean! The advantage of an early bath is that the coat tends to blow, and a day in between gives it a chance to settle. I bath mine the day before the show. I do not actually bath the whole dog – just the legs and feathering and any of the other white parts that need attention, and I find this quite satisfactory. Normally, I use a shampoo formulated specially for white coats. Some dogs have a sensitive skin, and in their case, I use a good quality human shampoo. If the dog is short of coat, try a shampoo with a conditioner incorporated, and bath the whole of the coat the night before the show. As the TV advertisements tell us, it gives a little body and glamour to the hair!

Page 16 The Starter Barks/15 Jan 1994

Bad Hair Day

By Sandra Ilmanen, Education Committee

Hints for dealing with. . .
A Bad Hair Day

Our Welshies' sleek, shiny, red coats are one of their prettiest features. But on occasion, after a bath, they can look like a sheep ready for shearing! The pretty neck appears to be a giant lion's ruff and perky curls fluff up the area above their tail.

The traditional solution for this is to "towel" the dog's coat. This is done by placing a bath towel lengthwise along the dog's back (on a smoothly brushed coat) and then pinning the towel in place at the throat, chest, and tuck-up with diaper pins. After a length of time (with luck and a sleepy dog) you will end up with a (mostly) smooth back.

Some years back I was introduced (Thanks, Carol!) to an alternate method. Besides resulting in a sleek coat, it does NOT involve pointy objects and provides great comic relief to everyone who sees the dog.

After using my hair dryer to blow the coat dry, I dress the dog up in panty hose. Yep -- two pairs per dog.

A) Front half of dog - front pair of panty hose.

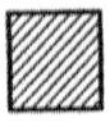

A-- Front Pair

B -- Back Pair

Note: Cut small hole for the ear to be pushed through on each side.

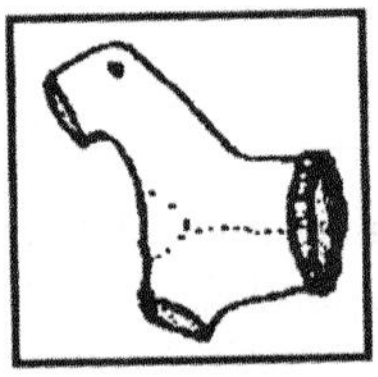

‹‹-- This leg is cut off and placed over the neck and head.
‹‹-- Waistband.

‹‹-- Other leg cut off rather short. Both front legs go through the opening.

B) Rear half of dog -- rear pair of panty hose.

‹‹-- Cut small hole for tail.

‹‹-- Waistband

‹‹-- Cut off both legs of panty hose. Put one dog leg in each panty hose leg hole.

I take care to be sure the coat is laying flat and straight under the panty hose and leave it on the dog as long as necessary to flatten things out. Adjust the panty hose size to the size of the dog -- a too-tight waistband will result in a "groove" in the coat.

It does NOT involve pointy objects and provides great comic relief to everyone who sees the dog.

Once, I left the panty hose on the dog until we got to the show. The resulting hilarity as Rio looked out the car windows caused several near-accidents on the highway! As we unloaded the car at the show, people were choking with laughter. Now I take the panty hose off the dog prior to leaving home.

I towel-dry my dogs, as they object strongly to electric hair dryers, and as long as they stay in a warm area, they come to no harm. Sometimes a dog will have a part of its coat which will not lie down.

On the opposite page you will see *A Bad Hair Day*, reproduced by kind permission of the Welsh Springer Spaniel Club of America, Sandra Ilmanen (Education Committee), who wrote the article, and Carol Krohn (President), who introduced the 'alternate method' idea to Sandra.

Many years ago, a breeder gave me this useful tip for the hind leg feathering: use a ladies' heated roller to shape it correctly.

What You Need to Take to the Show

- Grooming equipment
- Copy of schedule, and passes if sent
- Towel
- Food and drink for yourself
- Collar and lead
- Show lead
- Water bowl and bottle of water
- Titbits
- Poop scooper/plastic bags
- Ring clip for your number
- Club badges (optional)

Many exhibitors take a cage for the dog at an Open Show, but it is not always possible to use them, depending on space available.

For Championship Shows, where dogs are benched, you will also need a rug and benching chain.

Your First Show

Wear something comfortable, and take something warm to put on. It is usually a long day, possibly a long journey,and the last thing you want to worry about is yourself. Dogs can look very different to a judge if they have you as a background in an outfit which complements their beautiful red and white coats. High heels for the ladies are really not at all practical, nor plunging necklines and very short skirts. I feel that an exhibitor owes it to the judge to be dressed in a respectable manner, just as I would expect a dog to be clean for the judge to handle.

In these days of traffic hold-ups and delays, it is essential that you leave yourself enough time to get to the show in an unflustered state. Make sure you know exactly where you are going, which motorway exit to take, and which road number to look for.

On arrival, give your dog the opportunity to relieve himself. Don't forget the poop-scooper/plastic bag for cleaning up after him; the public is becoming more and more anti-dog, and all dog owners must be vigilant about this.

Then make your way to the entrance. Only entered dogs are allowed into shows.

You will find catalogues available at the entrance or just inside the showground. If you have not already paid for one, you will probably want to buy one to see what the entry is like, and how many are in the classes in which you have entered your dog.

Now find the loos!

At Open Shows, dogs are usually unbenched, and you are in charge of your dog on a lead, and the dog can go with you anywhere within the showground. You will need to look for details and a plan of where and when your breed is scheduled to be judged. Make your way to the ring. You may be lucky and find some spare seats available at the ringside. Probably there will be other Welsh Springers nearby, and it is a good time to introduce yourself, have a chat with other exhibitors, and pick up any useful tips. Experienced showgoers should be only too happy to help novices.

The judge and stewards will be at the table in the ring. Groom your dog (this should only be a quick brush and comb, as you will have prepared your dog the night before the show), and make sure that you are wearing your ring clip for your number. At the appointed time, the steward will call in the first class. If this is your class, enter the ring with your dog, and collect your number from the steward – make sure that you know what it is before you go in! The stewards will then indicate where you are to stand for the judge. Experienced exhibitors will know the procedure, so follow them, and stand at the end of the line. You then have the advantage of watching them so that you know what you will be expected to do. Probably this is just what you have learnt at the training classes: standing the dog, probably moving him round the ring, with each dog being individually assessed and moved, and then standing the dogs again for the judge to make his decisions.

The winner of the class will be called into the centre of the ring, followed by the others probably down to 5th place, standing in line from left to right as they face the judge, and the awards are handed out. The first prize winners remain for the judge to write his notes for his critique for the dog press, while the steward calls in the entries for the next class. If you have entered more than one class, the steward will ask you to stand with your dog with any other 'seen' dogs in another part of the ring, until the judge has seen all the new exhibits. You will then be asked to join those for the judge's selection. As he will already have seen your dog, you will not be required to come forward for full inspection, but you will probably be asked to move your dog again. Listen carefully to anything that the judge says and, above all, keep your eye on the judge at all times! When you move your dog, remember that it is not a race. Try to establish which is your dog's most becoming gait and, once you have established that, stick to it. Get a friend to move the dog when you are practising at home, so that you can see how he will move in the ring at different speeds. You want steady movement, at a moderate speed, so that the dog's stride and reach can be seen to full advantage.

The first prize winners from all the classes (if unbeaten in another class), will be called in for the judge to select the Best of Breed, Best Opposite Sex and possibly Best Puppy. After the judging, you may be able to take your dog with you and ask the judge what he thought of your dog. You may not like what you hear, but accept the comments graciously and try not to show any displeasure. Dog showing should be fun, and you are only seeking a judge's opinion on your dog. Another judge on another day could bring a different result, and that is the whole essence of dog showing.

Later in the day, the Best of Breed and then the Best Puppy winners will be called into the main ring, for another judge to select the Best in Show. Sadly, the pressures of today and the need to get home have resulted in ringside spectators at this exciting stage of a show being rather thin on the ground, and the excellent opportunity of learning more about other breeds is missed.

chapter 9
Judging

After you have been in the breed for several years, you will have formed opinions on the type of dog that you like, and will probably be ringside judging with all the other spectators. You will be considering whether or not you would like to judge yourself and, in due course, you may be asked to judge a few classes at an Open Show. You will then have to ask yourself whether you feel that you have the depth of knowledge of the breed, conformation, movement and breed type, and also if you have the confidence to stand alone in the middle of a ring and make an independent judgment of the dogs, without influence from others.

From time to time, the Breed Clubs will hold seminars, and these present the best opportunity for the potential judge, both in the knowledge offered and in the chance to get your hands on good dogs. No one knows everything, however experienced they are, and such gatherings offer the ideal opportunity to ask questions without feeling stupid and inadequate.

Stewarding

An excellent way to learn about a breed is to offer to act as a trainee ring steward, and it is a requirement for judging at the highest levels. You do not have to pass any tests to do this, and Show Societies are always looking for more stewards, particularly younger ones. You will have the opportunity not only to learn about ring procedure but also to familiarise yourself with the judging book, so that if and when you do tackle your first judging appointment, it is not completely strange to you. Some judges will comment on the exhibits as they return to the table between classes, and you may get the chance to ask why one was favoured rather another. Be patient, though, as judging is absorbing, and you may have to wait until the task is completed before the judge is ready to talk. As the individual assessment of each dog is usually done in front of the table, you are given a wonderful opportunity to watch the judge closely, and then you are very well placed to see how the dogs move.

If there are two ring stewards, the various tasks will be agreed between them. They will consult with the judge as to where he or she would like the dogs to stand. If judging is taking place outside, the judge will probably like Welsh Springers to be stood with the sun on their backs so that their beautiful red and white coats are shown to advantage. Stewards should make sure that the exhibitors know when judging is about to commence, and then it is the exhibitors' responsibility to be in the ring for judging. Ring numbers will be handed out at the beginning of each class. At benched shows, the numbers are usually left on the dogs' benches. The stewards check each class to make sure that the correct dogs are in the ring according to the catalogue, and any absentees must be noted in the judge's book. When all is in order, the stewards retire to the table whilst judging is in progress. The judge does not have access to the catalogue until judging is completed.

Once the judge has pulled out and placed the winners, the steward hands him the judging book and pen, or a dictaphone if this is used, and the judge enters the winners' numbers in the book. The steward enters the numbers on the steward's card, usually provided by the Show Society.

Prize cards and any other awards are handed out by stewards, and the numbers of winners should be announced clearly. Many stewards also record the results in the catalogue, so that a completed copy can be handed to the judge at the end of his task. The stewards also have to place in order any dogs that the judge has seen in previous classes, and inform the judge, agreeing with him where these dogs are to be stood. While the following class is being judged, the stewards remove the completed slips from the judge's book, displaying one on the awards board for spectators' use, and keeping others for the Secretary's office.

When all classes have been completed, the steward calls for all the dogs that remain unbeaten to return to the ring for the judge to select the Best of Breed, and possibly Best Opposite Sex and/or Reserve Best of Breed. The Best Puppy award will then follow. All the judge's slips in his book must be signed by him, and it is the stewards' responsibility to see that the book is completed, that the slips are removed from the book, and those for the Secretary's office are safely delivered. Another vital piece of equipment, usually to be found under the table, is the bucket and shovel, to deal with any mishaps. Some exhibitors expect the stewards rather than themselves to attend to their dogs' mistakes, although I do not agree with this principle.

Breed Standards

Breeders and judges are ruled by Breed Standards. They are the ideal that we endeavour to interpret. Different judges will give different interpretations, but a good dog stands out above all the others. Some judges will have started their judging careers at an early age, possibly having grown up with dogs and other animals. Others come into it later in life, maybe when they have more time to devote to it. All rounders – those who started their judging careers as a specialist judge in one or two breeds, and then graduated to judge many breeds – see the whole dog, and have a good eye for a dog, judging on soundness and overall appearance and quality. The specialist judge will compare each dog point by point with the Breed Standard, and each dog against another, looking more for type and the finer points of the breed. Overseas the Breed Standard is based on ours, although some countries are more rigid on some points. It is helpful to refer to the diagram on page 108 while reading the Standards.

Our Breed Standard has remained much the same since it was first composed. I quote from *British Dogs* (1903) by Drury and Others:

To Mr Williams, of Ynisygerwn, the writer is indebted for the following notes, which are a supplement to the description of this variety, promulgated by a committee of the Welsh members of the Sporting Spaniel Society:-

The Welsh 'Spaniel', or 'Springer', is also known and referred to in Wales as a 'Starter'. He is of a very ancient and pure origin, and is a distinct variety, which has been bred and preserved purely for working purposes. The show-bench has therefore in no way affected him, and he retains his beauty and his working properties. The true original colour is red-and-white (of varying shades). The standard points adopted for this variety of Spaniel by the Kennel Club are as follows:

Skull – *Fairly long and fairly broad, slightly rounded, with a stop at the eyes.*

Jaws – *Medium length, narrow (when looked at downwards), straight, fairly square, the nostrils well developed, and flesh-coloured or dark. A short, chubby head is objectionable.*

Eyes – *Hazel or dark brown, medium size, intelligent, not prominent, not sunken nor showing haw* [the third eyelid or membrane in the inside corner of the eye].

Ears – *Comparatively small, covered with feather not longer than the ear, set moderately low and hanging close to the cheeks.*

Neck – *Strong, muscular, clean in throat.*

Shoulders – *Long and sloping.*

Fore Legs – *Medium length, straight, good bone, moderately feathered.*

Body – *Strong, fairly deep, not long, well-sprung ribs. Length of body should be proportionate to that of leg.*

Loin – *Muscular and strong, slightly arched, well coupled up and knit together.*

Hindquarters and Legs - *Strong; hocks well let down; stifles moderately bent (not twisted in or out), not feathered below the hock on the leg.*

Feet – *Round, with thick pads.*

Stern – *Low, never carried above the level of the back, feathered, and with a lively motion.*

Coat – *Straight or flat, and thick.*

Colour – *Red- or orange-and-white (red preferable).*

General Appearance – *Symmetrical, compact, strong, merry, active, not stilty, built for endurance and activity.*

Weight – *Between 30lb and 42lb.*

We can compare this with today's Breed Standard, reproduced by kind permission of The Kennel Club:

General Appearance: *Symmetrical, compact, not leggy, obviously built for endurance and hard work. Quick and active mover, displaying plenty of push and drive.*

Characteristics: *Very ancient and distinct breed of pure origin. Strong, merry and very active.*

Temperament: *Kindly disposition, not showing aggression or nervousness.*

Head and Skull: *Skull of proportionate length, slightly domed, clearly defined stop, well chiselled below eyes. Muzzle of medium length, straight, fairly square. Nostrils well developed, flesh coloured to dark.*

Eyes: *Hazel or dark, medium size, not prominent, nor sunken, nor showing haw.*

Ears: *Set moderately low and hanging close to cheeks. Comparatively small and gradually narrowing towards tip and shaped somewhat like a vine leaf.*

Mouth: *Jaws strong with perfect, regular and complete scissor bite, i.e. upper teeth closely overlapping the lower teeth and set square to the jaws.*

Neck: *Long, muscular, clean in throat, neatly set into sloping shoulders.*

Forequarters: *Forelegs of medium length, straight, well boned.*

Body: *Not long, strong and muscular. Deep brisket, well sprung ribs. Length of body should be proportionate to length of leg. Loin muscular and slightly arched. Well coupled.*

Hindquarters: *Strong and muscular, wide and fully developed with deep second thighs. Hindlegs well boned, hocks well let down, stifles moderately angled, neither turning in nor out.*

Feet: *Round, with thick pads. Firm and cat like, not large or spreading.*

Tail: *Well set on and low, never carried above level of back, customarily docked. Lively in action.*

Gait/Movement: *Smooth, powerful, ground covering action; driving from rear.*

Coat: *Straight or flat, silky texture, dense, never wiry or wavy. Curly coat highly undesirable. Forelegs and hindlegs above hocks moderately feathered, ears and tail lightly feathered.*

Colour: *Rich red and white only.*

Size: *Approximate height: Dogs 48cm (19in) at withers. Bitches 46cm (18in) at withers.*

Faults: *Any departure from the foregoing points should be considered a fault, and the seriousness with which the fault should be regarded should be in exact proportion to its degree.*

Note: *Male animals should have two apparently normal testicles fully descended into the scrotum.*

Changes over the Years

It was not until the Annual General Meeting of the Welsh Springer Spaniel Club in 1967 that the words 'which has been bred and preserved purely for working purposes' were deleted. This coincided with the registration explosion in the breed, when the showing side really took off.

In the 1920s and 1930s, the jaws were 'strong, neither under- nor overshot', and this continued until 1982, when the 'scissor bite' was introduced, and this was reaffirmed in 1986, when The Kennel Club produced revised Breed Standards for all breeds, so that each Standard had the same headings. I have, however, found several references where level mouths are required for our breed, in common with other spaniels, setters and retrievers.

The description for the ears as 'covered with nice setter-like feathering, and shaped somewhat like a vine leaf' seems to have appeared after the Second World War. There is no mention of it in the Welsh Springer Spaniel Club's Minutes of meetings of the time, but it was included in the official Breed Standard of 1949. Some debate was recorded in 1967 as to whether this should be retained, but the majority of the Club Committee were in favour, and it is still there today. It is of interest that Clifford Hubbard, in his book *Dogs in Britain* (1948) says of the Welsh Springer: 'The ears are set fairly low, pendant, rather small (for a spaniel) and pear-shaped (unlike other spaniels), with the feather finishing not longer than the leather (the flap of the ear); the muzzle is of medium length, more pointed than in the English Springer, with well developed flesh-coloured nostrils and level mouth.'

The colour of the nose has varied a little. Flesh coloured appeared as standard until 1990, when 'brown to dark' was substituted, but in 1991 this was changed back to include flesh coloured.

In 1927, the weight was given as 33–40lb (15–18kg) (*Pedigree Dogs*, edited by C C Anderson), and this was still included by C A Phillips (*Hounds and Dogs,* 1932), and again in 1938 by Edward Ash *(New Book of the Dog)*. No height was given.

In 1949, the well-known breeder, Mrs Margery Mayall, at a Committee Meeting of the Welsh Springer Spaniel Club, wished it to be recorded that she considered that the Welsh Springers being shown at the time were 'as a general rule too big'. The Minutes report: 'After discussion, it was decided not to incorporate a weight or height limit into the Standard, but the matter should be left to the individual judge. If the smaller ones were put up, the larger ones would eventually disappear'. Despite this, the official Standard included the weight as 35–45lb (15–20kg), and this remained until 1967, after which it has not been included. At the Committee Meeting in March 1950, the well-known judge, Mr Pete Painter, expressed disappointment that the ideal height was not included in the new Standard of Points drawn up by The Kennel Club. Apparently, the general feeling was that the height should be included, instead of the weight, 'particularly at present, as dogs as big as English Springers were receiving awards at shows'. It was then decided that 18in (45cm) should be the ideal height, this decision to be placed before The Kennel Club. It was not implemented, and at subsequent Annual General Meetings of the Welsh Springer Spaniel Club, the question of height and weight came up regularly.

It was not until 1969 that the height was given as: 'Dogs to be approximately 19in (48cm) to the shoulder and bitches approximately 18in (45cm) to the shoulder'. In 1971, this was altered again: 'A dog not to exceed 19in in height at the shoulder and a bitch 18in, approximately'. This remained until 1983, when the present wording was adopted.

In 1907, the coat was described as 'thick', and this was in the Standard until 1982. The word 'dense' was included in 1986. C A Phillips in 1932 quoted the coat as 'dark rich red and white', and that remained in the Standard until 1967. The following year, it appeared as 'rich red and white only', as it is today.

Until 1982, 'Faults' were included individually in the Breed Standard. These were: coarse skull, light bone, long or curly coat, bad shoulders, poor movement, and 'a short chubby head is objectionable'. I feel that we have lost some very valuable points by generalising on faults, and not actually drawing attention to them in our present paragraph on faults as we have it in today's Standard.

I have only found one reference to assessing the Welsh Springer on a points system. In *Modern Dogs (Sporting Division)*, Third Edition Vol ll 1906, Rawdon Lee gives it as follows:

Positive

Head and expression (including eyes)	*15*
Ears	*10*
Neck	*5*
Body and loins	*15*
Legs and feet	*15*
Stern and its carriage	*10*
Coat and colour	*15*
General appearance	*15*
Total	*100*

Negative

Light-coloured eyes (undesirable)	*15*
Curled ears (very undesirable)	*20*
Coat (curly, woolly, or wiry and bad colour)	*20*
Carriage of stern (crooked or twisted)	*25*
Top-knot (fatal)	*20*
Total	*100*

The Welsh Springer is described as being particularly hardy, handsome to look upon, a clever retriever and persevering worker, less afraid of gorse, prickles, and thorns than any other spaniel, docile, and possessed of excellent olfactory organs. 'What more can be required of a spaniel?'

My interpretation of the Breed Standard

Judges will interpret the Breed Standard slightly differently. This is just as well, for if we all had the same interpretation, with the same winners every time, there would be little point in dog showing! I shall now try to explain how I interpret the Standard – how **I** judge a Welsh Springer, not **how** to judge one. I do not regard myself as one who knows everything about the breed but, over the years, I have received so much help that I hope that I may be able to help others to fill in their own knowledge.

By coincidence, we had Jane Painter, one-time Secretary of The Welsh Springer Spaniel Club and daughter of Breed Specialist Pete Painter, as a student on our farm. When, unbeknown to them, and not knowing of their connection with the breed, we chose a Welsh Springer as our family dog and bought our first birth in 1965, purely as a pet, they took us in hand, and it was really through Pete that we caught the showing bug.

He was a man who passionately believed in maintaining the 'old type' of Welsh Springer, and I owe my interpretation of the Breed Standard to him, and to the great breed experts, Harold Newman (Pencelli) and Cliff Payne (Tregwillym).

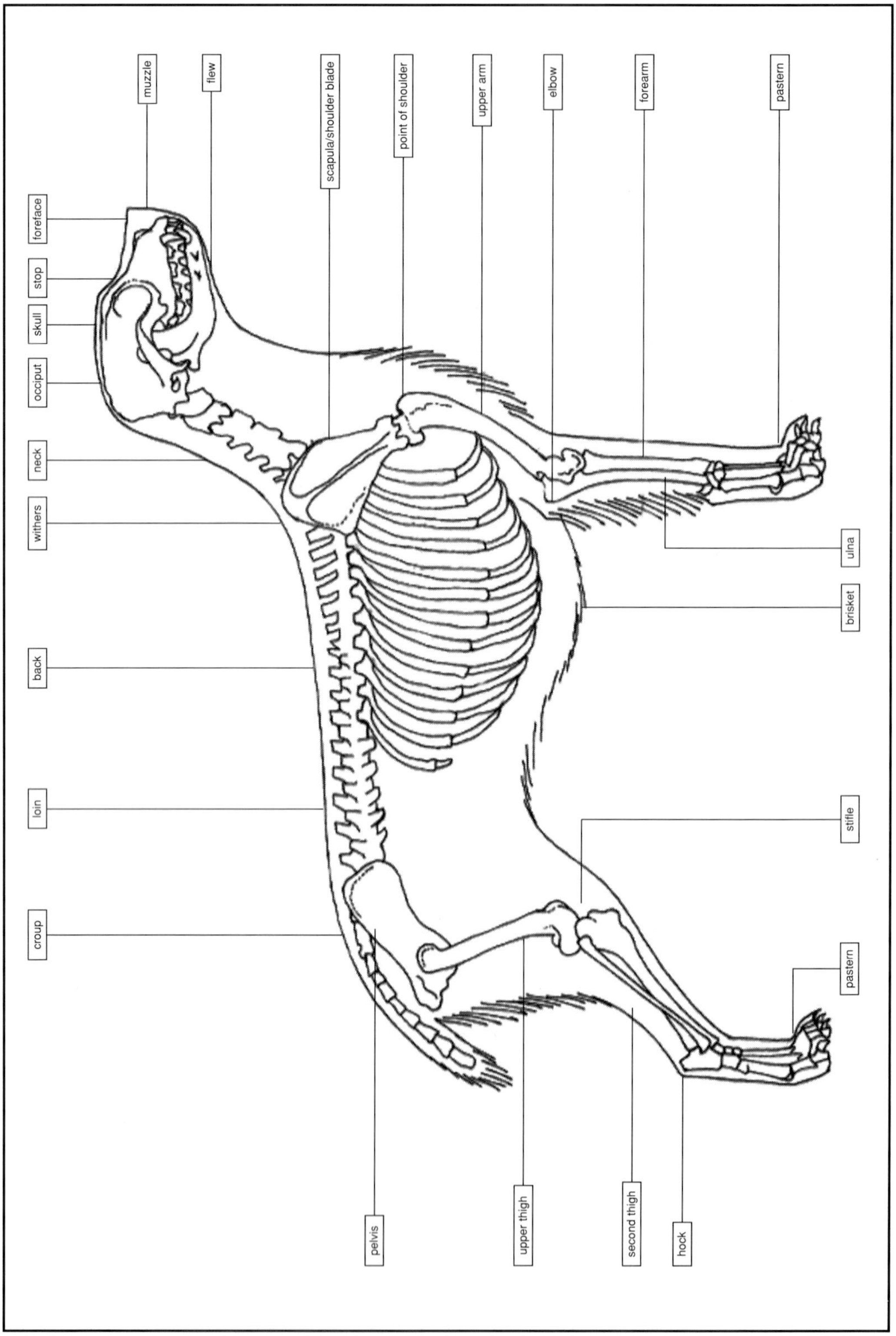

Fig 9.1: Points of the Welsh Springer Spaniel.

The 'old type' to me is a dog of substance, well built for its job, and free moving.

Over the years, there has been a tendency towards a more elegant Welsh Springer, with wide variation in type, sometimes rather fine boned and racey, and, in my opinion, good movement is not always given enough consideration.

These, then, are my comments on the breed standard, section by section.

General Appearance

Symmetrical, compact, not leggy, obviously built for endurance and hard work. Quick and active mover, displaying plenty of push and drive.

As the exhibits enter the ring, here is the judge's opportunity to see if any dog catches his eye. In a large class, the judge may notice that one dog stands out for its quality and ring presence. It may not be the eventual winner, but it already has a lot going for it. When it comes to assessing the dog, I try to give the exhibitor a chance to get himself and the dog settled. If I feel that the dog would benefit by altering a leg position a little, I will then re-position it; there could be a more even piece of grass nearby of which the exhibitor might not be aware, and I would then suggest that the dog is placed there for my inspection.

I begin by standing back and viewing the dog from a few feet away, so that I see it as a complete entity. I shall be looking for type, overall balance, topline, angulation, and general soundness, how the dog is built, whether it is well boned, but not too heavy to move freely. It should not look racey, that is, slightly built and long in the leg. It always has to be borne in mind that a Welsh Springer is a working dog and should, therefore, look as though it could do a day's work in the field.

The topline is very distinctive. It should never fall away, but should flow from head to tail without interruption, with the arching over the loin. A good way to describe the topline is that it forms a slight 'S'.

The dog also has to be looked at from the other side, again standing back. It is surprising how different a dog can look and, as there is no rule that states which way the exhibitor handles his dog, the head can be facing to the right or to the left. This is not always the case, particularly overseas, where some judges insist that the dogs' heads should face to the right and this, of course, must be complied with. Some exhibitors find it more comfortable for themselves and/or their dogs to face them the opposite way, and it is up to the exhibitor to place the dog to its best advantage, and for the judge to find out what is beneath.

The view from the front then follows, again standing back a little. Here I shall be looking for a good straight front, well boned, with the elbows well tucked in, and toes neither turning in nor out (see fig 9.4 on page 114).

To complete my initial inspection, I will go behind the dog, noting the muscles of the hindquarters which need to be well developed for push and drive, and the alignment of the bones. On my way back to the dog's head, I will look down on the dog from above, to see how its body is made.

Characteristics

Very ancient and distinct breed of pure origin. Strong, merry and very active.

The history of the breed has already been dealt with. I like to see a happy Welsh Springer in the ring, one who greets me with a wag of the tail, and does not clamp its tail when on the move. Those of us who keep our dogs in the house do have some disadvantage, and I was told many years ago that our dogs would never show as well as kennel dogs, as our dogs' home lives were far too exciting compared with going to a dog show. Although they love going to the shows, lying in the kitchen by the Aga while Mother is cooking, digging up the garden, and having wonderful walks round the fields must surely be far more fun!

Temperament

Kindly disposition, not showing aggression or nervousness.

I always approach a dog quietly, from the front, extending the back of my hand to its nose, and I will start to assess the dog's temperament from the reaction that I receive. It may have a suspicious look in its eye, and back away from me. That could be due simply to lack of experience, and can be expected with puppies and young dogs. I make some allowance for this in the showring, which can be a very awesome occasion, but any sign of aggression, such as lifting of a lip, growling when handled, or genuine nervousness, has no place in Welsh Springers. The majority are family dogs, loyal and devoted, always wanting to be with their owners, and one must be able to live with them. A dog or bitch with a suspect temperament should never be considered in one's breeding programme.

Head and Skull

Skull of proportionate length, slightly domed, clearly defined stop, well chiselled below eyes. Muzzle of medium length, straight, fairly square. Nostrils well developed, flesh coloured to dark.

This is where the judge will start 'to go over the dog', a strange term to the newcomer, perhaps, which means the examination of the dog in detail. If you are exhibiting the dog, you are 'going under' the judge.

When assessing a dog's head, I always start by holding it gently with both hands, and looking at the expression, making eye contact, and talking quietly to the dog. I shall again be assessing the dog's temperament and experience at this stage. I will ask the age of the dog, as maturity and furnishings can vary quite considerably. In a mixed class of dogs and bitches, there is nothing wrong in asking the exhibit's sex, as this can help as you progress in your assessment, and before you reach the rear end. When it comes to an Open class, age is not of great significance to me; some Welsh Springers mature very early, but many do not reach their prime until four or five years of age, or even later in some cases, and grey hairs on the face have little affect in my assessment of a dog. The head is the most important feature in any breed, distinguishing it from all others, and from which one can form an instant liking or disliking of a specimen. My father, who was in the Cavalry in the First World War, used to quote to me: 'A sensible head means a sensible horse', and I apply this to dogs as well. It is the first thing that you see, and you have to live with it, so it is imperative to me that it should be beautiful and aristocratic. I want to be able to see straight away whether I am handling a dog or a bitch, so I am looking for masculinity or femininity in the head. A narrow, fine head is weak, whilst a heavy head gives a coarse appearance. The head should be in proportion to the body. It may look big because the neck is short or thick.

Markings on the head can be quite deceptive. There is no requirement for specific marking: it does not have to be symmetrical. A wide white blaze can give a coarse look, and a narrow one the appearance of a fine head, when in fact neither is the case, and it is up to the judge to see through that. You may see a few exhibits with no white blaze between the eyes, which is rather less attractive, but nevertheless quite permissible.

It is said that A T Williams' Llanharran Welsh Springers in the 1900s had a distinctive spot on the top of their heads – The Llanharran Spot – and this is still seen today, although the majority of head markings have the red at least partially joined on the top of the head. Our first Welsh Springer, Polly Garter of Doonebridge, had the spot; I am always thrilled when a puppy is born with one, and am instinctively drawn to it.

The skull should be slightly domed, not with an exaggerated occiput, which is the prominent bone at the top of the skull. To ascertain that it is of proportionate length, the distance between the end of the nose and the stop (the depression where the nose and skull join) should be the same as from the stop to the occiput. My 'tutor judge', Pete Painter, told me that the measurement across the top of the skull between the ears should also be the same length. This will give a well-proportioned Welsh Springer head, allowing brain room, and I always bear that in mind. The stop should be clearly defined, but not overdone, giving a duck-like appearance, and should rise gradually. The chiselling is the well defined moulding beneath the eyes or muzzle. If it falls away below the eyes, it gives a snipey look, and indicates weakness. The muzzle needs to be square, and the underjaw strong, to fulfil the purpose of the breed as a working gundog.

The nostrils should be well developed for scenting and good breathing. Small nostrils are associated with short, flat ribs, and lack of chest capacity. Welsh Springers with flesh-coloured nostrils are very much in the minority nowadays. We have one ourselves, a bitch, who has been very successful in the showring. Many people agree with us that the colour of her nose suits her rich colouring and dark hazel eyes. Cliff Payne (Tregwillym) always says that the flesh coloured nosed Welsh Springers make the best workers, and I have heard this from others who have worked their dogs for many years. There is nothing to say that the 'butterfly' nose (a mottled nose of two colours) is not acceptable either.

The Eyes

Hazel or dark, medium size, not prominent, nor sunken, nor showing haw.

The Welsh Springer's eyes should be well set, not so close together as to give a mean expression, nor too wide apart on the side of the head. They should not protrude so that they are objectionable to look at, and should have tight rims; showing haw is not suitable for a working dog, and is unattractive. The eyes should have a soft, almost apologetic, expression, showing intelligence and honesty. Judges usually seem to favour the dark eye, and the very dark, almost black, eye is becoming more common. The hazel colouring is equally correct; but a light, or 'gooseberry', eye gives a very hard expression, and is not acceptable.

Ears

Set moderately low and hanging close to cheeks. Comparatively small, gradually narrowing towards tip and shaped somewhat like a vine leaf.

The ears should lie flat, and be level with the eyes as you look through the head from the nostrils. They should never be below the level of the eyes, nor should they extend beyond the nose. If they are thick and not clean cut, they contribute to a plain head. The movement of the ear indicates temperament. A nervous dog will move its ears a lot, while the ears of a sluggish, lazy and inactive dog's are usually still.

A vine leaf: the 'pattern' for the ears of a Welsh Springer Spaniel.

The significant feature of a Welsh Springer's ears is the shape: 'somewhat like a vine leaf' (see previous page). Of course, not everyone can find a vine leaf to compare it with; 'pear shaped' is another description which fits the bill just as well. Welsh Springers' ears do vary in size and hair texture, but their shape should always be the same.

Mouth

Jaws strong with perfect, regular and complete scissor bite, that is, the upper teeth closely overlapping the lower teeth and set square to the jaws.

When the judge looks at the teeth, he will be inspecting the alignment and the 'bite'. The 'scissor bite' is when the front upper teeth closely overlap the lower teeth. When the front upper teeth protrude over the lower teeth, it is known as 'overshot', giving a weak chin or slack jaw. If the front lower teeth extend beyond the front upper teeth, the jaw is 'undershot'; then you will get a heavy foreface, and the wrong expression. A 'level bite' is when the upper and lower teeth meet. I do not object to the level bite: it was acceptable when we started in the breed in 1965, and I feel that it does not impede the dog's function. Many other features, if incorrect, are of far greater importance. Many judges share this view, while for others, it is elimination in their assessment.

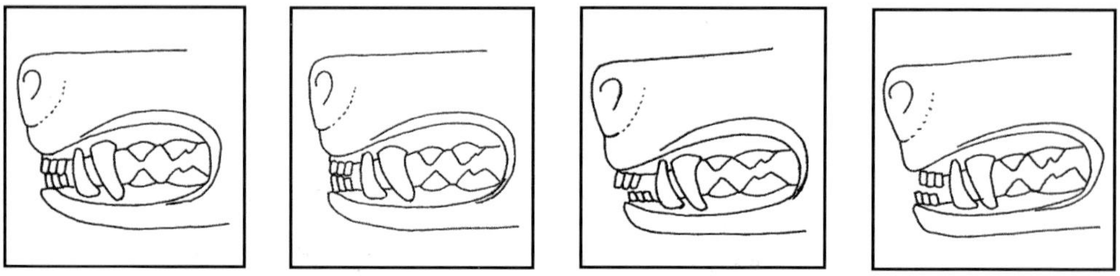

a: Scissor b: Level c: Overshot d: Undershot

Fig 9.2: Bites.

Neck

Long, muscular, clean in throat, neatly set into sloping shoulders.

A long neck is attractive, and a necessity for the working dog, so that he can pick up the game almost in his stride when retrieving. It should not, however, be swan-like. A long neck usually goes with a good sloping shoulder, and a short neck with an upright shoulder. Short necks are impractical, as the dog will almost fall over in retrieving, and the muscles do not function as well in lengthening the stride. A muscular neck helps the dog to contract or extend his stride, to shift his weight, change speed, and vary the weight carriage from front to back.

Throatiness is ugly, and there should be no loose skin around the throat. A clever handler will conceal this, so I make sure that I have the dog's head in my hands, not shared with the handler's.

The neck should fit neatly into the long, sloping shoulder, giving power and strength for greater extension of the forearm, when the front leg is raised higher to allow completion of a stride before the foot strikes the ground. The head will normally be held proudly, so that the neck flows smoothly into the topline. A straight shoulder means that the front leg moves less freely, giving a short, terrier-like movement rather than the free, easy movement, incurring the least effort which is what I am looking for.

I have found that muscle development has a considerable effect on a dog's movement. Too much muscle under the shoulder blade forces it away from the rib cage, and the upper edges of the shoulder blade become too far apart, giving a coarse appearance to the withers, and forcing out the elbows. If there is too much muscle on the outer surface of the shoulder blade, it impedes free and supple movement. Some exhibitors sometimes express surprise when told that their dog has too much weight on the shoulder, perhaps not realising that it affects the front movement. The late doyen of the breed, Harold Newman (Pencelli) told me that you should not be able to get more than the width of two fingers between the withers. If it is more than that, the dog will be wide in front, and I always put this theory into practice when judging.

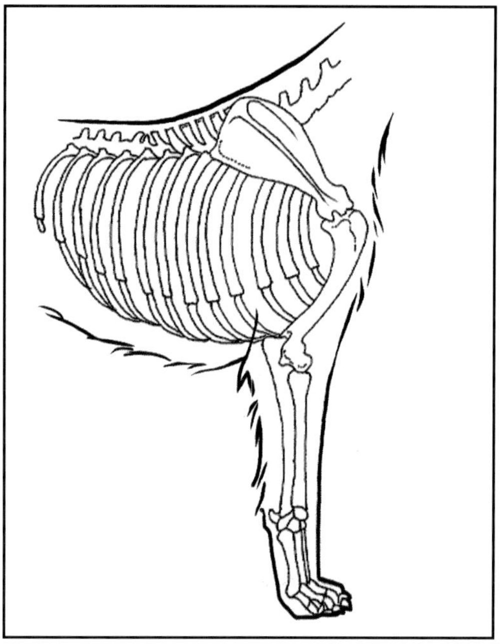

Fig 9.3: Front angulation.

Shoulders and front angulation often pose a problem to the novice judge.

The heel needs to be under the centre of the shoulder blade, in a straight line. Experts tell us that the shoulder blade should slope from the junction with the upper arm at an angle of approximately 45 degrees, when the dog is standing naturally, with its feet under the body, and that the upper arm is approximately the same length as the shoulder blade.

Your eye can tell you a certain amount, but this is where you need to run your fingers down the shoulder blade and upper arm, so that you can actually feel the angulation. To help in your understanding of a good shoulder, make a point of watching the hunter classes at a big horse show, or go to the collecting ring before judging starts and have a look at the way the horses are put together. Better still, ask the rider if you can run your hand down the horse's shoulder. There is the enlarged version of a dog's shoulder, without any extra furnishings.

Forequarters

Forelegs of medium length, straight, well boned.

The front legs should be straight, well set into the body, and well under the dog, not at the corners of the body, and with the elbows well tucked in (see fig 9.4 overleaf). The legs should never be fine and spindly, but have the appearance of strength and quality, and be well muscled. 'Well boned' means the substance of the bone, and this is gauged below the knee. If it is good there, it will be good throughout. I lift the dog's leg towards me for my assessment and, as the leg drops, I look to see how it returns to position, with elbows well tucked in. This will give me the dog's natural front leg standing position, and I then have some idea of what front movement is likely to be.

Another theory, which I have found to be the case with my own dogs, is that 'bone' can also be assessed in the dog's tail. A good, thick tail, which is, of course, an extension of the spine, goes with good bone elsewhere, and vice versa with the fine-boned tail.

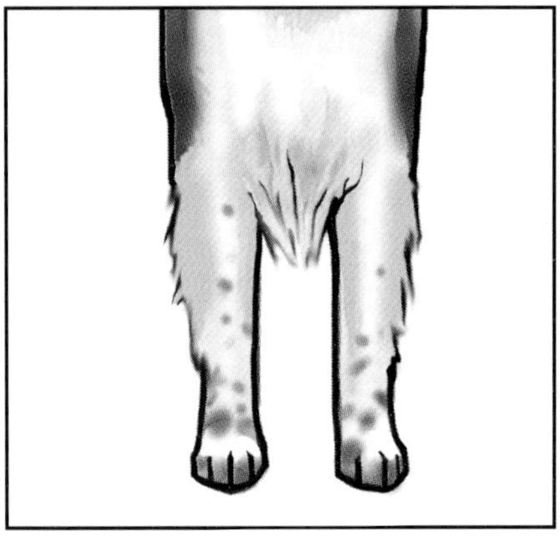

a: Front too narrow.

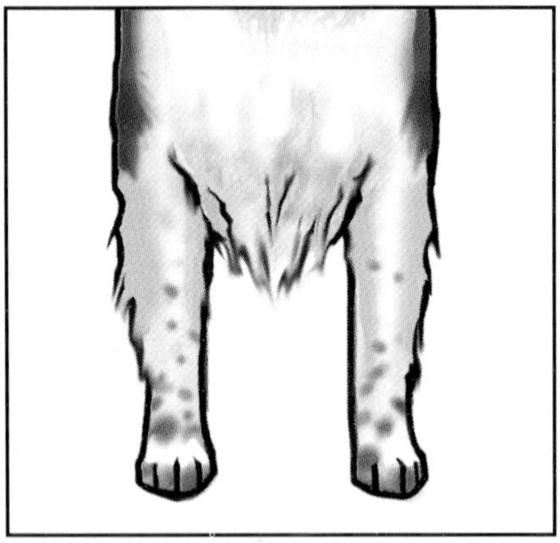

b: Front too wide.

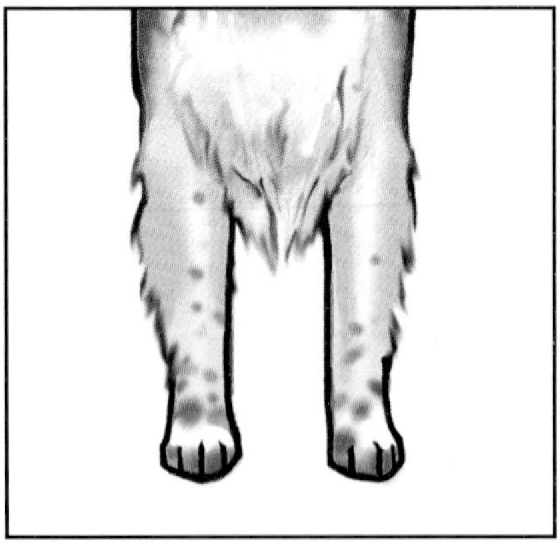

c: Good front.

Fig 9.4: Forequarters.

The pasterns (see fig 9.5 opposite) are the shock-absorbers. Although there is no mention of them in the Standard, they need to be firm, strong and flexible, and slope gently, as that prevents knuckling over as the foot touches the ground. A dog that is down on the pasterns indicates that it is weak or out of condition. This can be remedied by road work to a certain extent. After raising a litter, we generally find that returning to good firm pasterns takes some time in the bitch's recovery to full condition.

Body

Not long, strong and muscular. Deep brisket, well sprung ribs. Length of body should be proportionate to length of leg. Loin muscular and slightly arched. Well coupled.

The Welsh Springer should have the appearancc of a dog that is totally in proportion. If he appears long in the body, ask yourself whether it is because the legs are too short? Or does he look short in the body because the legs are too long? There is a saying that the length of two and a half heads equals the topline, which equals the distance from the withers to the ground. This may be so, but I prefer the theory that the chest cage should reach to the point of the elbow, and this is half the height of the dog from the ground; and that the height from the wither to the ground is the same as from the wither to the croup, or root of the tail. I then have what I consider to be the correct Welsh Springer. I allow a little extra length of body for a bitch, bearing in mind her duty in life of carrying, and then rearing, a litter.

There needs to be a good deep brisket and well sprung ribs, giving plenty of heart room for the bellows and the pump. Your best view of the rib cage can be obtained as you stand over the dog and work your way down the body. Some Welsh Springers appear to be 'slab sided' in their adolescent stage, and many need much more time to mature in this direction.

I also want a good hand's breadth between the top of the forelegs. The fine boned, narrow fronted Welsh Springer is not what I am looking for.

The next point to note is the loin, which is the part of the body between the last rib and the

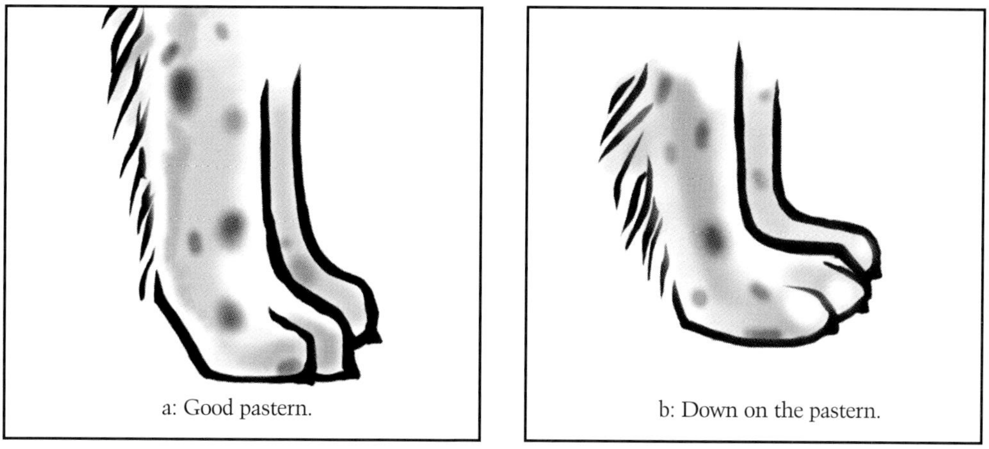

a: Good pastern.

b: Down on the pastern.

Fig 9.5: Pasterns.

croup. The loin should not be over-long – a good guide is the width of your hand - and should be strong and muscular, to give spring and force. It should be slightly arched, a point which is so typical of the Welsh Springer, and tends to be forgotten today. The back should not be roached, forming a 'hump', nor hollowed, which indicates a weakness.

The term 'well coupled' denotes the joining of the front and hind parts of the body at the loin.

Hindquarters

Strong and muscular, wide and fully developed with deep second thighs. Hindlegs well boned, hocks well let down, stifles moderately angled, neither turning in nor out.

Strong, muscular hindquarters are a good indication of the dog's ability to work. To test the strength, I put my hand on the hindquarters and press down to see what resistance I get at the stifle joint. The hindquarters should feel strong, firm and well muscled. They should have a rounded appearance when viewed from the back and from the side, and you should be able to see and feel the muscles in the second thighs, inside and out, something which is often lacking due to insufficient exercise.

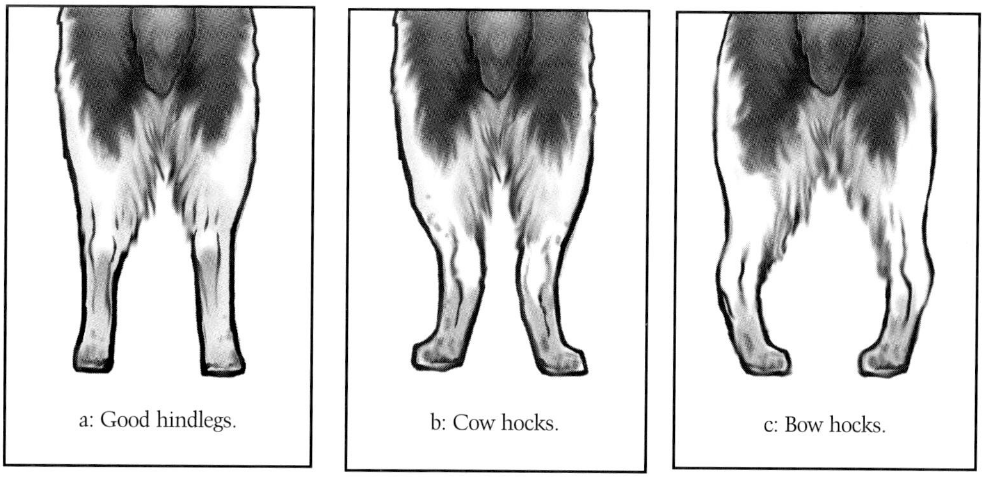

a: Good hindlegs.

b: Cow hocks.

c: Bow hocks.

Fig 9.6: Hindquarters.

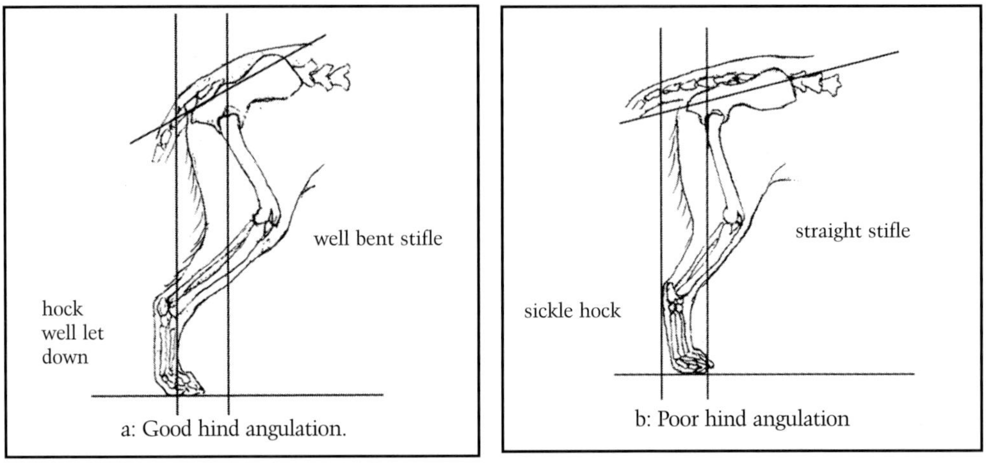

Fig 9.7: Hind angulation.

The stifle joint must be large and wide, and should work with suppleness and a flowing motion. The hocks correspond to our ankles, and the point is our heel. You will hear the expression 'hocks well let down', and may wonder why they have to be so. They improve the leverage action, and are needed for endurance. They go with great length of stride, as does a good turn of stifle. High placed hocks and straight stifles produce a short stride, and often a stilted action. If the angulation is too great, the stifle joint is pushed back behind the buttocks, not under the dog's body, and this gives an unnatural topline. Over-angulation can affect the co-ordination of the hindlegs with the front legs.

As in the forequarters, the pasterns need to be firm and flexible.

I am looking for the long, smooth stride, covering the ground with the least effort. Cow hocks and bow legs are a sign of weakness, and the bones and the joints will not be in a straight line from the hip, through the hock and down to the pad.

Feet

Round, with thick pads. Firm and cat like, not large or spreading.

'A dog is only as good as his feet' is an excellent quotation. The Welsh Springer's feet should be cat-like and pliable, compact and light, with deep, rough pads.

The front feet are larger than the hind because they have to take the weight, whereas the hind feet do the driving. I return to a horse quotation: 'No foot, no horse', a very true saying which applies equally to the dog.

The hare foot is long and narrow, with the toes well separated. This is incorrect for the Welsh Springer, but is tending to creep into the breed.

Tail

Well set on and low, never carried above level of back, customarily docked. Lively in action.

The tail should never be carried above the level of the back. It should be set slightly lower than the back and, as you run your hand over the croup, you should be able to feel it as a steady continuation of the spine, flowing from a well-muscled croup. The tail is still docked, leaving approximately a third on, but an undocked tail is not to be penalised, nor if it is docked too long or too short – that is not the dog's fault. Docking is now banned in a number of countries, and may only be carried out by a veterinary surgeon in this country. Personally, I do not think that a Welsh Springer looks right with an

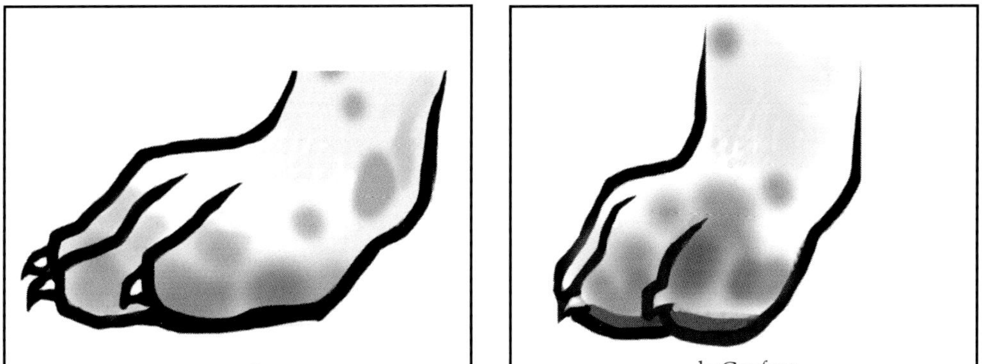

a: Hare foot.

b: Cat foot.

Fig 9.8: Feet

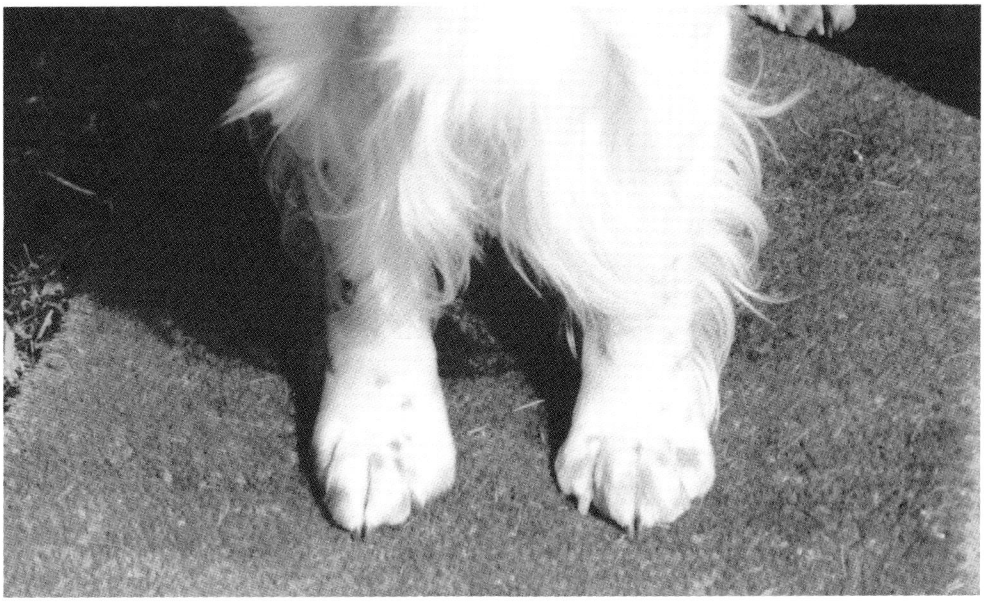

An example of the cat-like feet that are correct for a Welsh Springer Spaniel.

undocked tail and when judging, I have to train my eye to stop at the point where I would expect the tail to finish. I am not aware that any decision has been reached on the ideal length, carriage or feathering of the tail of an undocked Welsh Springer, which I have found very variable in those that I have judged abroad. Docking of spaniels' tails has been carried out for centuries, as can be seen in the old pictures. Because of their purpose as working dogs, they are expected to seek out game in the thickest of cover, and the lively action can result in damage to a full-length tail. I believe this is still the case today. My dogs are not trained to the gun as such but, as with many other Welsh Springers, their exercise includes walks in woods and fields, and the possibility of some interesting prey always draws them to the thickest of bramble patches and hedgerows. How would their tails fare if they had not been docked?

The tail is the barometer of the dog. I do not expect a Welsh Springer's tail to have quite the rapid action of a Cocker's tail, but it should be lively and indicate pleasure and interest.

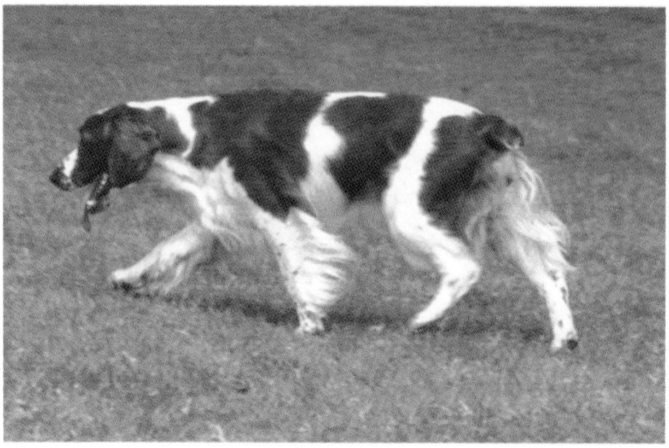

Good, free movement. Photo: Robert Smith

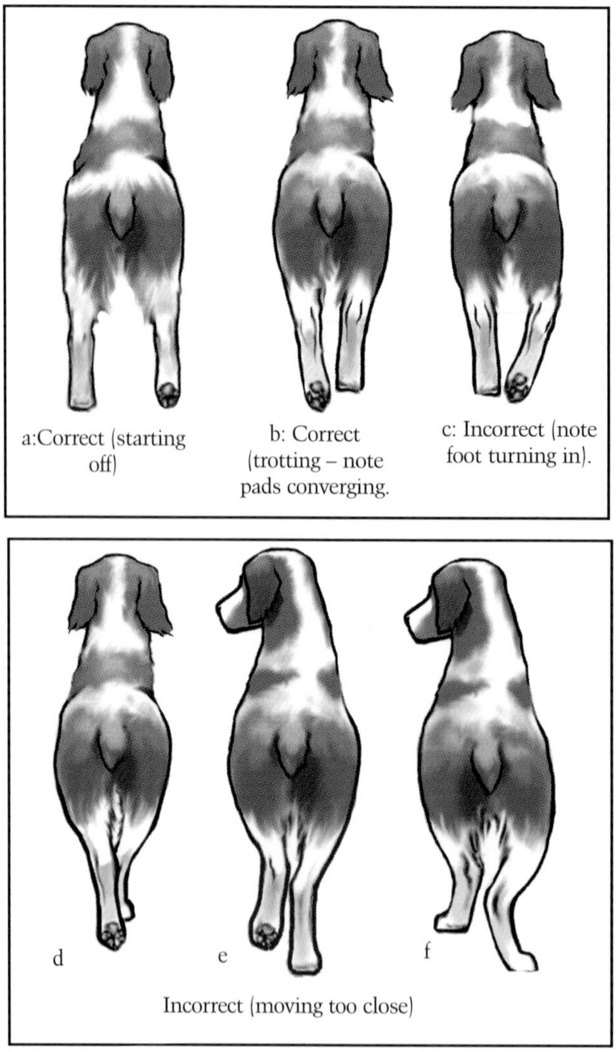

Fig: 9.9: Movement – going away.

Gait/Movement

Smooth, powerful, ground covering action; driving from rear.

This is your vital test when you are judging. You have been over the dog while it stands, and to complete your assessment, you will be hoping that the dog on the move is as good as it appeared on inspection – or that your suspicions were justified.

Judges seem to vary on the importance that they give to movement. To me, good movement is fundamental, and has always been a subject of great interest and study, not just in the canine world, but in the human race (the athlete and the ballet dancer), and in all forms of wild life, which we can see so beautifully via our television screens today. Much can be learnt, too, by reading books on conformation and movement, and there is no better place do this than by visiting The Kennel Club library in London, which houses in excess of 10,000 books about dogs.

I like to start my judging by asking for all the dogs to be moved round the ring once, sometimes twice, if the ring is rather small. This gives the dogs a chance to settle down, and for me to see how they look as a group. I feel it is a pity that not all judges ask for this, when movement plays such a big part in assessing a dog. In the United States, I noticed that much more emphasis is put on movement, and the final selection in a class is made while the dogs are on the move.

Having gone over an individual dog, it is usual for

the judge to ask for the dog to be moved in a triangle, thus assessing movement as it goes away, from the side as the dog crosses the top of the ring, and then back again for the front view. As you look at the dog going away from you, the bones from the hip to the pad should be in a straight line, with plenty of drive, and the hocks should not be turned in (cow hocked) or out (bow hocked) (see fig 9.6).

As the dog moves across the top of the ring, observe the topline, which should be maintained all the time without roaching (curving upwards) or dipping in the back, and notice the head and tail carriage, the amount of ground that is covered, and the drive from the hindquarters, with flexibility in the hocks. A dog carrying too much weight will 'roll' as it moves. As the dog comes towards you, it is important that the joints and bones from the shoulder to the pad are in a straight line, that the elbows are well tucked in, and that the feet do not turn in or out.

As the dog moves faster, you will notice that both front and hind legs incline inwards towards a central line under the body, so that balance is maintained. The whole sequence of joints and bones should remain in a straight line.

Many judges will then ask for the dog to be moved 'straight up and down', that is, away from the judge and back again, really giving the dog a last chance. If a dog paces (the legs move together on the same side instead of diagonally), the exhibitor is usually aware of it and corrects the dog as it is a fault, but, if not, I always ask them to go again, and explain why. Hackney action, with high action of the front legs, is also a fault, caused by poor front angulation.

I like to see a Welsh Springer moving on a loose lead at a moderate speed, not racing round the ring. A dog that is strung up on a tight lead immediately incites my suspicion. Ask yourself why, and then ask the exhibitor to go again, this time with the dog on a loose lead. If your request is not complied with, you know the answer – there is something wrong with the dog's movement!

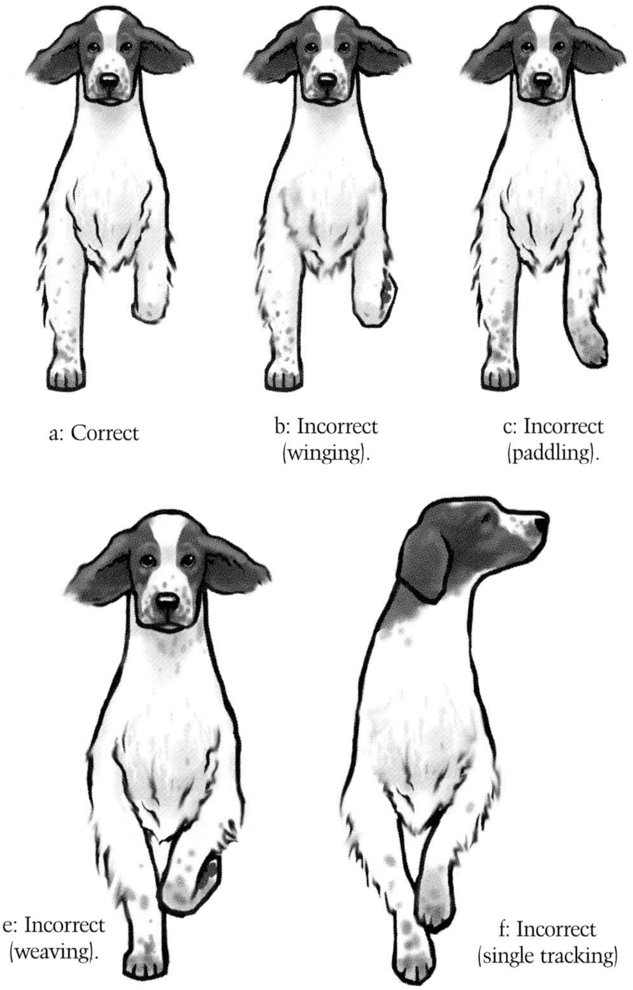

Fig 9.10: Movement – coming back.

Coat

Straight or flat, silky texture, dense, never wiry or wavy. Curly coat highly undesirable. Forelegs and hindlegs above hocks moderately feathered, ears and tail lightly feathered.

A Welsh Springer's coat should never be curly or wavy, but straight, smooth and silky, with a bloom. It should be dense in texture, a feature which is tending to be forgotten. Some have very thin coats, which would not be practical for a dog that works and retrieves in water. Some people say that dogs who live indoors will never have good furnishings. Forget it! The texture and density of our own dogs' coats varies considerably, and some coats grow faster than others. When it comes to trimming for a show, I can do one up to five days before the day, while another I will leave until perhaps three days before. Some grow profuse feathering, which will need attention, but others will hardly need any. And, as I have said before, they all live in the house.

It is quite normal for puppies to have woolly coats on their bellies and down their legs, and it is not a cause for concern. It will all be replaced in due course with a normal coat, and is best left to fall out on its own, without plucking or stripping.

Feathering grows on the ears, the back of the forelegs, down the neck and below the breastbone, under the body, and on the hindlegs and tail. In the showring, it is customary for surplus feathering to be trimmed off the ears, to give a smart appearance to the dog and, in particular, to reveal the 'vine leaf' shape of the ear. The tail feathering is also trimmed to the tail's shape. This is described in detail in chapter 6.

Colour

Rich red and white only.

This is the important distinctive feature between the Welsh Springer and its English cousin, which can be any other colour and white, but never red and white. There are various degrees of red, all of which are acceptable. You will see in old pictures of the breed that often there was much more white than we see today, a feature which I for one find eye-catching. I have also been told that many who work their Welsh Springers like them to have more white, so that they can be seen more easily, and some like the feathering left on the end of the tail, especially if it is white. Freckles are to be expected, especially on the face and legs, but can be unattractive if they are too profuse. In my opinion, some judges place too much importance on markings. Markings can certainly create an illusion, and some are definitely detrimental to the overall appearance of a Welsh Springer. White hindquarters can make the dog look high on the rear, and white on the loin can make the dog look long in the back. A competent judge should be able to evaluate the dog itself, not be influenced by its markings. Only where there are two dogs of equal merit would I place the one with better markings above the other.

Size

Approximate height: dogs 48cm (19in) at withers; bitches 46cm (18in) at withers.

In our present Breed Standard, we are given the approximate heights at the withers for dogs and bitches. This gives the judge some leeway and, for me, the most important point is that the dog should be balanced. If he is slightly over or slightly under the given heights, it is still acceptable to me. I beg to differ with some judges who consider that it is not correct if a dog is over the approximate height, but one well under the approximate height is correct. I feel that, in both cases, one has to weigh up whether or not the dog is balanced, and presents a picture of a true Welsh Springer.

If you want to measure your own Welsh Springer, make a hoop out of firm wire with a height of 48cm (19in) for a dog, or 46cm (18in) for a bitch. Then all you have to do is get the dog or bitch to stand naturally, and slip the hoop over its head to the withers. You may be quite surprised at the result!

I feel it is a pity that the Breed Standard no longer gives any indication of the weight that one can expect an adult Welsh Springer to be. In the past, various figures were given, the last being 35–45lb (15.9–20.4kg) in the 1950s, but weight was dropped completely in 1968. When asked, I always give these figures, as I believe that they are still about right today.

Faults

Any departure from the foregoing points should be considered a fault, and the seriousness with which the fault should be regarded in exact proportion to its degree.

Fortunately for us, the perfect dog has still to be created, and breeders are left attempting to achieve that goal. This means that every dog must have at least one point which is not quite perfection. A good judge will not condemn a dog for one obvious fault when it has many good points, but will take the dog overall, putting everything into perspective.

Note

Male animals should have two apparently normal testicles fully descended into the scrotum.

This is still in the Standard, but it is now permissible for a dog to be shown without this requirement in this country. Permission to do so has to be sought from The Kennel Club, and this also applies to spayed bitches.

A beautifully presented champion:
Cliff Payne's Sh Ch Golden Tint of Tregwillym.

My Interpretation of the Breed Standard Put into Practice

In 1993, a several judges were asked by the *Kennel Gazette* (the journal of The Kennel Club) to select the all-time greatest Welsh Springer Spaniel, and the dog nominated by most of us was Cliff Payne's Sh Ch Golden Tint of Tregwillym (see page 121).

I have always considered that this Welsh Springer adhered the most closely to the Breed Standard, although I never had the pleasure of judging her; only competing against her. I felt that she typified the breed in every way. She had substance and elegance, was beautifully constructed, and with the correct topline, with the arching over the loin. In the showring, she never put a foot wrong, and we all knew that we were up against it as soon as she entered the ring; if we managed to beat her, we had really made it. She gained her title in 1966 and reigned supreme in the showring for several years, with 33 Challenge Certificates to her name, and was the record holder of her time.

The present breed record holder for bitches, winner of 42 Challenge Certificates, is Christine Knowles' Sh Ch Northoaks Sea Mist of Menstonia, or Ziggy. Bred by Christopher Anderson, she is sired by Sh Ch Dalati Sibrwd, out of Menstonia Moonlight Mist. I awarded her the Challenge Certificate when I judged her as a youngster in 1991, and I am delighted to be able to use her – now a mature and very beautiful lady – to demonstrate how I judge a Welsh Springer.

Photo 1

Photo 2

Photo 1: Ziggy is presented to me, and I am standing back for my first impression and assessment.

My first observation here is the beautiful topline, which flows from head to tail without interruption, forming a slight 'S'. Note the arching over the loin, which is so typical of the breed, and is a feature which I feel very strongly should be preserved. There is quality and substance but not coarseness, overall balance, a rectangular appearance, with good angulation. Nothing is exaggerated, and she is in beautiful coat and condition.

Photo 2: A judge needs to look at the other side of an exhibit, and again I stand back to make my assessment. With Ziggy, I still get the same impression, and there is nothing that offends my eye. Note the excellent shoulder placement, with the her forelegs well under her. As far as markings go, although different from the other side, Ziggy looks equally good from both sides.

Photo 3

Photo 4

Photo 5

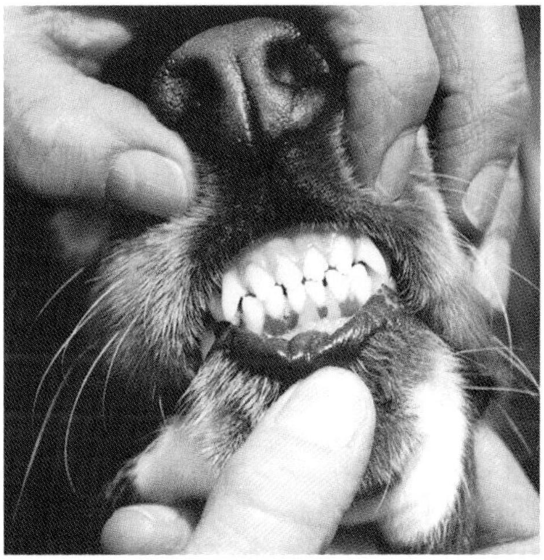

Photo 6

Photo 3: This view shows the beautiful straight front, and the good bone.
Photo 4: The view from the back shows Ziggy's well-muscled hindquarters and straight legs. At this stage, I will also look down at her from above.
Photo 5: I am now down at eye-level, looking at the typical Welsh head, the ear set, and the gorgeous expression in her eye, the chiselling, the muzzle and the nostrils.
Photo 6: This is the examination of the teeth, with the scissor bite.

Photo 7

Photo 8

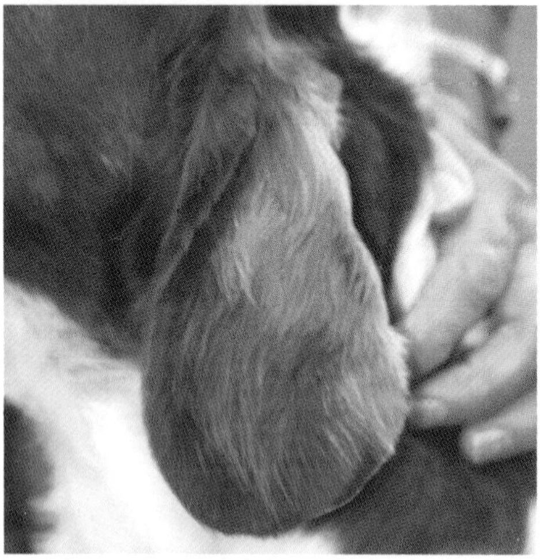

Photo 9

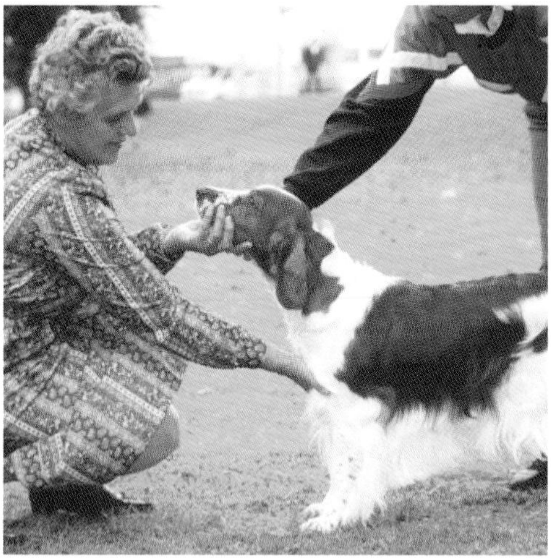

Photo 10

Photos 7 and 8: These demonstrate the well-proportioned head, requiring the same distance between the end of the nose and the stop, and the stop and the occiput.
Photo 9: This shows the attachment and the shape of the ear: 'shaped somewhat like a vine leaf', and lightly feathered.
Photo 10: Here I have run my hands down the neck from the throat, and am feeling between the forelegs to assess the depth and breadth of the brisket.
Photos 11 and 12: I am lifting the leg, feeling the bone and the foot, and will watch how the leg falls when I drop it. This will show me Ziggy's natural foreleg position, and whether or not the elbows are well tucked in. It will also give me some indication of the likely front movement.
Photo 13: Christine goes to Ziggy's head, while I feel the withers and shoulders.
Photo 14: The elbows are well tucked in, and I am continuing my examination of the shoulders.
Photo 15: Feeling the spring of rib and the depth of chest.
Photo 16: Here I am feeling the loin and muscles, noting the hand's width in the flank.

Photo 11

Photo 12

Photo 13

Photo 14

Photo 15

Photo 16

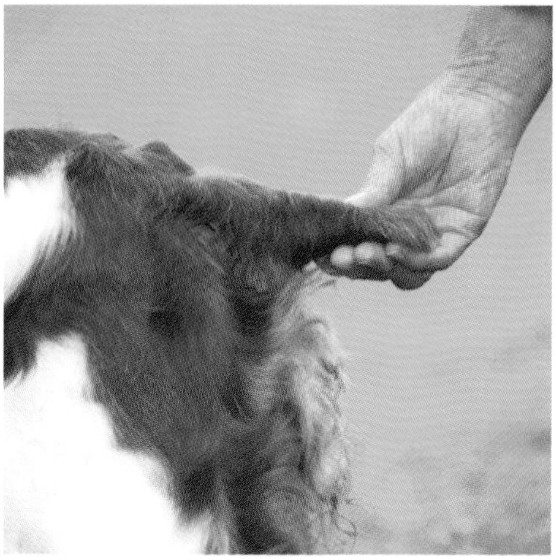

Photo 17

Photo 18

Photo 19

Photo 20

Photo 21

Photo 22

Photo 17: I am examining the tail and the way it is set, a steady continuation of the spine, flowing from the croup.
Photos 18 and 19: Feeling the angulation of the hindquarters, the stifle and hock joints, and the muscles. I want a good, round and muscular back-end.
Photo 20: I have finished my 'hands on' examination, and Christine moves Ziggy away from me. I am watching her free movement and drive, and her happy tail action.
Photo 21: Across the top, and Ziggy strides out, never losing that lovely topline and the correct tail carriage.
Photo 22: Ziggy comes back towards me, alert and happy at the end of her demonstration.

The American Breed Standard

When I visited America in 1984, I spent many happy hours discussing the breed with the renowned professional handler, and 'father' of the breed, the late Laddie Carswell. I asked him if he would write me his view on the American Breed Standard. This is what he said:

No one seems to know when the standard which we use for Welsh Springer Spaniels today was adopted. It has only a few minor differences from the one used by you in England today. If one compares both with the 'Points of the Welsh Springer' from the Sporting Spaniel, both appear to be a paraphrasing and re-grouping of words. I find both standards most descriptive of the breed: short and not wordy -- as are most of the modern standards written in this country today. It was written for and by people who were involved in animal husbandry and breeding, and knew the meaning of the words used, rather than the wordy and explicit attempts today, to write for the general public to know what a particular breed of dog should look like. I recall what your Mr Lloyd of English Cocker (of Ware) fame told me about English Cockers. 'They are square within a square'. Recalling Mr Lloyd's words, I read in our Welsh standard what I think gives the perfect picture of a Welsh: it is a square within a rectangle.

The square is formed – ground to the top of withers, and withers to tail set. The rectangle is formed in profile – from the ground vertical to the nose and top of the head, from there horizontal to the tail and vertically down to the ground.

I believe that the square within the rectangle is explained and written into the standard, but overlooked by many.

Attention is called to the withers in the standard, 'Neck and Shoulders' – long, muscular, clean in throat, set neatly into long sloping shoulders. 'Body' not long and length of body proportional to length of leg and well balanced. That pretty much makes a square of the body to me.

The rectangle or profile of the dog is formed again in 'Neck and Shoulders' by referring to the neck as long, muscular, clean in throat set neatly into long sloping shoulders. In 'Head and Skull', skull proportionate, of moderate length, slightly domed with clearly defined stop and well chiselled below the eyes. Muzzle of medium length, straight, fairly square, the nostrils well developed and flesh coloured or dark, a short chubby head is objectionable. In 'Appearance', a symmetrical, compact, strong, merry, active dog, not stilty, obviously built for endurance and activity.

Thanks again to Mr Lloyd, I find that the use of the square and rectangle applies to most dogs. The use of them seems to determine the type, character, or carriage of the breed. It controls the whole front assembly of the dog. The length ratio of the two upper bones of the leg and the angle of them, and thus into the shoulder blades and withers, thus the hole that the neck will come out of, and the carriage and placement of the head on it. This not only makes the type of front the dog should have, but also makes possible the movement that the dog should have to do the job it was created for. Many times when an attractive dog catches my eye standing in profile, by itself or posed, and something does not make the right picture for the breed – I get my answer as to what is wrong from my use of the proper grouping of geometric figures that the breed should have.

The best examples I can give off-hand are the Welsh – a square within a rectangle; the Brittany – a square within a square; the English or Gordon Setter – a square within a rectangle, and the Irish Setter which is more a square within a square.

Laddie wrote that for me five years before the present Official Breed Standard for the Welsh Springer Spaniel, from the American Kennel Club, was approved. It is reproduced here by kind permission of the Welsh Springer Spaniel Club of America.

General Appearance: *The Welsh Springer Spaniel is a dog of distinct variety and ancient origin, who derives his name from his hunting style and not his relationship to other breeds. He is an attractive dog of handy size, exhibiting substance without coarseness. He is compact, not leggy, obviously built for hard work and endurance. The Welsh Springer Spaniel gives the impression of length due to obliquely angled forequarters and well developed hindquarters. Being a hunting dog, he should be shown in hard muscled working condition. His coat should not be so excessive as to hinder his work as an active flushing spaniel, but should be thick enough to protect him from heavy cover and weather.*

Size, proportion, substance: *A dog is ideally 18–19 inches in height at the withers and a bitch is 17–18 inches at the withers. Any animal above or below the ideal to be proportionally penalized. Weight should be in proportion to height and overall balance. Length of body from the withers to the base of the tail is very slightly greater than the distance from the withers to the ground. This body length may be the same as the height but never shorter, thus preserving the rectangular silhouette of the Welsh Springer Spaniel.*

Head: *The Welsh Springer Spaniel head is unique and should in no way approximate that of other spaniel breeds. Its overall balance is of primary importance.*

Head is in proportion to body, never so broad as to appear coarse nor so narrow as to appear racy. The **skull** *is of medium length, slightly domed, with a clearly defined stop. It is well chiselled below the eyes. The top plane of the skull is very slightly divergent from that of the muzzle, but with no tendency toward a down-faced appearance.* **Eyes** *should be oval in shape, dark to medium brown in colour with soft expression. Preference is for a darker eye though lighter shades of brown are acceptable. Yellow or mean-looking eyes are to be heavily penalized. Medium in size, they are neither prominent, nor sunken, nor do they show haw. Eye rims are tight and dark pigmentation is preferred.* **Ears** *are set on approximately at eye level and hang close to the cheeks. Comparatively small, the leather does not reach the nose. Gradually narrowing towards the tip, they are shaped somewhat like a vine leaf and are lightly feathered. The length of the* **muzzle** *is approximately equal to, but never longer than that of the skull. It is straight, fairly square, and free from excessive flew. Nostrils are well developed and black or any shade of brown in colour. A pink nose is to be severely penalized. A scissors* **bite** *is preferred. An undershot jaw is to be severely penalized.*

Neck, topline, body: *The* **neck** *is long and slightly arched, clean in throat, and set into long sloping shoulders.* **Topline** *is level. The loin is slightly arched, muscular, and close-coupled. The croup is very slightly rounded, never steep nor falling off. The topline in combination with proper angulation fore and aft presents a silhouette that appears rectangular. The* **chest** *is well developed and muscular with a prominent forechest, the ribs well sprung and the brisket reaching to the elbows. The* **tail** *is an extension of the topline. Carriage is nearly horizontal or slightly elevated when the dog is excited. The tail is generally docked and displays a lively action.*

Forequarters: *The shoulder blade and upper arm are approximately equal in length. The upper arm is set well back, joining the shoulder blade with sufficient angulation to place the elbow beneath the highest point of the shoulder blade when standing. The forearms are of medium length, straight and moderately feathered. The legs are well boned but not to the extent of coarseness. The Welsh Springer Spaniel's elbows should be close to the body and its pasterns short and slightly sloping. Height to the elbows is approximately equal to the distance from the elbows to the top of the shoulder blades. Dewclaws are generally removed. Feet should be round, tight and well arched with thick pads.*

Hindquarters: *The hindquarters must be strong, muscular, and well boned, but not coarse. When viewed in profile the thighs should be wide and the second thighs well developed. The angulation* *of the pelvis and femur corresponds to that of the shoulder and upper arm. Bend of stifle is moderate. The bones from the hocks to the pads are short with a well angulated hock joint. When viewed from the side or rear they are perpendicular to the ground. Rear dewclaws are removed. Feet as in front.*

Coat: *The coat is naturally straight, flat and soft to the touch, never wiry or wavy. It is sufficiently dense to be waterproof, thorn-proof, and weatherproof. The back of the forelegs, the hind legs above the hocks, chest, and underside of the body are moderately feathered. The ears and tail are lightly feathered. Coat so excessive as to be a hindrance in the field is to be discouraged. Obvious barbering is to be avoided as well.*

Colour: *The colour is rich red and white only. Any pattern is acceptable and any white area may be flecked with red ticking.*

Gait: *The Welsh Springer moves with a smooth, powerful, ground covering action that displays drive from the rear. Viewed from the side, he exhibits a strong forward stride with a reach that does not waste energy. When viewed from the front, the legs should appear to move forward in an effortless manner with no tendency for the feet to cross over or interfere with each other. Viewed from the rear, the hocks should follow on a line with the forelegs, neither too widely nor too closely space. As the speed increases the feet tend to converge towards a centre line.*

Temperament: *The Welsh Springer Spaniel is an active dog displaying a loyal and affectionate disposition. Although reserved with strangers, he is not timid, shy, nor unfriendly. To this day he remains a devoted family member and hunting companion.*

This Standard was approved on 13 June 1989 and became effective on 1 August 1989. I find it very informative, and should be helpful to all Welsh Springer enthusiasts. As can be seen, it is much more verbose than ours. I regret that a pink nose is to be severely penalized, when that was one of the distinctive features of the original Welsh Springer. It makes interesting and helpful reading for all those who are enthusiasts of the breed.

Hints for the Novice Judge

Some words and expressions in dog judging can be somewhat bewildering to the novice: 'an eye for a dog', 'balance', 'quality', type' and 'soundness'. These are all important when assessing a dog.

To have an 'eye for a dog', one needs to be able to look at a dog and see his overall virtues, almost at a glance, whether or not he is in peak condition, or shown to his full advantage. A 'balanced' dog is well proportioned, and each part is in proportion to the others as a whole, so that there are no exaggerations. A dog that has 'quality' has refinement, and all his parts flow beautifully together to give an air of aristocracy and bearing. 'Type' refers to the breed characteristics and features, conforming to the Breed Standard. A 'sound' dog stands and moves correctly, with no disabilities (see picture overleaf).

When it comes to interpreting the Breed Standard, I recommend that it is read frequently, imprinting what one is looking for in one's mind, looking at the top dogs, memorising what is seen, and visualising; practising all the time subconsciously with any animal, and reasoning out why it is built the way it is, and its function. Train yourself to memorise – stare at a dog, and see it with your eyes shut. Base your judging on visualising the dog which you feel most closely conforms to the Standard, and which gives you the most satisfaction in looking at it, then add good movement and quality. Keep that in your mind's eye, and pick as many of that type as you can. Then you should have a good line-up, and the spectators can see what you are looking for. It helps if you keep certain points in the back of your mind: beauty, symmetry, style, personality, character, intelligence, alertness, bearing, showmanship and condition.

A well-balanced dog: Sh Ch Hillpark Hamlet.

Be positive, confident and strong minded. Stick to your decisions, and remember the words **integrity**, and **judge on the day**. Then you will go home happy that you have done what you consider was right on that day.

Your Judging Appointment

This does not start on the day itself, of course. First you may receive an invitation from the Secretary of a Canine Society by telephone; this should be confirmed in writing, and your acceptance should also be in writing. In due course, you will receive a schedule from the Secretary, with the details of your entry. It could be a record entry, or it could even be just one – on an extremely rare occasion, it has been none at all! Whatever it is, you are still duty bound to arrive at the show at the appointed time.

Well before the day, decide what you are going to wear. This is very important, as you do need to feel comfortable and look smart. For the ladies, remember that you will be bending down over the dogs, and therefore it is wise not to have too low a neckline or too short a skirt. You may be judging outside, so a full skirt is not to be recommended either. For the men, smart trousers with jacket and tie, or a suit, are the most suitable. In general, Welsh Springer and gundog exhibitors prefer to be outside, whatever the weather, so go prepared for that as well. Do not forget your feet: smart but flat heels, ladies, are the order of the day as, believe me, a day spent judging on hard concrete can be lethal.

You will need to check that you have all the information sent to you from the Society, and that you know exactly where the venue is. Getting lost on the way is the best way of upsetting your equilibrium. You will be feeling nervous: we all do, otherwise we are not really keyed-up for the job ahead.

The last thing to do at night, however experienced you are, is to read the Breed Standard to refresh your memory so that, when you enter the ring, you have a clear picture in your mind of what you are going to be looking for. You may not find it, but at least have that clear picture uppermost in your mind.

On the Day

Leave yourself plenty of time. We all know what travelling is like nowadays, whatever the method. It is far better to arrive an hour early than to arrive in a flustered state just when judging is due to begin. If your appointment is a long away from home, you may be offered overnight accommodation. If not, try to find a bed somewhere near the venue.

At the Show

You will probably have a judges' car park ticket so, as you near the venue, look out for any notice directing you to the Judges' and Officials' Car Park. Having parked, make your way to the Secretary's table, to report your arrival. You will be given your judging book, and told in which ring you will be judging. One of the Society's officials will probably welcome you, and you will be offered a cup of coffee. You may also be introduced to your steward. It may seem obvious, but a trip to the conveniences should not be overlooked at this stage!

Now is your opportunity to wander round the Show, and find your ring. Make your way there about 10 minutes before you are due to start, and your stewards will probably be waiting for you. You will know all about the procedure in the ring from the exhibitors' side; you may not be quite so familiar with the other side, and the judging book may be strange to you. Your steward may now ask you to sign the judging book. There is a space at the bottom of the page for this, below the spaces for the winners' numbers and usually judges just use their initials. It is customary to do this before you actually judge the classes, mainly to save time. Some prefer not to do it beforehand, which is strictly correct, as you would be signing something which has still to be undertaken.

The book has a page or pages for each class that you are judging, with the name and number of the class, and the numbers of the dogs entered in that class. There are usually four columns: the first is for the dogs' numbers, with space below for you to make notes on your winners and this remains in the book for you to take home with you. The other columns are perforated; one is for the awards board at the ringside, and the others will be collected for the main awards board and the secretary's use. When you make your placings, you should fill in all the columns, but many stewards will do this for you, once you have entered the first column. The last page in the book is for the final awards: Best of Breed, Best Opposite Sex and Best Puppy. At Championship Shows, the numbers of the winners of the Challenge Certificates also have to be entered. The stewards will make sure that in the excitement, this final page is not left in your judging book when you go home!

You will need to confer with the steward and decide where you want the dogs to stand. This is not only so that you can see them to advantage, but remember that the ringside spectators will want a good view, too. If judging is to be outside, there is nothing better than to have Welsh Springers standing with the sun on their backs, so that is something to be taken into consideration when selecting the position.

Ten o'clock arrives, and judging is due to begin. You will be nervous, but try to appear to be calm, and in command of the job ahead. I always go with the principle that if you are not keyed up, you will probably not do a good job. Remember that you should always be consistent when you are judging, giving each exhibit the same amount of time and attention, whether or not you like the dog. Everyone has paid the same fee for those few minutes in the ring.

The stewards are responsible for ring procedure and for looking after all your needs, keeping you informed about absentees, the number of awards available, which dogs you have already judged, and any awards that they might have received, providing you with your judging book at the end of each class, and handing you a catalogue at the end of the proceedings. Many stewards will mark up the catalogue as the judging progresses. Make sure that you thank your stewards, and be ready to talk to any exhibitors who might come up to the table at the end. Then you can retire to lunch, and have a look at the catalogue for the first time, to see what you have done.

If you can possibly stay on for the Group and Best in Show judging, this is invaluable for your own experience and gives moral support for your breed. The Society's Secretary will probably appreciate it if you convey your thanks for a happy day, either verbally or in a letter afterwards, and should you be claiming any travelling expenses (agreed when you accepted the appointment), now is the time to collect them from the Treasurer. Most Societies, apart from Championship Show Societies, do not pay expenses nowadays, as Dog Shows are run on very low profit margins, and you are gaining experience by accepting their invitation to judge.

To complete your judging appointment, you are left with one more task: writing a critique for the canine press. Although this is not obligatory, exhibitors expect to read what the judges have to say about their dogs, and it is little to ask for, when they have supported you and asked for your opinion. The sooner you can get this done after the day of the show, the easier you will find it to write. Some judges use a dictaphone for their critiques, but they can go wrong, or you could forget to turn it on, so I would always recommend using a pen to make notes for your critique.

Try to make your reports on the dogs as interesting as possible. You can begin by giving your opinion on the breed as a whole on the day, and then give the individual class results, explaining why you preferred a certain dog over a lower placed one, emphasising the virtues and minimising the faults.

You must always keep a record of your judging appointments, with full details of the numbers of dogs judged, as you will need these if you are asked to complete a judge's questionnaire. I also include the names of the dogs who took the top awards on the day. It makes very interesting reading at a later date, when one you picked out as a puppy reaches the dizzy heights and gains his title.

chapter 10
Breeding

Before deciding that you want a litter, there are certain questions that you will have to ask yourself: Is my bitch suitable for breeding? Have I got enough time, and can I cope? How much will it cost? Can I afford it? Have I got the right facilities? Can I find suitable homes for the puppies?

It is imperative that you can answer all these questions positively, before you embark on breeding a litter.

Before You Start

Before considering breeding from your bitch, consult her breeders to find out whether they consider that she is a good specimen. She will be carrying their affix in her pedigree name, and they will want to feel happy that she is being bred from.

Temperament

Temperament is of primary importance. If your bitch does not have a good temperament, I would strongly recommend that you do not breed from her. However beautiful any Welsh Springer, if you cannot live with it, it is no good to you or anyone else. Temperament should be foremost in any breeder's mind when planning a litter. Very few puppies will be going to show homes or to live in kennels; it must always be remembered that the majority will be living as part of the family.

The Costs

Many believe that breeding dogs is a profitable business, particularly when they hear how much people pay for a pedigree puppy, but how many have gone beyond that and thought how much it all costs?

The bitch should be checked by your veterinary surgeon to ensure that she is in good health. Her booster vaccinations must be up-to-date, so that the puppies will receive protection from their mother until their own vaccinations are given, usually when they are 10 weeks old. She will also need to undergo examinations for hereditary diseases of hips and eyes, which are arranged with the veterinary surgeon. These examinations are organised by the British Veterinary Association and the Kennel Club, and are known as the BVA/KC Scheme for the Control of Hereditary Diseases. If everything is satisfactory, you can then progress further.

Most Welsh Springers whelp without problems, and you will have a beautiful litter of happy, healthy puppies. However, there are occasions when you have to consult your veterinary surgeon, both before, during and after whelping, and this will have to be taken into account in your costings. At the very worst, the bitch may have to have an emergency Caesarean Section – a very expensive procedure, and possibly resulting in no live puppies. This is a very rare occurrence but tragedies do sometimes occur, and it should always be borne in mind as a possibility. It could be that you rear only one puppy, which you are going to keep, and you have nothing to sell.

Having a litter is a very time-consuming undertaking if the puppies are to be well reared and socialised. If you are not prepared to give them your full attention for the duration of their rearing, then you should not consider breeding a litter. Plenty of time will have to be allocated to prospective puppy buyers, some of whom will probably want to see the puppies on more than one occasion. Not only will they be assessing you as a suitable breeder, but you will be assessing whether they are suitable owners for your treasured puppies.

The Stud Fee

This will vary according to how well known and successful the dog is. You can usually expect to pay a fee of at least half the selling price of a puppy. At one time, stud dog owners would take pick of litter in lieu of the fee, but this custom does not apply today. It is more than likely that you will have to travel some distance to use the dog.

Equipment

These are the basic requirements for the actual whelping, and they do not have to be costly. We have a home-made wooden rectangular whelping box, measuring 102cm (40in) x 71cm (28in), with 22cm (8½in) sides and a raised floor. Some breeders recommend having a small 'creep' – a small shelf half way up and all round the box, so that the puppies can creep under it. When we were breeding litters of pigs every week throughout the year, we always had a creep area for the piglets, but as yet we have not found it necessary for puppies. Our Welsh Springer bitches are devoted and very careful mothers.

Whelping boxes last for years – we are only on our second one in over 30 years! After each litter, we scrub and disinfect the whelping box before storing it inverted, ready for the next time. In the early days, we always used newspapers to line the whelping box during the actual whelping, but now have found the absorbent green-backed rugs (as used in hospitals) excellent for the job, with newspaper underneath. You will need to start saving your newspapers as soon as you know that the bitch is pregnant, as it is surprising how many are needed for puppy rearing. It is advisable to have two of the rugs cut to fit the whelping box, one in use, and one in the washing machine.

You should also have a good pair of surgical scissors, a premature puppy feeding bottle (available from pet stores or your veterinary surgeon) and some specially formulated milk powder. Some breeders use infra-red lamps, but this should not be necessary if the bitch is whelping in a heated room. The room will need to be at a constant temperature of 21°C (70°F), for approximately two weeks, when the puppies are becoming more active. The temperature is then reduced to 18°C (65°F).

Feeding

You will have to consider the cost of feeding the bitch extra high-quality food in the last weeks of her pregnancy. Once she has whelped, her feeding costs escalate rapidly before weaning, after which she will still need feeding, and the puppies will need food as well.

Worming

Worming is inexpensive, but it is most important that the bitch should be wormed before she is mated, and that the puppies are wormed at least three times before they leave you.

Registering the Puppies

The puppies should be registered at The Kennel Club, so that the registration certificates are ready to hand to the new owners. This takes several weeks, so it is advisable to send in the application form in good time. We usually wait until the pups are about three weeks old, when they should be well established, and weaning is in progress.

Insurance
We also include insurance to cover up to six weeks after the puppies leave us, as it is during these first few weeks in their new homes, in a different environment, that puppies sometimes seem to need veterinary attention.

Tattooing
We have always tattooed our pedigree lambs, and these numbers remain with the animal for life. We now have all our puppies tattooed in their right ears at six weeks and entered in the National Tattoo Register, so that they are always identifiable. It is quick and easy, relatively inexpensive, and can be read by anybody. On the Continent, this is now the accepted form of identification. Alternatively, you can have the puppy microchipped, which is popular but more expensive, and the chip has to be read by a special scanner.

Facilities
A large house and garden are not essential to having a litter of Welsh Springers. You will need a quiet room where the bitch can whelp and rear her puppies. When the pups are about five weeks old and becoming active, they will need a restricted area to play in outside. A kennel or shed, with an escape-proof run (Welsh Springers are remarkably good escapologists!) or the garage are ideal. You need tolerant neighbours, too, as young puppies make considerable noise when they are playing, barking with a high-pitched tone, quite early in the morning!

Homes for the Puppies

This is another very important consideration. Established breeders will have a waiting list for their puppies, but they will have made their reputation. Before you make the final decision to breed a litter, it would be advisable to have several prospective owners for your puppies. You can advertise the puppies, or you can join one of the Breed Clubs and have the litter put on the Secretary's list of puppies available, but it is foolish to rely entirely on this. You are still responsible not only for producing and rearing a fine healthy litter, but for laying the foundation for the puppies' future, and doing your best to ensure that they are going to suitable homes.

Other Factors

After the bitch has been mated, she will lead a normal life until five weeks into her pregnancy. The gestation period is nine weeks. It is not a good idea to send a pregnant bitch off to kennels while you go away on holiday. You should be looking at living at home from the time that she is mated to the day the last puppy leaves you, at least four months later, or longer if there are any unsold puppies, or a new owner wants you to keep the puppy for an extra week or so. Should a puppy be going abroad, it usually has to be at least 12 weeks old before it can travel.

It is not everyone's idea of pleasure, having to come down in the morning and clear up, once the pups are weaned but not house trained; nor is the devastation that occurs in the garden to everyone's liking, but it can all be restored in due course, and the fun that the puppies get out of doing it far exceeds the disappointments of seeing one's best summer annuals strewn like confetti on the lawn!

Code of Practice

The Breed Clubs have a Code of Practice, which includes advice on breeding, and a copy should be obtained before any decision is made. The Code is not obligatory, but acts as a guideline. It is recommended that bitch should be two, or preferably three, years of age before she is bred from. Some would say that the latter is getting rather late, especially if the bitch happens not to take on the first mating, and only comes into season every eight or nine months.

So – once you have satisfied yourself that you can answer all these points positively, you are now ready to make plans for breeding your first litter!

Choosing the Stud Dog

The Novice Breeder

If you are a show-goer, and sit chatting at the ringside while the Welsh Springers are being judged, it goes almost without saying that before long you will hear people discussing breeding a litter and pedigrees, and then: 'Oh yes ... which dog are you going to use?' More time must be spent on that subject in dogdom than anything else, from those longest in the breed to the novice breeder. You can learn so much by listening to conversations, and advice will always be forthcoming! As a novice, first of all consult the breeders of your bitch and take their advice on a suitable stud dog for her. They will have expert knowledge of their own stock, and should have a good idea of all the stud dogs and their pedigrees, and which should tie in best with your bitch's line.

It is easy just to use the dog down the road; he is so handsome, and it is so convenient for you to take the bitch to see him. I have had desperate telephone calls from novice owners who have done just that, and the dog, a family pet, now perhaps seven years old, will not oblige. What should they do? It is almost impossible to advise in such circumstances. My advice is that if you pay the stud fee to an experienced stud dog owner, you will be paying for that experience and for the use of the stud dog. It will all be done professionally – and you need not watch if you don't want to. Also, should the bitch not take to that particular dog, as does sometimes happen, the chances are that there might be another stud dog whom she will accept. The dog should also have been successfully tested under the BVA/KC Scheme for the Control of Hereditary Diseases.

Once you have made your decision about the stud dog, speak to the owner, and ask if he or she is prepared to let you use the dog on your bitch. This is not a foregone conclusion, and must be established early on. Be prepared to give details of the bitch's pedigree because, although you will know all about this experienced breeder and his dogs, the reverse is not necessarily the case. You also need to ascertain at this stage what the stud fee will be. Once agreement is reached, you will make the necessary arrangements with the stud dog owner.

As soon as your bitch comes into season, inform the stud dog owner, and confirm the possible date for the mating to take place. This is not only a courtesy, but essential, particularly if the dog is being used widely, as his timetable will need to be planned as well. It is customary for the bitch to be taken to the stud dog at the appropriate time, not for the stud dog to visit your bitch.

The Dedicated Breeder

Much thought needs to be given to the choice of a stud dog. You have a good bitch, who has done well in the showring. Now you will hope to breed something from her that will be even better, and start to establish your own line.

It is universally acknowledged that the perfect dog has yet to be bred so, as a breeder, you will have that challenge before you. Always look at your bitch extremely critically, and then ask yourself questions about her: what would you like to improve? What would you hope to perpetuate and retain? Above all, remember that temperament must be your foremost consideration.

Regular show-goers will be looking at the dogs in the ring, particularly the puppies and juniors, with a view to the future. Pedigrees need to be closely analysed and discussed, and combinations worked out, bearing in mind what one is looking for in the next generation. A litter of puppies will be a mixture: some like the sire, some like the dam, and some a mixture of both sire and dam.

Results of available health examinations will also have to be considered, and progeny should be studied as well. With the relatively small gene pool in Welsh Springers, it will not always be the case that the stud dog or the brood bitch have the ideal health test results. They may have so much else going for them in type, conformation or temperament that breeders will need to get everything in perspective to maintain the Welsh Springer that has been for so many centuries. The well-known dog does not always produce the best offspring. Just because he has done well in the ring does not necessarily mean that as a sire he is better than the dog who is rarely shown but has all the right bloodlines to produce what you are looking for. Be brave – some 'experts' will tend to question you as to why you are going to use that dog. Nevertheless, if you have decided that he is the right dog for your bitch and the owner has agreed, go ahead and use him! However, it must never be forgotten that any fault or virtue in the offspring must always be attributed to both sire and dam. There is always a temptation to praise or blame just the stud dog, and this is totally unjust.

Care of the Stud Dog

You should only be contemplating using a dog for stud purposes if he has the following qualities: he is a good example of the breed, he is sound and has passed the necessary health requirements for hips and eyes, and has a good temperament. Hip X-rays cannot be scored under the BVA/KC Scheme until the dog is 12 months old. My vet recommends 15 months as the ideal age for hip X-rays. Once that and the other examination results have proved to be satisfactory, the sooner a young dog is used at stud the better. It is advisable to let the dog have his first experience at stud with a proven, even-tempered bitch, as he could lose his confidence if he has an unfriendly first encounter.

The stud dog should be kept in good health, fed on good quality food, and given plenty of exercise.

If your stud dog is due to mate a bitch, it is advisable not to feed him until the mating is completed, as he will probably vomit his meal if he is fed beforehand.

The Brood Bitch

I am never very happy when I hear people say: 'my bitch is not good enough for showing, but will make a very good brood bitch.' She may well do, but she can also produce a litter of puppies with just the same faults that she has herself. The best brood bitches are usually well built, with enough length of body to carry possibly eight or nine puppies, have at least eight well-spaced teats, are even-tempered, show no signs of being shy or nervous, and are good eaters. You will certainly not want to have the worry of trying to persuade the bitch to eat, either when she is heavily pregnant or when there is a beautiful litter of puppies lying in the nest, draining the milk bar. There is nothing like mother's milk, and this can only be produced if she is consuming plenty of quality food. As with stud dogs, brood bitches should undergo the necessary health examinations, with satisfactory results, before a litter is planned. She needs to be in good health at the time of mating, not carrying too much weight, wormed, and with vaccinations up to date.

Establishing a Line

There are three ways of establishing your own line or strain: in breeding, line-breeding, and outcrossing. None is guaranteed to produce the perfect dog, but that should be the ultimate aim of all breeders, and you must be prepared for disappointments as well as successes.

Line-breeding

In order to establish their own line, breeders will often line-breed. This is where the dog and bitch are not very closely related but share some of the same ancestry, and the names of a dog or bitch, or the same affix, may appear several times in the pedigree. Breeders will line-breed with the idea of strengthening the good points in their own stock, having studied pedigrees and the various lines over many years. As you double up on the good points you are, of course, doubling up on bad points, some of which you may not have known about until you make the combination. These points need to be borne in mind. The best results usually occur when third and fourth generations are combined, such as grandparent to great-grandparent. An excellent example of line-breeding in Welsh Springers is the Dalati line, established by Noel and Dodo Hunton Morgans, in the heart of Wales. In the 12 February 1988 edition of *Dog World*, Simon Parsons (now the Editor) told the success story, and has given me permission to reproduce it:

27 Show Champions from One Bitch Line

Surely the ambition of every serious breeder is to produce an outstanding bitch line, one that comes up with top class stock generation after generation. Owning a super stud dog is all very well, but without good bitches, or rather good brood bitches, a breeder's progress soon comes to a dead stop.

You can't develop a good line of bitches unless your bitches produce bitch puppies. But even given this, it's all too easy to 'lose your line', as so many breeders have found out.

It may be a cliché, but it's all too true: 'getting to the top is hard, staying there is harder'. A period of whelping problems, selling or exporting rashly, an injudicious mating or two – and a quality bitch line can quickly evaporate.

So, what an achievement then, to produce, entirely in direct female line from your first bitch, 27 British title holders within just 20 years.

Such is the record of Dodo and Noel Hunton Morgans of the Dalati Welsh Springers. Living near Llandovery, in the beautiful Towy valley, these two Welsh-speaking school teachers (now retired) have built up a line of bitches which has benefited not only them, but a host of other kennels. Twelve of the 27 champions bred at Dalati have been made up by other people, many of them novices. And even more important, they have gone on to found other kennels, successful in their turn.

Rather than go into every step of their breeding programme, which would make over-complicated reading and can be analysed in any case from the chart below [not reproduced here], I will try to explain how the kennel's success was achieved. Perhaps I should point out that Dalati has never been an enormous establishment, averaging around eight to ten dogs.

Experience

Although the Hunton Morgans went straight to the top in Welsh Springers, they were no novices in the dog world. For several years, they had bred Dalmatians with some success, including several

Ch Dalati Del. Photo: Anne Roslin-Williams

Sh Ch Dalati Braint.

champions in Europe. So by the time they went into the breed in which they made their name, they had a basic background in showing and breeding.

An Eye for Conformation

And here Dodo emphasises how valuable their Dalmatian apprenticeship was. This breed has no coat or frills to disguise the basic make and shape. So a badly made dog became anathema to them, and they determined to breed shapely Welsh Springers, something the breed did not always excel in.

Choice of Foundation Bitch

Obviously luck plays a big part. Indeed, they originally wanted a gundog for Noel to work! So they approached Hubert Arthur, who at that time owned a top kennel of Welsh, and fell in love with a mature bitch,from whom Hubert had already had a litter, called Freesia of Hearts. They did not worry about her pedigree – all they wanted was a worker. After several months, Hubert let them buy Freesia. 'She had a lovely head,' says Dodo 'and was beautifully made. But she would not make the best of herself in the ring, and could have been a darker colour. However, she did have one thing above all – **quality***.' An eye for quality, that is another essential. As it happened, Freesia did not develop into a working gundog. so they gave up that idea, but as a brood, she was brilliant – with, as it happened, an inspiring pedigree, a double granddaughter of Ch Statesman of Tregwillym, and from three generations of bitch title-holders.*

A Little Luck and Encouragement from the Top

Freesia was mated to Hubert's Sh Ch Diplomat of Hearts: Hubert was to have the pick. A bitch puppy stood out, but after Dodo's persuasion, Hubert took another leaving the Hunton Morgans with Dalati Anwylyd. their first show champion.

Use Only The Best Dogs

At the time, the breed's top dog was Sh Ch Bruce of Brent, a BIS winner. A similar type to Freesia, he excelled in depth of colour and combined with her extreme quality, produced the kennel's first champion, Dalati Swynwr, plus Sidan, a marvellous brood. Bruce also bred two show champions to Anwylyd. Ever since, the kennel has only used top class dogs, whether their own or other people's.

Perseverance

This, incidentally, is the English equivalent of the Welsh word 'Dalati'. At the time, the breed was dominated by several top kennels who were hard to get past. The early Dalatis won countless reserve CCs and their first CCs came mainly from all-rounders. (Swynwr's from Novice at his first show, beating his sire, Bruce, into reserve). But they persevered, and were eventually accepted in their turn.

Identify your Weaknesses

Fronts and shoulder blades were a problem in the breed at the time, so the Dalatis used Sh Ch Athelwood Daiperoxide, who excelled in these areas, and helped them to fix the conformation they aimed at. To Sidan he sired Ch Dalati Del (15 CCs, and a great worker)(see previous page) and Sh Ch Delwen and Dyma Fi.

Don't be Tempted to Keep a Stud Dog Too Soon

In fact, the Dalatis did not keep a dog themselves until Sh Ch Dalati Braint (1976) (see previous page). Several promising males before him were exported, notably Dyma Fi, whom hardly anyone wanted to use, until it was too late!

Intelligent Line-Breeding But Not Too Close

Before he was exported, Dyma Fi mated his aunt, Anwylyd, twice, producing four show champions. Among them was the unforgettable Rhian, an outstanding winner, and 'the one we are still trying to recreate,' say the Hunton Morgans. This essay into line breeding proving successful, the Dalatis have continued the same way, with outstanding results from such matings as uncle – niece, or grandmother – grandson.

Know your Background

Only after several generations of line-breeding, finding out what is in the background, did the Hunton Morgans retain a male. Sh Ch Dalati Braint (by Rhian's brother Math ex Ch Del) had the movement they wanted. He is the breed's leading sire, with nine titleholders among his offspring.

Since then, they have three further generations of the male line – Sh Ch Cais, Sh Ch Sioni, Sh Ch Tomi, and all from the same bitch line too. Sioni is current top sire.

Occasional Outcrosses

They used the renowned Pencelli dogs for their quality, coming up first with Ch Fflur, a great worker, and then again to produce three show champions in one litter, all starting off novice owners with their first Welsh Springers. Recently, successful outcrosses have been made to the long-standing Tregwillym kennel, whose lines were behind their first bitch.

Establishing a Type

The 'Dalati type' has not evolved deliberately, merely a result of their concentrating on breeding the conformation they admire. Good ribbing and angulation are priorities; a super head is desirable, but they will accept a reasonable one in a superbly made dog.

Campaigning the Stock

The Hunton Morgans believe in showing as widely as possible – today, it is usually Noel who shows the dogs, while Dodo stays home with the others. The occasional defeat may disappoint but does not worry them unduly: 'There are always 20 other judges watching, who will think "that one was unlucky today".'

Although they would be too modest to say so, immaculate presentation, quiet but effective handling, and a knowledge of when a youngster is ready to bring out, also help.

Sh Ch Dalati Sioni (see pedigree overleaf). Photo: Sally Anne Thompson

Generosity with Young Stock

A small kennel cannot keep all its promising youngsters, and Dalatis have become champions in many countries.

No less than 12 British Dalati-bred show champions have been made up by ten owners – and not one of them had previously made up a Welsh Springer. Indeed, several of them had never previously even owned a Welsh Springer! And some have gone on to found their own highly successful kennels, breeding their own champions.

Of course, as in any kennel, there have been setbacks – the great Rhian, for example, was a disappointment as a brood, producing just one litter (though even this produced a Show Champion). But the Dalati story in general has been one of remarkable achievement, all thanks to just one original bitch, Freesia of Hearts.

Since that article was written, the Dalati kennel's successes have continued, with the outstanding contribution coming from Sh Ch Dalati Sioni (see picture on previous page and pedigree below). He gained his title in 1983, and went on to win 18 Challenge Certificates, but his main attribute was as a stud dog. He was top stud dog of all breeds

Pedigree of Sh Ch Dalati Sioni

Sh Ch Dalati Cais	Sh Ch Dalati Braint	Dalati Math	Int Ch Dalati Dyma Fl
			Sh Ch Dalati Anwylyd
		Ch Dalati Del	Sh Ch Athelwood Daiperoxide
			Dalati Sidan
	Sh Ch Dalati Cerian	Int Ch Dalati Dyma Fl	Sh Ch Athelwood Daiperoxide
			Dalati Sidan
		Sh Ch Dalati Anwylyd	Sh Ch Diplomat of Hearts
			Freesia of Hearts
Sh Ch Dalati Fflur	Sh Ch Roger of Pencelli	Sh Ch Bruce of Brent	Benefactor of Brent
			Bronwyn Trixie
		Sh Ch Marie of Pencelli	Priory Major
			Bonny Legent
	Ch Dalati Del	Sh Ch Athelwood Daiperoxide	Nobleman of Tregwillym
			Atalanta of Athelsone
		Dalati Sidan	Sh Ch Bruce of Brent
			Freesia of Hearts

in the United Kingdom in 1992, and sired 23 Show Champions among his British offspring, including the current breed record holder, Sh Ch Russethill Royal Salute over Nyliram, and his influence on the breed will continue for many years to come through his descendants. In the pedigree of Sh Ch Dalati Sioni, note that Ch Dalati Del is the granddam on one side of the pedigree, and the great granddam on the other. The Hunton Morgans have now had 33 home-bred Show Champions (including two full Champions) in direct line to their first bitch. What an achievement!

In-breeding

In-breeding is mating very close relations together, such as brother to sister, mother to son, or father to daughter. This should be left only to the very experienced breeders. You may be duplicating the genes for the good points of a combination, but you are also duplicating any genes which are carrying faults, and these can be very hard to eradicate in the future.

Out-crossing

This is where a dog from another line is introduced into the breeding programme, and this will be followed with the breeder returning to using a dog from the bitch's own strain in the future. This enables new blood to be introduced, strengthening any weaknesses in a line, but great care still needs to be taken in selecting the dog to minimise the chances of introducing undesirable points.

The Bitch's Season

The bitch's season lasts for approximately 21 days. There is bleeding for about the first 10 days (pro-oestrus), and then it becomes less profuse and almost colourless (oestrus). However, this is not always the case, and bleeding can continue right to the end of the season, whether or not the bitch is successfully mated. The first season can take place any time after six months of age. Usually our bitches come into season when they are about eight or nine months old, but it can be much later, even up to two years old. They will drop their coats about two months beforehand, and the new coat will be coming through nicely when the season is due. You will be able to establish your bitch's cycle, and have some idea of when to expect her next season, probably between six and eight months' time but, again, that can vary and some bitches only come into season once a year.

A very close watch should be kept on the bitch when the season is expected; Welsh Springers do seem to be meticulous about keeping themselves clean when the season starts, and the bitch may pay particular attention to her vulva, so keep a very close eye on her. Watch for the enlargement of the vulva, which will probably be about a week before she comes into season. You can dab her vulva daily with a kitchen towel when you have your suspicions because, whatever happens, you really need to know the exact day when the season started if you want to breed from her. You may also find that the bitch is a little excitable when her season is due.

Deciding on the correct day for the mating is always of some concern, not only for the novice, but for the experienced breeder as well. It is all too easy to decide to take the bitch on Saturday for your own convenience, when really she was ready on the previous Thursday, or will not be ready until the following Tuesday. This is when you **have** to put yourself out to suit her, and not expect her to fit into your life.

No two seasons are exactly the same. A bitch can ovulate and be ready for mating on the seventh day in one season, and on the 15th day in another. On one occasion, when we were mating one of our bitches to our own stud dog, the days passed, and I was anxiously awaiting the arrival of **the day**. They were running freely together, so were free to please themselves. Although the bitch appeared to be standing between the usual 10–14 days (oestrus), as she had for previous matings to other dogs, this time, our dog took no interest in her whatsoever, despite her flirtations. I was convinced that we had missed the day. Wrong! On the 17th day, there they were – and the promised litter duly arrived. Wise old dog! In the majority of cases, successful mating will take place between days 11–13. You can be fairly confident that the bitch will not conceive up to nine days into the season, and after about 16 days – but it is not guaranteed! We had one bitch who had very protracted seasons, and on one occasion was found to be ovulating when tested at 23 days!

Once the season is over, the vulva returns to its usual size, and the bitch returns to her normal self (anoestrus).

Bitches continue to have seasons throughout their lives. We find that, although the season lasts for the normal three weeks, as she gets older often there is no sign of blood, and she may present herself ready for mating without any prior evidence, apart from an enlarged vulva, and cleaning herself more thoroughly than normal.

The Mating

When the bitch is ready for mating, she will stand very squarely, and turn her tail sharply to the right or the left as you run your hand down her back towards her tail - in fact, she is presenting herself. If any dogs live nearby, they will certainly be ready and waiting, so it is advisable never to let your bitch out of your sight as the season progresses. Your vet can carry out blood tests to ascertain when your bitch is in oestrus (ready for mating). If you have more than one bitch, they will probably come into season at the same time, and will mount each other as if they were mating; this also helps you in deciding on the correct day for your visit to the stud dog. It is not advisable to use any medicinal preparation to deter dogs' interest during the season if you intend to breed as, even if this has been stopped several days before the bitch is ready, it can still put the dog off. This is something which first-time breeders often do not think about. Some breeders have their bitches vaginally swabbed to check for any infection, but opinion now is that this is unnecessary, as bacteria are always present and no harm can be done to the dog by being in contact with them.

Having ascertained that your bitch is ready for mating, notify the stud dog owner – you will already have made contact when the bitch first came into season – and make the necessary arrangements.

As soon as you arrive at the stud dog's home, allow your bitch to relieve herself. Dog and bitch will be introduced. This could be in the garden, a garage, or a kennel run. We always allow ours to have a play first. The bitch will probably have had a long car journey, and is in a strange place, so this is an opportunity for her to relax.

She will probably flirt and encourage the dog at first, and then perhaps reject his early approaches. He will investigate her vagina and, if the time is right, she will allow him to mount her, her tail will turn to one side, and the penetration will be attempted. If you are staying while the mating takes place, you will probably be asked to hold your bitch's head, while the stud dog's owner gives his attention to the dog. Some stud dogs object to any intervention and will only perform if they are left to their own devices. With a maiden bitch, it is quite likely that she will yelp when the dog's penis penetrates, and she may need to be muzzled if she snaps at him. However, she should never be forced to be mated. Perhaps some more play and flirting will encourage her, and then she will allow the dog to mate her. Penetration can be made easier if the vagina is lubricated first, or it may be that you will have to stay overnight or come back next day for a successful mating to be achieved.

Assuming that all is going as it should, the dog will hold the bitch round her body with his front paws as he attempts to mate and, once he has penetrated fully, his penis swells, and the muscles of the bitch's vagina tighten around it. This is known as 'the tie', and the sperm is ejaculated as a result of the dog's thrusting movements. They cannot separate until the bitch's muscles relax. Often the dog will lie on the bitch for a few seconds when they have tied, after which he will turn, still tied, so that dog and bitch are facing in opposite directions. He can do this himself, but it is customary for his owner to lift one of his hind legs over the bitch's haunches. At this stage, many stud dog owners will hold all four of the hind legs together for the duration of the tie. The bitch's owner can then relax. For me, as the dog's owner, it is time to settle myself on an old milking stool, which we used when we were hand-milking cows many years ago, and then conversation can begin.

The tie can last for just a few minutes or up to an hour, so you want to be comfortable, and be wearing plenty of clothes if this is all happening out in the garden, and weather conditions demand it. The bitch accepts it all to begin with, but the novelty soon wears off, and she may try to get away; hence the necessity, in my opinion, for the two to be held together until they separate. On one occasion I visited some kennels with a bitch who was left with the stud dog unsupervised, but my bitches are special to me, and this is the beginning of a special event so, for me, it is not an experience that I would recommend.

It is possible to have no tie, and yet have a litter, as long as the sperm has been ejaculated satisfactorily, but it is more likely that there will be a litter if there has been a good tie.

At the end of the mating, both dog and bitch will clean themselves, and the bitch should be returned to the car and offered a drink. At this stage, it is usually time for a cup of tea or coffee, and the stud dog owner is paid the stud fee. A receipt should be given, and also a signed form confirming the mating, which will be required for the puppies to be registered at The Kennel Club in due course. If you are offered a repeat mating, and can return the next day or two days later, it is as well to do so, but it is not essential. Should the mating not result in any puppies, it is customary for the stud dog owner to offer a free service next time the bitch is in season; but payment is for that one service, and once that has taken place, the stud dog owner is not obliged to offer another opportunity.

Misalliance

If it should happen that your bitch is accidentally mated when you were not planning a litter, she will need to be taken to the veterinary surgeon within 48 hours for an injection to prevent her from conceiving, and this will result in her coming back into season for a further three weeks. It is interfering with nature, as is administering drugs to prevent a bitch from coming into season in the first place, which is an alternative choice. Both can result in future difficulties in getting a bitch to conceive. It is quite impossible, as is sometimes heard, for a bitch to produce mongrel puppies in a future planned litter if she has had a misalliance with a mongrel on an earlier heat.

False Pregnancy

This can happen when a bitch has not been mated or is not in whelp after mating. She will have all the signs of being in whelp, make nests, 'mother' toys and produce milk. Usually it is not a problem, and everything will return to normal, but it is worth removing anything that is being 'mothered', and try not to sympathise too much with the bitch. However, if the symptoms persist, veterinary attention may have to be sought. A remedy I have had suggested to me for reducing the milk is to rub the udder with camphorated oil.

In my invaluable little book dated 1893, *The Dog: Its Varieties and Management in Health and Disease* by 'Stonehenge', is a section on 'Diseases of Parturition', and I quote:

If the bitch has been 'put by', as it is called, and is not in whelp at the end of nine weeks from her 'heat', she will be fat and indolent, with her teats full of milk. At this time it is better to take a little blood from her, and to give her a smart purge once or twice, together with vegetable food; after which she will generally recover her health and spirits, and become much as usual at the expiration of another month or five weeks. This ought to be fully considered in the case of all sporting dogs".

The Pregnancy

The length of pregnancy (the gestation period) is about 63 days, but puppies can arrive several days early, or be overdue. If the bitch is more than two days overdue, consult the veterinary surgeon. A whelping chart can be found in appendix B, so that you can work out when you could expect your litter to arrive.

The bitch's season will continue as usual for about a week after she is mated, and the greatest care must be taken that she does not get mated to another dog. Any other bitches you have will be very interested in her as, of course, will any dog. He will know that another dog has achieved what he had hoped for, so you need to be exceptionally vigilant at this time.

Once the bitch's season is finished, to begin with there is not much to indicate whether or not she is in whelp, apart from her appearing to be rather self-satisfied and contented. Her vulva remains a little larger than usual, often with a slight colourless discharge, right to the end of the pregnancy. I have heard of cases where a coloured discharge occurred throughout the pregnancy and puppies have still arrived safely, but it would be safer to report this to the veterinary surgeon at once.

All breeders have their own ways of dealing with their bitches' pregnancies: this is **our** way. Having a litter of puppies is always a great excitement in our household. Usually we have only one litter a year, and it is a very special event. We expect to devote a lot of time to raising a litter, and we know that nothing much else will get done while the puppies are around. I like to think that I can tell if a bitch is pregnant at three weeks by a slight alteration to the shape of the rib cage when I look down on her. Probably this is because we live in very close contact with all our dogs and they are so much part of our family. It is possible for an experienced person to palpate the bitch's abdomen 28 days into the pregnancy, when foetuses about the size of a golf ball may be detected. Alternatively, the bitch can be scanned by ultrasound (see photo opposite). We do not normally do this, as we feel that there is nothing to be gained by doing so unless the vet recommends it for a medical reason. Either she is in whelp or she isn't, and there is not much we can do about it.

Usually, by five weeks I shall have a fairly good idea whether a bitch is in whelp because, at this stage, her teats will be more prominent and pink, and I would hope to see that the shape of her rib cage was beginning to broaden.

By the time the sixth week comes, the bitch is beginning to ask for more food. Her diet will be of high quality, richer in protein than normal, and she will be getting two meals a day, with some milk if she wants it. Much work has been done in recent years by the feed companies to produce correctly balanced feeds. We now use complete feeds, where no further additives are required, and find them very satisfactory. For many years, we used the traditional method of feeding half good-quality meat and half biscuit, adding extra calcium as advised by the manufacturers, and some breeders still prefer to do this. Sometimes the bitch will go off her food for a day or two, but this is not a cause for alarm at this stage. If she is having a large litter, her abdomen will be enlarging quite quickly but, if there are only one or two puppies, there could be very little apparent change, so don't give up hope.

When our bitches are pregnant, they continue to lead the same active lives, go on walks with the other dogs as usual, and they regulate their activity as time progresses. They may even want to go for a walk on the day that they whelp, and I see no reason why they should not do so.

By the seventh week, the bitch will often lie stretched out on her side and, at this stage, the puppies can be seen moving. If you place a very gentle hand on her, you can feel the heads and legs moving, which is always very exciting. Towards the end of the pregnancy, the teats will be enlarging, and the hair around them will thin out. Trim back any profuse feathering around the vulva and the teats. The vulva will also enlarge, and the whole area around it will become pink and soft. If the bitch is carrying a large litter, she will probably have a strained and drawn look on her face as well. Should she be unable to finish two large meals, it is worth offering food little and often, as she will probably find it more comfortable.

About two weeks before the puppies are due, we clean and disinfect the whelping box. Our bitches whelp in the study; a utility room or spare bedroom is just as good. Once the whelping box is in place, the study is for the expectant mum, and is hers alone. The other dogs seem to realise that they are not permitted to enter, and the bitch settles down quite happily. The whelping box is placed in the darkest corner of the room. We have an easy way of making it draught-proof and private: a large Victorian fireguard is placed

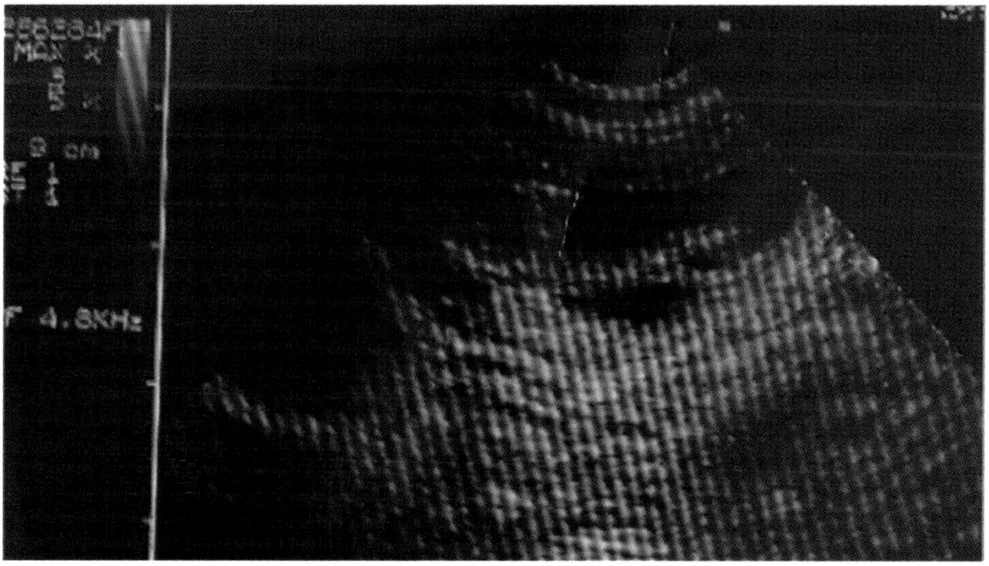

Scan of bitch six weeks in whelp.

down one side and partly across the ends of the whelping box, and draped with a blanket, which is securely attached once the whelping is finished. The room temperature is kept at 18°C (65°F) until the whelping begins, when it is increased to 24 °C (75°F). The box is lined with plenty of newspaper and a blanket – not the fleece one, which is reserved for the actual whelping. You can use an infra-red lamp: this should be hung securely, well above the bitch, and in such a position that she can get away from it if she gets too hot. We use them for sows and litters on the pig farm, but have not found them necessary with our bitches.

Now is the time to assemble the other equipment for the whelping. This is my list:

- lots of newspapers;
- at least two towels;
- a box of tissues;
- weighing scales;
- pen and paper;
- clock or watch;
- pair of surgical scissors;
- petroleum jelly;
- premature feeding bottle and teats, and bitch milk replacement powder from the vet or pet supply shop;
- plastic sack for soiled newspaper;
- a torch, and a mattress, sleeping bag and pillow for me!

The Whelping

Three or four days before whelping, you will notice that the puppies will 'drop' from the rib cage and move to the back, behind the ribs. The milk will start to come into the teats several days before whelping. About 24 hours before she whelps, the bitch will start to tear up the newspaper in her bed, scratching the carpet, panting, and becoming generally restless. Then you know that things are on the way. Her temperature will have dropped several degrees, perhaps down to 36°C (97°F). The normal temperature for a dog is 38°C (100.5°F).

She will probably refuse her food; she may vomit a frothy substance or pant and shiver; there may be a mucous discharge from the vulva; and she may want to go out frequently to relieve herself. Some of our bitches will have done all these for two days before a birth but, as long as she is not straining, do not worry.

Photo 1: This photo shows the bitch's udder the night before whelping. Note the enlarged vulva and teats, with only a little of the feathering around them.

I always accompany a bitch if she wants to go outside, just in case she decides to go under the garden shed, dig a hole under a bush, or even produce a puppy on the lawn. If you are lucky, the whelping will take place during the day but, more often, it takes place in the still of the night, so I always settle down in the sleeping bag on my mattress (with torch readily available) as soon as the bed-making starts, just in case. It is not essential to be present at the births, but I would never forgive myself if things went wrong and I was not there at the crucial time. However, it is not a time for a family gathering, as the bitch does need peace and quiet.

The first sign of the second stage of labour is the 'breaking of the waters', and this can take place anywhere, such as on your bed or on one of your new conservatory chairs, as has happened to us. The arrival of the first puppy will not be far away, so now is the time to try to settle the bitch in her whelping box, which is easier said than done. Invariably

Photo 1

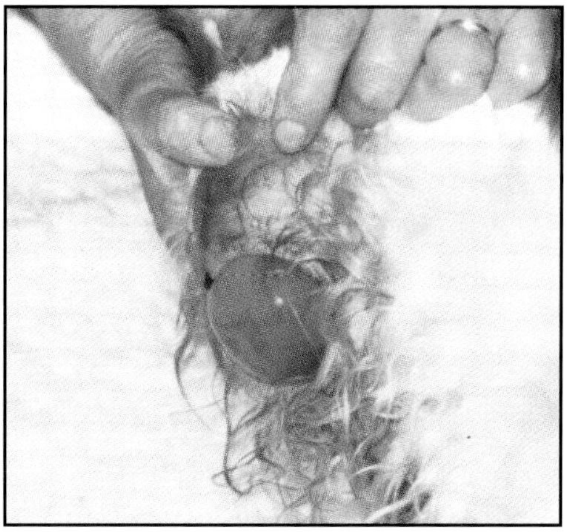

Photo 2

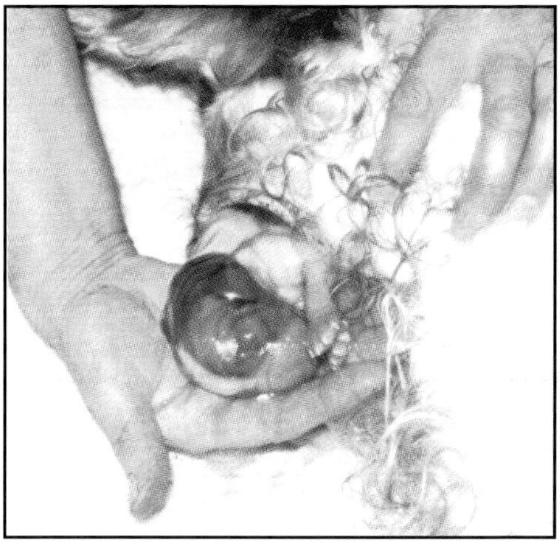

Photo 3

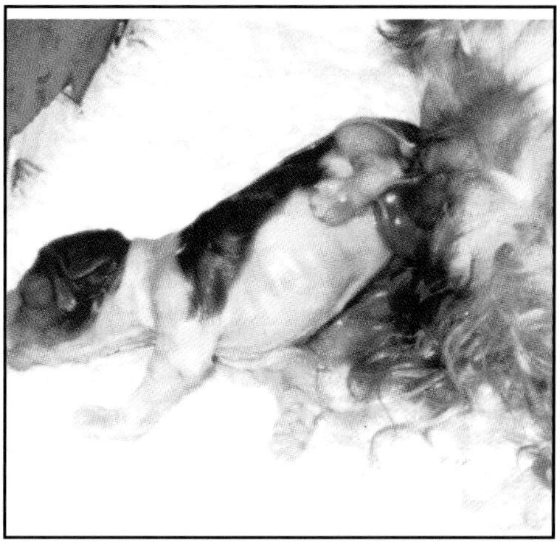

Photo 4

she seems to prefer anywhere but the box to begin with but, once the first puppy is safely in the bed, all should be well.

Photo 2: Usually, within half an hour of the waters breaking the bitch will be straining, and the first foetal sac can be seen, with a bulge behind it which is the puppy.

Photo 3: One more push, and the membrane enclosing the puppy breaks, and the head and front feet emerge. Note the pink nose and pads on the feet.

Photo 4: Another push, and we are nearly there. You can see the black placenta (afterbirth), still attached to the puppy. This puppy was able to start breathing straight away, as the membrane had broken as it emerged. If the membrane is still intact, break it quickly with your fingernail, wipe the mucous off the puppy's nose and mouth with a tissue, and open its mouth with your forefinger. Unless this is done, the puppy cannot breathe.

Photo 5 (see overleaf): In no time, the puppy is becoming mobile. The bitch may be licking hard at her vulva and, if she can reach it, she may break the membrane herself as the puppy emerges.

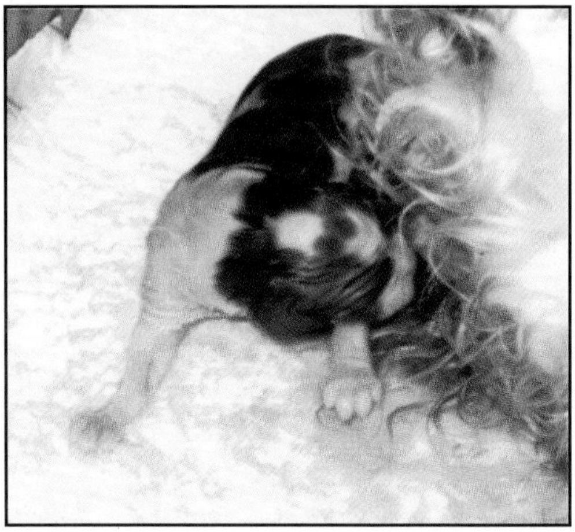

Photo 5

Photo 6

Photo 7

Photo 6: The placenta has come away with the puppy. It is very dark, looks rather like liver, and is about the same size as the puppy itself. We allow our bitches to eat the placentas; it is a natural thing to do as they are very nutritious. The disadvantage is that they do seem to act as a laxative. Placentas do not always come away with the puppy (maybe two will come with the next puppy) but it is important to keep a record of how many placentas arrive as they can cause a problem if they are retained.

Photo 7: The bitch will generally break the umbilical cord by biting it, and here you can just see the end of it below her tongue, as the puppy is making its way to the milk bar. Some breeders cut the cord with sterile scissors but, if I have to intervene, I prefer to squeeze the blood back along the cord, towards the puppy, and gently tear it off, as far as possible away from the puppy. (It is most important to have well scrubbed hands and short finger nails.) The bitch will then continue to sever the cord back to where she wants it. It is important that the puppy is dried as quickly as possible with a towel, and then returned to the mother, as it must not be allowed to get cold.

Photo 8: The mother will wash her offspring continuously, each new arrival and those that have already be born, as they often get soiled again. She is really quite rough with the puppies, turning them upside down in her enthusiasm. Here, the puppy is urinating, probably in response to her stimulation. Some breeders take the puppies away from the bitch and keep them warm in a box until whelping has finished. We leave ours with the bitch, putting them in by her udder, so that they start sucking as soon as possible after birth. In the farming world, piglets are always put in by the sow's udder, as it is supposed to stimulate both the milk flow and the production of another piglet.

Photo 8

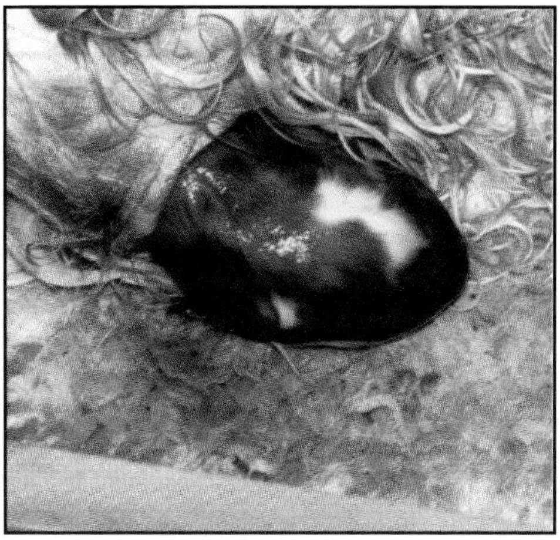

Photo 9

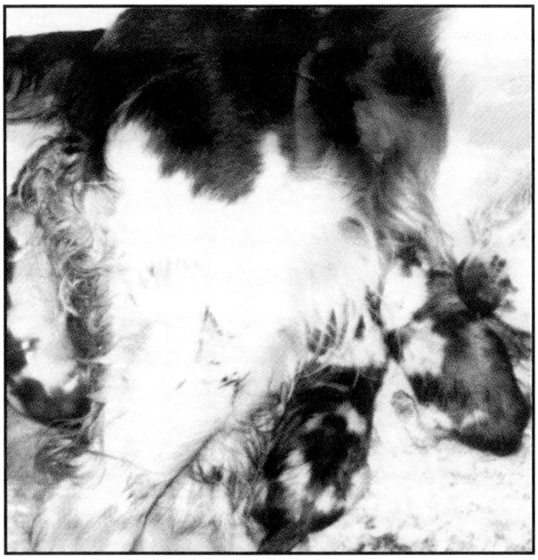

Photo 10

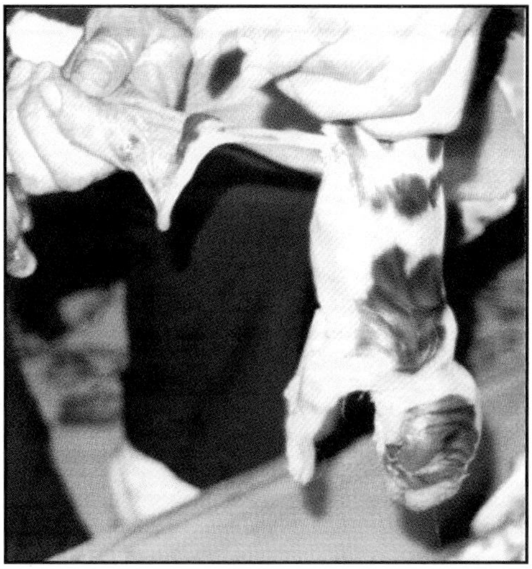

Photo 11

Photo 9: This puppy is being born rear first. This is not unusual, and does not cause problems. You will have to be extra careful to see that the puppy's mouth is clear, as the membrane will probably not break as the puppy emerges. Puppies are born deaf and blind. Welsh Springers' markings are already there, as they will be when the puppy is an adult, but not the freckles – they come later.

Photo 10: Three puppies are already at the milk bar, as the next puppy is arriving. This is a rear presentation, with the puppy's head still inside.

Photo 11: This puppy was born rear first, complete with placenta. Having cleared the membrane from the mouth, I then hold the puppy upside down, and swing it gently to clear any mucous away, until the puppy cries. Then it is a quick rub with the towel, and back to mum to cut the cord.

Photo 12

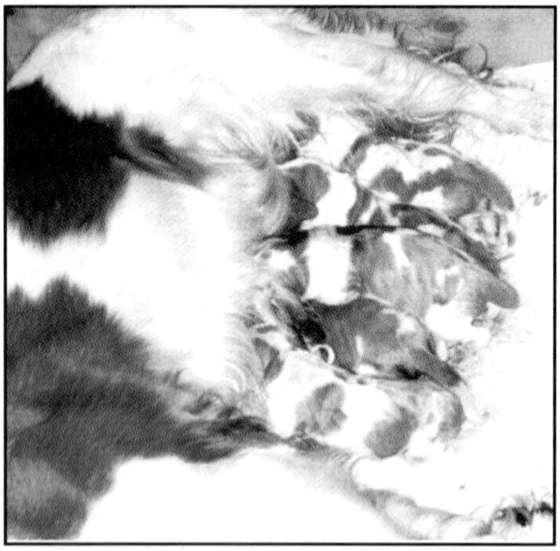

Photo 13

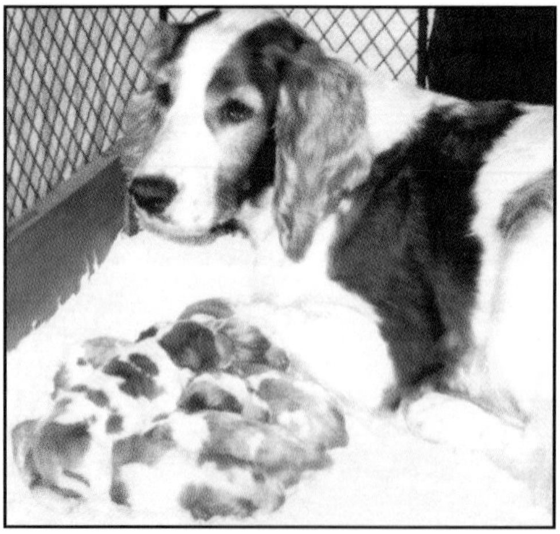

Photo 14

Photo 12: The puppies are now settling round the udder, while mother continues to wash and tidy up the cord.

Photo 13: All finished now: the fleecy blanket and the newspaper underneath have been changed, and mother and family are doing well.

As the whelping progresses, you will find that quite a lot of green fluid is expelled. This is quite normal and, if you are using the fleecy blanket, the fluid will pass through to the layers of newspaper underneath. I change the newspapers during the whelping, hence the suggestion that a dustbin sack for the soiled paper should be part of your equipment. Also, should there be a dead puppy, this will need to be removed from the bitch straight away and her attention drawn back to those already at the milk bar.

During whelping, we offer our bitches glucose and water to drink, and when all is over, we give a light meal. We find that top quality canned total food, recommended for rearing and maintenance, is very appetising; the bitch will be tired after her hard work, and this is easy for her to eat. Milk puddings, chicken and scrambled egg are also very acceptable. She will not want to leave her family, and all meals are fed in her bed, so that she does not even have to stand up. Then, before she settles, she is persuaded to go out to relieve herself -- and persuasion it is, because the bitch is always adamant that she cannot leave her young, and almost has to be dragged out on a lead. Then it is back to bed.

Photo 14: After a nice rest and a good meal, mother and family are very contented with life.

Not all bitches will allow their owners to assist when they are whelping, but mine are very domesticated (spoilt!), and I like to think that I give them encouragement and moral support when they need it. One of them would actually turn round and present me with her pups into my hand. Bitches may stand or lie down to produce their pups. In the series of photographs, the bitch was lying down, and allowed me to raise her rear end for the camera. I wonder how many would be so trusting.

Bitches' seasons vary, pregnancies vary, and whelping, too will vary. Sometimes, everything seems to go smoothly and it is all over in a short time during the day. We always keep a record of everything that happens during the whelping: the following is one that I would call a textbook whelping, with a good average-sized litter of three dogs and three bitches:

6 October 1995

6.10pm	The bitch's waters broke.		
6.20pm	Bitch (1) born, head first.	Weight: 368g (13oz)	Placenta.
7.20pm	Bitch (2) born, rear first.	Weight: 382g (13½oz)	No placenta.
7.30pm	Dog (1) born, head first.	Weight: 410g (14½oz)	2 placentas.
7.40pm	Bitch (3) born, head first.	Weight: 396g (14oz)	Placenta.
7.48pm	Dog (2) born, head first.	Weight: 425g (15oz)	Placenta.
7.59pm	Dog (3) born, rear first.	Weight: 368g (13oz)	Placenta.

I also record identification markings as the pups are born. One tends to think that it will be easy to remember which is which, but it is surprisingly difficult. I make a note of the head markings particularly, and then record a brief description of where the red patches are, not just 'heavily marked', 'red on left shoulder', or 'almost completely white', as there may well be others that will fit that description. Each puppy is examined as it is born in case there is any deformity, such as cleft palates, and a note is made if there are any hind dew claws, as well as the normal ones in front. If you keep a record like this as the whelping goes along, you will have all the information available in case you have to call a vet at any stage. Also, it is always of great interest to look back for comparison when you are expecting further litters in the years to come.

The litter above was the perfect whelping, and there are many variations on that theme, nearly always with the safe arrival of a happy and healthy family.

The following litter was born in 1980. I did not make a note of when the waters broke, when the placentas arrived, or how the puppies were presented at birth.

7.55am	Bitch (1) born.	Weight: 396g (14oz)
8.05am	Dog (1) born.	Weight: 325g (11½oz)
8.17am	Bitch (2) born.	Weight: 354g (12½oz)
8.35am	Dog (2) born.	Weight: 396g (14oz)
9.06am	Bitch (3) born.	Weight: 354g (12½oz)
9.44am	Dog (3) born.	Weight: 368g (13oz)
10.05am	Dog (4) born.	Weight: 382g (13½oz)
11.00am	Dog (5) born.	Weight: 382g (13½oz)
11.48am	Bitch (4) born.	Weight: 368g (13oz)
12.38pm	Dog (6) born.	Weight: 382g(13½oz)

This was a very big litter of 10 puppies, all of very good weight, averaging 371g (13.1oz). As luck would have it, a collie bitch, Kala, belonging to one of our farm staff produced an unexpected litter of four pups under a shed on the same day. Two of the pups were put down, and we decided to see if Kala would accept two of our Welsh Springer puppies, once she had been safely re-housed inside the shed. While she was away from the nest, we rubbed our two largest dog pups in Kala's bedding, rubbed their heads and noses in a little of her milk which we had drawn off, and tucked them in with her own pups. She accepted them and, although they were a little smaller than those reared by our own bitch, they re-joined the rest of the litter when they had been weaned, a pair of beautiful rogues.

Each whelping is different, in our experience, even with the same bitch, and it is very easy to get anxious when things are not going quite as you expected. Keep calm, and don't panic!

A question frequently asked is: how will I know when the bitch has finished whelping? The obvious feature is that she no longer has a full abdomen, and she looks hollow in the flanks. Once the task has been completed, she will lie down on her side and have a rest, with her puppies sucking at the milk bar. If she does not settle, you know that something is not right.

At the end of the whelping, not only will the bitch need a rest, but you will probably be ready for one, too, after witnessing one of the great wonders of nature. I never cease to marvel at the way animals instinctively know what they have to do. The minute that a pup is born, it knows that it must make its way to the milk bar to survive, and the mother knows that she must sever the cord and stimulate the pup to breathe by licking it continuously, and directing it round to her udder. For me, it is another night in the sleeping bag on my mattress on the floor, so that I am there if the bitch should accidentally sit on a pup, or one gets lost in the bed.

From then on, I shall be keeping a close watch on both mother and babies, and I inform the stud dog owner of the new arrivals.

Whelping Problems

It is as well to be aware that things do not always go according to the text book. If the waters break, the bitch has contractions and is distressed, but no puppy arrives, ring your vet. You will probably be asked to bring her to the surgery: the journey could very well put the whole thing in motion, and you could have the first puppy born in the car! It is always difficult to know when to contact your vet during whelping; it is a good idea to let the surgery know that you are expecting a litter, and it is courteous to give them a ring when it is all over. If you are at all worried during the pregnancy or the whelping, you can always ring the surgery for advice and reassurance.

Whelping can take several hours; sometimes, the bitch will have two or three puppies, and then rest for perhaps two hours before the next one is born. It sometimes helps to take her out in the garden to relieve herself, when there is a gap, but take a torch with you if it is dark, just in case a puppy arrives on the lawn. The activity may well stimulate her and, once she is back in the nest, the next puppy may arrive. However, if more than two hours have passed since the last puppy was born, there are no signs of anything further happening, and you can still feel puppies in the bitch's abdomen, it is best to ring your vet. The bitch may have just be having a rest, she may be having difficulty with a pup, or she could be suffering from inertia of the uterus and need a little help to get her going again.

Towards the end of a whelping, particularly if it is a large litter, a puppy may not get going and may appear to be dead. Do not give up hope. Clear the nose and mouth with a tissue, and gently swing the pup upside down to clear the mucous, as described earlier. Then rub his chest with the towel, watching for even a small gulp; make sure again that you cannot hear any mucous, and continue rubbing until he starts breathing regularly. Then put the pup back with his mother, but keep a constant watch on him, and rub the chest again if the breathing does not appear to be quite regular. I have, on one occasion, given successful mouth-to-mouth resuscitation to a puppy, which was a great thrill.

However, if a puppy is starved of oxygen for too long, there could be brain damage, and it is better to let him go. I am not a believer in rearing very weak puppies: there are enough dogs in the world already, and it is far better to enjoy a litter of strong and healthy puppies.

If at any time the bitch is straining, and no puppy arrives after an hour, again ring your vet at once. It is just possible that a puppy has stuck on its way out, and you could lose not only that puppy but also others that might be following. Sometimes, when you think that all is finished, and the bitch has settled down for the night, there is a late arrival the following day. You might be lucky and have a live puppy, but it is quite likely that puppy will be dead.

Experienced breeders will know their bitches, and whether they can cope with a situation or will need to seek veterinary assistance. Assisting with difficult births in sows on numerous occasions, and in lambing with my Hampshire Down ewes, has stood me in good stead when it comes to whelping, should I need to make an internal examination in consultation with my vet. If a puppy seems to be stuck half way out, you can assist the mother by very gently pulling the pup downwards as she strains. However, I would never advise the novice breeder to make any internal examination of the bitch. Always consult your veterinary surgeon. On rare occasions, a bitch will have to have a Caesarean Section, when the vet considers that there is no alternative. A puppy may not being presented correctly, or the bitch may have uterine inertia and, despite treatment, the uterus has ceased to contract. A Caesarean is a costly exercise, which we have experienced on just two occasions. I actually assisted at one of these and revived the pups as they were being extracted. It all happens very quickly, and is very exciting if all is well. Both bitches recovered remarkably well and returned home to settle down and feed the pups straight away.

From Birth to Eight Weeks

Puppies need to be kept warm, and the mother will arrange herself around them. Welsh Springers are usually excellent mothers and are remarkably adept at getting in and out of bed without injuring the family. When you pick up puppies, they should be firm and feel full. They make a contented humming noise if all is well. If one is making a wailing sound, or is limp when you pick it up, its stomach and feet are purple and the mother is not bothering with, it is probably nature telling you that something is wrong and the vet should be consulted.

Make sure that all the puppies are feeding, particularly if there is a smaller one that could get knocked off the teat, usually by one of the big boys. If we have a large litter, I try to put the smaller ones on to one of the back teats every time I go into the room. The teats at the back of the udder, nearest the vulva, are the largest, and sometimes the smaller puppies have difficulty in attaching themselves to the teat when the udder is full. This only lasts for a few days, after which they should be able to cope. The pups will feed frequently, and it is essential that each puppy gets some of the first milk, called the colostrum, which is rich and creamy and contains antibodies which give them a good start in life.

There are occasions when the bitch has problems after whelping, and she does not seem to be quite her normal self: perhaps lethargic, not wanting to eat, running a temperature, and not very interested in her family. A placenta might be retained, or an infection have occurred in the womb, and it is advisable to have her checked over by the vet within 24 hours of whelping, just to make sure that all is well and that the uterus is shrinking. Experienced breeders will know whether to consult the vet: provided all the placentas have been passed, there is no longer a heavy green discharge (which will smell very unpleasant), and the bitch has settled well, it is probable that a consultation is not necessary.

The udder should be inspected daily, to make sure that all the teats are being used. Some of our bitches have double teats at the back, which newly-born pups do not always find easy to drink from at first. If the teats are very full, try bathing with a warm wet flannel, and express some of the milk, then encourage the bigger puppies to drink. Once they use the teat regularly and become stronger, the problem should be overcome. If it persists, and the teat becomes inflamed and hard, it could turn into mastitis, which is very painful for the bitch and could result in the loss of that teat for ever. It needs urgent veterinary attention and usually responds well to antibiotics.

Our other dogs are always intrigued with what is happening behind the study door, and I get a tremendous amount of attention when I emerge and re-join them. However, the door is kept shut for the first few days, as the bitch does not need anything extra to worry about. She has a full-time job on her hands looking after her family as it is. Our bitches are very good natured and love to show off their families to friends and family, but this is exclusive to those they know, and no one is allowed to pick up the puppies.

The fleecy blanket is changed at least twice a day. If the bitch is a good mother, she will keep the puppies and the bed spotless until the puppies start on solid food. She will eat all the puppies' faeces, and lick her young as they urinate. For several days after whelping, she will still have to be dragged out to relieve herself; and after such an occasion, she will have her rear end washed and dried before she returns to the bed. We make sure that she has plenty to drink (being careful with milk, as she may have loose faeces), and offering her light meals for the first three or four days, gradually increasing to four meals a day, and feeding two or three times her usual amount, depending on the size of her litter. The food must be of good quality, high in protein, as this produces the milk for her family. Our bitches will get freshly cooked chicken, scrambled egg or cooked fish at this stage for their protein ration, mixed with cooked rice or a good biscuit meal. Canned milk puddings also form part of their diet. We weigh our puppies daily for the first week, and then every week until they go, by which time, we expect them to weigh a minimum of 3.6kg (8lb). This is the lightest that we will let them go, and often the pups, particularly the dogs, are considerably more than this.

On the first day after whelping it is not unusual for puppies to lose a little weight, but this is soon regained, and they should put on weight daily. We find that the weight gain varies: the larger the litter, the slower could be the gain, but we like to see the puppies double their birth weight within a week.

On the second or third day, the puppies' pads and noses will start to go black. The mother will increase her food intake, although still on a fairly light diet of top-quality food, either canned or home-cooked, and some milk. Some bitches cannot take a lot of milk, as it gives them diarrhoea; others refuse water in favour of it, so you have to use your common sense. We will also start to reducc the room temperature to about 18°C (65°F). You can tell if the puppies are not warm enough: they will lie huddled together, probably crying. If they are happy, they will be lying contentedly and quietly together.

With a large litter of puppies, or if the mother is short of milk, you may have to supplementary feed some of the smaller puppies. This is quite easy to do by using a premature feeding bottle, obtainable from your vet, and a specially formulated milk powder.

It is important to use the formula exactly as directed by the manufacturer. The pup

Dam with two-and-a-half-week-old litter.

Sitting up to feed the puppies.

should be held in one hand on your lap, with the bottle supported in its mouth at a similar angle to the natural feeding position, so that the pup can 'paddle' with its front legs, just as it would on its mother's udder. When it has finished, the pup will need to be stimulated to pass urine and faeces, either by the mother or by yourself. To do this, rub the aperture with a damp cloth, and you will soon get results. It can then be returned to 'mum' and the rest of the family. On one occasion, one of our bitches had a haemorrhage two days after whelping, and was unable to feed her litter of 11 puppies. With a bereavement in the family, my time was inevitably going to be very full, and my once-in-a lifetime vet took mother and young to be cared for at the surgery until after the funeral. A routine was set up, where the mother suckled four of the pups, four were on bottle feeding, and the others had a rest. Every two hours, they were rotated, and this continued after they came home, until we could start weaning at two and a half weeks of age. I then learnt what it was like to feel tired! The story had a happy ending – we reared all 11 successfully, and the bitch reared another litter perfectly normally in due course.

Between the third or fourth day, when the tail is still cartilage, the puppies' tails are docked, and the dew claws from the front, and the back if there are any, are removed. Docking is a very quick process, and we have no evidence that it impedes a puppy's growth in any way. The pup will return to its mother, who will continue to tend it as before. As I have said elsewhere, Welsh Springers have had their tails docked for centuries. They are a working breed whose job in life is to go into dense undergrowth and flush out the game. Even if they are not worked, they still have that instinct, and a

The first solid meal.

A lively bunch at four weeks.

long, flowing tail is totally impractical. Docking their tails at such an early age is surely far less traumatic than an adult having its tail amputated under general anaesthetic after it has been damaged. I know of several instances where this has occurred. Breeders used to do the docking themselves but, since 1993, docking has had to be done by a veterinary surgeon. Not all vets will do it: to obtain a list of those who will, you need to become a member of the Council of Docked Breeds (see Useful Addresses). We have our puppies' tails docked by two-thirds plus 'a whisker', where there is a natural reduction in the shape of the tail. If possible, we like to leave a little white at the end.

It is quite normal for the bitch to have a brownish discharge from her vulva after whelping, and this will probably continue for most of the lactation, quite heavily to begin with, and then reducing to odd spots in the bed. It should never have a strong aroma – if it does, consult your vet.

For the first week, the bitch will feed her young lying down, after which probably she will sit up to perform the task. The puppies are becoming more mobile, and have no difficulty in finding the milk bar. The bitch will want to go for short walks and, at this stage, she is beginning to show off her family to our other dogs. The study door will be left open during the day, with a low barrier to keep them at bay – they are more than fascinated, particularly if we have run on one from the previous litter who has never seen puppies at home other than itself and its siblings!

When the puppies are about 10 days old, their eyes will be opening, but they are unable to see much until they are about four weeks old. Their nails will have grown, and need to be cut carefully with nail scissors; while they are feeding, they pummel their mother's udder, and can make her very sore if they are not attended to.

When the puppies are $2\frac{1}{2}$–3 weeks old, they are getting on their feet and beginning to move around the bed. They can hear, and will start to climb out of the whelping box.

Picture of contentment.

Now is the time for them to be moved to a larger area – ours come into our busy farmhouse kitchen. They need to be socialised, and get used to people, as well as sounds and activity. Family and friends come and go, but prospective new owners are not encouraged to visit yet; they always expect the puppies to be running around, so it is better if they can possibly wait for another fortnight. I talk to my puppies right from the start. They cannot hear me to begin with, but later they begin to recognise my voice, and come out of their bed when I call them.

We fence off the end of the kitchen, leaving a lower part for the bitch to jump in and out. The sleeping area with the fleecy blanket is at one end, with newspaper underneath and covering the whole of the pen. This is the beginning of house-training and, very soon, the puppies will be walking out of their bed on to the newspaper to relieve themselves, and making their way round the pen. Newspapers are in great demand at this stage, and need changing constantly. The bitch will be getting 4–5 meals a day, depending on the size of the litter; she will need about four times her usual quantity of food, still of the highest quality, and we give as much variety as we can to help her to produce the quantities of milk that she is required to give. She will also be given calcium tablets night and morning while she is lactating. Plenty of fresh water is always available, and we put a small bowl of fresh water in the puppies' pen as soon as they move into the kitchen.

Weaning

We usually start to wean our puppies when they are three weeks old. This may be earlier if it is a large litter but, as long as the bitch is doing well and the puppies are contented, we leave it to the bitch until then. The first meal is aptly known as 'sticky time' in our household: a small quantity of specially formulated puppy porridge is made up according to the instructions, in small trays, and the puppies are introduced round the edges of the trays. Of course, they walk into the food and get it all over them, but they soon learn to lap, and the mother will go in and wash them all as they return to the milk bar. That is the beginning of weaning. The puppies take to it very easily even though they are wobbly on their legs, and by four weeks, they are having four meals a day.

Depending on the size of the litter, the quantity fed to the bitch will gradually be

Five weeks old, and they've found another friend.

reduced, as the puppies eat more solid food. Once they are on to solid food, the mother will no longer clean up the bed; house training will be progressing, and constant newspaper changing will be the order of the day. We take the puppies out of their run to feed them, at the same time changing the newspaper completely and replenishing the water bowl.

They are fed their puppy food to appetite and, once the greedy ones look full, they are put back into the run, to allow the slower eaters to have their share. Their weights are still monitored, although not daily. You can see if a puppy is not doing as well as the others and needs to be watched or requires special attention given to it: this is where home-rearing is so important.

A walk around the garden.

At three weeks, the puppies are wormed for the first time and, very soon after, the worms will be there on the newspaper. It is our experience that all puppies are born with worms, and our puppies are wormed three times before they go to their new homes at eight weeks of age. Various worming remedies are available from vets and pet stores, and these should be used according to the instructions.

'Human's are there to be climbed over...'

The mother will now have allowed the rest of the dogs to come into the kitchen and inspect her babies. They seem to know that they are allowed so far, but never to cross the threshold of the puppy pen. However, they are never allowed in the kitchen without our supervision.

By the time the puppies are four weeks old, the mother may be standing up to feed them, and their first teeth will be coming through. They will bark and play together, and their ears will start to darken in colour, with freckles coming through on the legs and stomach. Some puppies born with rich, dark red coats sometimes become much lighter in colour. There is no need to worry; the red will start going dark after a few weeks, and we find that the lighter ones often finish with a darker coat than some of the others. Also, when they are about three months old, some puppies grow very fluffy coats,

'... and so are mums!'

Follow my leader.

particularly on the flanks and hind legs, but this falls out by about eight or nine months, and we never attempt to trim it.

Registration

Once the pups are established on their solid food, we register them with The Kennel Club, using the green form received from the stud dog owner on completion of the mating. A list of preferred names for the puppies is given, all with our Hillpark affix, together with alternatives should the names not be available. Each litter has a theme for naming, which makes it easier for us to identify when owners contact us in subsequent years with news of their wonderful Welshie, or a request for another puppy to keep the old dog company before it is too late. Processing the registrations normally takes about three weeks, so that new owners can have their puppies' registration certificates when they collect their puppies. Pedigree forms need to be compiled, and are easily obtainable from dog food manufacturers, pet shops, Breed Clubs and specialist canine printers. We always hand write our pedigrees on our own forms, as we feel that it is more personal. It takes about 20 minutes to complete each one, so this is the time when I start writing!

Growing Up and Moving Out

We are now at the five week stage, and the puppies are beginning to be well socialised. Children will be encouraged to come in and play gently with them, and they will be used to the television, the telephone and the vacuum cleaner. Most households have their radios on during the day, so we accustom our pups to that as well, classical and jazz! **But** they are also becoming rather unpleasant to live with, particularly first thing in the morning! The time has come for them to move out to an indoor kennel and run, with a pophole out to an outside fenced run. If it is cold enough to need one, an infra-red lamp hangs above a large plastic dog bed (or two, if it is a large litter) in the sleeping area. The bed is lined with the fleecy blanket as before, and the floor of the kennel is covered with newspaper, with fresh water always available. The bedding is changed constantly, and the newspaper consumption is enormous, so we will have saved them for weeks beforehand, and have regular bonfires to dispose of them when used. The whole kennel will be

A quick snack in tandem.

disinfected every day as well, and the feed pans washed immediately after use. The puppies settle very well, and soon learn to make use of the whole indoor pen as a play area, but they do not go out into the run just yet.

If you are using a garage for this stage, start by confining the pups to a small area, with a draughtproof bed at one end, providing heat if necessary, and enlarge the exercise area as the pups settle in.

The mother will still want to visit her brood and feed them periodically, usually standing up. She may want to spend the night in the kennel, in which case, she will be given a bed raised off the floor, so that she can get some peace.

Dinner in the garden.

'What's this white stuff?'

The puppies will continue on their increasing diet of specially formulated puppy food, but we introduce other foods as well, so that by the time they leave us they should eat any type of food: fish, scrambled egg or minced meat, mixed with puppy meal for one meal, or a canned milk pudding. We always used to raise our puppies on this type of meal, but now there are such good specially-prepared puppy foods on the market, and the results are so excellent, we have changed our practice and have been very pleased with the puppies that we have reared on them.

After the puppies have had a day or two to get used to their new surroundings, we open the pophole door into the run. If it is a nice day, the puppies are let into the garden for a short play and, from then until they are ready to leave us at eight weeks old, we spend a lot of time with them, watching them as they develop, playing with them, and making sure that each one receives the attention that it requires. Like children, each one is different, with a different character, and the quieter one may need to be encouraged, while the bully may need to be suppressed. They need plenty of sleep, but they also need plenty of socialising. We encourage children to come in, and they can play with the pups as long as they are gentle, but they are never left unsupervised. Pups love playing with people, and climbing over them and the mother will show them how to play as well. Children need to be shown how to hold puppies, and realise that they are fragile, and will 'break' if dropped. It is safest to hold them in the crook of the arm, and support underneath their bodies, holding their front legs between the fingers. You must also teach this to the children of your prospective purchasers.

By six weeks of age, they can run almost as fast as you can, and will come when you call. They will be more adventurous every day, exploring and enjoying new experiences.

We endeavour to have our puppies weaned by six weeks, but this is not always easy, as our bitches often seem very reluctant to give up, and have to be kept away.

Just once, we had two litters of the same age (see picture opposite). Never again – we were exhausted!

If the weather is kind, we feed the puppies in the garden, with water available outside as well. In this way, they are already outside to relieve themselves after the meal, and are nearly house-trained. They will use the newspaper in the pen at night, when they are shut in, and we find that they tend to use one area of the paper. Puppies are very hardy, and even snow does not do them any harm once they are active and running around.

If it is not possible for the puppies to go outside, newspaper soiling will be much heavier, needing frequent changing, and we then spread a thin layer of fine wood shavings under the newspaper as well.

Worming is carried out again at five and seven weeks, by which time there will probably not be any evidence of worms, but further worming must be done after the puppies go to their new homes. It is now possible to have puppies tattooed in their right ears at the age of six weeks. This is a quick and permanent means of identification, and the puppies are then on a national tattoo register at a very reasonable cost, should they at any time get lost, or, worse still, stolen. Our last four litters were tattooed here at home, and we have found the service very efficient and satisfactory. Microchips are also very popular for identification, and details can be obtained from your veterinary surgeon.

Meeting the Owners

Prospective owners will be telephoning and wanting to know when they can come to see the puppies. Three weeks is the very earliest for us, and preferably five weeks, when the puppies are running around and becoming interesting and fun, so if the first visit is booked for five weeks, no one will be disappointed. If you are not keeping a puppy yourself, you can let the purchasers choose theirs then, although, by the time they come back at eight weeks, the pups will look so different that probably the owners will not recognise them! Our method is always the same: we make a list of prospective owners as we receive the orders. They can then come and see the puppies, but no choice is made until the pups are ready to go, when they are selected by their new owners in list order; if, for example, they are third on the list for a bitch, they have third choice of bitches. We find that this works very well, and it also enables us to have the choice of the whole litter until that stage, should we be running on puppies for ourselves or to go abroad.

Once a prospective owner has booked a puppy, for the benefit of both parties we ask for a deposit and issue a receipt, with details of the outstanding balance, and how many puppies of the selected sex will be available for the purchasers to choose from on the day of collection. At the same time, we give our information leaflet, which includes full details of the puppy's diet, what equipment will be required before the pup is collected, and as much guidance as we can to help make the owners and the pup's new venture together a success. This gives the owners a chance to make a list of questions which may need to be answered beforehand, and we are always open to suggestions from new owners for additions or alterations to our leaflet. Some will want to come back again – and again – before the day of collection, and you must be ready to spend a great deal of time with them. Some stay for three hours! In this way, you are getting to know them, and it helps both you and them to confirm that they have made a correct decision in purchasing one of your cherished puppies.

The Day of Departure

The day of collection has now arrived, and each of our puppies will have an envelope to accompany it on its first journey. Like many other breeders, we insure our puppies for the first six weeks from the date of sale, and the necessary certificate will be issued. The envelope will also contain the tattoo certificate, an update on feeding, dates of worming, literature on the Breed Clubs, the handwritten pedigree, and the registration certificate, which will have been signed on the reverse ready for the new owners to transfer the pup to their own name at The Kennel Club, should they wish to do so. As our bitches are up to date with their vaccinations before whelping, our puppies will also have some immunity to diseases, and will not need their first vaccination until they are 10 weeks

Hillpark Starlight Express at eight weeks: a picture for the family album from a new pet owner.

old. We ask purchasers to check with their own veterinary surgeon on this, as opinions differ, and some prefer to start the course straight away. It also provides an opportunity for the new owners to check that all is well with their puppy. To complete the envelope, once the payment is settled, a receipt is issued. A small pack of puppy food is made up for each new owner, sufficient for the first few days, so that the puppy is at least started on the same diet as it is used to, together with a tablet for the next worming administration. We also ask that, should the puppy have to be re-housed for any reason at a later date, we are contacted immediately so that we can place the pup in a suitable new home. Then it is time for the farewell, with a request that we should be kept informed on the pup's progress, and offering help with any queries or problems that the new owners might have at any time. And finally, we ask for a photograph, in due course, for 'the family album'.

Dutch Sh Ch Wesley of Rowan's Residence, top-winning Welsh Springer in the Netherlands, owned by Ria Horter. Photo: Wim van Vugt.

chapter 11
The Working Welsh Springer

Throughout its history, the Welsh Springer has been recognised as a working dog. It has a reputation of having a wonderful 'nose', and the ability to do a full day's work and still be ready to get up and go again. The Welsh Springer is different from the English Springer: the Welsh Springer is the same whether he is required for showing or working, whereas there are two distinct types of its English cousin, the larger show type (larger than the Welsh Springer), and the field trial working type (smaller than the Welsh Springer). The working instinct is very strong in our breed, and whichever line you choose, you will probably find that the breeders have sold puppies for working as well as for the showring – and, of course, as wonderful pets and companions.

Throughout the century, there have been those who have been committed to promoting the dual-purpose Welsh Springer. In the early days, A T Williams did so much to promote the breed and get it recognised at The Kennel Club (see chapter 1) as well as, amongst others, Mrs Greene and her famous Longmynd dogs. Col Downes Powell's O'Matherne kennel was very prominent before the Second World War and, after the War, great enthusiasts included Frank Hart (Denethorp), Harold Leopard (Rushbrooke), Mrs Mayall (Rockhill), Mrs Morriss (Stokecourt) and Cliff Payne (Tregwillym).

Gordon Pattinson, MBE.
Photo: John Curtis

Although support for competition on the working side always appears to have been rather poor, nevertheless there has been a strong nucleus of enthusiasts, and Welsh Springers that have gained their titles in the showring have qualified in the field to take the title of Champion. Towards the end of the 1960s and early 1970s, one of these enthusiasts was **Gordon Pattinson**.

Now in his 80s, still he recalls vividly his times spent wild fowling and rough shooting with his Tidemarsh dogs – 'bred for brains and beauty' – two of which, Ch Tidemarsh Rip and Ch Tidemarsh Tidemark, became full Champions. Rip had the distinction of being awarded Best in Show at the Welsh Springer Spaniel Club Championship Show in 1971, as well as being regularly shot over. Gordon has offered me an article which he wrote at the time on his working Welsh Springers, from which I quote.

I make no claim to be an expert, either in the field or in the show ring, just an enthusiastic amateur exhibitor and shooting man, with some 15 years' experience of working spaniels. I have, however, strong views that gundogs should be capable of the work for which they were originally bred and, therefore, feel one should breed from stock with working blood not too far back in the pedigree. I also contend that one can have both brains and beauty in a working dog, which is what I aim for in my breeding policy.

A spaniel seemed the correct choice for me as a shooting companion, as my type of shooting is mainly of the rough variety, with a considerable amount of wild-fowling; this requires my dogs being able to quarter, hunt thick cover, flush game and retrieve, and also be good in water. Cockers seemed rather small for wild-fowling conditions, and there is such a difference in size and appearance between the field trial English Springer and the show specimens, that I felt neither could serve my dual purpose of shooting field and show ring. I finally decided on the Welsh Springer, a handsome but very workman-like spaniel, and I have never regretted this choice.

Training time is one of the most satisfying and enjoyable periods of spaniel ownership. It is then one can get to know one's dog, and can adapt one's training methods to its particular needs. This makes a very interesting pastime during summer evenings, and can create a good understanding between man and dog. I found the book Dog Training by Amateurs by R Sharpe of great help to me in my training efforts. Attendance at a training course is also to be recommended, especially for those who have had little or no experience in gundog training.

At the end of each summer, various Gundog Societies organise working tests; these give one a target for the end of the summer training period, and a most enjoyable day out; here one can see the results of training in competition with other dogs and handlers, and learn a great deal from watching others perform. These working tests, particularly for puppies and novice dogs, do not demand the very high standard required in field trials, and even a novice can anticipate some success, providing he has reached a satisfactory understanding with his dog. Field trial work demands specialisation, and is perhaps beyond the scope of the average amateur spaniel handler. The standard for spaniels requires dogs to be so keen and fast, that one feels the whistle should never be far from the mouth, just in case one might lose control! To maintain this standard on an ordinary shooting day would, I feel, mean continual concentration on the dog, to the detriment of my full participation in the shoot. I have settled, therefore, for something perhaps less spectacular or 'racy', but more suited, I feel, to the needs of the everyday shooting man.

I am a comparative newcomer to the showring, but have found that this does give one a wonderful opportunity to meet other enthusiasts and breeders, with whom to share notes and compare the standard of your dogs with others in the breed. Also, who does not enjoy exhibiting a dog of one's own breeding which one feels is a real eye-catcher?

The qualifying tests give one an opportunity of seeing what your show spaniel can achieve in the field, and if you are fortunate enough to own a dog which can gain its three Kennel Club Challenge Certificates, it will enable you to claim full championship status.

I thoroughly enjoyed my first attempt at Spaniel Tests. Unfortunately, drawn as number one, I had no example to follow. However, the judges were most helpful, and all they require is that your spaniel will hunt cover, flush and retrieve game tenderly; steadiness is not essential for this test. I was most fortunate in being 'presented' with a most spectacular retrieve by my dog; he was hunting on the far side of a thick hedge, when a pheasant was flushed on the gun's side and, obviously hit, the bird flew over the hedge and my dog, and across low over a large grass field and out of sight around a corner of a high wood. I would have 'dropped' my dog (if I could), as it seemed an impossible unmarked retrieve, but the judge told me to let him go, indeed I could not have stopped him! On rushing through the hedge to the open field, I saw my dog disappear 300 yards down the field into the end of the big wood. My heart was in my mouth, I anticipated pheasants flying out in all directions, and being very unpopular with the keepers and all concerned. However, to my joy, after some two minutes, my dog jumped out of the wood into the field. I immediately whistled and, exceeding all my expectations, as he approached at a fast pace, I saw indeed he had the pheasant. This he delivered alive, gently, to hand. This was the end of my test, and it made a most

Ch Tidesmarsh Rip wild fowling.

memorable occasion. Indeed, I would have been hesitant in sending an experienced dog on such a retrieve, and this was only the second pheasant Rip (only 16 months) had retrieved in his life. On the whole, the tests asked were much simpler, and the birds shot fairly close to hand in thick cover, not demanding a very severe test of the dog or handler – a standard which should be attained by anyone with reasonable training, and a biddable dog.

My enjoyment in shooting is largely governed by the prowess of my dogs, and there is particular joy in shooting over an active and merry Springer, working rough cover. I would much prefer to leave the gun at home and work the dog, than go shooting without a dog at all. All of my happiest shooting memories are not of days of exceptional 'bags' or good 'left and rights', but of spectacular work or retrieves by my dogs. I well remember my first Welsh Springer bitch, on her first outing, partridge shooting; a 'runner' dropped in thick reed over a deep fleet, her first 'live' retrieve and across water, after three experienced dogs had failed; and next season, her hunt and retrieve of a wounded cock pheasant. This was in a newly planted wood covered with dense bramble, almost impenetrable; I dropped the bird some 40 yards away and managed to get her on the line, from then on the dog was invisible and on her own, all I saw was the cock pheasant popping out of the bramble about 2–3 feet in the air, on about five occasions, as she pursued him round the 10 acre block, and eventually emerged in about the only clearing, where I stood, with him tenderly in her mouth.

I have memories of the big freeze-up in January 1963, when the Medway Estuary froze, and the strayway was solid pack ice, of the retrieve by my puppy of a beautiful drake Pintail across the ice into the tide and floes, and the struggle back. Again, I remember my present bitch, Rhoda, and the 'tipped' Teal dropped by a friend well over the far side of a wide creek at high tide. After the failure of his dog to cross, and ten minutes later, I remember her swimming for the unseen retrieve, her perseverance in finding and taking up the line 80 yards or more across and into the marsh, and disappearing into various rills in the gathering dusk, and the successful return to hand. At the end of this season, during a cold spell, when the high spring tides 'churned' the whole marsh, Teal and

Wigeon were flighting low against the gale across the sea, in the lea of the mound where we had been driven by the tide. Every bird we dropped was well out into the sea, which was very rough, and necessitated long, bitter swims and retrieves, often against the ripping tide and wind; without Rhoda, we would hardly have picked up a bird.

These memories to me are the reward and fulfilment of breeding and training, and the understanding between my dogs and me, that makes their companionship such a privilege and pleasure.

In the 1970s, there was enough support for a separate working section to be formed in the Welsh Springer Spaniel Club, with Gordon Pattinson as its chairman, and the enthusiasm of Angie Lewis (Riscoris), Eileen Falconer (Hackwood), Dolly Leach (Presthill), and Ray Plunkett (Clankerry) created a great impetus for the working side of the breed.

Eileen Falconer (Hackwood) is an ambassador for the dual-purpose Welsh Springer, and in recognition of many years' dedication to the breed, she has been made an Honorary Life Member of the Welsh Springer Spaniel Club, as has Gordon Pattinson.

Some years ago, Eileen and her husband and family moved from the south east, where she had been picking up regularly on several shoots, to Somerset. There, the local shoot manager was very reluctant to accept Welsh Springers on the shoot. Eileen asked if she could go along for a trial period on the day, and if he did not like what he saw at lunch time, they would go.

By the end of the day, they were asked to stay for the whole of the season, and received an invitation to two other shoots.

Sadly, in recent years, due to debilitating health problems, Eileen has had to curtail her activities, but she still picks up regularly on local shoots, and still has an eye for a good dog. She now finds that she is unable to manage Welsh Springers, and has had to turn to English Springers, an easier breed to train and work. I had the opportunity of reminiscing with Eileen, and hearing a little of how she has achieved her ambitions.

Ramblings with Eileen Falconer

We had our first Welsh Springer, to avoid it being put in a bucket, in 1968. That was Hackwood Susan. The man who had her was on an estate, and I chose the puppy out of the litter; I was totally ignorant as to what I was looking for.

She was initiated into an early life of rabbiting with Keith (Eileen's husband), whose father was gamekeeper at the Hackwood Estate near Basingstoke. She used to go to the other end of the cover, and hunt it backwards to Keith. When she started yapping, you knew that there was a rabbit in front of her.

After going to a carnival exemption show, and coming away with a prize, with a totally untrimmed dog, I was 'hooked'. A further award, from a well-known Welsh Springer judge – Mr Peter Painter – later encouraged me to go on. As Sue had no obvious faults, we bred a litter from her, and kept two puppies, Hackwood Echo and Hackwood Skylark, and both turned out to be good dual purpose dogs.

Eileen Falconer and Ben.

Hackwood Echo.

I did not know of any training classes for gundogs in the vicinity, so used the local library, and read all the books that I could find on the subject. Eventually, I used two books: one Gundogs – Training and Field Trials by Peter Moxon, and the other specifically on spaniels by Joe Irving. Both I felt tackled the subject with common sense, and were straightforward in their approach to tuition.

We muddled through the lessons, going wrong many times, but learned very early to watch the eyes and expression. This, together with the response from the dog in basic obedience, is the epitome of training. The aim is for a command to be given once, to be obeyed instantly, and the dog to **enjoy** *doing it. I try to keep the interest in the lesson, and the dog alert, which also ensures that the trainer is attentive! The eyes can give away sometimes a second's advantage to a moment's wickedness; if the trainer can spot it and rectify the problem immediately, life is made much easier.*

Once the obedience has been mastered, lessons are alternated with a quiet walk through meadows or woodland. The dog should work fairly close, with the trainer talking quietly to it, and if the relationship is good between them, the ability to find game and 'stop' to the find should be fairly easy to master. By the word 'game', I refer literally to anything that moves, initially, and that progresses to using the wind, quartering across it, and finding, perhaps, a rabbit, pheasant, hare or partridge. This sounds easier said than done, but with perseverance, the same result can be achieved with ground where game has recently moved, and the 'stop' whistle can be used effectively. The 'stop' whistle, incidentally, has always been for me: one quick 'pip', rather than a blast on the whistle.

I now know not to underrate the intelligence, nose and natural instincts of the "Welshie", and respect them for these qualities. All the dogs that I have trained work with me as a team, and I love them for it.

In 1975, I bought Hillpark Sea Breeze (later 'of Hackwood') – Amy – (Sh Ch Progress of Pencelli ex Sh Ch Hillpark Pollyanna). I was looking at her from the dual-purpose side, and she was a quality-looking puppy, and had the background, pedigree and temperament to produce what I was looking for. The theory behind it was that there were Tregwillym and Pencelli lines, which would keep the dual-purpose, and also maintain the quality.

Amy had considerable success, and, with the idea of promoting maturity, I felt that she would benefit from having a litter. With the dual-purpose context in mind, I mated her to a really good tempered working dog at that time, Dolly Leach's Riscoris Evan of Presthill, and produced a fine litter of good quality puppies, from which, at the age of six weeks, nobody had the chance to purchase Hackwood Kingfisher – Ben [see page 38]. *His intelligence stood out, and the look in his eyes said exactly what he was thinking, as it does in most dogs. He never ran straight forward, not because of his lack of temperament or confidence, but he seemed to be contemplating how to avoid all the terrible rush of puppies in front of him - deciding what to do, and then doing it.*

Amy went on to mature well, achieving the Dual-Purpose Dog of the Year award in 1976.

Hillpark Sea Breeze of Hackwood: Dual Purpose Dog of the Year, 1976.

I was very fortunate to have such a dog [as Ben], *and he collected from both sides of his pedigree the best qualities to make what he was: a really good tempered, naturally instinctive, devoted dog. He was the end product of building up an early relationship, never being allowed to do anything wrong, and, hopefully, always channelling his thoughts in the right direction.*

Ben won numerous awards in the showring and in the field, including one Challenge Certificate, and the first Field Trial held by the Welsh Springer Spaniel Club after its revival in 1983, repeating this achievement the following year. He sired over 400 puppies.

There are Welsh Springers in all lines who will work. They do tend to be more intelligent than English Springers, and are inclined to be very wilful and, therefore, create their own downfall. Having said this, Welsh Springers are, in my experience, far more purposeful when it comes to scenting and finding game. They are unlikely to go in cover without game being present, and this again presents a disadvantage in competition with English Springers, from the onlookers' and judges' point of view. In my opinion, we have lost the constructive criticism of the breed, and are somewhat lacking in promoting the competitive edge into our Field Trials and Working Tests.

If you are going into the realms of training the Welsh Springer, you have got to say it and mean it, and be strong. A dog must never win: you have always got to finish on a successful note. Give a command once only, and if you fail, then you have to make the dog do it, otherwise it has won, whatever age it is. If the dog does not come when called, go and get it. You must be positive in your approach to training any dog, regardless of breed, but it must be rewarded with the same intensity with which the lesson is conducted. You must never treat a dog harshly.

'If you know where it is, why don't you go and get it?'

I would start playing with a puppy as early as eight weeks of age. Take the

Puppy retrieving at eight weeks.

puppy into the garden, and it will soon learn that the only way it can continue playing with a toy, such as a ball, or a paint roller, is if it brings it back to you, when it will have most fun, hence the retrieve.

The fun will continue, and the puppy will finish the 'lesson' on a good note. This is the follow-on through to its adult life, where retrieving anything and everything will be quite normal. The play time is with you and the puppy, and it is natural for the puppy to want to be with you. Incorporate the word "fetch" because it is a natural follow-on again, and you must keep on talking to the puppy all the time.

It is possible to achieve anything which a dog does not want to do by patience and perseverance, and talking quietly to the puppy, endeavouring to be sensitive as to how it feels, and perhaps trying to do something another way. In my opinion, you cannot start training too early, because, although it seems like play at the time, you are generating the dog's thoughts and actions into a positive future as a wholly disciplined dog.

I do not introduce the dummy straight away. First of all, you persuade the puppy to go into shallow water and gain confidence. If puppies are with adult dogs, they will copy them.

Use the play technique of retrieving as early in life as possible.

The whistle commands are never implemented until the puppy or young dog has taken it in, and is explicitly obeying all voice and hand commands. In this way, you are building up your relationship with the dog. It is then an easy matter to change from voice and hand, to hand and whistle, and making the commands easily understandable and accepted by the now confident young dog.

I have never agreed that the Welsh Springer should be compared to an English Springer, which quarters to hunt [see page 179]. *The Welsh are totally different in that they instinctively line-hunt, and in virtually all cases, they have to be taught to quarter. The intelligence that they exude, when asked to retrieve a running bird, has never failed to impress me, and I have seen them on numerous occasions beat their English cousins on this on live game. Having picked up on a number of shoots now over the last 25 years with Welsh Springers, I have no hesitation in saying that they are my first choice for a working dog.*

Modern Enthusiasts

In recent years, we have had more devotees who have had great success with their dual-purpose Welsh Springers, and have gained high awards in competitions. Under the guidance and enthusiasm of John Phillips (whose Ch Wainfelin Born Free gained her title by winning both in the showring and in the field), Pat and Derek Dean (Pasondela), Christine and Andrew McDonald (Northey), Julie Revill (Julita), and Gill Tully (Highclare), have all made up Welsh Springers into full Champions. This is a formidable team, and all have done much to promote the working Welsh Springer. The working section of the Welsh Springer Spaniel Club of South Wales was formed in 1983, led by John Derrick, who is the present chairman of the strong contingent there, and is proving to be very successful in the showring as well. The Welsh Springer Spaniel Club and the Welsh Springer Spaniel Club of South Wales hold working tests and Field Trials, and Julie Revill, Gill Tully and John Derrick have been outstanding in their achievements in these in recent years.

Hackwood Kingfisher retrieving a pheasant. Photo: Gillian Harris

Regular training classes are held in various parts of the country, open to anyone who is interested in furthering the natural ability of their dog, whether or not they intend to work him. Those who have gained their knowledge and experience in the field are very generous in encouraging and helping others, and one who regularly takes training classes for the South Eastern Welsh Springer Spaniel Club is **Julie Revill**. Some take place on our farm, and they become a social occasion as well, with everyone enjoying their picnic lunch and tea and coffee after the classes sometimes augmented with hot soup, when the temperature is below zero! Here she is at work.

WSSC Field Trial 1993.

Training with Julie Revill

You will need:

- *whistle: black plastic, available from most gundog shops, on a lanyard*
- *rope slip lead.*
- *dummies: one small canvas puppy dummy, one large canvas of about 1lb in weight, which will also float.*

Welsh Springers are certainly not the easiest of dogs to train, but once the effort has been made and success follows, you

First shooting day of the Welsh Springer Club of South Wales.

Julie Revill with Julita Rainspeckle.

will derive great satisfaction and enjoyment from a well-trained and happy dog. What follows is purely my own way of training; I have found it works for me, and some, or all, of it may work for you. You may find you only use some of my suggestions, and that you discover other ways of gaining the same results – that's fine, whatever suits you and your dog is the way to go.

I do, however, have three Golden Rules:

1 *Make* **all** *training fun – if either you or your dog do not feel like it, don't do it. You will gain nothing, and could create problems that will take many months to eradicate.*

2 *Always try to set up a situation where your dog can hardly fail to do what you ask of him, and always finish on a good note, even if he just sits when told to – loads of praise and encouragement.*

3 **Never** *treat your dog harshly; if he goes wrong it is probably* **your** *fault, due either to Rule 1 or 2. Welshies do not respond to harsh treatment; my usual punishment method is to pick him up by the extra skin either side of the neck, hold him close to my face, and keeping eye contact, shake him slightly and growl at him (yes, growl!) saying 'No' (or whatever is appropriate for his 'sin').*

Bearing these rules in mind, you have brought your new 'baby' home at around eight weeks of age; start training **now**. *'No' is the first word he will learn; make sure you mean it, and make him obey. This can be followed by asking him to 'sit' or 'hup', before he gets his meals or treats; and, of course, whenever he is playing in the garden, call him to you, using just one word 'come' or 'here', using body language to encourage him, crouch down and open your arms to give him a lovely cuddle when he throws himself at you. These simple commands are starting training without him being aware of it. Naturally, you will try to get him to walk to heel when you take him out on a lead; with him on your left, swing your arms as in marching, and the lead will be jerked slightly to keep him from dashing ahead, and equally from dropping behind. Use 'heel' as your command to bring him close to you. In this way, you can very easily have a happy puppy, who will walk nicely to heel, sit on command, and come when called by the time he is a few months old.*

A major problem with Welshies seems to be the retrieve – they love to hunt, but really can't be bothered with retrieving unless trained correctly right from the beginning. My way is thus: when he is around 3–4 months old, he will enjoy chasing a rolled-up sock or puppy dummy, so we use this game to start the retrieve. Use a long hallway or narrow room so that there is no escape; hold puppy at one end, telling him to 'wait' (he won't understand, but the word will remain in his brain), throw the toy/dummy down the hall, and then allow puppy to go and get it, telling him to 'fetch it'. He will dive on it and pick it up; now lots of encouragement to come back to you with it. He will attempt to rush past you, but you can catch him, and tell him how wonderful he is for bringing this lovely article to you (yes, I know it was totally unintentional, but he will remember the pleasure when you are pleased with him, and want to repeat it – hopefully).

Do not be tempted to 'have another go' if your first try is successful; stop whilst you are winning, and leave it until the next day or so. **Never** *get cross if he doesn't retrieve: just forget the exercise, and try again another day, but only one retrieve two or three times a week whilst he is little.* **Don't** *be tempted to try this game outside until he is a lot older. You will have to decide when a retrieve outside is possible, but it must not be before he is steady on most commands, and you can* **stop** *him on the whistle, and recall him to you.*

He is walking nicely to heel on the lead, and sitting on command, so it is time to introduce the whistle. Learn to use this correctly, and give short, sharp 'toots', using your tongue to shorten the blast.

When walking your pup to heel, stop, and instead of the verbal command, use a sharp 'toot' on the whistle; this may need reinforcing with the verbal command to begin with, but he will quickly learn to sit to whistle. You can then bring in the first of the hand signals he will need to learn. As you whistle him to 'sit', turn to face him and hold up your hand, palm open, towards him. I call this 'the brick wall' – the dog is not allowed to pass it, and it **should** *stop him in his tracks! Eventually, this hand signal can be used to stop him at distance, hopefully even without the whistle command.*

Instill each of these commands into your pup before moving on to the next. I cannot emphasise enough that the time taken now will pay great dividends in the future.

Now that he is stopping on the whistle, you can risk letting him off the lead. However, this should be a gradual process; first walking him to heel (on lead), just drop the lead over his back, and continue walking along, stopping, starting and so on. When you are happy that he is still obeying you, remove the lead, and continue the exercise as before. Well done – now we can move on.

Sit him comfortably, telling him to 'stay' or 'wait' (whichever command you have chosen to use), and step back only a pace or two, hold your hand up as you step away, reinforcing your command, and pushing the palm of your hand towards him at the same time. Immediately return to him, still using the command 'stay', and give him enormous praise, but without allowing him to move from the sit if possible. If he breaks the stay, gently place him back on the same spot, and start again. Increase the distance very slowly as and when he is ready, until he is steady at a good 15 paces, returning each time and praising him. This may well take a few weeks to perfect, but must not be hurried; steadiness is extremely important in a gundog.

Obviously, you will reduce the number of reinforcements of command as the pup gets better at the exercise, until, hopefully, one command at the onset is all that is required, and you can stand well away from him, just holding up your hand to keep him in his position (the brick wall).

On perfection of this exercise, you may allow about one recall out of 10 stays. When doing this, use three or four short sharp 'toots' on the whistle, and crouch down, opening your arms to encourage him in – usually he will gallop straight at you, and throw himself upon you with great joy. Do not discourage him at this stage by attempting to make him sit before you praise him, as this may inhibit him coming straight to you later on with his retrieves. Remember, loads of praise and cuddles each time.

By the time the pup has perfected all these exercises, you will probably want to try a short retrieve in the garden. So, sit him down and give him the command to 'wait' (not forgetting the hand signal), stand to the right of him, and put your right foot just in front of him; this creates another small barrier to reinforce the command. Now throw out the dummy only about 4 yards or, preferably get a friend to do this for you, all the time reinforcing the command to wait.

When you are ready, move your foot away, and tell him to 'fetch'. Hopefully, he will dive on it just as he always has done, and come rushing back to you (you may use the recall whistle if required, to encourage him, and, of course, body language).

Do not take the dummy from him immediately; *try to get him to hold onto it whilst you praise him to the skies, eventually taking it from him with whatever command you plan to use.*

Early stages of training: stay whilst on a lead.
Photo: Tony Wickenden.

If he fails to retrieve, go back to indoor training. If he retrieves and dashes off with his prize, use the recall whistle and body language, and encourage him in. If he retrieves it and then drops it, try to send him back to 'fetch', and give loads of 'good boy, come' and so on, the minute it is in his mouth. If he retrieves it and stands and looks at you, turn and make out that you are running away; hopefully, he will run after you, and you can turn and praise him for returning to you. If none of these things work, return to basic training!

Now the pup is interested in retrieving, do **not** *do more than one or two retrieves. Between allowing him to retrieve, throw the dummy out a number of times and, leaving him on the 'stay', fetch it yourself. A good exercise at this stage, to assist with steadiness, is to sit him comfortably, and then throw dummies over his head and well past him, telling him to 'stay' each time, walk round him whilst throwing dummies, picking them up as you come to them, and throwing them over him again.*

When he is really steady to this exercise, you can allow the dummy to fall nearer and nearer to him (making very sure it **never** *hits him, as this can put back his training by many weeks). Allow* **one** *retrieve as a reward at the end of the exercise.*

You now have a steady dog, who obeys your whistle instantly, and retrieves a dummy happily! Good – we can move on to hunting, or quartering. First you need to teach him to 'seek'. This can be done with the use of a favourite toy or a fluorescent coloured tennis ball. Throw it a short way into grass or light bracken and, when he retrieves it to you, throw it into cover again. Continue this, making exciting noises and telling him to 'seek it'. This exercise can be enlarged upon by hiding the toy in increasingly difficult places, with lots of praise when he finds it and returns it to you.

Now we will try hunting, or quartering, which, as the word suggests, is to teach your dog to work the ground methodically and seek out any game (toy) that may be there. Ideally, when you are working your dog into the wind, he will move from side to side just ahead of you in a figure of eight, that is, send him to your right and forward, then back to you, out to the left and forward and back to you.

Dog sitting as dummy is thrown.

This is the best way of covering the ground thoroughly as you move slowly forward. The 'turn' whistle command is used here: send him out, and move slightly to your right with him to encourage him. Just as he moves past you, turn to move to your left, giving two sharp 'toots' on the whistle and encouraging him to follow you. Repeat on your left, giving lots of encouragement all the time. The clicking of fingers can often encourage a dog to follow in the direction you require. You can use a longish line to assist with this exercise if necessary, However, I have to say that I have usually found that this causes me to get tangled up, rather than assist the dog! When he has got the idea of what you want, encourage him to 'seek seek' and get his nose down, looking for the ball you have been playing with previously. Ensure

Sending the dog for the retrieve (also called 'casting off').

Teaching the dog to 'quarter' (hunting in a tight pattern).

that occasionally it is there for him to find!

Working your dog with the wind behind you will result in him quartering differently. He will be pulled forward and then will work back to you, criss-crossing in front, but this is more complicated and for more advanced training, as is using a side wind. Suffice it to say that whilst training, try to work **into** *the wind at all times to begin with. Gradually, he will learn to quarter faster, and to use his nose to find nice smells in bracken and bramble; encourage him to hunt right into thicker and thicker cover until he is thoroughly covering the ground.*

Using the wind when retrieving is really very simple. Pick up a little grass to allow it to blow away; you can see which way the wind is blowing, and always send your dog into the wind to assist the scenting of the retrieve article.

Once the basic canvas dummy is fully accepted, you can wrap a little bit of rabbit fur around it, or attach a pheasant wing, both of which will help him to learn to retrieve game eventually.

Let us now return to the 'stop' whistle. You will remember that the puppy was taught to sit with a single whistle and hand held up high. Now try this whilst he is hunting freely. He should stop, sit and look at you for a command as soon as you blast the whistle at him. If he does not: back to basics, and remind him of what is required. Now that he is running freely, he may well put up a bird or rabbit by mistake, and you do not want to have to chase him into the next county, or across a main road. Ensure that the lesson is very well learnt. **Nothing** *is more important.*

Next we will look at distance control. You would use this if you were sending him to find a 'hidden' or 'unseen' retrieve. The control will be by use of hand signals; the dog has already learned the 'stop' or 'stay there' command with the hand held high, palm towards the dog, so sit him with a fence or wall behind him, step a few paces away from him, and throw out the dummy to the left and one to the right of him – hold him steady with your hand. Decide which dummy you want retrieved; if you have the right hand up, send him for the right hand one. Throw the arm out to the right, palm outstretched, at the same time move your right foot slightly to the right, and bend your body slightly that way as well, saying 'fetch' firmly as you move. The body language is very important here: you are almost throwing yourself, and him, towards the dummy. He should go for the correct dummy and bring it to hand. If he goes in the wrong direction, attempt to stop him with whistle or command 'no', and send for the correct dummy. If he reaches the wrong dummy, let him bring it to

'There it is!'

you, but do not praise or chastise him; just start again from the beginning. When this lesson is well learned, you will be able to stop your dog at distance, and re-direct him wherever you want him to go.

There is just one other hand signal required for total control, and this is the signal to go 'back', (or whatever command you wish to use). Sit the dog in front of you, a few feet away and facing you; now throw the dummy over his head, behind him. Using the hand you are holding up to keep him steady, bring your arm back a little to just behind the shoulder (keeping it high), and then throw the arm forward, moving one foot towards the dog, at the same time telling him to 'get back' (or whatever command you use). He should then turn around and go straight to the dummy he knows you threw behind him. Repeat a couple of times, and return to this exercise every few days, to remind him.

Another good exercise here is to walk him to heel, dropping a dummy at some point, but keeping the dog walking to heel until you are some 20ft past it, stop, sit him, turn to face him, and send back for the dummy. When you feel he is sure of what you require of him, place three of four dummies out in your area about 12ft apart without him seeing them. Send him 'Back and fetch', and he is almost bound to find one! Remember Golden Rule No. 2: lots of praise. Do not let him find the others: go and collect them yourself. Combining the stop, back, and right and left hand signals, you should now be able to send him for any hidden retrieve.

'Fetch!' Photo: Tony Wickenden

When working on the distance control, it can be quite illuminating to put yourself in the dog's place; in a field of long grass, crouch down to the dog's level and look to the position you would be in, and you will see that the dog's area of vision is really small. You will also see why the hand signals need to be with the hand held high, and the signals very definite to ensure that the dog understands what is required of him.

You may require your dog to work in water, this is a natural thing for many Welshies to do. However, occasionally they do need encouragement to swim and retrieve from water. The best way in my experience is to put on a pair of waders and go in with him, preferably whilst he is still young. Swimming will only be learnt by gentle guidance – no throwing in please. I had a reluctant swimmer once who only finally gave in when gently pulled across a narrow, shallow stream on a long line once or twice. This did the trick, but a helpful companion is obviously required to do this. Once Welshies have enjoyed a short dip, they usually love it, and it can become difficult to keep them out of water of any sort! If retrieving from water, never let the dog rush in; he must wait until told to enter the water, and to go in gently, rather than throwing himself in (hidden objects can be

Presenting the retrieve.

very dangerous). He should be encouraged to bring the dummy out of the water and right to you before shaking, so do not stand close to the water's edge; stand back a few feet to encourage him to you. However, waterproof clothing is highly recommended for this exercise!

It is possible that your dog will be required to retrieve over a wall or fence, so it is a good idea to include jumps in your training. Start with low ones and build slowly, using the same command at all times, such as 'over' or similar. Even jumping into the car can be used as training, if you always use the same command. Once the dog is jumping happily, try a simple retrieve over a jump, making sure that he has no choice but to return over the jump!

Most aspects of basic working training have now been covered, except for the 'drop to shot', and this is the one aspect you must **never** *do on your own. Ask a friend to shoot a starting pistol or*

Free run when training session is finished.

John Derrick's Mynyddmaen Tegwyn with a Pink Foot Goose.

Welsh Springer Spaniel Club of South Wales Tregwillym Day 1989:
the Welsh Springer Spaniel Club and Minor Breeds teams.

similar, from a very great distance to begin with, whilst you hold your dog on the 'sit' close to you, making lots of encouraging noises. No doubt he will look up when he hears the shot: keep him sitting, and tell him what a good fellow he is. If he accepts this, try firing the pistol a little nearer, and again nearer still. For the first lesson, do not allow more than three shots, and keep all of these well away from him. Leave it a few days, and try again, until he looks up whenever he hears the shot but accepts it as part of life. The refinement is to get him to 'drop to shot' whilst hunting freely, and again you need a friend to assist with this. Many dogs drop automatically into the sit when they hear the shot whilst on the move, but you can reinforce it with the stop whistle if necessary, remembering to praise him abundantly when he complies.

Remember to go back over early training frequently, and never rush ahead to the next exercise until you feel your dog truly understands, **and obeys** *the previous one. Remember always the Golden Rules and have fun; there is nothing more satisfying than watching your dog out working, obeying your commands, doing what he was bred to do. If you ensure that every lesson is well learned, you will have years of fun with your Welshie.*

Recipe for a 'Tummy Warmer' – Sloe Gin

Supplied by Eileen Falconer and Julie Revill

one litre of gin
1.8kg (4lb) sloes
0.9kg (2lb) sugar
almond essence
optional extra: 1 bottle of cooking sherry

Method

Freeze sloes
Remove after three days, pour over the gin, add sugar..
Shake madly every day – in fact, every time you pass in the kitchen, tasting as you go.
After two weeks, add approximately one teaspoonful of almond essence.
Leave a couple of months.
(Extra tip from Eileen: add a bottle of cooking sherry.)
Strain through muslin, to get as clear as possible.
Leave as long as possible!

A Hackwood puppy retrieving in the water.

chapter 12
Welsh Springers Abroad

At present there are no quarantine regulations for the importation of dogs from the United Kingdom into overseas countries, apart from short periods in Australia and New Zealand. This has enabled overseas breeders to take full advantage of utilising new blood to improve their stock. Many British breeders would welcome the opportunity of importing stock themselves, but with the statutory quarantine period of six months, one has to consider the vast expense involved before coming to that decision.

There is an international network of breed devotees, many of whom know each other personally through visiting or by correspondence. Once Welsh Springer people get together, it is hard to get a word in as, wherever you go, all have the same enthusiasm for and interest in the breed. It's an ever-open door!

The system of judging varies from country to country, but the British Breed Standard is generally adhered to, and British judges are often given the honour of judging the breed overseas, particularly at the Breed Club show, where they attract very large entries. In Scandinavia and Europe, the judge dictates a critique to a secretary on every dog exhibited, mentioning both good and bad points; one copy of the critique is given to the exhibitor, and another is sent to the relevant Kennel Club. This inevitably limits the number of dogs that can be judged on one day. The British system is different: there is an unlimited number of dogs (apart from Crufts Dog Show, where dogs have to qualify), and only the 1st and 2nd placements remain after each class for the judge to make notes (1st place only at Open Shows). It is to be hoped that judges will then submit written critiques to the weekly canine press for publication, but they are under no obligation to do this. In the United States, the system is different again, working on a points system. Awarding Challenge Certificates and gaining titles differs from country to country and, when judging overseas, judges have to be acquainted with the rules appertaining to a particular country.

Docking of tails is no longer permitted in Scandinavian countries and, with no guidelines in the Breed Standard, there appears to be no uniformity in length, feathering or carriage of Welsh Springers' tails.

Welsh Springers are found in many countries, and have a very enthusiastic following, some countries having their own Breed Clubs. They are particularly strong in the United States, the Netherlands, Sweden and Finland; other European countries, Canada, Australia and New Zealand also have very active devotees. Perhaps the most surprising country to have a long interest is Czechoslovakia, now the Czech Republic and Slovakia. It is impossible to mention every successful breeder and dog by name in each country. With the help of devotees from the various countries, I have endeavoured to give a general account of the Welsh Springer internationally in a very abbreviated form.

It appears that although the Welsh Springers were in existence in a number of countries early in the century, it was not until the 1950s that they began to find favour and become established.

An explanation of the various abbreviations is in appendix B.

The United States of America

A Short History

Contributed by Adrienne Bancker, with thanks to Beth Marley (Canada) for the researched and documented details.

In the United States, the Welsh Springer Spaniel was formally recognised by the American Kennel Club in 1906, although red and white spaniels have been seen in earlier illustrations or paintings (some as early as 1712). The Missippi Valley KC Shows (3–6 April 1911) recorded an entry of four Welsh Springer Spaniels: three bitches and one dog, all owned by A A Busch. The Welsh had been imported from Mrs H D Greene's and Mr R Hughes' kennels. It is interesting to note that Welsh were being shown 10 years before American Kennel Club (AKC) classes were available for English Springer Spaniels.

The first Welsh Springer registered with the AKC was Faircroft Bob, owned and bred by Harry B Hawes of Kirkwood, Missouri. Bob was registered in 1914; at the time, the breed was listed by the AKC as Welsh Springer. Bob's sire, Faircroft Snip, was also registered in 1914, as were four littermates, but his dam, Faircroft Sue, was not registered until 1915. Another early supporter of the breed in the United States was Hobart Ames of Connecticut, who imported his shooting dogs from the kennels of A T Williams. One of the last of the Llanharran strains, Marged O'Matherne, a bitch, was imported in the 1920s to a sportsman in the mid-west.

Probably the most famous introduction of the breed to America came in 1950, when Dorothy Ellis and four of her adult Downland Welsh and one puppy flew from England to New York to exhibit at Westminster, Hartford and Boston. There was much attention and publicity, including a television interview with Edward Everitt Horton. In Miss Ellis' reminiscences, she remarked that, fortunately, one of her dogs went Best of Breed at each of the three shows. The first American Champion to be registered, Am Ch Holiday of Happy Hunting, was a son of two of the Welsh Springers Dorothy Ellis brought over.

Also in the 1950s, I J Smith imported dogs from the Rockhill kennels of Marjorie Mayall. The Welsh Springer Spaniel Club of America owes a debt of thanks to I J, as he prepared the first brochure devoted to the breed, a six page document covering its history and characteristics.

English Sh Ch & Am Ch Trigger of Tregwillym.
Photo: William Brown

In the early 1960s, Bert and Edna Randolph of Randhaven kennels owned or bred eight American champions. They also hired a handler to assist them in showing their rare breed – D Lawrence (Laddie) Carswell. Laddie imported English Show Champion Trigger of Tregwillym in 1962. He then proceeded (in his words) to 'show that dog everywhere he could reach', in order to introduce and educate the American judges and public on the breed. Laddie earned the nickname 'Mr Welsh Springer Spaniel' by his continual efforts to keep Welsh Springers in front of the judges' eyes.

In the 1970s, the breed started its rise in popularity. Although still low in AKC registrations (the breed was ranked in the 100s), Welsh Springers were found in shows across the United States, and occasional group placements were achieved for those dogs being campaigned. In 1977, the first book about the breed, *The Welsh Springer Spaniel History, Training, Selection and Care*, by William Pferd III, was published. Am CH Sylabru's Cimri Aberystwyth became the first Welsh to win a group. He was a grandson of Trigger of Tregwillym, bred by Sylvia Foreacre and owned by Sue Spahr.

The Welsh Springer Spaniel Club of America (WSSA) held its first A-OA (conformation and obedience) match. It was won by Sylabru's Caitlin of Whimsy, a daughter of a British import dog, bred by Sylvia Foreacre and owned by Adrienne Bancker. Highest Score in Match was won by Deckard's Cymru'u Un, a son of a British import bitch, bred by William and Jane Pferd and owned by Adrienne Bancker.

In 1980, the WSSCA held its first National Specialty, with an unbelievably huge (for that time) turnout of 64 entries. It was a freezing cold, miserable day in April at the Penn Treaty Kennel Club – the dogs loved it! Am Ch Randail Taffy of Sylabru was Best of Breed, a daughter of a British import sire, bred by Sylvia Foreacre and owned by Jane Randolph. Best of Opposite Sex was Am Ch Hillpark Caesar, a British import, bred by John and Anne Walton, and owned by Frances and Carl Bloom. High in Trial was Ch Deckard's Cymru'u Un, UD, still owned by Adrienne Bancker.

As it turned out, the 1980s became a decade of many firsts for the Welsh Springer Spaniel in American show competition. In 1986, for its 25th anniversay, the WSSCA

Am Ch Sylabru's Cimri Aberystwyth.

Am/Can Ch Fracas Little Caesar. Photo: John L Ashbey

held its first independent specialty. The show was won by Am/Can Ch Fracas Little Caesar, a dog bred and owned by Frances and Carl Bloom, and the son of two British Hillpark imports. Best of Opposite went to Am Ch Nimue of the Lake, a daughter of a British import, bred by Richard and Pat Pencak, owned by Barbara and Adrian Nunn. High in Trial went to Truepenny Lady Cyfeillgar, a daughter of a Dutch import who was himself of two British parents, and was also the breed's first all-breed High in Trial winner. She was bred by Marion Daniel, and owned by Shirlee O'Neill.

Perhaps, however, for the American dog show scene, the greatest accomplishments and strides were gained by Am/ Can Ch Fracas Little Caesar. 'Little C', as he was known, was handled by Laddie Carswell (or Laddie's daughter, Candy), to become the first Welsh Springer Spaniel to win an all-breed American Best in Show, the first (and only one so far) to win Best in Show at the American Spaniel Club and, some 37 years after Dorothy Ellis made her trip to Madison Square Garden, the first Welsh Springer Spaniel (and only one so far) to place in the group at Westminster.

The Welsh Springer Spaniel in the United States Today

Author's comments.

In the 1990s, it is common to see a Welsh Springer placed in and even winning the Sporting Group. Am Ch Rysan's First Round Kayo, bred and owned by Sandra and Richard Rohrbacher, and Am Ch Royailes Kool Ham Luke, bred and owned by Nora

Am Ch Bachgen Dewr of Pencelli.

Carlton, are multiple Best in Show winners. The breed can also be proud of its first Master Hunter, Briallu Crossfire, bred by Barbara Smith and owned by Chuck Urland. Glyndwir Fwyn Celsey UDX, Can UD, is the first Obedience Trial Champion (OTCH), bred by Janet Ing, and owned by Chuck and Cathy Soule. From 1990 to 1996, of the seven WSSCA National Specialties, four of them had British breed specialists as judges. All seven Best of Breed winners so far can claim that at least one parent or grandparent is of British origin – proof that the American Welsh Springer Spaniels continue to retain the ties of their heritage.

In the 1970s, new blood was imported from British kennels: Tregwillym (Payne), Pencelli (Newman), Brent (Perkins), Hillpark (Walton), Dalati (Hunton Morgans) and others contributed to the foundation of many of the leading American kennels today.

Other imports from the United Kingdom in the 1980s were from the Dalati, Brent, Tregwillym, Goldsprings (Ordish), Hillpark, Northey (McDonald), Delkens (Spate), Cwrt Afon (Morgan), Wainfelin (Young) and Topmast (Phillips) kennels, and also from Holland and Scandinavia.

Our Sh Ch Hilllpark Gemmabelle went over to Virginia in 1982, and soon gained her American title as well, only the second Welsh Springer to hold both titles.

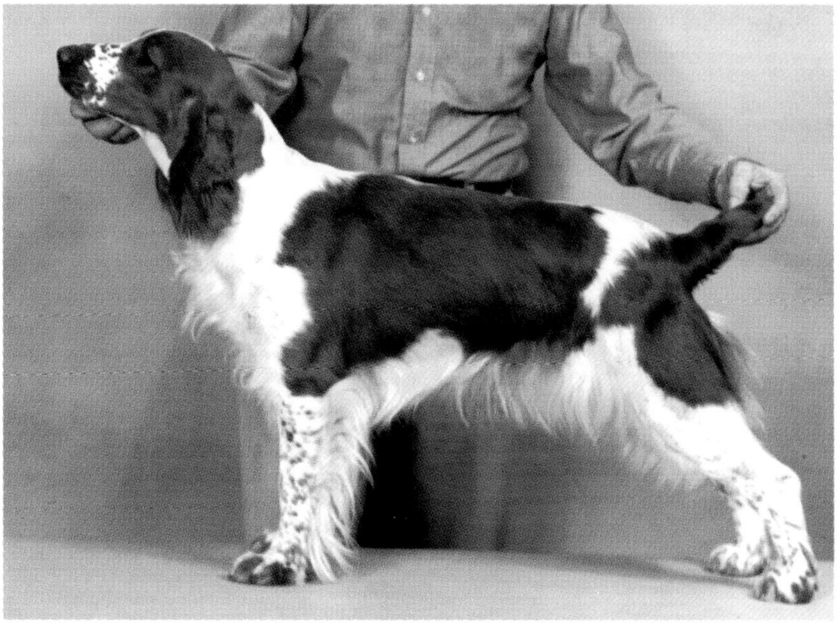
Am Ch Olympian Rhonda Redhead.

Over the years, many outstanding breeders and exhibitors have represented many kennels. These have included Sylabru (Foreacre), Pickwick (Seamans), Wynfomeer (Cummings), Olympian (Preston), Killagay (Christie), Deckards (Pferd), Statesmans (Riese), Tydaky (Krohn), Truepenny (Daniel), Sudawns (Spahr), Fracas (Bloom), Limberlost (O'Keefe), Aurora's (Kuhn), Bu-Gwyn (Hamaguchi), Rysan (Rohrbacher) and Saga (Ilmanen).

Breed judging is carried out on a points system, a stated number of points being awarded at shows according to the number of dogs being exhibited. A dog earns the title of American Champion once 15 points have been gained, which must include at least two major wins. A major consists of a win where 3, 4 or 5 points are accumulated at one time. Frequently, the dogs are handled by professional handlers, something which is almost unknown in the United Kingdom, where we all tend to prepare and handle our own dogs.

I had the great honour of judging at the 1994 WSSCA National Specialty in Georgia, with an entry of 101 dogs; some had travelled great distances by air from all over the country. In the Best of Breed class, where they are all Champions, there were 37 dogs and bitches to judge. Once a dog gains its title, it has to enter the Champions class – hence my enormous entry – and what a spectacle! Inevitably, there were a number of different types, but I was very impressed with the general quality. My Best of Breed winner was Am Ch Statesman's Llanharan Abbey, a beautiful bitch bred by Gary, Susan and Meghen Riese, and owned by Dan and Marta Stoneman. My Best Opposite Sex was Carl Bloom and Neil MacRitchie's Am Ch Fracas Trade Mark, a son of Ch Fracas Little Caesar, grandson of our export, Am Ch Hillpark Brutus – so it was 'in the family'!

There is an increasing interest in the working side. The first sanctioned working tests for Welsh Springers were held in the 1980s. Ned Cummings (Wynfomeer) has helped me here: he tells me that in 1993, the AKC introduced Hunting Tests for Spaniels. Only English Springers, American Cockers and English Cockers have Field Trial ratings. There are three Standards of Performance: Junior Hunter, Senior Hunter and Master Hunter. The following three dogs are the only ones to obtain Master Hunter titles: Briallu Cross Fire MH, Ch Briallu Shotgunner's Sam MH, and Ch Wynfomeer's Lu-C Nor'Easter CD, MH (see opposite page). Two of the three are bench champions. Other spaniel breeds cannot claim this percentage of dual dogs.

Obedience is also very popular, where dogs can gain CD, CDX and UD titles.

The end of an era for the Welsh Springer Spaniel Club of America came in 1995, with the death of Past President and elder statesman, Laddie Carswell. He was regarded as **the** expert on the breed in the States, and I was honoured to be included in his large circle of friends. On my three trips to his country, I had wonderful discussions about the breed with him, and was always enthralled with his deep knowledge, and his understanding of anatomy, conformation and movement, which he was always so willing to impart. He had such a wealth of experience and so many wonderful dogs, spanning many years.

Laddie was a professional handler, who achieved fame at the Westminster Show (the equivalent of our Crufts) in 1963, when he handled an English Springer to Best In Show. He had many great successes with Welsh Springers over a period of 30 years, as a breeder, handler and owner. Amongst them were notably Am Ch Felicia's Dylan, who gained his title in 1965, won 23 Best of Breeds in the showring and sired six Champions; and Am Ch Peter Dewi Sant of DL'Car, who gained his championship in 1974, and was Best of Breed 33 times. Perhaps his greatest star, certainly in recent times, was American and Canadian Champion Fracas Little Caesar, with whom Laddie had such an affinity, and always presented to perfection. Laddie selected him as a puppy, taking him on to the greatest heights, already recorded in Adrienne's history above. When Dodo Hunton Morgans, of the famous Dalati kennel, went to the States to judge at the Breed Specialty in 1988, she awarded 'Little C' Best of Breed. Sadly, Laddie died soon after I had written to him, asking for his help with this section of my book, and I was too late.

Am Ch Statesman's Llanharan Abbey.

The Start of it All

Here is Miss Ellis' story of how it all started with her and, subsequently, for the Welsh Springer in America.

In the distant days before the last war, I had the good fortune to fall deeply in love. The object of my affections was a waif called Freckles with a rather doleful expression and large arresting black eyes. He was a foundling who had been taken to be looked after in a

Am Ch Wynfomeer's Lu-C Nor'Easter CD, MH.

London basement room for two weeks, then destroyed unless a home had been found for him. The looker-after, a run-down officer of small means and expensive drinking habits, financed by two elderly ladies, could not bring himself to destroy Freckles, so he extended the hospitality at his own expense for a further week and sought among his cronies someone to relieve him of the burden. The congenial spirit who took it on somehow dropped his own identity and became known as 'Master', such was the compelling domination of Freckles. They occupied a flat belonging to me – that was how I met them. When I learned that Freckles had to be left alone all day whilst Master worked, I took over day-time adoption and he returned to Master at night.

One day when I was walking him over Hammersmith Bridge and passed a march of ex-Servicemen from Wales, I heard a shout 'Look, there's a Welsh spaniel', whereupon a dozen or so left the march and dashed over to have a closer look. Thus I learnt that Freckles was a Welsh Springer. I went to the Agricultural Hall to Crufts Show (the only dog show I had ever heard of) to see what his legitimate family looked like and, although I saw some fine looking dogs, somehow there was nothing quite so handsome as Freckles.

The war broke out and Master was recalled to the Army, leaving behind him Freckles, whom I came to regard as my own. One unhappy night in 1941, two of my houses of flats received direct hits in an air raid, and five people were killed. Over that disastrous night I like to draw a veil, but the following morning, amid the debris and survivors, appeared Master. He was very sorry for our distress, and wished us well but, being in London for a Court Martial, with a car, he had thought it a good opportunity to collect Freckles. I felt stricken; having got so used to Master's absence for the past year, that I had quite forgotten him and his claim on the dog. So we parted, for good it seemed, as I felt I never wished to see Master again anyhow.

Some two years after, I casually met a friend, who, in course of conversation, said 'I suppose you read of Major –'s suicide?' It has been held against me that my immediate reply was 'What happened to the dog?'. My friend did not not know. 'Where was he stationed?' 'Basingstoke,' was the answer. I wrote and begged for Freckles, getting grudging permission to collect him. The Officers' Mess had adopted him. Begging and scrounging enough petrol to get there, I called at the Mess. Freckles approached me suspiciously, sniffed, then threw back his ears and rushed, yelping, up and down the room several times, after which he jumped into my car and sat waiting for me. Freckles spent that night on my bed, and did so for the rest of his life. A strange thing was that he had turned completely white. Old age, of course, would partly account for it, but I have had many dogs live to great age, and none has so completely lost colour.

At this time I was living in Stanmore, Middlesex, having not only a large garden, but good country walks, so I felt I should like a wife for Freckles. Alas, everyone had stopped breeding, and it took me two years' continuous effort to find a young bitch in North Wales which I was glad to buy on trust, and a charming little thing she turned out to be. She got lost on her war-time railway journey, and it was nearly 24 hours later when I managed to track her down. She leaped out of her box, as bright as a button and full of gaiety. She earned her name of 'Fussy'. She was to become the first mate of Harold Newman's famous Dewi Sant, and gave me 10 pups as her first litter. Later, I was to move to Sussex, where I have several acres of land, and Freckles was to spend his last days with many of his race.

But for Freckles, the first American Welsh Springer champion would have been of other lineage.

The Netherlands

I am grateful to Ria Horter for all her help with this section.

Kamp Ch Plattburn Proclaim.
Photo: Marinus Nijhoff

The first Welsh Springer was registered by the Dutch Kennel Club in 1911. He was a dog called Mist, offspring of Mrs H D Greene's Longmynd Morgan and Longmynd Myfanwy, born in 1908. However, there appears to be no further knowledge of the breed in the Netherlands until 1951, when Red Rascal of Downland, bred by Miss Ellis, was shown for the first time. This was followed by the import of a bitch, Hal Leopard's Rushbrooke Rhoda, and the first litter from these two was registered in 1955. Between then and 1969, fewer than 30 litters were registered. The first well known kennel was J Heins' Fen Bjirkhieming's; his daughter still breeds a few Welsh Springers today.

There followed the import of a number of very influential dogs and bitches from England: several from Ken Burgess' Plattburn kennel, most notably Sh Ch Plattburn Peewit, Kamp P Pinecob, Kamp P Partner and Kamp P Proclaim; Jonathan of Brent from Hedley Perkins; Sh Ch Kamp Dalati Delwen and Kamp Dalati Derw from the Hunton Morgans; and Vi Buchanan's Reliance of Krackton, all of whom had a great influence on the breed.

Hedley Perkins (Brent) judging the
1980 National Gundog Show in the Netherlands.
Dutch Sh Ch Dalati Derw (left) with Dutch/Lux Sh Ch Dalati Si-Lw.
Photo: Marinus Nijhoff

Two Dalati dogs from the Hunton Morgans, Iago and Aled, played their part when they joined Mr and Mrs Huisman's kennel. They did not gain their Champion titles, but were very successful with their offspring.

Mrs Cox Ohmstede-Evers started the Speldermark kennel in 1968 with Sh Ch Kamp Plattburn Peewit and Sh Ch Kamp Dalati Delwen. Jonathan of Brent was the foundation dog of Mrs A H Raad's Tassel kennel, and was used considerably at stud. Two Plattburn dogs, Kamp P Pinecob and Kamp P Partner, were imported by J G J van Elteren, of the Dusky's Starter kennel in the late 1960s. They produced 23 litters, and set the foundation of a new and modern type of Welsh Springer in Holland.

Koos van Wijngaarden (Isselsteyn's kennel) imported several Plattburn dogs, and Dutch Sh Ch Dalati Derw, the most famous Dalati dog to go to Holland. He was European Spaniel Champion in 1978 and World Champion in 1979, 'a lovely dog, beautiful temperament, very hard to beat in the showring – Big Winner!' Stock from this kennel provided a very good example of sound and typical Welsh Springer Spaniels.

In 1978, a much-needed new blood line (and a new type) arrived from England at the Lissenbergs' van Snellestein kennel. This was Sh Ch Bramblebank Calamity Jane, bred by Val Roach. I had given her her first Challenge Certificate at Windsor in 1977, and she gained her title at Crufts in 1978, judged by Mary Payne (Tregwillym). Her 'partnership' with Reliance of Krackton produced Kamp Valentijn van Snellestein, who was a great influence on the breed in Holland and also in the United States when he was over there for a few years. In the late 1970s to mid 1980s, the van Snellestein kennel dominated the show ring, not only in Holland, but all over Europe. Behind this was the exceptional talent of Ria Lissenberg-Horter (now Horter), as both breeder and exhibitor.

Dutch Sh Ch Blessed Boleyn van Berdenstein
Photo: Marinus Nijhoff

Dutch/Lux Sh Ch Nyliram Mr Dark Horse.

Other influential imports from the Hunton Morgans' Dalati kennel included Si-Lw, and Sawel, litter brother to the top stud dog in Britain, Sh Ch Dalati Sioni, joined the van Dillen's Our Loyal Welsh kennel.

Many of the top British breeders exported stock to Holland in the 1980s and early 1990s: Dalati, Delkens, Wainfelin, Northey, Ferndel, Mapleby, Russethill, Haregate and others have contributed, and are still contributing, to the strength of the Welsh Springer as it is there today. They have played their part in establishing some of the most successful breeders, including: Miss M Crucq's Of The Half House, Ben and Monique van Bindsbergen's (now Monique van Bindsbergen-Geurts') van Berkenstein, Ine v d Beulen's Inma's, and John and Lia Doejaaren's van Mussel's kennels. Mapleby Post Master and Northoaks Sea Sun Flower are well-known stud dogs of the era.

Dutch Sh Ch Blessed Boleyn van Berkenstein was born in 1990, the product of a very successful blend of Dalati and Wainfelin lines (Dalati Sinsir ex Wainfelin Miss Money Penny), one of three Show Champions.

France has also had an influence on the breed, with several dogs and bitches bred by Mme Bolze (Des Terres Froides) being shown and used for breeding in Holland. Marie-Madeleine van Grinsven based her Of the Yasmin Garden kennel on a mixture of French and Dalati lines.

The influence of the van Snellestein kennel and Ria Horter still continues today, and many of the well-known kennels have that blood as a basis of their lines. After a break, Ria Horter (Of Rowan's Residence) has now returned to the Welsh Springer scene, and she has imported stock from a number of British kennels. The most successful is Dutch and Lux Sh Ch Nyliram Mr Dark Horse (son of Sh Ch Russethill Royal Salute over Nyliram, the breed record holder in Britain at the present time). He was the best Welsh Springer in the Netherlands in 1993, 1994 and 1995, and is the breed record holder on the Continent.

Welsh Springer Spaniel Club in Nederland Clubmatch, 1997.

Sh Ch Barco Van 't Slekkerhout. Photo: Ben van Bindsbergen

In 1976, the Welsh Springer Spaniel Club in the Netherlands was formed. It is a very flourishing Club with about 700 members, and there is always a large contingent of its enthusiasts at the ringside at Crufts and the Welsh Springer Spaniel Club's Shows in England. The Club produces an excellent magazine six times a year, and holds an annual Championship Show, at which many British judges have had the honour of officiating, usually with an entry of about 100 dogs.

I judged their first Clubmatch in 1979, and made a return visit with Doreen Gately (Russethill) in 1997. Our Best in Show was the British import, Kamp Northoaks Sea Sun Flower, bred by Christopher Anderson (Weslave Weeping Willow ex Northoaks Sea Breeze), the top winning Welsh Springer of the year, with the veteran, Kamp Wainfelin Miss Money Penny (Sh Ch Wainfelin Barley Mo ex Wainfelin Tuppenny Piece) Best Opposite Sex, another British import.

Some genetic defects were causing problems in the 1970s and, in 1974, nearly 8% of Welsh Springer dogs and bitches were epileptic. By careful breeding, this was reduced to 5.5% by 1984, and has now reached an acceptable figure of 2%.

One of the few Show Champions from parents both bred in Holland was Monique van Bindsbergen's Sh Ch Barco van 't Slekkerhout, world champion in 1989, a big winner in the late 1980s, and frequently used for breeding.

The first Welsh Springer in Sweden:
N DK UCH Linkhill Five To One.

INT N UCH Mustela F Publikan.

INT S N UCH/S JCH Trigger Bonnie Lass.

Sweden

I am indebted to Yvonne Scheppstedt Schill for contributing this section:.

The first Welsh Springer in Sweden was Linkhill Five to One , bred by Ann West, and imported in 1963 by Mrs Marianne Ahrenback-Hermelin of the Mustela kennel. She had 12 litters; her first in 1965 was from another import from Cliff Payne's kennel, Gay Boy of Tregwillym. Five to One was the dam of three International Champions, all with awards in Field Trials.

There were other imports from England in the early years, which had a great influence on the establishment of the Welsh Springer in Sweden, and were the foundation of all the big kennels of the time: Mustela (Mrs Marianne Ahrenbeck-Hermelin), Maroon (Mrs Ann-Sophie Everhed), Himledalen (Mrs Anita Norberg), Corydon (Mrs Rigmor Grant Carlson) and Trigger (Mrs Catarina Hultgren).

Mrs Sophie Everhed (Maroon) bred 3l litters, the last in 1985. She imported Jemima of Tarbay, and several dogs from the Hunton Morgans' Dalati kennel, Dalati Anian being the first Welsh Springer to win Best in Show at the Swedish Club Show in 1978.

In the 1970s, Tidemarsh Ruff, bred in England by Gordon Pattinson, joined Anita Norberg's Himladalen kennel, which was founded in 1970, and is still active today. It had many big wins and top placements in progeny groups during the 1970s and 1980s. Nearly 70 litters have come from this kennel.

Mrs Grant Carlson (Corydon) imported four dogs, the most important being S UCH Rebecca of Basildon and Benefactor of Brent, and had 20 litters under the Corydon prefix, the last in 1988. Her most successful dogs were Corydons Despot, and Corydons Noble, sired by Pencelli Mwyn, a dog bred by Harold Newman and given to Mrs Birgitta Thoresson.

The Himledalen kennel, 1980.

Kennel Trigger was started by Mrs Catarina Hultgren in 1971. She imported several dogs from the United Kingdom, which were of great importance to the breed: Chiltern Haig of Huttons and Wainfelin Countryman, both used by many breeders at stud; N UCH Nutbourne Red Flash and Highwinder Miss Lucy of Hackwood (who had five field trial awards), both daughters of Hackwood Kingfisher, winner of two field trials in the United Kingdom, and Trigger of Stokecourt, given to the kennel by the late Dorothy Morriss, so well known for her working dogs. Mrs Hultgren has also exported dogs, notably to France, and Denmark, where DK UCH Trigger Osborne has had a great influence on the breed. There have been many successful dogs from this kennel over the years, with champions in showing, obedience and field trials. INT S N UCH/ S JCH Trigger Bonny Lass (see opposite) is the only field trial champion to date, and N UCH Trigger Winston one of the very few full champions. Trigger dogs are frequently used at stud, and the kennel is still of major importance in the breeding of Welsh Springers in Sweden.

Several other well known breeders founded their kennels in the 1970s. Mrs Kristina Anjou (Vindhaxans) had her first litter in 1973, and she is still active in the breed. Her foundation bitch was Himledalens Bonny (N UCH Bryn of Tarbay ex Maroon's Holly), and she was mated to Tidemarsh Ruff. Out of this combination came her successful bitch, N UCH Vindhaxans Bettina. N UCH Vindhaxans Hemingway is a very successful stud dog, and I extolled the virtues of Vindhaxans Vanilla when I awarded her Best in Show at the Swedish Club Show in 1993.

Margareta Edman (Clumbrolds) started her kennel in 1976, using a bitch from the Corydon lines, Corydons Honey Bee. She imported Welsh Guide of Tregwillym, sire of her most well known dog, INT SF N UCH Clumbrolds Purpurdod. He was exported, with INT SF N UCH C Flitiga Lisa, to Kennel Rwyn in Finland, where they had a great influence on the breed.

Rigmor Langstrom (Dalsvedens), started in 1977 with Carmen, a bitch sired by Dalati Cai ex Himledalens Bonny. Her most successful dog is Dalsvedens Othello, twice Best in Show at the Swedish Club Show.

The 1980s and 1990s have seen the emergence of several new and very successful kennels. There has been a continuation of importation of new blood from most of the major British lines, and also from Norway and Finland. Dogs are to be seen everywhere

Merry One's Into the Light.

in Sweden, and their owners are very vigilant about cleaning up behind their animals. At Club Shows, the whole family, humans and dogs, arrive and set up camp at the ringside for the day, which means that from a very early age, the dogs are integrated and very much part of the family. When I judged the Swedish Club Show in 1982, my Best in Show actually went to a dog from Finland, sired by one of our Hillpark dogs in that country. I felt at that time that a good foundation had been laid for the breed in Sweden. On my return visit to judge again in 1993, I was most impressed with the progress made, and noted with envy the general quality of the breed, particularly in stud dogs. The Swedes appear to have been fortunate in not having any major disease problems and, as a result, their breeding stock was, in my opinion, stronger than our own. What British judges have to accustom themselves to are the undocked tails in Sweden. Docking is now banned in Scandinavia, but I found that exhibitors bent their dogs' tails back for me, to make them look as though they were docked, so that I really noticed the wide variation of tail shape, feathering and tail carriage only when the dogs were on the move.

Bjorn and Yvonne Skeppstedt Schill started their Merry One's Kennel in 1985, with a bitch called Loranga (Trigger Oliver ex Keepsake Cleopatra). They have met with considerable success in shows, as well as in obedience, tracking and field trials.

Merry One's Christmas Candy made history in 1992, being the first Welsh Springer to receive artificial insemination with fresh semen in Sweden. The sire was the famous Int Ch Delkens Turul, belonging to Marjo Jaakkola in Finland. At that time, the borders between Sweden and Finland were closed, and this was the only way that the mating could be accomplished. Merry One's Grace and Glory, a product of the combination, was very successful in the showring, winning Best In Show at the Club Show in 1996. From a litter sired by the dog N UCH Vindhaxans Hemingway out of Merry One's Candy came Merry One's Into The Light, who was runner-up in the Best All-Rounder Welsh Springer Competition in 1995. Her litter brother, Am Ch Merry One's I'm a

Grimmhills Sleeping Beauty, BIS at the Swedish Spaniel & Retriever Club.

Statesman, was exported to United States, and was the first Swedish-bred Welsh Springer to gain this title.

Freckles Kennel was started by Carina Arvidsson in 1986. Her foundation bitch was N UCH Triggers Wait and See (Chiltern Haig of Huttons ex N UCH Nutbourne Red Flash). Freckles Welsh Springers have achieved success in the showring and in field trials, Freckles Inspiration being the top field trial dog in the breed, and Freckles Miss Decibell the Best All Rounder, in 1995.

Multi Ch Metzgard's Moonlight Valley winning the Champion of Champions Contest in 1990.

Marita and Rolf Carlsson's Grimmhill's kennel also started in 1986, and is of particular interest to me, as they imported our Hillpark Edwardian Mint to be their foundation bitch. Their kennel is not one of the larger ones, but they now have four generations. Their biggest success so far was when Grimmhill's Sleeping Beauty (see below opposite) won Best in Show at the Swedish Spaniel and Retriever Club Show in 1996, one of only five Welsh Springers to claim this distinction.

Annica Hogstrom and Karin Brostram, of Don's kennel, had their first litter in 1989, and have met with outstanding success in the showring, with many different dogs. A number of dogs have been imported from different kennels: Metzgards from Norway, and Weslave and Beradene from England. Their foundation bitch was Weslave Winter Breeze JW, bred by John and Joy Hartley, who is not only very successful in her own right, but also a brood bitch that has really put a stamp on her offspring. One is Don's Thunderstorm, group winner and twice Best in Show at the Swedish Club Show; and another, Don's Treasure, who was Best in Show at the Club Show in 1995. The most famous import (from Norway) is the well-known multiple Best in Show winner, N UCH NV–88, 89, SV–89--92–94, NV-94 Metzgard's Moonlight Valley. Don's were the first kennel to take the step into Europe and compete successfully at the World Winners Show in Belgium, where Don's Coq Rouge took the top award in 1995.

The foundation bitch for Gudrun Jonsson's Hammalgardens Kennel was Kabos Frida of Music (Don-Pedro ex Maytorp's Goosberry Girl). The kennel was started in 1990, and a number of dogs have been imported both from England and Finland. The most well-known is Dalati Curig (co-owned with Jens Carlsson of Kennel Art-Wave). INT/SF UCH KW-92 Tri dyw 92 Uro-Jifex, a group winner, and co-owned with Tiina Mattila, Rwyn Galloise, Rwyn Talisman and Rwyn Talita, all Best in Show winners. Other imports from England have come from Weslave, Pamicks and Cleevemount.

Kennel Hillcrofts, owned by Agneta and Bert Mansson, was founded in 1990: their foundation bitch was Clumbrolds Trollslanda (Metzgards Moonlight Valley ex Corydons Dheila). They have also imported dogs from Weslave and Metzgards, and have met with considerable success in the showring.

Other kennels have started in the last few years, and time will tell what will be their contribution to the breed. For 20 years, between 180 and 200 Welsh Springers were registered every year, but there has been a big increase in the past few years: in 1995, there were 264.

There is a Welsh Springer Spaniel Club in Sweden. The annual Club Show is the biggest event of the year, and there are also a few open shows every year, where different Swedish breeders are invited to judge. A few years ago, the Club started a Club Championship, with competition in obedience, tracking and field trials, all in the same weekend. It has become very popular, and it is hoped that it will continue.

On the working side, Field Trials in Sweden are always held like a proper shoot, with live game. Welsh Springers always compete with all the spaniels, including the 'working Springer'. Since the English Springer of 'working type' was introduced at trials, the requirements have increased immensely. To qualify as a full Champion in Sweden, apart from gaining three Challenge Certificates, a dog has to win a 2nd in the open class at a trial, and this is very difficult. The trials include field work, water retrieve and tracking. About 30 dogs have received awards at field trials since 1985.

Finland

My husband and I visited Finland in 1988, when I was judging the breed show near Helsinki. We stayed with Welsh Springer friends and visited other owners, and we were interested to see that every home had made special provision for their dogs: a ledge or shelf with blanket alongside one of the living room walls, specially for the dogs. Those of us who have our dogs with us in our homes probably have our dogs' beds in various parts of the house, but this special arrangement appeared to be the routine in Finnish homes, and they certainly lived with their dogs. Many of the handlers at shows are young, and they are very proficient and most enthusiastic.

I made a return visit to Finland to judge the breed in 1995, and I found that I had given Best of Breed to a daughter of my best dog on my first visit! There are some really good dogs and bitches in Finland, resulting from some sensible breeding over the years, and imported dogs from the United Kingdom have had a big influence.

Miss Marjo Jaakkola has sent me her story of Welsh Springers in Finland:

The first Welsh Springer Spaniels were imported to Finland in 1967 from Sweden by Mrs Misse Puolakkainen, of the famous 'Of Skyway' kennels. These two bitches, Int Ch Mustela T Pomperipossa and Int Ch Mustela T Pompadour (Plattburn Pimlico ex Mustela F Tirana), became the foundation of the breed in Finland. Their first litters were born in1968, when both bitches were mated to Swedish dogs. From these litters came the first Finnish-bred champions, Of Skyway Peggy, Pansy and Puppet. SF UCH Of Skyway Puppet was the foundation of Mr Eero Santala's successful breeding under 'Gritty's' prefix.

INT SF UCH Hillpark Cleopatra.

There was great interest in this new breed: 15 were registered in 1968, 11 in 1969 and 38 in 1970. New blood was needed and, in 1969, Mrs Puolakkainen imported two dogs and a bitch from Cliff Payne's Tregwillym kennel in

England: Nobleman, Ambassador and Golden Charm of Tregwillym.

In the early 1970s, Tuulikki and Reino Makitalo started their Sinsir kennel by importing a bitch from Sweden, Lundkullas Liv (Richard of Brent ex Mustela F Tirana), who had a very strong Brent background from Hedley Perkins' kennel. Later on, Brad Brent was imported to the Sinsir kennels, together with INT SF UCH Hillpark Cleopatra (Dewi of Tregwillym ex Sh Ch Hillpark Pollyanna) (see previous page) from the Waltons.

INT SF N UCH Hillpark Robin Goodfellow.

At this time, the hard work in establishing this new breed was done by Of Skyway, Gritty's, Sinsir and Lucas kennels. The first Finnish-bred Welsh Springer Spaniel to gain the Finnish Winner title was SF UCH Lucas April (Bryn of Tarbay ex Destiny of Skyway).

A very important year for Finnish Welsh Springers was 1975. Mrs Puolakkainen was fortunate to import a valuable stud and show dog from Great Britain: INT SF N UCH SFV–76,–77–79 Dalati Dyma Fi (Sh Ch Athelwood Daiperoxide ex Dalati Sidan). His excellent breed type was passed on to many of his successful offspring.

Other imports included Int Ch Dalati Helgi, Int Ch Pencelli Hapus, Pencelli Proceed and INT SF N UCH Hillpark Robin Goodfellow from Great Britain, and Int Ch Envoy, Int Ch Clumbrolds Red Star and Int Ch Clumbrolds Purpurdod from Sweden.

In 1984, INT SF N UCH NORD-V–85,–86W–87,–88 Delkens Turul (Delkens Penniko ex Sh Ch Delkens Teralea) came to the ownership of Miss Marjo Jaakkola from Ken and Del Spate's kennel. His importance to today's Welsh Springers in Finland is prominent. He was a top winner in the showring, winning gundog groups at

INT SF N UCH NORD-V-85,-86,-87,-88 Delkens Turul.

The first time a Welsh Springer Progeny Group went BIS at the Helsinki International Championship Show. Int Ch Delkens Turul (far left) with progeny. Photo: Finnish Dognews

International Championship level, but made his biggest mark on his winning progeny (see picture overleaf), siring over 30 champions and many top winners in the breed, and he is behind many Welsh Springers in Finland.

The most successful breeder of Welsh Springers in Finland is Mrs Tiina Mattila with her Rwyn kennel. Her breeding started in 1977 with INT SF N UCH SF OBCH Gritty's Lily (Int Ch Dalati Dyma Fi ex Int Ch Gritty's Debutant). Mrs Mattila has bred over 50 champions, many international champions and numerous top winners, including SF UCH SF V–94 Rwyn Notre Dame (Int Ch Rwyn Xavier ex Int UCH SF W–90 Rwyn Galloise). One of the most successful brood bitches from this kennel was INT SF N UCH NORD V–87, EUR V-91 Clumbrolds Flitiga Lisa, who was by the very successful stud dog in Finland, INT UCH SF V–84 Envoy, out of Clumbrolds Beaubelle. Besides being an influential brood bitch, she was an excellent show bitch, going Best of Breed at 10 years of age at the European Winner Show in Finland in 1991.

INT SF DK EST UCH SF V-91 Sprightly Xylophone.

The Sprightly kennels of Mr Hannu Suonto started with the litter sister of Int Ch Gritty's Lily, Int Ch Gritty's Luminary. They have also bred several champions, the best known being INT SF DK EST UCH SF V–91 Sprightly Xylophone (Int Ch Delkens Turul ex Int Ch Sprightly Rusty Rose – pictured opposite below). She is the top winning Welsh Springer ever in Finland, with several group wins, Best in Show wins and placements.

Mrs Sari Kauppinen's Rocbee Welsh Springers started in 1985 with her foundation bitch INT SF N UCH Sprightly Ruby (Int Ch Envoy ex Ch Sprightly Pin-up Girl) and has bred several champions and winners, including group winner Rocbee Up-To-Date and Omt SF N UCH Rocbee Jonathan.

Other kennels that have bred several litters and champions include That Way, Llawen, Mawredd, Real Braf, Sweetie-pie, Lucky Moor and Twist And.

In the last few years, registrations of Welsh Springers in Finland have been around 150–180 per year.

France

Mme Brigitte Bolze tells the story of Welsh Springers in France.

The first Welsh Springer to be registered in France was a bitch imported from Britain, Peridot of Tarbay, bred by the late Dr Rickards. That was in 1958, and Peridot was in whelp to Sh Ch Mikado of Broomleaf when she was imported, giving the first litter in France. The breeders of the eight puppies were Dr Drouillard and his wife, very well known in the Cocker world. A bitch, Hilda du Valcain, was kept from the litter, and bred some successful puppies with the second English import, Myrddin Dewr. She ended her life in the home of the father of the Welshies in France, L R Veignat (Pilou), who fell in love with the breed and did a great deal for it and French breeding.

The first des Fretillants litter was born from Hilda and Dewr in July 1963, and a bitch was kept, Merry des Fretillants. She was bred with TR CH B Deri Day of Linkhill, from Ann West's kennel (Ch Ambassador or Linkhill ex Ch Katrina of Linkhill), which produced TR CH B Pat des Fretillants and his brother, Ch Porros des Fretillants, who was very successful in Eastern Europe. The mating was repeated, and resulted in TR CH B Quetzal des Fretillants, the Best Spaniel at the championship in Paris. Pilou Veignat had a few top-quality litters, keeping the real dual-purpose breed. All his champions were qualified in Field Trials, a working prize (TR: Trialler), which is necessary for a dog to qualify for the title of French Champion (CH B), or International Show Champion (CH IB). He exchanged dogs with Eastern countries, Hinckeldeyns and Grunda lines in particular, and bred several champions: TR CH B Usnee des Fretillants, TR CH B Jasmynn des Fretillants, and TR CH B IB Sharlotte des Fretillants, who was the most important brood bitch for the breed in France. Pilou was a very good judge, in shows and field trials, and judged in many countries, including Britain. He passed away in 1990 while still very young, leaving the minor varieties in France without a mentor.

I will never forget how Pilou Veignat let me choose the best of the only two puppies in a litter, having driven 3000km for the mating with the Dutch Ch Valentijn van Snellestein. That was Sharlotte, and all the French Welshies of the last 15 years have come down from her. Her litter brother, Sosie des Fretillants, was Best of Breed at the World Show in Madrid in 1984. Her successful offspring included TR CH B IB Monaco, Italy, Swiss Ulex du Mas de la Ranche, whose dam was daughter of the great import CH B IB FT Pencelli Gelert (Roger of Pencelli-Paula Girl of Pencelli, bred by Harold Newman). He was the first Welsh Springer to become a French Field Trial Champion, and is the sire of TR CH B Siani de Vaccares.

TR CH B IB Allowin des Terres Froides.

Sharlotte had a great influence on the breed in Europe. She was mated to Lux, Dutch, German Ch Idriss Cymro van Snellestein twice, resulting in six champions: TR UCH B IB Averell des Terres Froides, Best of Breed at the World Show in Brno in 1990; TR CH B IB Swiss Dutch Italy Lux Allowin des Terres Froides; TR CH B Alois des Terres Froides; UCH B IB FT Carlotta des Terres Froides, winner of four CCs in Field Trials; Dutch/Lux Ch Christophe des Terres Froides, and Dutch Ch Charlotte des Terres Froides. She also had a very successful litter by DK CH Trigger Osbourne.

TR CH B IB Averell des Terres Froides.

Of the next generation, Averell sired TR CH B IB Dalton Ma du Mas de la Ranche, best bitch at the World Show in Berne in 1994, and Swiss Ch Dalton Joe de Mas de la Ranche, reserve at this show. Averell is also father of the English litter, Torcello Esprit de Corps, Entente Cordais, Quelle Chance and La Petite Fleur.

From Allowin came TR CH B IB Swiss Chadock des Terres Froides, Best of Breed at the World Show in Berne in 1994, and a Best in Show winner. The sire was Dutch Ch Dalati Sawel. From a mating with Dutch Ch Nicolaas van Snellestein, Enguerrand des Terres Froides was Best in Show winner in Belgium. A further litter resulted from a mating with UCH B IB FT Trigger Red Baron (Trigger Dusty ex Highwinder Miss Lucy of Hackwood), a Swedish import, a real dual-purpose stud dog, producing TR CH B IB Gillie des Terres Froides and Gertrude des Terres Froides, a championship winner. Carlotta had two litters, the first with Multi-Champion Delkens Turul, producing Geromine des Terres Froides, reserve at the Dutch Club Match; and the second with TR Fabian Z Drsne Planiny, which produced TR CH B Iol du Val D`Arroux and TR CH B Irlys du Val D'Arroux, Best of Breed at the World Show in Brussels in 1995. From the same mating of Idriss with Sharlotte, Coralie des Terres Froides produced Ellowin du Mas de la Ranche (by Nicolaas van Snellestein), Best Bitch at the World Show in Barcelona in 1993, and by Pupsaint Parker, TR CH IB Heulwen du Mas de la Ranche.

In the next generation, Chadock is the father of CH DK IB French Duke des Terres Froides (by Mynnidmaen Bronwen), who was very successful in Denmark, and Erg de la Font de Se, well used at stud in Czechoslovakia.

So you can see that French breeding is of top quality in Europe, often winning the great international competitions, despite having only 40 Welshies born every year. Most Welsh Springers in France are used for hunting, and breeders are very careful about preserving the dual-purpose breed. Many are at the top level in Field Trials, and many have won the Field Trial ticket or the reserve. These include Sharlotte des Tretillants, Ulex du Mas de la Ranche, Allowin, Carlotta, Dorothee and Gille des Terres Froides, Irlys du Val D'Arroux, and the two imports, Dual Ch Pencelli Gelert and Trigger Red Baron.

The first Special FT Stake for Welsh Springer Spaniels in France.

Every year, we have special Field Trial stakes for Welsh Springers and in 1995, when only 20 puppies were born in the year, 16 Welshies competed at the same time, some of them from the Netherlands and Italy.

In 1992, Trigger Red Baron was 6th best Field Trial Springer winner (English and Welsh), winning a reserve at the French Cup.

We do not have many entries at shows – about 10 for a club match or championship.

In 1995, a new stud dog joined the French stock, having won well in Sweden: N UCH Inu Goya Ferrymaster (Ch Ferndel Fun at Inu Goya ex Ch Inu Goya Cloudberry).

Denmark

Merethe Andersen and Finn Nielson of Kennel Gallois have sent this brief history of Welsh Springers in Denmark.

Kennel Hoje Mon was the first to introduce the Welsh in Denmark. The owners, Ingelise and Ivan Selberg, had been at a field trial in Wales and were completely carried away by this breed. As a result, they imported their first Welsh bitch, Maroon Lotta, from Sweden in 1973, followed in 1974 by a bitch, Dalati Denol, and in 1975 a dog, Dalati Dyma Fi, from the Hunton Morgans in Wales.

These dogs were the breeding foundation until 1980, when two more Welsh Springers were imported from Sweden and Holland respectively.

Triggers Osborne and Rosa van Snellestein were the start of two new kennels, Sweet Chester, owned by Mette and Lars Kruuse, and Danebod, owned by Kirsten Hahn and Ove Noraett. The breeding foundation in Denmark is, therefore, a combination of Swedish and Dutch bloodlines. This is even more intensified by the fact that two more were imported from Holland: in 1988, Brynmore van Snellestein (Kamp Wessel v Dee Weidezoom ex Winsome Wendy v Snellestein), and in 1990, Booze Boleyn van Berkenstein (Dalati Sinsir ex Wainfelin Miss Money Penny), the breed record holder in Denmark, owned by Lena Sorensen. He won Best in Show at the Club Show in the Netherlands in 1993, and was shown by Mrs van Bindsbergen.

Booze Boleyn v Berkenstein. Photo: Lena Sørensen

In 1991, Kj Groth imported a French dog: French Duke des Terres Froides. This initiative adds a new bloodline to the Danish population of Welsh Springers, and others have been imported from Holland, Great Britain, Finland and Sweden during the past few years. As a result, the bloodlines in the population of Welsh Springers in Denmark vary considerably, and tend to go in different directions. From 1982 to 1994, the average number of registered Welshies is only 28 a year. During the last three years, 143 dogs have been registered, of which seven have been imported, so the number is increasing, and the number of the breed in Denmark is about 300–350.

It is only in recent years that you see Welshies in field and retrieving trials. They now enter in the picture from time to time, and it is quite obvious that in the years to come, more will attend the trials, as people become more and more aware of the importance of the dual-purpose dog.

Fourteen shows are held each year, seven international, and seven arranged by the Spaniel Club. At each show 7–10 Welsh Springers are entered, and the number is increasing as more litters are bred. Every dog receives a written judgment at the end of the show, giving the good points as well as the faults, and thus showgrounds are where the dogs are judged, and where there is the opportunity to use the written critiques as a guide when planning further breeding. The dogs are also presented with coloured ribbons to put on their leads, so that spectators can easily tell the placings of the dogs on the day.

DK UCH Cwrt Afon Harri.

Marethe Andersen and Finn Nielson registered their Gallois kennel in 1989, and their foundation bitch was from Kennel Chester, mating her to NL CH UW89 Northey Over the Rainbow from Holland (bred by Christine McDonald in England). Three years later, a bitch from that litter was mated to Sh Ch Ferndel Paper Moon (bred by John Thirlwell, also in England). In 1992, they imported DK Ch Cwrt Afon Harri from Len and Kath Morgan in Wales. He has been very successful in the showring, and his owners are enjoying seeing him working in field and retrieving trials.

Kennel Red and White's was started in 1987 by Birte Bjorn, with Sweet Chester's Corin (DK UCH Triggers Osborne ex DK UCH Chessie) from Lars Krusse's kennel. A bitch, Danebod's Diana Bianca (daughter of DK UCH Rosa van Snellestein) came a year later, and she has proved to be very successful in the showring and in the field. Her full title is DKCH KBCH BDSG91 INCH BDSG92 KBHV92 BESG93 VDHCH Danebod's Diana Bianca! Birte Bjorn writes: 'Bianca has all the qualities of a good show and breeding bitch. She is intelligent, loves to be in the centre of the showring, moves happily and fast, is a wonderful companion on travels, which she enjoys, because it means

DKCH KBCH BDSG91 INCH BDSG92 KBHV92 BESG93 VDHCH Danebord's Diana Bianca.
Photo: Marianne Bolsen.

meeting a lot of people. She has also inherited the hunting gene, and likes retrieving. She is a wonderful representative of the breed, and is an excellent brood bitch.'

A third import to this kennel is DK UCH KBHV95 Nikita Boleyn v Berkenstein from Holland: 'a very typical Welsh, nearly without any faults'. Birte Bjorn offers one outstanding dog from his Red and White's kennel: DK UCH Baffin at Last, jointly owned by Jesper Poulsen and Karin Larsen; he is a brave hunting dog, with successes in qualifying, field and retrieving trials.

In 1991, Lena Sorensen imported DK UCH Hillpark Sweet Song (Sh Ch Fiveacres Firecrest ex Hillpark Serenade). She went to just three shows and gained her title, and also passed the obedience test. She has had two litters: one by Danebods ed von Pax and the other by Kamp. Northoaks Sea Sun Flower (Holland). In 1992, Hammalgardens Lou Lou was imported from Gudrun Jonsson in Sweden and, a year later, Hammalgardens Jiggery Pokery joined the kennel, with Norwegian import Inu–Goya Fun Day.

DK INT UCH Sweet Chesters Hannibal.

Thomas Clausen started with a dog bred by Lars Kruuse, Sweet Chesters Hannibal (DK Ch, Int Ch Brynmore van Snellestein ex DK Chessie); he was Dog of the Year in 1992.

In 1995, Hammalgaardens Leader of the Pack (Weslave Wild Card ex Rwyn Galloise) joined the kennel.

Since 1970, 23 Welsh Springers have been imported to Denmark.

Hinckeldeyns Aar: the first Welsh Springer in Czechoslovakia (now the Czech Republic and Slovakia).

Czech Republic

For many years, I corresponded with Frantisek Liml, of the Grundon kennel in Kostelec nad Orlici, Czechoslovakia. His reports on Welsh Springers in his country regularly appeared in the Welsh Springer Spaniel Club Year Book, and were read with great interest. I am indebted to him for the information that enabled me to write the history of the breed in his country, but saddened by the fact that he is no longer with us to see it in print.

In 1963, Mr Liml imported Hinckeldeyns Aar (out of Rushbrooke Ringlet from Hal Leopard in England, and bred by Harry Hinckeldeyn in Germany), the first Welsh Springer in the country.

The following year, the first bitch arrived, Bright Poppet of Hearts (Brancourt Bang ex Brancourt Belinda – see previous page), bred by T Hubert Arthur.

These two were a gift from Mr Harry Hinckeldeyn in Hamburg. Three litters

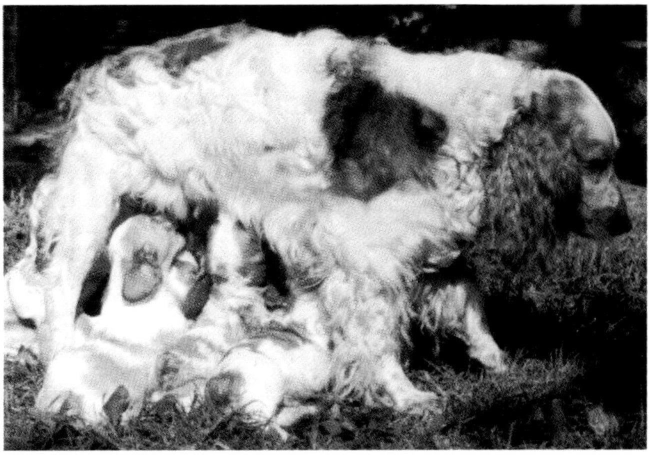

Bright Poppet of Hearts, the first Welsh Springer bitch in Czechoslovakia.

Charming.

Int Ch Mackie Grunda.

Reliance of Krackton.

were bred from this partnership, resulting in 13 dogs and 5 bitches being reared. According to the breeding rules at that time, no more than six puppies per litter were permitted to be raised, and six dog puppies had to be destroyed.

Aar then became sterile and, if breeding was to continue, a new dog or bitch had to be imported. As a result, Hinckeldeyns Elk (Porros des Fretillants ex Rhiannon of Tarbay) was imported from Germany, who was an outstanding dog.

In 1971, M Veignat in France sent Ugo des Fretillants to Mr Liml. In exchange, he received Flok Grunda (a son of Elk). In the same year, Mr Hinckeldeyn brought a dog from Holland to Mr Liml: Charming (Rushbrooke Ringer ex Dusky). This dog won six CACIBs, although he was only 45.5cm at the shoulder. The present KC standard gives an approximate height of 48cm.

The first International Champion, bred by Mr Liml, was CACIB, CACIT Mackie Grunda, who gained the title in 1971.

In 1973, Mr Hinckeldeyn sent another dog from Holland, Duskys Starters Ede (Reliance of Krackton ex Duskys Starters Deborah), so further breeding was assured.

Later, more dogs were imported from France, Holland and Sweden. A limit on breeding programmes was a condition: only a member of the Union of Czech Hunters could be a breeder, so breeding was confined almost entirely to hunters. Also, dogs and bitches could only be included in the breeding list after taking part in a show, and only dogs with minimum marks of Very Good (2nd place), and bitches with Good (3rd place) could be included.

It was also necessary to take a test for suitability for hunting, called 'autumn exams.' This was based on a demonstration of inherited and congenital qualities: a good nose, seeking in front of the gun, tracking, volume of barking on a scent or barking at an animal which can be seen, and fearlessness after a shot. This also included awareness of vermin (a cat in a cage), but that was phased out. It also consisted of retrieving furred and feathered animals, such as rabbit and pheasant, and retrieving birds such as duck from deep water. Since 1990, only the first part of the exam – natural ability, demonstrating inborn and inherited qualities – has been required to get the breeding certificate. It was no longer necessary to be a member of the Union of Czech Hunters (today called the Czech–Moravian Union of Hunters), so that those that do not hunt can breed dogs too. But another condition was added: the dog had to be successful at a higher standard show – National, Club or International.

Int Ch Lucky Leicester of the Half House retrieving a wild boar.

Dogs, both male and female, can take part in other special tests in predominantly wooded areas (seeking wounded animals), and water tests for wild duck. Tests are also held where dogs work in fields, woods and water as well, lasting two days.

Every year, the Milena Sterbove Memorial is organised, for dogs that have got the highest marks at previous general tests, and the winners of this is awarded the title of CACIT or Reserve CACIT. Seven Welsh Springer dogs and one bitch have gained the title of CACIT, and 26 dogs and 18 bitches have gained CACIBs in the showring.

In competition with other hunting spaniels in the Czech Republic, Welsh Springers are doing very well. For example, at the autumn tests in 1989, they were placed as follows:

	lst	**2nd**	**3rd**
Welsh Springers	35%	24%	20%
English Springers	24%	24%	24%
Cocker Spaniels	21%	27%	14%

Welsh Springers are highly valued for their excellent barking when they pick up the animal's scent, brilliant nose, and willingness to work in water. They proved their qualities at seeking animals of all sizes, including boars.

Int Ch Lucky Leicester of the Half House was imported by J Frencl from Minka Crucq in Holland (Delkens Rebel Reeba ex Hylon Nana of the Half House).

Ch CSSR Betty Jifex.

The Tracking Dog Breeders' Club has about 300 members who are breeders of Welsh Springer Spaniels. Approximately the same number of breeders are not members of the club. About 130 registered dogs and bitches are kept for breeding. Bitches may not be used for breeding after they have reached eight years of age; there is no age limit on the use of dogs for breeding. Each year, 120–150 puppies are born and there is no longer a limit on the number of puppies reared. Breeding is managed by a Breeding Adviser who advises the bitch owner of three suitable dogs.

These people are responsible for the introduction of breeding standards in the Czech Republic: Mr Harry Hinckeldeyn (Germany), Mr Veignat and Mr Mainard (France), Mrs Minka Crucq and Mrs Horter (Holland) and Mr Rolf Kindstrand (Sweden).

Mr Liml also told me that there has been a breeder of Welsh Springers in Poland for several years, and that there is also a kennel in Cyprus.

Slovakia

There are only three or four breeders of Welsh Springers in Slovakia. About 20 puppies are registered each year. There is still a condition that a dog or bitch must have a Field Working Certificate before it can be used for breeding.

Mark Hamer, former Chairman and now a Vice President of the Welsh Springer Spaniel Club in the United Kingdom, gave me this information, following a visit to the Janek family. Their first bitch, Linda of Lamaca, gained the title of Champion in the showring in 1984, but unfortunately was run over subsequently. She had Plattburn and French blood on her sire's side and was from a Czech bitch. Two puppies have been imported from Rolf and Kiki Kindstrand's kennel in Sweden, and these have been successfully bred from.

Canada

Beth Marley, a voracious statistician and breed correspondent, has furnished me with the information to write this section.

In 1949, the first Welsh Springers to be registered in Canada were a bitch, Countess Hobo of Dale, and a dog, Prince Bohunk. They were owned by Mr J R H Kirkpatrick of Kitchener, Ontario. No litters produced were from them, and nothing was heard of their owner until 1996, when he arrived at a show to see the Welsh. He had been in England to look for a puppy. His first Welsh was a wedding gift from his wife; he was with the Royal Navy during the war, stationed in Trinidad, and took the dog with him. They moved to Canada after the war, and he imported the third Welsh Sopringer from Boston in the early 1950s. Countess Hobo was bred by Mr W H Rann fof Great Britain, and was imported in 1945; Prince Bohunk was bred by Mr D E R Griffith in Wales in 1943.

Twenty years passed before the first Welsh Springer litter was registered. Eve Carter of Schomberg, Ontario, imported Rona of Pencelli from Harold Newman's kennel in

South Wales. This was the foundation bitch of the Ghost Inn kennel. She was in whelp to Nobleman of Tregwillym, and was litter mate to Sh Ch Marie of Pencelli and Am Ch Bachgen Dewr of Pencelli. Most puppies born today in Canada go back to Rona and Nobleman. Nobleman was exported to Finland in 1979.

Four from that first litter of ten puppies gained their titles: three Canadian Champions and one American CD. They were Can Ch Ghost Inn's Fashion Plate, owned by Mrs Carter; Can Ch GI Peredur O'Coedmawr, owned by Mrs Peggy Saltman who lived in Newfoundland; Can Ch GI Sweetheart, owned by Jim McIvor in Ontario; and GI Matador CD, the seventh Welsh Springer to earn an obedience title in North America, owned by Helen Mateer of Tennessee, .

The foundation dog of the Ghost Inn kennel was Can Ch Tidemarsh Roger, imported from Gordon Pattinson in England (Stokecourt Sam ex Lingholm Rhoda).

Another import from the United Kingdom., Knockmains Glenlossie (Sh Ch Dalati Briog of Walgoreg ex Canisbay Heather of Knockmains), bred by Jock Beattie, gained his CD in 1996 and has now gained his Championship title.

Can Ch Ghost Inn's Peredur was the foundation

Ghost Inn's Autumn Glory.

Can Ch Ghost Inn's Peredur O'Coedmawr.

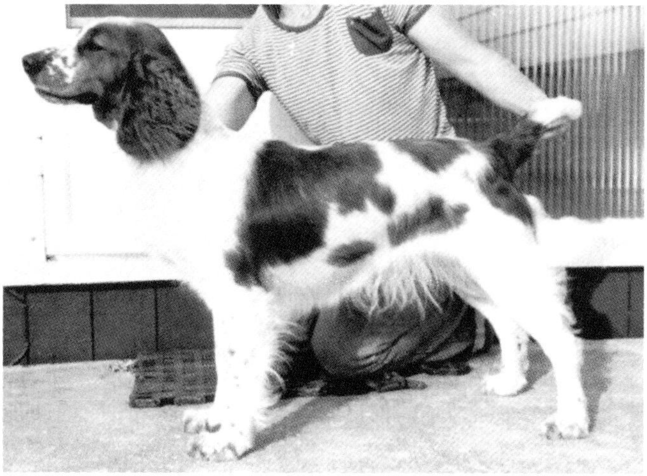

Can Ch Coedmawr Ceri Elen.

of **Newfoundland** Peggy Saltman's Coedmawr kennel, which has produced many of Canada's top Welsh, and holds several breed records. Peggy has owned and shown the breed longer than anyone in the country. She describes Peredur (see previous page) as the nicest Welsh she has ever owned. He had good structure, a great personality, and produced fine puppies. He had a successful career, taking Best Canadian Bred Puppy in Group at the Newfoundland KC Show, and gaining his title in 1969.

Peggy had imported her first Welsh, Ceinwen of Tregwillym, from Cliff Payne's kennel in Wales in 1962. Ceinwen was the third Welsh registered with the Canadian Kennel Club, and the first to earn a Canadian title. In the early 1960s, a handful of the breed was being shown in the United States, and only Ceinwen in Canada. She enjoyed an outstanding show career, gaining two Group lsts, two Group 2nds, two Group 3rds, and three Group 4ths – a Canadian record for a Welsh that stands today.

Unsuccessful attempts to breed Ceinwen to Peredur led Peggy back to Wales for another bitch, Tregwillym Merionwen, and from her and Peredur, she had three litters. This was the beginning of the Coedmawr line of Welsh Springers (see picture of Can Ch Coedmawr Ceri Elen on previous page).

Coedmawr Welsh were the foundation of breeding programmes in Quebec and Western Canada, and two-thirds of all Canadian Welsh have Coedmawr in their background. They have proved themselves in show, obedience, tracking and hunting, and are behind more than half the group placements awarded to Welsh at Canadian shows. In 1979, another import from Cliff Payne, Tregwillym Delightful Prince, joined the kennels, and he too gained his title.

In **Ontario,** Can Ch Ghost Inn's Sweetheart was the foundation bitch for Jim McIvor, producing 20 puppies, and is famous as the dog on the Cheese Milk Bones box.

Through occasional breedings, and a readiness to share his knowledge of and enthusiasm for the breed, Jim has played a major role in the establishment of Welsh Springers in Ontario. His dogs accompany him to work every day, and are wonderful breed ambassadors.

Can Ch Ghost Inn's Sweetheart.

Gerry and Nan Curry's Havenbrooke kennel was founded with a bitch, Velka Klajdoyka of Havenbrooke (by Hillpark Sky Rocket, imported from our kennel in England by Jim McIvor, to a Czech bitch), and a dog was imported from Czechoslovakia in 1990, Nero Z Hejlicku. Sky Rocket was by Sh Ch Hillpark Mr Polly out of Sh Ch Hillpark Reverie.

Welsh Springers in **Quebec** started in 1975, when Andree Plante imported three month old Shanvana Yevan (Dalati Dyma Fi ex Tamara of Mottisfont) from Mrs S E Read's kennel in England. The following year, Can Ch Coedmawr Seren Aur (Can Ch Ghost Inn's Peredur O'Coedmawr ex Can Ch Tregwillym Merionwen) became a 'Springer Gaulois'. This group-placing bitch from Peggy Saltman's first litter had been number two Welsh in Canada in 1974. The third import was Kenwater Poppy (Golden Shot of Tregwillym ex

Dayhouse Golden Privet) from D E Phillips in England, and the foundation of her Roseraie kennel was complete.

Between 1976 and 1979, six Welsh Springer litters were born in Quebec, almost certainly the only ones ever whelped in that province. Shanvana sired five of the six litters, and was double grandsire of the sixth. Seren was the dam of two of the litters; Poppy was dam of three. The sixth litter was sired by a Seren son out of a Poppy daughter.

At a time when few Welsh were being shown in North America, it is remarkable that almost one-third of those born in Quebec were shown. Five completed championships; three gained obedience titles, and Can Ch Rose de Mars CD was a group-placer, and was Canada's top Welsh in 1978. In 1977, Andree Plante's home was burned. Six dogs died: Seren was one of them. Andree gave Can Ch Kenwater Poppy to Madeleine Magnan, who owned Prince du Portage CD from the first Roseraie litter. Poppy was bred to Can Ch Shanvana Yevan once more, and from that litter, Madeleine kept Dalati Yevan, who made breed history in 1982 when he became the first undocked Welsh to gain a Championship in North America.

Can/Am Ch Bankdam's Bobby Dazzler.

After the devastating fire, Andree Plante stopped breeding and showing Welsh. The last litter to be born in Quebec (Sieur Picco de la Roseraie ex Can Ch Rose de Mars CD) was bred by Michel Bouchard in 1979.

One of the earliest supporters of Welsh Springers in Canada was Gordon Wilkinson who, with his wife Shirley, was a pioneer in establishing the breed in **Western Canada**. Their first Welsh, Can Ch Bankdam's Taffy Bark, was the first of the breed to gain a championship west of Ontario. Taffy was joined by Coedmawr Megan of Bankdam in 1976 and by Am Ch Pencelli Pandour in 1978 to form the foundation of Bankdam Welsh Springers. All three gained their Canadian championships: two were group placers, and Megan is the first and only Welsh to have won a BPIG. Gordon was a founder member of the first Welsh Springer Spaniel Club of Canada, and its first president. The club held successful boosters in British Columbia in 1978 and in Saskatchewan in 1979, with entries of seven and nine.

The first Taffy–Megan litter produced a dog that is, arguably, the top Welsh ever bred in Canada. Can & Am Ch Bankdam's Bobby Dazzler (see previous page), owned by Sally Pearson of British Columbia. Through Bobby, Bankdam influence continues to be felt. The top Welsh Springer in Canada in 1993, 1994 and 1995, the top Welsh in the United States in 1994 *and* 1995, Best Bitch at the WSSCA National Specialty in 1995, and America's top obedience Welsh two years running all have Bobby as a great-grandsire.

In 1983 Can & Am Ch Killagay Court Jester became the first Welsh Springer to be awarded Best in Show in Canada. His great-grandmother was Can Ch Rona of Pencelli's litter sister, Can Sh Ch Marie of Pencelli; his sire was Am Ch Pencelli Tomas, his dam Am Ch Killagay O'Kintyre, and he was bred by Connie Christie in Virginia.

After more than 30 years, only two or three litters are registered a year. Most Welsh born in Canada are sold as companions, a few go to hunting homes, a few more are shown. In 1968, nine were registered; 15 in 1978; 36 in 1988; and 25 in 1995. Despite their proximity to the United States, until recently, the breed in Canada has developed almost entirely independently of our neighbour to the south. In addition, interest in the breed in Canada is now, and always has been, confined to a few isolated pockets.

Stud Book

By law all dogs sold as purebred in Canada must be registered with the Canadian Kennel Club. The CKC Stud Book is a record of registrations. The 'Foreign Dogs Registered by Breed' section of the Stud Book includes dogs registered with the CKC for the purpose of showing in Canada, as well as imports. Between the years 1968 and 1984 inclusive, no stud book was published by the CKC.

Australia

I have received the information for this section from the New Zealand Kennel Club, Mrs Frances (Bobbie) Hitchcock, former President of the Welsh Springer Spaniel Club of New South Wales, and Jim and Sue Simmonds.

It appears that some Welsh Springers were exported to Australia before the Second World War. Although there were some reports of them in various parts of the country, they were lost from the gundog scene. No records were to be found, and it was not until 1973 that two Welsh Springers were imported by Mr and Mrs S Jeffery (Talgarth) when they returned to Australia: a dog, Plattburn Paceman, and a bitch Plattburn Pi, bred by Ken Burgess. From this combination, the first litter was registered in 1974, and three of them were shown. One was owned by Sally Hartley of the Wildheart German Shorthaired Pointers and Golden Retrievers, and another she had in partnership with Bob Philp, a well-known breeder, exhibitor and judge of gundogs. The third, Talgarth Tim, was owned by Arthur O'Dell and Kevin O'Neill, and in 1975 he was the first Welsh Springer to win a Challenge Certificate at Sydney Royal Show.

Aust Ch Talgarth Cassandra CD.

Sue and Jim Simmonds (Pennlyon), purchased Talgarth Temptation (Holly) for Joyce Beaver, Sue's mother. Holly was the first Welsh Springer to win a Royal CC and Best of Breed at the Sydney Royal, in 1976. Two litters were bred from her: from the first, three went on to be Australian champions, and one a New Zealand champion. From the second came three Australian Champions, and Catriona O'Sullivan took Pennlyon Ester to CDX.

Talgarth Tasha (litter sister to Temptation, and bought by the Simmonds) also gained her title, and a CD (Companion Dog). From her only litter, she had three Australian Champions. Bobbie Hitchcock had a bitch from the first litter of the Plattburn combination, Talgarth Cassandra (see previous page). She gained her title in 1977, and her obedience title the following year, the first Welsh Springer to achieve this. Bobbie says: 'When we first started showing and obedience work, we were told to take the dog out of the ring, as it was for pedigree dogs. We were at that time the only Welsh in the ring for obedience work. However, we did educate the judges, and it was not long after that that there a few more Welshies in the ring.'

The Simmonds' first three litters were sired by Ch Pencelli Prospect (Rufus), imported in 1976 from Harold Newman's kennel in Wales. 'He was never very happy in the ring, but he was worth importing for his pups alone, and his beautiful, loving nature made him an absolute joy to live with.' Rufus sired nine litters, producing 27 Australian Champions and one New Zealand champion. He retired in 1981 at the age of 8½ with a Best in Group under Dr Harry Spira and 1014 Challenge points. He had 16 Group awards, a Reserve Best in Show and a Best in Show. He came out of retirement two years later on the Welsh Springer Spaniel Club's first picnic parade, and took Best Exhibit under Gundog judge Jim McCreadie – 'the only time Rufus actually enjoyed being shown'. Sue Simmonds considered Rufus' greatest success was an Open in Group at Canberra, when he beat a line-up of multi-BIS winners. Unfortunately, the only picture available does not reflect his quality.

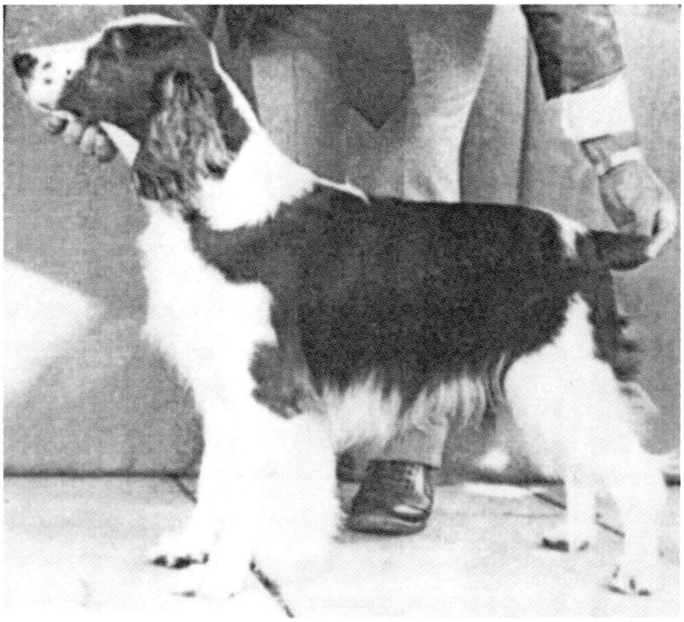

Aust Ch Pencelli Prospect.

Bobbie's Ch Talgarth Cassandra was mated to Pencelli Prospect to produce the first of the Rhiwderin lines. She then imported our Hillpark Cicero (Dewi of Tregwillym ex Sh Ch Hillpark Pollyanna) in 1979, and used him on some of the progeny of her first litter. His son, Rhiwderin Bryn, obtained his champion status in 1982, and his CD in 1986. Bryn was then mated to Mrs Tess Hay's Brynderyn Blaenaf; this resulted in Ch Rhiwderin Talgarth. He was due to be trialled in 1987, but Bobbie was unable to continue as a result of a car accident. The Brynderin kennel was founded on Rhiwderin and Pennlyon stock.

Cliff Bilston from Victoria had a puppy from the Pennlyon kennel, sired by Ch Pencelli Prospect; he not only showed Welsh Springers, but worked them in the field. He also owned labradors but, after seeing the Welsh work, he soon had only this breed in his kennels. He wrote of his untrained Welsh bitch retrieving on a duck shoot 'in fine style'.

In 1981, New Zealand Ch Dalati Heledd was sent to be mated to Ch Pencelli Prospect, and two of the offspring became Champions. Heledd was then mated twice to Pennlyon Fergus, and Champions were produced from both these litters.

From this information, one can see that the Pennlyon and Rhiwderin kennels contributed greatly to the establishment of the Welsh Springer in Australia.

In 1978, Bob Lott from Adelaide imported Dalati Gammath from the United Kingdom to go with his Pennlyon stock. At about the same time, Scott and Eira Taylor imported into New Zealand Sh Ch Tregwillym Golden Gem and her grandson, Tregwillym Taliesin, from Cliff Payne's kennel. The Taylors moved to Victoria and New South Wales, where they established the Nantyderi kennels, and these imports are in many pedigrees going back over a number of years. They also imported NZ Ch Warwick Red Handed and NZ Ch Levana Adam Laird from New Zealand; the Forbes imported Dalati Myfanwy from the Hunton Morgans in Wales, and the Swaingers imported Levana Cymry from New Zealand, while Levana Benson went to Peter Montgomerie.

Mr and Mrs P Lawless' Bryndoain kennel in New Zealand was based on Northey blood, imported from Christine McDonald in England, and Peter Jones imported Bryndoain Brigadier (who later gained his title) to become the foundation dog of his Plattwood kennel in Sydney. Four other Bryndoain Welsh Springers were imported by various breeders in Australia.

In 1984, the first Welsh Springer to arrive in Australia in whelp (to top sire Sh Ch Dalati Sioni) was Sh Ch Beaconside Siw. She was imported from John Thirlwell in England by Sylvia and Bill Crozier (Slyvkin) and Mary and David Forbes (Milwrmlaen), and was the foundation bitch of their jointly-owned HenEpil kennels in New South Wales.

Since then, new blood from many of British lines has been imported, and new kennels continue to emerge. The number of registrations remains quite low, at about 100 per annum.

In 1982, Bobbie Hitchcock and Tess Hay produced the first Welsh Springer Spaniel Social Club newsletter. Fifteen people from nine kennels attended a meeting of those interested in the breed, with a view to forming a Club. Eighteen members were present on 7 November 1982, when the Constitution of the Welsh Springer Spaniel Club was adopted, with Bobbie as President and Tess as Secretary. Originally, it was 'of Australia', and subsequently 'of Australasia'. On the same day, the Club's first Specialty Show was held. In 1984, the Welsh Springer Spaniel Club of New South Wales was adopted, and is the only Breed Club in Australia. A number of Open Shows were held annually, and the first approved Championship Show in Australia for Welsh Springers was held in 1989. Two Championship Shows have been held every year since. There are about 100 members of the Club at present, which include those from Australia, New Zealand and Asia.

Tail Docking

There are a few vets who refuse to dock tail. Bobbie Hitchcock prefers not to dock, and has requests for tails to be left on; she tends to dock two thirds of the litter. She writes: 'When the tail is in full feather, it is absolutely magnificent. Some people tend to hold the tail where it should have been docked, but I have been doing it the way the setters are shown; if it is a happy dog and wagging its tail, I let it sway. At present, the issue has gone underground.'

New Zealand

I asked Conrad Hardy of the Ap Daffyd kennel to tell us about the breed in his country.

The advent of Welsh Springers in New Zealand started in the mid 1970s, with the importation of Talgarth Tarragon (Plattburn Paceman ex Plattburn Pi) by Mrs Val Giblin, from the combination of breeding in Australia by Mr and Mrs Jeffrey from their two United Kingdom Plattburn imports. They were so taken with 'Ben' that they decided to import a bitch from the United Kingdom, and thus start the first of many New Zealand-bred Welsh Springers. The bitch they purchased in 1976 was Dalati Heledd (Sh Ch Progress of Pencelli ex Ch Dalati Fflur) from Noel and Dodo Hunton Morgans. 'Della', as she was known, became the first Champion in New Zealand, and progeny from her first litter became the foundation for Bryndoain kennel of Pat and Sue Lawless, and also of the Warwick/Nantyderi kennels of Scott and Eira Taylor.

From this first litter came the first New Zealand-bred Champion, NZ Ch Levana Alvin, as well as the first Field Trial qualified dog, NZ Ch Levana Ambassador QC; Alvin gained his QC at a later date.

The first shows in New Zealand had mainly three dogs, Alvin, Ambassador and litter brother Adam Laird, competing for Best Dog. Bitches were even less numerous: Levana Amy was the only one being shown.

During the late 1970s, there were three more importations from the United Kingdom to increase the lines available, as each kennel started on a path to develop their own type. The first to arrive were from Mr H C Payne's kennel were Sh Ch Tregwillym Golden Gem (Golden Shot of Tregwillym ex Sh Ch Golden Tint of Tregwillym), and her grandson, Tregwillym Taliesin (Dewi of Tregwillym ex Tregwillym Golden Honey). These two were subsequently mated, and produced NZ/Aust Ch Warwick Red Handed, who became the first Welsh Springer to attain a Best in Show Specialty at Championship level.

Another import to appear at the same time was Titoki Kiri (Sh Ch Plattburn Pinetree ex Dunwill Gill). She attained her NZ title, and was mated once, although the progeny did not breed on successfully.

At the end of the 1970s, Mr and Mrs Taylor moved to Australia with their Tregwillym-based stock, to start their kennels based at Tamworth. In 1980, a dog from the Australian-based Taylor kennels came to New Zealand, and was to become the biggest winner at All Breed level in New Zealand. He attained top honours at Group and In Show level in his six-year show career, the height of which was winning three Best in Show All Breeds, and with them the title NZ Grand Champion/Australian Champion. This dog was Nantyderi Red Demon Imp (Aust/NZ Ch Levana Adam Laird ex Sh Ch Aust/NZ Ch Tregwillym Golden Gem).

During this period of initial breeding, a few problems came forward, namely fitting, hip dysplasia, entropion (inwards-turning eyelids) and poor temperament. The main concern for breeders at this stage was the health of the breed, with people looking overseas for help to improve the base stock that we all had started with. A watershed year was 1981 with the importation of Northey Sauterne (Sh Ch Dalati Braint ex Byrony of Banlieue) and Northey Walnut (Sh Ch Goldsprings Bright Spark of Selworthy ex Northey Stonechat). From these dogs came the basis for the Bryndoain Kennels of Pat and Sue Lawless, the start of Yasha Kennels for Yvonne Ash and her daughter, Anthea and, latterly, Ap Daffyd kennels for Conrad Hardy. From the first mating of NZ Ch Northey Sauterne to Ch Levana Alvin QC came Aust Ch BryndoianBrigadier, who became the start of the Plattwood Kennels of Peter Jones and Kevin O'Neil in Australia. From these kennels stock has been imported/exported between both countries.

In 1983 came another first for Welsh Springers: the importation of a bitch in whelp. Northey Sangara (litter sister to Northey Sauterne) was in whelp to Sh Ch Golden Boy of Tregwillym. From this mating another kennel started on its way: Debbie and Murray Christensen's Shogun lines.

During the mid 1980s, one dog came to the fore as a top winner at All Breed and Specialty level. Ch Yasha Arbennig (NZ Ch Northey Walnut ex Ch Bryndoain Candytuft) was a great ambassador for the breed but, alas, did not produce any offspring.

NZ Ch Highclare Golden Wonder.

At the end of this decade, we had a chance to meet and show under Christine McDonald. To this day she has had the largest assembly of Welsh Springers ever – 27 – and there is a photo to prove it. The day was memorable, as it was the first time that we had all been together with everything that we had, including lots of veterans. In 1990, we were treated to a visit by Mark Hamer, who judged an Open show for the Auckland Spaniel Club. This was the first time that a Welsh Springer specialist had been able to judge at a recognised show.

I must mention two dogs at this time who would play a great part in the future, both from Australia. The first is Aust/NZ Ch Plattwood Progressor (Aust Ch Bryndoain Brigadier ex Aust Ch Balcraig Blazeaway), who was in New Zealand on lease, and whilst here was used on a couple of occasions, leaving some nice progeny behind. The second to mention is the bitch Slyvkin Iolanthe (Dalati Capten of Michandra ex Country Maid of Ferndel). She was chosen by Mrs Ash, and has been bred from, thus introducing new lines to our gene pool.

Some more stock was imported in 1991 from both Australia and the United Kingdom. A top winning dog in the form of Aust/NZ Ch Penbryn Braint (Aust Ch Janoda Thomas ex Plattwood Perfecta) hit the show scene by storm, and left his stamp on many of his offspring. Our first British import for some years arrived in the South Island kennel of Christine and Gordon Snow. Menstonia Martyka (Sh Ch Ringleader of Haslemount ex Menstonia Martinique) was shown and titled, and has since produced offspring to another English import also owned by the same kennel, Russethill Raincheck (Sh Ch. Fiveacres Firecrest x Russethill Renate) who also became titled. Christine and Gordon's Tregaron kennel is the only breeding kennel in the South Island.

This brings us almost to the present day. In 1993, Scott and Eira Taylor of Nantyderi returned to New Zealand from Australia, thus bringing back some of the older lines which had not been used for some time. Also, we welcomed the arrival of Graeme and Bonnie Scales from England. With them came two imports, NZ Ch Highclare Golden Wonder (Ch Northey Whittington ex Highclare Special Formula) (see previous page), and Pasondela Blue Spar (Sh Ch Dalati Siwbrd ex Ch Northey Showboat).

Since this time, there have been two more imports for Graeme and Bonnie: Kazval Bondalero (Ferndel Freshman ex Sh Ch Canisbay Captivation of Kazval) and, most recently, the first bitch from Sweden, Don's Here There Everywhere S UCH Don's Thunderstorm ex Beradene The Winter Breeze). The last dog to mention as a British import is my own Aust/NZ Ch Aranwr Pryderi (Sh Ch Wainfelin Barley Mo ex Dalati Prydwen). Hopefully, with this new stock and recent arrivals,we will have a wider scope in breeding, as it has introduced dogs that have not been in the New Zealand pedigrees before.

It is now 20 years since our first importation. Altough we may be small in number, and the furthest away from the originating country, we are a dedicated group, striving to continue to promote our breed as a merry, all-purpose, healthy dog, to be enjoyed in every facet of the dog world.

In conclusion...

I find it most interesting to read how all the countries have founded their kennels in so many different ways. No doubt the breed will grow from strength to strength all over the world.

chapter 13
Breeders Past and Present

Notable Breeders of the Past

Colonel J Downes Powell (O'Matherne)

Colonel Downes Powell was the 'Father of the Breed', founding the Welsh Springer Spaniel Club in 1922, and nurturing it through to his death in 1958. His obituary is included in Chapter 2: Development of the Breed.

Richmond Championship Show, 1951.
(Left) Hal Leopard with Ch Rushbrooke Runner.
(Centre) Judge: E Turner.
(Right) Dorothy Morriss with Stokecourt Saki.

Hal Leopard, 1990.

H J H Leopard (Rushbrooke)

From 1947–1963, Mr Harold Leopard was Secretary of the Welsh Springer Spaniel Club; then he was Chairman for four years, and finally President until 1975. He joined the Club in 1929, and before the First World War he had been Assistant Secretary. His Rushbrooke Welsh Springers were well known as highly successful dual-purpose dogs. Rushbrooke Racer was the Welsh Springer of the Year in 1950, with several Certificates of Merit at Field Trials, whilst Ch Rushbrooke Runner was the second post-war Champion in the breed, and Dog of the Year in1951. Runner typifies the best in the breed – the dual-purpose Field Trial and Show Bench winner. The Rushbrooke kennel was one of the dominant kennels on the working side for many years.

In 1965, a special General Meeting of the Welsh Springer Spaniel Club was held, when it was announced that a new Club, the Welsh and English Counties Spaniel Club, had been formed for those interested in Field Trials for spaniels. The new Club was sponsored by the Welsh Springer Spaniel Club, and it was agreed that the Field Trial Committee of the Club should be appointed to serve as committee of the new Club. Mr Leopard became its Secretary, and continued as the Delegate to the Field Trial Council, a post which he held until 1974.

Mrs Marjorie Mayall (Rockhill)

Mrs Marjorie Mayall died in 1956. She was one of the greatest supporters of the Welsh Springer Spaniel that the breed has ever had; the dogs were part of her life.

She joined the Welsh Springer Spaniel Club in 1923, soon after it was formed, and her Rockhill affix, which became so well known, is to be found in many pedigrees if one goes back far enough.

Apart from achieving great success in the showring, she was a great enthusiast of the working dog. Her first Welsh Springer was a bitch called Adcombe Flush. At her first show, where the judge was Col Downes Powell, she won the Bitch Challenge Certificate and, a few months later, she had awards at the Club's Trials.

It is recorded that, with the exception of the War years of 1939–1945, there was hardly a Championship Show where Welsh Springers were classified without entries from the Rockhill kennel, and Mrs Mayall regularly ran dogs at the Club's Field Trials with great success.

The Rockhill Welsh Springers were always 'true to type, and no one knew better than she the correct points of the breed, although she could never be persuaded to judge,' so her obituary read. Her best known winners were Ch Mair O'Cwm before the war, and Ch Rockhill Rhiwderin after the war.

Rushbrooke Kennels, 1951.

Ch Rockhill Rhiwderin, CC and BOB Crufts 1960.
At that time he was owned by Frank Hart.

Rockhill Welsh Springers, 1939.

It can be seen in old photographs of the Rockhill dogs that they had well broken red and white coats, and this feature was passed down to our first Welsh Springer, Polly Garter of Doonebridge, a granddaughter of Ch Rockhill Rhiwderin.

Frank Hart (Denethorp)

Denethorp Driag (left) and Danny, 1952.

Frank Hart was one of the great breeders of dual-purpose Welsh Springers in the years after the Second World War. He had seen the breed before the First World War but, at that time, he was working English Springers and was not interested in the showring.

In 1943, he bought a bitch puppy, Treorchy Megan, from Harold Newman and she met with great success in the showring. She had five litters, one by Harold Newman's Deri Di, and four by the famous Dewi Sant. Harold Newman had one of the puppies, Denethorp Dido, who gained her title and was a great winner in the showring, with 11 Challenge Certificates to her credit. That was in the 1950s, when there were about 10 sets of Challenge Certifiates on offer each year. Now 27 sets are awarded annually. Another of the puppies was bought by Captain and Mrs Mayall, Rockhill Rona, the dam of the great Ch Rockhill Rhiwderin, another very big winner of the time. Riwderin came back to Frank Hart after Mrs Mayall's death and went on to win his 12th Challenge Certificate.

Denethorp dogs had considerable successes in Brace classes and Frank Hart was very proud of his pair, Ch Denethorp Driag and Denethorp Danny. He considered Col Downes Powell's Ch Marksman O'Mathern the best Welsh Springer that he had ever seen. Of his own dogs, his choice was Ch Denethorp Danny, who was awarded a Certificate of Merit and was a very fine gundog.

Frank Hart took a great interest in our own progress from the time that we came into the breed with a bitch sired by his famous Sh Ch Denethorp Dihewyd, and was always generous with help and advice. He told me that he expected his dogs to be out working one day and in the showring the next, and he had an abhorrence for severe trimming.

Denethorp blood was also behind Ken Burgess' very successful Plattburn kennel.

Towards the end of his life, we called on Frank Hart at his home in Lancashire. Although he had little sight, he was watching the Test Match on television, another great interest of his. At his request, we brought in two of our dogs who were on holiday with us, and my lasting memory of Frank Hart is seeing his hands going over the dogs with tears in his eyes. They were offspring of the dog to which he had given Best of Breed at his last judging appointment in 1975, Sh Ch Hillpark Mr Polly, grandson of Sh Ch Denethorp Dihewyd.

Ann West (Linkhill)

Ann West's Linkhill was very successful in the 1950s and 1960s. Sh Ch Belinda of Linkton was the first of the kennel to gain her title, and was the dam of the big winnner, Sh Ch Arabella of Linkhill.

Arabella was mated twice to Cliff Payne's great sire, Ch Statesman of Tregwillym, and from the first litter came the outstanding winner, Sh Ch Deri Darrell of Linkhill, who was the breed record holder of the time, with 26 Challenge Certificates to his name. When we came into showing in the 1960s, having the same surname initial meant that we were benched near Ann West, and the red cards and green CCs demanded admiration. We joined in with the celebrations at Crufts – and the whiskey – after Deri had won Best of Breed for the fifth year in succession; three times he was Reserve in the Gundog Group, and also had the distinction of going Best in Show at WELKS in 1964. We had our own personal interest too, as Deri was great-grandsire of our bitch, Polly Garter of Doonebridge, so we were justly proud.

On the repeat mating of Arabella to Statesman, there was another big winner, Sh Ch Liza of Linkhill, who won nine CCs.

Sh Ch Belinda of Linkton.

Linkhill Welsh Springers at home.

Harold Newman (Pencelli)
I wrote an obituary to this great man when he died in 1980. His death marked the end of an era in the Welsh Springer world; when the Pencelli kennel came to an end after 51 years, it was an irreplaceable loss to the breed.

Harold's life with dogs started in 1925 with Sealyhams, and in 1929 he bought his first Welsh Springer. Then followed Cocker Spaniels, Welsh Terriers, Wire and Smooth Fox Terriers, Corgis, Setters, and Pointers, and Beagles – and Welsh Springer Spaniels.

Harold's first big winner in

Sh Ch Easter Parade.

Sh Ch Progress of Pencelli.

the 1930s was Sh Ch Dere Mhlaen, son of Ch Marksman O'Matherne, followed by many other title holders, with such great names at Sh Ch Dewi Sant, who appears in every pedigree today, Sh Ch Easter Parade (see previous page) and Show Champions Roger and Progress, who had such an influence on the breed, both in this country and overseas.

Harold built up a reputation for exporting first class stock, and was justly proud of the titles which they gained. He was particularly proud of Sh Ch Roger's son, Australian Champion Prospect of Pencelli, who was such an outstanding success out there in promoting the breed. There were others in Holland, Sweden, the United States and Canada. Am Ch Hillpark Caesar, Sh Ch Progress's son, had won Best of Breed at their Westminster show three years running, and Harold had a new champion in Finland just a week before he died.

One of his proudest moments was at Windsor Championship Show in 1979, when Progress took first place in the All Breeds Progeny class, a very popular win.

Harold Newman joined the Committee of the Welsh Springer Spaniel Club in 1948, and was elected President in 1975, a position which he held until his sudden death. He was a very popular judge, both in this country and overseas, and he judged the breed twice at Crufts. He had a wealth of knowledge and experience, which he gave so freely to all who sought it, always encouraging new breeders and exhibitors, and promoting the breed whenever he could.

We had regular correspondence over a number of years, and on many occasions I was welcomed by Harold and his wife, Betty, at their Treorchy home. His letters summed up one of the great men of Welsh Springers; pride in his own dogs' achievements all over the world, and help and encouragement to an enthusiastic newcomer. In a letter in 1980, Harold told me about the days when he started Miss Ellis (Downland) in the breed just after the Second World War, when:

there were no Welshies to be seen anywhere, and I worked hard for her and the breed then. Although working, I would slip away late on the Friday in my little Standard 9 car down to St Mary's by Friday night, do up all the dogs, and the following morning you would find me in either Surrey, Sussex or Kent. I did this so much that the people were asking, 'Where does that little fellow live?' When I look back, I just can't think how I did it, and remember, winter as well as summer, and no heaters in the cars either in those days – lucky my car never let me down. I had some great wins, and I suppose I did a lot to put the breed on the map.

What an understatement!

I remember, when I started showing, being taken to the ringside and told to 'watch that little man, Harold Newman – he puts them down to perfection; he could win a first prize even if it looked like a donkey!' I am privileged that that little man became a great personal friend and adviser and, like so many, I am deeply grateful for all he did for the breed.

Cliff Payne (Tregwillym)

Cliff Payne is the other 'great name' of our time – or rather, Cliff and Mary are, for although it was Cliff whom we all saw in the ring, it was Mary who was behind the scenes, and between them they built up the world-famous Tregwillym kennel. Sadly, the partnership ended in 1997, with the passing of Mary at the age of 89 years.

Sh Ch Token of Tregwillym. Photo: C M Cooke

Cliff originally had a Welsh/English crossbred to shoot over in the early 1930s, but in due course, he decided to look for a Welsh Springer. In 1938, he bought his first Welsh Springer, already trained, from the Keeper at Llangibby. The dog was a tremendous worker, but unfortunately he drowned. After much searching, Cliff came across a litter of six Welsh Springer puppies, five bitches and a dog, bred by Mr D E R Griffiths, and he bought them all.

It was not until five years later that Cliff and Mary started breeding Welsh Springers. Their first litter, sired by Goblin O'Gwmro out of Griff, the foundation of the Tregwillym kennel, and it was during the War years that they started showing, when the dogs were handled by Mary. The Tregwillym kennel had great success in the 1950s in both shows and field trials, and in 1956 came the first champion, Sh Ch Token of Tregwillym. There followed many great winners: Sh Chs Tulita and Topscore, and Show Champion and American Champion Trigger, who went to Laddie Carswell in the United States, 'the reintroduction of the Welsh to the American dog shows'. Mandy qualified in the field as well, thus gaining the title of full Champion, as did Statesman, one of the greatest sires of all time.

Ch Statesman of Tregwillym, one of the greatest sires of all time.

Other well-known Show Champions followed: Golden Tint, Amber Rose and Golden Gem. In 1976, Sh Ch Contessa of Tregwillym had the distinction of winning Best in Show at the Ladies' Kennel Association Championship Show, when the judge was Dr Esther Rickards, the Chairman of the Welsh Springer Spaniel Club.

Tregwillym dogs are behind so many of the successful kennels of the past and of today, and are renowned for their soundness and temperament. Such big winners at Sh Ch Deri Darrell of Linkhill (described by Cliff as the best Welsh Springer he had ever seen), Ch Rockhill Riwderin, Sh Ch Diplomat of Hearts, and Ch Krackton Surprise Packet were all sired by Tregwillym dogs, as was our own Sh Ch Hillpark Pollyanna. The one-time breed record holder, Mansel and Avril Young's Sh Ch Wainfelin Barley Mo was sired by Tregwillym Mint, and so was the famous Sh Ch Dalati Sarian, bred by Noel and Dodo Hunton Morgans.

My personal favourite was Sh Ch Golden Tint of Tregwillym, another breed record holder of her time. In 1993 a number of judges selected her most frequently as the all-time greatest Welsh Springer from the past or present from anywhere in the world. Another choice was Sh Ch Contessa of Tregwillyn, and yet another, Sh Ch Golden Gem of Tregwillym.

Cliff has always been generous to any who sought his help, and I have many happy memories of staying at The Old Rectory at Henllys, witnessing the spectacular sight of the largest kennel of Welsh Springers in the world, and listening by the hour to Cliff and Mary as they reminisced, displaying such deep knowledge of and enthusiasm for the breed. Both judged the breed for many years, and I was very pleased to be awarded Challenge Certificates by both of them. Both were invaluable members of the Committee of the Welsh Springer Spaniel Club, before the formation of the Welsh Springer Spaniel Club of South Wales, when they were elected Joint Life Presidents, a highly respected and admired couple in the Welsh Springer breed.

Dr Esther Rickards, OBE, MS, MRCS (Tarbay)

Dr Rickards, or 'The Doc' as she was universally known, was Chairman of the Welsh Springer Spaniel Club from 1967 until her death in 1977. As Harold Newman wrote, 'The Club will be all the poorer with her passing', and as the Secretary of the Club myself for six of her years in office, I can say that she was a great leader, a wonderful adviser, and one who commanded respect from all. Some of the older members of the Club will recall the Annual General Meeting after her passing; as we were mourning her passing, suddenly there was a tremendous clap of thunder – she was still with us!

Dr Rickards was a woman of many parts: highly respected by the medical profession, where she served on hospital committees, a Suffragette, a superb needlewoman, a music-lover and, above all, she had a great knowledge of dogs and dogdom, and was a highly respected member of The Kennel Club. She also had a great sense of humour.

Shadow of Tarbay.

Before the War, Dr Rickards' Tarbay Cockers were world famous, and there were Irish Water and Sussex Spaniels before some very successful Welsh Springers came along. She was a founder member and later Chairman of the Windsor Gundog Society and Windsor Championship Show Society, and became President of the European Spaniel Congress, having played a major part in its formation.

During her last illness, 'The Doc' kept in regular touch with me from her bed, still concerned with the welfare of the Welsh Springer Spaniel Club, which was so typical of this great character.

Sh Ch Stokecourt Jonathan, BOB Crufts 1951. Fox Photos.

Mrs Dorothy Morriss (Stokecourt)

Mrs Morriss' Stokecourt kennel was well known for its dual-purpose qualities, and particularly for the working side. Stokecourt Beau was the foundation dog of the kennel, originally said to be a Cocker when Mrs Morriss bought him in 1945, but later registered as a Welsh Springer, and he went on to win a Challenge Certificate in 1948, as well as being a very successful working dog. All the Stokecourt dogs worked, and there were three Show Champions, Jonathan, Gillian and Judith.

Stokecourt Sam, 1968.

Probably the best-known Stokecourt dog was S. Sam, who was behind the best workers of the time, and had 12 Certificates of Merit and many awards in the field to his name. When I came into the breed, I soon became aware that if you wanted a working Welsh Springer, Stokecourt Sam had to be in the pedigree somewhere, and he passed on his good looks to his progeny as well.

Mrs Morriss' guidance and enthusiasm for the working Welsh Springer inspired the revitalisation of the working side of the Welsh Springer Spaniel Club in the 1970s, which culminated in the first Club Field Trial being held in 1983, after a break of 23 years. From 1980 until 1984, Mrs Morriss was President of the Welsh Springer Spaniel Club. She was a highly respected judge in the showring as well as in the field.

Ken Burgess (Plattburn)

In the 1960s and 1970s, Ken Burgess and his Plattburn kennel was a very strong force in the world of Welsh Springers.

Ken started breeding and showing Cocker Spaniels in the early 1950s, but having seen Cliff Payne's Ch Statesman of Tregwillym, he turned to Welsh Springers. His foundation bitch was Patmyn Pie Powder and, as a result of a mating with Ch Rockhill Rhiwderin came Sh Chs Plattburn Penny and Paramount, the start of a long string of title holders. Sh Ch Plattburn Progressor, with 12 Challenge Certificates to his credit, and Sh Ch Kaliengo Flash (by Sh Ch Plattburn Perchance out of Plattburn Pansy) with 16 CCs were two of the 'greats'. But Sh Ch Plattburn Probability, winner of 32 CCs, 6 Gundog Groups and BIS at the West of England Ladies' Kennel Society All-Breed Championship Show in 1980, was the outstanding Welsh Springer of the time.

Plattburn stock was used extensively at stud, and was exported to many parts of the world, where it was very influential in establishing the breed.

Sh Chs Plattburn Paramount, Progressor and Penny.

Welsh Springer Spaniel Club Championship Show 1980.
BIS: Sh Ch Plattburn Probability with Ken Burgess.
BOS: Sh Ch Pantyscallog Proud Lass with Gareth Burke.

On many occasions, I travelled up to Ken's home in Yorkshire and enjoyed and appreciated his forthright and honest opinions. He is a true Yorkshireman – blunt and to the point! He is what farmers call 'a good stockman', and has had vast experience in showing many varieties of livestock: racing pigeons, rabbits, goats, bantams, and several other breeds of dogs, apart from Welsh Springers. I feel it is a pity that we no longer see Plattburn dogs in the ring, although Ken still takes the stage as a respected judge of the breed.

Breeders of Today

Some exhibitors come and go every year, others remain enthusiasts, and are dedicated to their hobby. Below is a list of kennels with their title holders representing the breeders of today.

Cwrt Afon
Owners: Kath and Len Morgan.
Sh Ch Cwrt Afon Llion is the most recent of the eight title holders from this kennel, which started in 1972 with Cliff Payne's Tregwillym stock. Four were made up in the United Kingdom, two in the United States, one in Denmark and one in France. The most successful was the bitch Sh Ch Cwrt Afon Poeth Goch, who gained her title in 1986 and won nine Challenge Certificates.

Sh Ch Cwrt Afon Llion.

Dalati
Owners: Noel and Dodo Hunton Morgans.
This is the most successful and influential kennel of the era, and it is featured in Chapter 10.

Ferndel
Owner: John Thirlwell.
John Thirlwell started showing Irish Setters while still at school. He bought his first Welsh Springer in 1976; Sh Ch Dalati Gwent became his first champion. He has had 10 Welsh Springer champions so far, seven of which he bred, and another three made up by other exhibitors. Ferndel stock has also been very successful overseas.

Goldsprings
Owner: Barbara Ordish.

Sh Ch Ferndel Paperlace. Photo: CMJ

Barbara Ordish was given her first Welsh Springer, Krackton Arabella, in 1968. She bought Hillpark Trampoline from the author in 1970, who produced Sh Ch Goldsprings Guillemot, sired by Harold Newman's great stud dog, Sh Ch Roger of Pencelli. Guillemot had the distinction of winning Best in Show at the Welsh Springer Spaniel Club Championship Shows in 1975 and 1977. There have been two further Show Champions, and five American Champions from this kennel.

Sh Ch Goldsprings Vagabond. Photo: Gibbs

Highclare

Owner: Gill Tully.

Gill Tully started her truly dual-purpose kennel in 1983, and has met with many successes in both the showring and in the field. Her foundation bitch was Delkens Tamble. Strands of Gold is the most successful dual-purpose Welsh Springer of the time, with many Challenge Certificates and Field Trial awards to her credit, and she has a daughter who has gained her title: Sh Ch Highclare Search for a Star. Highclare Special Formula, also a daughter of Delkens Tamble, excelled in Field Trials and Working Tests, and there have been several exports from the kennel which have met with considerable success; this includes a champion in New Zealand.

Ch Highclare Strands of Gold.

Hillpark
Owners: John and Anne Walton
Our foundation bitch was Polly Garter of Doonebridge, bought as a pet in 1965, and all Hillpark Welsh Springers descend from her.

Polly Garter of Doonebridge.

Julita
Owner: Julie Revill.
Julie Revill started showing dogs at the age of three, and bought her first Welsh Springer in 1983. Ch Julita Jaunty Reveller is a home-bred full Champion, and there has also been a Junior Warrant winner. Rainspeckle won the Welsh Springer Spaniel Club Field Trial in 1993, has numerous other awards in Field Trials and working tests, and has been the top working dog and runner-up in the dual-purpose 'Dog of the Year' competition. Apart from being particularly successful in the field, Julie has also consistent winners in the showring. The emphasis in this kennel is the dual-purpose Welsh Springer Spaniel.

Julita Ryvanda.

Kazval
Owner: Frank Whyte.
Captivation was the foundation bitch of the Kazval kennels, and she has produced offspring which have gained their titles in this country and overseas. Rated 'the best' by her owner for 'her true Welshie temperament and courage to get over a severe car accident at seven months,

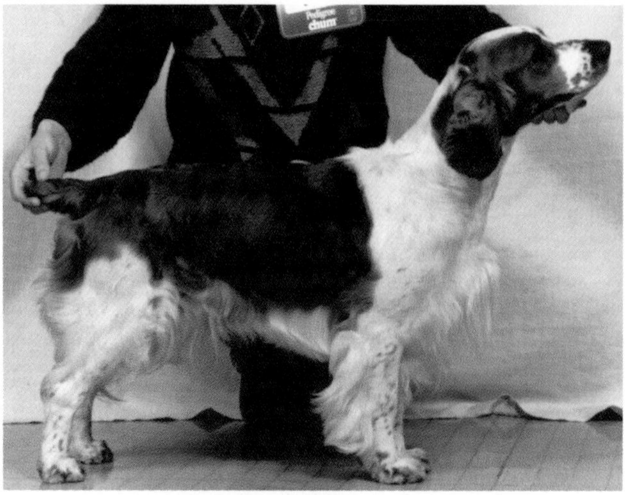

Sh Ch Canisbay Captivation of Kazval. Photo: Gibbs

Sh Ch Dalati Brig of Knockmains.

Sh Ch Mapleby Post Haste.

and still be the extrovert character she is, passing on her infectious personality.'

Knockmains
Owner: Jock Beattie.
Brig was the first Welsh Springer in the kennel, born in 1975. Jock says, 'Although not quite so active in the shows and dogdom now, we will always have a Welsh Springer Spaniel at Knockmains'. He is one of our most respected judges, and judged our breed at Crufts Dog Show in 1996. Can Ch Knockmains Kinlossie is the most recent dog from this kennel to gain a title.

Mapleby
Owners: Philip and the late Margaret Bye.
This kennel was founded in1980 with the purchase of Stagarth Little Phoebe from Major Don Charles, as a pet. She proved to be an excellent brood bitch, producing a further title holder, Sh Ch Mapleby Cymreig Cyfaill, owned by Steven Pick, and two others with Challenge Certificates to their name. Post Haste's most notable success was Best of Breed at Crufts at Crufts' centenary show in 1991.

Menstonia
Owner: Christina Knowles.
Christine started her kennel in 1975 with a rescue dog which was going to be put down at her vets. She had to visit the library to find out what he was. She had always had German Shepherd Dogs

before, and thought that she would like a matching pair. She went to a few shows, decided what she liked, and booked a puppy from Cliff Payne (Tregwillym). She has bred six British Champions and two overseas Champions, one in Australia and one in New Zealand.

Sea Mist is the Bitch Record Holder in the breed, with 44 Challenge Certificates, and is featured in Chapter 9 on Judging. She was a puppy back from a bitch which Christine bred and let go to Christopher Anderson on breeding terms – to make a further Menstonia Show Champion.

Sh Ch Northoaks Sea Mist of Menstonia. Photo: Robert Smith.

Melladomina Molly Mu.

Melladomina

Owner: Tricia Lazenby.

Tricia started in the breed in 1971, and has had six generations of home-bred bitches. She aims to qualify Molly Mu in the field, to gain her full Champion title. Molly's grand-dam, Ch Melladomina Jessie Meade, completed her title in 1984.

Sh Ch Mynyddmaen Graig Coch (see next page). Photo: EBW

Mynyddmaen

Owners: John, Jayne and Clare Derrick.

The first Welsh Springer for this dual-purpose kennel was Bronymaen of Wainfelin, the 7th birthday present for Clare in 1979. The first litter was bred in 1982, which produced Sadie Red Flash, who was very successful in the field and the showring. John has worked dogs since his teens, and has won many Field Trial awards with a number of different Welsh Springers. Jayne's grandfather, Mr George Tomlins, showed the breed in pre-war years.

Now his great-granddaughter, Clare, successfully handles and works a Mynyddmaen youngster. Graig Coch is the first of the kennel to gain a title, excelling in the showring, and with awards in working tests to his name. He was the Welsh Springer Spaniel Club Dog of the Year (Bench and Field) in 1995 and 1996.

Ch Northey Stormcloud.

Northey
Owner: Christine McDonald.
Christine bought her Brent foundation bitch, Byrony of Banlieue in 1976, and showed and worked her with some success, including winning a Challenge Certificate and Working Test awards. All Northeys are descended from her, including eight title holders in the United Kingdom, four of which are full Champions, and four Show Champions. Stormcloud was Best in Show at the Welsh Springer Spaniel Club Championship Show in 1986, and Sh Ch Northey Silver Cameo from Zamberlan (owned by Jane Hopkins) was top Welsh Springer in 1996. Dogs from this kennel have been sent to New Zealand, the United States, Holland and Finland and many have won their titles.

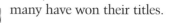

Dutch Sh Ch Northoaks Sea Sunflower.

Northoaks
Owner: Christopher Anderson.
This kennel was started in 1988 with Christine Knowles' Menstonia blood. It has the distinction of breeding Sh Ch Northoaks Sea Mist of Menstonia, the breed bitch record holder. Sea Sunflower is the 1997 top-winning Welsh

Springer in Holland, and Doreen Gately (Russethill) and I awarded him Best in Show at the Dutch Club's 1997 Championship Show. Another bitch from the kennel has gained her title: Sh Ch Northoaks Sea Glympse of Menstonia, owned by M D Greenwood.

Pamicks Araminta.

Pamicks

Owners: Pam and Mick Tew.

Pam and Mick started in 1979 with their foundation bitch, Delkens Jane Eyre. The first from the kennel to gain a title was Sh Ch Pamicks Paprika in 1990, and there is also a Show Champion in Sweden, Pamicks Ten-a-Penny.

Russethill

Owner: Doreen Gately.

Doreen bought Delkens Toneia from Ken Burgess (Plattburn) in 1980, and all Russethill stock is directly line-bred from her. The well-known all rounder judge, Jimmy Cudworth, awarded her first Challenge Certificate and Best in Show at the Welsh Springer Spaniel Club Championship Show in 1984. She returned as a veteran at the Club Show in 1988, when I was judging, and I awarded her last Challenge Certificate. Her son, Sh Ch Russethill Ringmaster, owned by John Perry, was Best in Show.

Among the other title holders from this kennel is the current breed record holder, Sh Ch Russethill Royal Salute over Nyrilam, owned by Tom Graham. The most influential stud sire on the Russethill line

Sh Ch Delkens Toneia at Russethill.

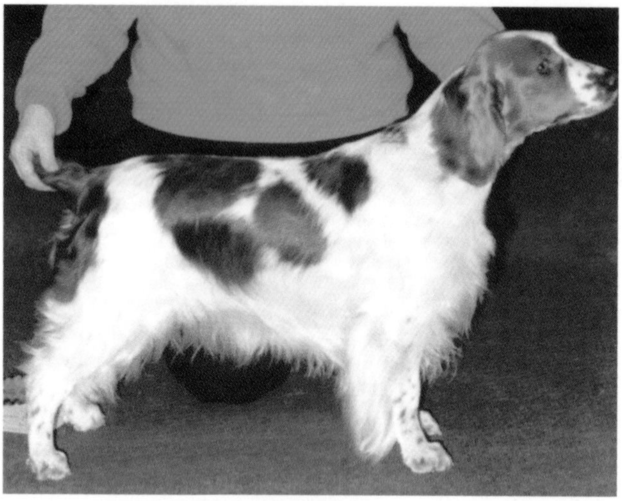

Sh Ch/Ir Sh Ch Solva Arabella.

Sh Ch Taimere's Tempra. Photo: David Dalton

Sh Ch Tarendes Air of Elegance JW. Photo: David Dalton

has been Sh Ch Dalati Sioni, the dog which Doreen used twice, and produced five Show Champions from two litters.

Solva

Owner: Mrs J M Luckett-Roynon.

Sh Ch/Irish Sh Ch Solva Arabella (Solva Don Carlos ex Russethill Rosalinda of Solva – see overleaf) won her title in 1992. Her greatest achievement was at Crufts 1992, when she was awarded Best of Breed. She won seven CCs and nine RCCs; also six Major Green Starts in Ireland, all with Best of Breed.

Taimere's

Owners: Lesley and Graham Tain.

Lesley and Graham began showing Welsh Springers in 1979, and all their dogs are bred back to a bitch from their first litter, Taimere's Tranquillity. Tempra was Best in Show at the Welsh Springer Spaniel Club Championship Show in 1995, and amongst their other title holders is Sh Ch Taimere's Tempest, owned by Michael McGrath, to whom I awarded Best of Breed at Crufts in 1994. Two dogs from this successful kennel have achieved Champion status: one in Ireland and one in the United States.

Tarendes

Owner: Sandra Jones.

Welsh Springers have been connected with Sandra's family since the late 1920s; her uncle, Robert James, showed and trained them. Amongst many

Sh Ch Wainfelin Super Trouper (see overleaf).

trophies, he won the John Davies Challenge Trophy outright, for Best Welsh Springer Spaniel at Field Trials, with Shot of Canonmoor in 1935, 1936 and 1937. He left the trophy to Sandra.

The first Welsh Springer in the kennel was Bensams Annwyl at Tarendes, bought in 1979. Sudden Impulse (by Sh Ch Wainfelin Barley Mo) joined the kennel, and was mated to Sh Ch Dalati Sioni, producing Air of Elegance. Her many awards include Reserve Best in Show at the Welsh Springer Spaniel Club Championship Shows in 1995 and 1996, and Best in Show 1996 and Reserve Best in Show in 1997 at the Welsh Springer Spaniel Club of South Wales Championship Show.

Wainfelin

Owners: Mansel and Avril Young.

This very successful kennel started in 1974 with a dog purchased from Cliff and Mary Payne (Tregwillym), who later gained his title at Crufts 1977 – Sh Ch Sandy of Wainfelin. The foundation bitch was Our Mistress Geannie of Wainfelin.

Mansel and Avril have had many Wainfelin title holders in this country, and others in Europe, the United States and Australia. The most famous was Sh Ch Wainfelin Barley Mo, the former breed record holder, who won 41 Challenge Certificates, and another of distinction from the same litter (sired by Tregwillym Royal Mint, ex Wainfelin Rhos Mair) gained her working qualifications as well. This was Ch Wainfelin Born To Be Free, owned by John and Pauline Phillips. Sandra Bell and Roy Palmer's Sh Ch Wainfelin Ace of Diamonds was Best of Breed at Crufts in 1997.

Super Trouper, another big winner, is seen in the photograph on page 239, handled by niece Hannah Young.

Weslave

Owners: John and Joy Hartley.

John and Joy's foundation bitch was Dalati Dethol, bred by Noel and Dodo Hunton Morgans. Out of her first litter, she had two Show Champions, Weslave Winter Mist and Weslave Will o' The Wisp, sired by Sh Ch Dalati Gwent. In 1987, Weslave Winter Breeze was exported to Sweden, where she became the all-time top winning bitch in breed. Out of her litter sister, Weslave Polly Flinders, came Sh Ch Weslave Wood Tiger, a dog which I chose as my Reserve Challenge Certificate winner when I judged at Crufts in 1994.

chapter 14
Memorabilia

Once one is obsessed with a subject, becoming a collector of items from the past is inevitable, and so it has been with me and Welsh Springers. Anything to do with the breed finds a home in my collection, from old newspaper cuttings to cigarette cards, postcards, stamps and photographs.

Old masterpieces are there to be admired in museums, stately homes and art galleries, and I am always on the look-out for red and white spaniels when I go to view them. Recently I went to an exhibition of paintings at the splended Bowes Museum at Barnard Castle in County Durham. There I spied a beautiful painting of *A Boy Sitting on a Dog's Back* by Claude-Antoine Fleury (French School, 1795–1822). The boy was riding the dog like a horse, his arm being characteristically licked by a dog with a head so similar to a Welsh Springer's.

There are reproductions and limited editions of prints by artists such as Maud Earl, particularly, of course, the two Longmynd Springers already referred to in Chapter 2 (see page 15). A series by Heywood Hardy (1843–1933) containing delightful country scenes, all with red and white spaniels, is readily available. I have four of them (there may be more): *By the Stile*, *A Chance Encounter*, *The Meeting* and *A Penny from the Squire*. I found these in a box in a general store, all framed, for the price of £15.

A Penny from the Squire, by Heywood Hardy (1843–1933).

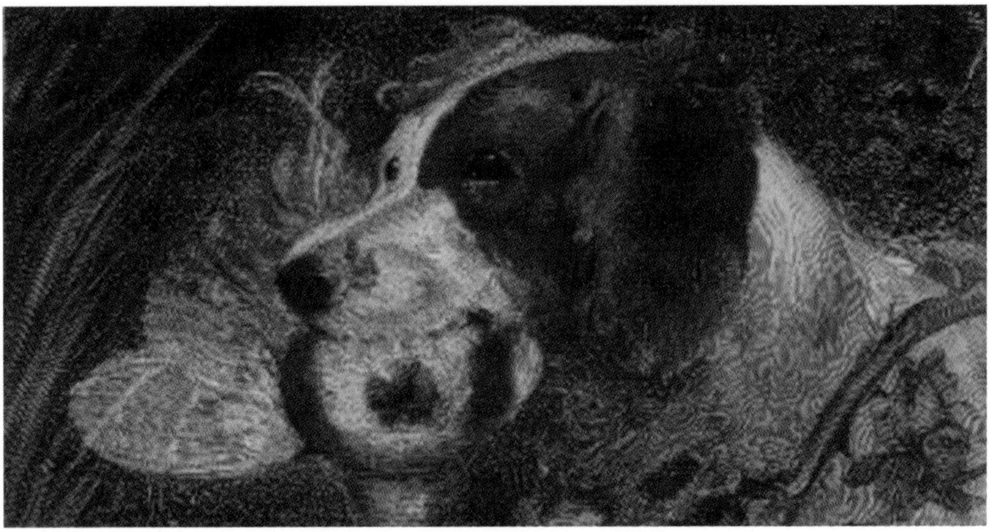

Partridge Shooting Retrieving (1840).

In an antique shop in the north of England, we found a beautful print, *Partridge Shooting Retrieving*, published by Joseph Rogerson, 1840. No mention of the breed, but so much like our Welsh Springer.

My real favourite is a reproduction of a painting by Frank Dadd, RI, dated 1893, which appeared in *Pear's Christmas Annual 1896*. There are the unmistakable Welsh Springers, before their recognition by The Kennel Club in 1902.

The dogs in this painting by Frank Dadd are unmistakably Welsh Springers.

Beswick *Puppies at Play.*

Antiques and Collectors' Fairs have become very popular in recent years, with programmes devoted to the subject on television, resulting in an increase in interest and thirst for knowledge. For Welsh Springer collectors, it is rather disappointing, but Beswick (Royal Doulton) has produced a delightful set of six ceramic figures in a series of *Puppies at Play* (nos 2946–2951). Although the figures are not catalogued as being modelled on any particular breed, their conformation and poses lead me to believe that a Welsh Springer played its part – and they are all definitely red and white although the catalogue calls them white and tan. From two expert sources, I have heard that they were thought to be terriers, but my second informant told me that she believed that they were Welsh Springers – and who am I to contradict her?

Paraguayan stamp.

Harvey May, an acknowledged master on Beswick ceramics, does not know who modelled the figures, but it may have been a Peggy Davies – a Welsh lady? They were part of a series of 13 character dogs, originally produced in fine china by Royal Doulton in the 1930s and remained with the Doulton stamp until 1985. The *Puppies at Play* were the most popular models and they were reissued as a series of six for about 18 months in 1987–1989 under the Beswick ceramic label.

Apart from the stamp issued by the United Kingdom Post Office in 1979 (see page 34), several countries have produced stamps illustrating Welsh Springer Spaniels in recent years. The Republic of Chad stamp (1973), with a picture of a mother and puppy, is well worth looking for. Vietnam produced a head study in 1990, and Paraguay showed a Welsh Springer in 1986.

Collecting cigarette cards is more rewarding. I have a series of four by Odgen's, part of the F Series of 420 subjects, photographs taken at the Sporting Spaniel Society Trials at Sutton Scarsdale, November 1901. Best of all is Mr A T Williams' team taking first in the brace or team stake. Mr Williams was the prime mover in persuading The Kennel Club to recognise the Welsh Springer Spaniel as a new breed in 1902. Others to look for are:

1923 R J Lea Chairman cigarettes. No 40 of a series of 50.
1929 and 1933 Players reproduced two from a painting by Arthur Wardle, RI: No 37 of 50 and No 15 of 25.
1931 De Reske Real Photographs 2nd series of 27, No 6 'Sportsman All', showing four puppies.
1936 Imperial Tobacco Co produced two versions of No 34 of 50, one by Ogden's and the other by Hignett.
1938 Gallagher, Welsh Springer Spaniel, No 27 of 2nd series of 48.
1938 John Sinclair's 2nd series of Champion Dogs – Ch Longmynd Marquis, No 3 of 52.
1939 John Sinclair again with a 2nd series of 54 Real Photographs, No 53 *Master Gun*.
1939 Senior Service Welsh Springer, No 3 of 48 dogs.
1940 Players Dogs. Series of 25 from paintings by Arthur Wardle, RI, No 20, *Two Welsh Springer Spaniel heads.*

In 1990, W D and H O Wills reproduced Lucy Dawson's painting of *Judy*, number 25 of 40 puppies. I have yet to come across one of the originals.

Belle and Glory of Gerwn, 2nd in brace or team stake.

Prince retrieving.

Hoar Cross Duchy.

Mr A T Williams' team.

Welsh Springer Spaniels (John Player).

There are also tokens for Spratts' Dog Soap (1926, No 36 of 36), and Pascall's Sweets and chocolates (1924, No 12 of 18), with a picture of Ch Longmynd Calon Fach.

Other picture cards are Godfrey Phillips' *Our Puppies*, No 30 in a series of 30 (1936); two similar pictures produced by Vims-Pet, The Molassine Co, Ltd, *Puppies*, No 46 of a series of 50 (1957 and 1967), and a further two similar pictures produced by Cadet Sweets, Dogs 1st series, No 1–25, No 12 (both 1958).

ABC Minors' Dogs, No 9 of a set of 17 (1957) is not really antique but collectable for its picture of a black and white Cocker-looking Welsh Springer Spaniel.

Old postcards of Welsh Springer Spaniels are rare. Two from the early 1900s feature Mrs Green's Champions, Longmynd Megan and Calon Fach, and I have one with a 1906 postmark entitled *Favourite Dogs – The Springer Spaniel*, a very white dog with red only on the head and a small patch on the side. Ch Cilsanws Rock (born 19.9.1906, Longmynd Mynd ex Cilsanws Dinah) is on another postcard, a well-made, typical-looking dog, with a lot of white on the body, which so often is the case with the old dogs.

It is well worth delving into boxes of old photographs and postcards at boot fairs and sales. I have made several useful 'finds' over the years, but I have not yet been fortunate in my search for old cards illustrated by G Vernon Stokes and Diana Thorne – I am still looking!

Selection of Cigarette Cards

Ch Maraglam Marquis (Barneys Cigarettes).

Welsh Springer Spaniel (Players cigarettes).

Welsh Springer (Chairman cigarettes).

Welsh Springer (Senior Service cigarettes).

Master Gun (Barneys Cigarettes).

Sportsmen All (de Reszke cigarettes).

Welsh Springer Spaniel (Hignett's cigarettes).

Welsh Springer Spaniel (Gallagher).

Postcard in the 'Our Dogs' series, showing *Longmynd Megan*.

Postcard entitled *The Springer Spaniel* from 'Favourite Dogs' series.

Appendix A
Whelping Chart

Serve Jan:	1	2	3	4	5	6	7	8	9	10	11	12	13	14	15	16	17	18	19	20	21	22	23	24	25	26	27	28	29	30	31
Whelp Mar/Apr:	5	6	7	8	9	10	11	12	13	14	15	16	17	18	19	20	21	22	23	24	25	26	27	28	29	30	31	1	2	3	4
Serve Feb:	1	2	3	4	5	6	7	8	9	10	11	12	13	14	15	16	17	18	19	20	21	22	23	24	25	26	27	28	(29)		
Whelp Apr/May:	5	6	7	8	9	10	11	12	13	14	15	16	17	18	19	20	21	22	23	24	25	26	27	28	29	30	1	2	(3)		
Serve Mar:	1	2	3	4	5	6	7	8	9	10	11	12	13	14	15	16	17	18	19	20	21	22	23	24	25	26	27	28	29	30	31
Whelp May/Jun:	3*	4	5	6	7	8	9	10	11	12	13	14	15	16	17	18	19	20	21	22	23	24	25	26	27	28	29	30	31	1	2
Serve Apr:	1	2	3	4	5	6	7	8	9	10	11	12	13	14	15	16	17	18	19	20	21	22	23	24	25	26	27	28	29	30	
Whelp Jun/Jul:	3	4	5	6	7	8	9	10	11	12	13	14	15	16	17	18	19	20	21	22	23	24	25	26	27	28	29	30	1	2	
Serve May:	1	2	3	4	5	6	7	8	9	10	11	12	13	14	15	16	17	18	19	20	21	22	23	24	25	26	27	28	29	30	31
Whelp Jul/Aug:	3	4	5	6	7	8	9	10	11	12	13	14	15	16	17	18	19	20	21	22	23	24	25	26	27	28	29	30	31	1	2
Served Jun:	1	2	3	4	5	6	7	8	9	10	11	12	13	14	15	16	17	18	19	20	21	22	23	24	25	26	27	28	29	30	
Whelp Aug/Sep:	3	4	5	6	7	8	9	10	11	12	13	14	15	16	17	18	19	20	21	22	23	24	25	26	27	28	29	30	31	1	
Served Jul:	1	2	3	4	5	6	7	8	9	10	11	12	13	14	15	16	17	18	19	20	21	22	23	24	25	26	27	28	29	30	31
Whelp Sep/Oct:	2	3	4	5	6	7	8	9	10	11	12	13	14	15	16	17	18	19	20	21	22	23	24	25	26	27	28	29	30	1	2
Served Aug:	1	2	3	4	5	6	7	8	9	10	11	12	13	14	15	16	17	18	19	20	21	22	23	24	25	26	27	28	29	30	31
Whelp Oct/Nov:	3	4	5	6	7	8	9	10	11	12	13	14	15	16	17	18	19	20	21	22	23	24	25	26	27	28	29	30	31	1	2
Served Sep:	1	2	3	4	5	6	7	8	9	10	11	12	13	14	15	16	17	18	19	20	21	22	23	24	25	26	27	28	29	30	
Whelp Nov/Dec:	3	4	5	6	7	8	9	10	11	12	13	14	15	16	17	18	19	20	21	22	23	24	25	26	27	28	29	30	1	2	
Served Oct:	1	2	3	4	5	6	7	8	9	10	11	12	13	14	15	16	17	18	19	20	21	22	23	24	25	26	27	28	29	30	31
Whelp Dec/Jan:	3	4	5	6	7	8	9	10	11	12	13	14	15	16	17	18	19	20	21	22	23	24	25	26	27	28	29	30	31	1	2
Served Nov:	1	2	3	4	5	6	7	8	9	10	11	12	13	14	15	16	17	18	19	20	21	22	23	24	25	26	27	28	29	30	
Whelp Jan/Feb:	3	4	5	6	7	8	9	10	11	12	13	14	15	16	17	18	19	20	21	22	23	24	25	26	27	28	29	30	31	1	
Served Dec:	1	2	3	4	5	6	7	8	9	10	11	12	13	14	15	16	17	18	19	20	21	22	23	24	25	26	27	28	29	30	31
Whelp Feb/Mar:	2	3	4	5	6	7	8	9	10	11	12	13	14	15	16	17	18	19	20	21	22	23	24	25	26	27	28	1*	2	3	4

• Adjust for leap year.

Appendix B
Abbreviations

General

AKC	American Kennel Club
Am Ch	American Ch
Aust Ch	Australian Champion
BVA	British Veterinary Association
CC	Challenge Certificate
Ch	Champion
Can Ch	Canadian Champion
BIS	Best in Show
BOB	Best of Breed
BOS	Best Opposite Sex
BP	Best Puppy
FT Ch	Field Trial Champion
Ir Ch	Irish Champion
JW	Junior Warrant
KC	The Kennel Club
NZ Ch	New Zealand Champion
OTCH	Obedience Champion (USA)
Sh Ch	Show Champion
WSSC	Welsh Springer Spaniel Club
WSSC of SW	Welsh Springer Spaniel Club of South Wales
WSSC of Am	Welsh Springer Spaniel Club of America

French Terms

CH B	French Show Champion
CH IB	International Show Champion
TR	Trialler

Scandinavian Terms

BIG	Best In Group
BIM	Best Opposite Sex
BIR	Best Of Breed
BIS	Best In Show
CACIB	International Challenge Certificate
Cert	Challenge Certificate
DK	Danish
EST	Estonian
HP	Prize of Honour
Int SF N UCH	International Swedish and Finnish Champion
Int U CH	International Show Champion
N UCH	Norwegian Show Champion
NORD	Nordic
NV	Nordic Winner
S UCH	Swedish Show Champion
SF	Finnish
SV	Swedish Winner
V	Winner

Registrations of Welsh Springer Spaniels taken from Kennel Club Records

1902	11
1903	25
1904	22
1905	56
1906	34
1907	31
1908	38
1909	45
1910	44
1911	37
1912	18
1913	17
1914	23
1915	14
1916	5
1917	6
1918	0
1919	2
1920	7
1921	7
1922	23
1923	62
1924	89
1925	127
1926	101
1927	136
1928	98
1929	114
1930	95
1931	118
1932	115
1933	107
1934	106
1935	100
1936	120
1937	121
1938	139
1939	56
1940	29
1941	29
1942	21
1943	31
1944	72
1945	107
1946	160
1947	166
1948	126
1949	116
1950	136
1951	102
1952	107
1953	99
1954	122
1955	82
1956	101
1957	143
1958	105
1959	139
1960	128
1961	153
1962	210I
1963	124
1964	195
1965	208
1966	157
1967	253
1968	229
1969	385
1970	335
1971	409
1972	357
1973	511
1974	452
1975	466
1976	240
1977	151
1978	463
1979	664
1980	767
1981	596
1982	670
1983	710
1984	648
1985	702
1986	715
1987	528
1988	516
1989	800
1990	599
1991	718
1992	491
1993	625
1994	562
1995	611
1996	609
1997	465

Appendix D
Crufts Entries and Judges

Definition	Year	Judge	No of dogs
Welsh Spaniels	1902	Mr W A Knight	9
Welsh Springers	1903	Mr S Smale	7
	1904		0
	1905	Mr W H David	6
	1906		0
	1907		0
	1908	Mr H Jones	10
	1909	Mr F E Schofield	14
	1910	Mr F E Schofield	16
Welsh Springers	1911	Mr F Gresham	9
(red and white)	1912	Mr F E Schofield	12
	1913	Mr F Gresham	5
	1914	Mr F Saunders	5
	1915–23		0
Welsh Springers	1924	Mr L Morgan	19
Springers (Welsh)	1925	Mr F Morris	25
Spaniel (Welsh Springer)	1926	Capt H Price Jones	9
	1927	Mr E Trimble	18
	1928	Mr A McNab Chassels	12
	1929	Mr J Alexander	12
	1930	Mr E Trimble	16
	1931	Lt Col Downes Powell	19
	1932	Major H E Doyne-Ditmas	17
	1933	Mr E Trimble	12
	1934	Mr D McDonald	28
	1935	Mr C Houlker	18
	1936	Mr D McDonald	12
	1937	Mr H Scott	13
	1938	Mr E Trimble	15
	1939	Lt Col Downes Powell	24
	1940–47	No show	
	1948	Mr E Trimble	22
	1949	No show	
	1950	Mr H Scott	16
	1951	Mr W East	29
	1952	Mr E Holden	22
	1953	Lt Col Downes Powell	29

Spaniel (Welsh Springer)	1954	Mr R R Kelland	29
	1955	Mr R R Kelland	25
	1956	Mrs G Broadley	40
	1957	Mr R R Kelland	24
	1958	Dr Esther Rickards	21
	1959	Mr A Badenach Nicolson	20
	1960	Mr A McNab Chassels	26
	1961	Mr Leo C Wilson	25
	1962	Mr J Braddon	21
	1963	Mr F Warner Hill	29
	1964	Mr H Newman	36
	1965	Mr H Leopard	26
	1966	Mrs G Broadley	41
	1967	Mr F Parsons	40
	1968	Mr F Warner Hill	34
	1969	Mr F Parsons	47
	1970	Miss C M Francis	56
	1971	Mrs L M Daly	59
	1972	Mr T Hubert Arthur	44
	1973	Mr A Badenach Nicolson	45
	1974	Mr H C Payne	40
	1975	Mr H Newman	44
	1976	Mr G W R Couzens	68
	1977	Mrs K Doxford	64
	1978	Mrs W M Payne	63
	1979	Mr M C W Gilliat	55
	1980	Mr E H Perkins	59
	1981	Mrs O Hampton	69
	1982	Mr T Hubert Arthur	87
	1983	Mrs J de Casembroot	69
	1984	Mrs D Arthur	82
	1985	Mr D Dobson	81
	1986	Mrs M J Mullins	101
	1987	Mr R Bebb	116
	1988	Mr J K Burgess	122
	1989	Mr E Froggatt	117
	1990	Mr P Green	121
	1991	Mr N Hunton Morgans	175
	1992	Mr R E Hood	159
	1993	Mr B J Mullins	157
	1994	Mrs A M Walton	187
	1995	Mr J M Phillips	173
	1996	Mr J Beattie	181
	1997	Mr R L Flye	178
	1998	Mrs D Leach	186

Appendix E

Breed Clubs Shows

Honorary Secretaries' addresses are obtainable from
The Kennel Club
1–4 Clarges Street
Piccadilly
London WlY 8AB
Tel: 0171 493 6651

The Welsh Springer Spaniel Club: The Parent Club

Presidents

1947–1951	Capt A Talbot Fletcher	1966–1975	Mr H J H Leopard
1952–1957	Commander A T Wilson	1975–1980	Mr H Newman
1957–1958	Col J Downes Powell	1980–1984	Mrs Dorothy Morriss
1958–1963	No one would accept the nomination	1984–1994	Mr N Hunton Morgans
		1994–1995	Mrs V N Buchanan
1963–1966	Mr Talbot Radcliffe	1996–	Mrs A M Walton

Chairmen

1947–1958	Col J Downes Powell	1977–1981	Mr N Hunton Morgans
1958–1963	Brig C P G Wills	1981–1986	Mr M S Hamer
1963–1966	Mr H J H Leopard	1986–1995	Mrs A M Walton
1966–1977	Dr Esther Rickards	1995–	Mr J M Phillips

Secretaries

Col J Downes Powell was Secretary from the time that the Club was re-started in 1923 until 1947.

1947–1963	Mr H J H Leopard	1971–1986	Mrs A M Walton
1963–1966	Major K E A Stephens	1988–1994	Mrs V N Buchanan
1966–1971	Miss W J Painter	1994–	Mrs L A Tain

Breed Club Shows

1971 First Championship Show

Judge: Dr Esther Rickards
Best in Show: Pattinson's Ch Tidemarsh Rip (D)
Best Opposite Sex: Mullins' Athelwood Lily The Pink

1972 Judge: Mr Derek Dobson
Best in Show: Pattinson's Ch Tidemarsh Tidemark (D)
Best Opposite Sex: Mullins' Sh Ch Athelwood Lily The Pink

1973 Judge:	Mrs Dorothy Morriss
Best in Show:	Newman's Progress of Pencelli (D)
Best Opposite Sex:	Mullins' Sh Ch Athelwood Lily The Pink
1974 Judge:	Mr J K Burgess
Best In Show:	Payne's Sh Ch Tregwillym Golden Gem (B)
Best Opposite Sex:	Newman's Sh Ch Progress of Pencelli
1975 Judge:	Mr F Warner Hill
Best in Show:	Ordish's Goldsprings Guillemot (B)
Best Opposite Sex:	Walton's Sh Ch Hillpark Mr Polly
1976 Judge:	Mr H C Payne
Best in Show:	Hunton Morgans' Sh Ch Dalati Rhian (B)
Best Opposite Sex:	Newman's Sh Ch Roger of Pencelli
1977 Judge:	Mr Harold Newman
Best in Show:	Ordish's Goldsprings Guillemot (B)
Best Opposite Sex:	Stratten's Sh Ch Goldsprings Bright Spark of Selworthy
1978 Judge:	Mrs A Badenach Nicolson
Best in Show:	Burgess' Sh Ch Kaliengo Flash (D)
Best Opposite Sex:	Ordish's Sh Ch Goldsprings Guillemot
1979 Judge:	Mr G W R Couzens
Best in Show:	Walton's Sh Ch Hillpark Reverie (B)
Best Opposite Sex:	Ravenhill's Sh Ch Derossé Lucky Sovereign
1980 Judge:	Mrs A M Walton
Best in Show:	Burgess' Sh Ch Plattburn Probability (D)
Best Opposite Sex:	Burke's Sh Ch Pantyscallog Proud Lass
1981 Judge:	Mr G H Pattinson
Best in Show:	Green's Sh Ch Tamaritz Toff (D)
Best Opposite Sex:	Morgan's Cwrt Afon Nia
1982 Judge:	Mrs D Hunton Morgans
Best in Show:	Powell's Sh Ch Blorenge Megan (B)
Best Opposite Sex:	McDonald's Ch Northey Woodpecker
1983 Judges:	Mrs V Yates (dogs); Mr G W R Couzens (bitches)
Best in Show:	Hartley's Weslave Will o' the Wisp (D)
Best Opposite Sex:	Hunton Morgans' Dalati Canig
1984 Judge:	Mr J Cudworth
Best in Show:	Gately's Delkens Toneia at Russethill (B)
Best Opposite Sex:	Hunton Morgans' Sh Ch Dalati Sioni
1985 Judges:	Mr R E Hood (dogs); Mrs Eileen Falconer (bitches)
Best in Show:	Walton's Sh Ch Hillpark Rosaline (B)
Best Opposite Sex:	Morgan's Delkens Teemo of Talliswen

1986 Judges:	Mr Mark Hamer (dogs); Mr Noel Hunton Morgans (bitches)
Best in Show:	McDonald's Sh Ch Northey Stormcloud (B)
Best Opposite Sex:	Young's Sh Ch Wainfelin Barley Mo
1987 Judges:	Mrs V Roach (dogs); Mr J Beattie (bitches)
Best in Show:	Hunton Morgans' Dalati Sarian (B)
Best Opposite Sex:	Perry and Iles' Sh Ch Russethill Ringmaster at Sierry
1988 Judges:	Mr J M Phillips (dogs); Mrs A M Walton (bitches)
Best in Show:	Perry and Iles' Sh Ch Russethill Ringmaster at Sierry (D)
Best Opposite Sex:	Gately's Sh Ch Delkens Toneia at Russethill
1989 Judges:	Mrs R Furness (dogs); Mrs V N Buchanan (bitches)
Best in Show:	Perry and Iles' Sh Ch Russethill Ringmaster at Sierry (D)
Best Opposite Sex:	Hunton Morgans' Sh Ch Dalati Sarian
1990 Judges:	Mrs P A G Hylton (dogs); Mrs M J Mullins (bitches)
Best in Show:	Jelley's Sh Ch Northey Wish Me Luck (D)
Best Opposite Sex:	Bye's Mapleby Post Haste
1991 Judges:	Mrs D Gately (dogs); Mr G J Burke (bitches)
Best in Show:	Hunton Morgans' Sh Ch Dalati Sioned (B)
Best Opposite Sex:	Thirlwell's Sh Ch Ferndel Paper Moon
1992 Judges:	Mrs J M Rees (dogs); Mr J K Burgess (bitches)
Best in Show:	Simpson's Heronsmere Rose Bowl (B)
Best Opposite Sex:	Young's Wainfelin Gwir Trysor
1993 Judges:	Mrs C McDonald (dogs); Mrs D Hunton Morgans(bitches)
Best in Show:	Gately's Sh Ch Russethill Royal Tan (D)
Best Opposite Sex:	Young's Sh Ch Wainfelin Gelli Fawr
1994 Judges:	Mr J S Thirlwell (dogs); Mrs P M Grayson (bitches)
Best in Show:	Graham's Sh Ch Kazval Kamal on Nyrilam (B)
Best Opposite Sex:	McDonald's Northey Wizard
1995 Judges:	Mr M Young (dogs); Mrs C Knowles (bitches)
Best in Show:	Graham's Sh Ch Russethill Royal Salute over Nyrilam (D)
Best Opposite Sex:	Jones' Pennylock Emma
1996 Judge:	Mrs L A Tain
Best in Show:	Hunton Morgans' Sh Ch Dalati Afan (D)
Best Opposite Sex:	Jones' Sh Ch Tarendes Air of Elegance
1997 Judges:	Mrs B Ordish (dogs); Mr D Dobson (bitches)
Best in Show:	Whyte's Kazval Bandito
Best Opposite Sex:	Bell and Palmer's Risinglark Kali

Welsh Springer Spaniel Club of South Wales

Breed Club Shows

1985 First Championship Show.

Judges:	Mrs C Sutton (dogs); Mrs W M Payne (bitches)
Best in Show:	Pickering's Tregwillym Twiggy of Freewheelin (B)
Best Opposite Sex:	Hunton Morgans' Sh Ch Dalati Sioni
1986 Judges:	Mr T J Davies (dogs); Mr G Morgan (bitches)
Best in Show:	Hunton Morgans' Sh Ch Dalati Sioni (D)
Best Opposite Sex:	Green's Ceindrych of Micarobian
1987 Judges:	Mrs E Falconer (dogs); Mrs O Hampton (bitches)
Best in Show:	Hunton Morgans' Dalati Tomi (D)
Best Opposite Sex:	Major and Mrs P Bye's Mapleby Bloedeuyn Aurora
1988 Judges:	Mr D Phillips (dogs); Mr M Young (bitches)
Best in Show:	Hunton Morgans' Dalati Sarian (B)
Best Opposite Sex:	Hunton Morgans' Sh Ch Dalati Sioni
1989 Judges:	Mrs P Woolf (dogs); Mr J Cudworth (bitches)
Best in Show:	Simpson's Russethill Rose Garland at Heronsmere (B)
Best Opposite Sex:	Hunton Morgans & Thomas' Dalati Tarian
1990 Judges:	Mr M S Hamer (dogs); Mr L Morgan (bitches)
Best in Show:	Perry & Iles' Sh Ch Russethill Ringmaster of Sierry (D)
Best Opposite Sex:	Thomas' Wainfelin Chantilly Lace
1991 Judges:	Mrs D Hunton Morgans (dogs); Mrs T Bebb (bitches)
Best in Show:	Young's Sh Ch Wainfelin Barley Mo (D)
Best Opposite Sex:	Thomas' Sh Ch Wainfelin Chantilly Lace
1992 Judge:	Mrs D Leach (dogs); Mr J Kenefick (bitches)
Best in Show:	Young's Sh Ch Wainfelin Pur Eirion (B)
Best Opposite Sex:	Graham's Sh Ch Russethill Royal Salute over Nyrilam
1993 Judges:	Mrs P M Grayson (dogs); Mrs V Roach (bitches)
Best in Show:	Graham's Sh Ch Russethill Royal Salute over Nyrilam (D)
Best Opposite Sex:	Mrs A Jones' Cwrt Afon Ceri
1994 Judges:	Mrs C Knowles (dogs); Mr N Hunton Morgans (bitches)
Best in Show:	Graham's Sh Ch Russethill Royal Salute over Nyrilam (D)
Best Opposite Sex:	Luckett-Roynon's Sh Ch Solva Arabella
1995 Judges:	Mr R D Watkins (dogs); Mr T R Bebb (bitches)
Best in Show:	Graham's Sh Ch Russethill Royal Salute over Nyrilam (D)
Best Opposite Sex:	Thirlwell's Sh Ch Ferndel Sweet Charity at Mariemead

1996 Judges:	Mr T Graham (dogs); Mrs A J Hartley (bitches)
Best in Show:	Esling's Dalati Digwydd (D)
Best Opposite Sex:	Jones' Sh Ch Tarendes Air of Elegance
1997 Judges:	Mrs J Rees (dogs); Mrs D Gately (bitches)
Best in Show:	Hunton Morgans' Sh Ch Dalati Afan (D)
Best Opposite Sex:	Sh Ch Tarendes Air of Elegance

South Eastern Welsh Springer Spaniel Club

1992 First Championship Show.

Judges:	Mrs D Hunton Morgans (dogs); Mrs A M Walton (bitches)
Best in Show:	Young's Sh Ch Wainfelin Gelli Fawr (B)
Best Opposite Sex:	Henson's Sh Ch Aranwr Siencyn to Yelenis
1993 Judges:	Mr L Morgan (dogs); Mr M Young (bitches)
Best in Show:	Knowles' Sh Ch Northoaks Sea Mist of Menstonia (B)
Best Opposite Sex:	McGrath's Taimere's Tempest
1994 Judges:	Mrs J Hawksley (dogs); Mr J Beattie (bitches)
Best in Show:	Graham's Sh Ch Russethill Royal Salute over Nyrilam (D)
Best Opposite Sex:	Jones' Pennylock Emma
1995 Judges:	Mrs V Roach (dogs); Mr J F Bowen (bitches)
Best in Show:	Young's Sh Ch Wainfelin Super Trouper (D)
Best Opposite Sex:	Knowles' Sh Ch Menstonia Muscatel

1996 no Championship status

1997 Judges:	Mr W Hatton (dogs); Mr M Bryant (bitches)
Best in Show:	Snowles' Menstonia Mustique (D)
Best Opposite Sex:	Derrick's Sh Ch Mynyddmaen Graig Coch.

Photo: Robert Smith

Appendix F
Champions of the Breed

A full list of Champions and Show Champions can be obtained from the Welsh Springer Spaniel Club's *Book of Champions 1902–1992*. Below is a list of those dogs which have gained their titles from 1992 onwards, kindly supplied by Dave and Babs Harding.

Champion	Sex	DOB	Sire and Dam	Breeder	Owner
Sh Ch Pamicks Rustic Spellbinder	D	17.6.86	Sh Ch Pamicks Paprika Delkens Jane Eyre	Owners	Mr & Mrs M Tew
Sh Ch Ferndel Alana	B	27.2.89	Sh Ch Ferndel Stroller Country Maid of Ferndel	Owner	Mr J .S Thirlwell
Ch Northey Showboat	B	15.1.88	Sh Ch Ferndel Stroller Ch Northey Stormcloud	Mrs C McDonald	Mr & Mrs D J Dean
Sh Ch Solva Arabella	B	16.12.86	Solva Don Carlos Russethill Rosalinda of Solva	Owner	Mrs J M.Luckett-Roynon
Sh Ch Dalati Briog of Walgoreg	D	26.3.90	Sh Ch Dalati Sioni Sh Ch Dalati Sarian	Mr & Mrs N Hunton Morgans	Mrs K M Gorman
Sh Ch Goldspring Vagabond	D	4.5.87	Goldsprings Nanook Goldsprings Kiri Anne	Owner	Mrs B Ordish
Sh Ch Heronsmere Rose Bowl	B	17.2.90	Dalati Curig Sh Ch Russethill Rose Garland	Owner	Mrs B Simpson
Sh Ch Menstonia Martini	B	19.8.91	Sh Ch Ferndel Stroller Menstonia Martynique	Owner	Mrs C Knowles
Sh Ch Tarendes Air of Elegance	B	5.3.91	Sh Ch Dalati Sioni Sudden Impulse at Tarendes	Owner	Mrs S M Jones
Ch Highclare Strands of Gold	B	10.6.89	Weslave Weeping Willow Delkens Tamble	Owner	Miss G A E Tully

Sh Ch Cwrt Afon Berwyn at Mariemaid	D	22.8.89	Cwrt Afon Meirion Cwrt Afon Eleri Wyn	Owners	Mr & Mrs L & Miss C Morgan
Sh Ch Russethill Royal Tan	D	26.2.90	Sh Ch Dalati Sioni Russethill Reverie	Owner	Mrs D Gately
Sh Ch .Serene at Cadehill	B	12.11.90	Ch Northey Whittington Sh Ch Ferndel Solitaire	Mr J S Thirlwell	Mrs C A Gibson
Sh Ch Dalati Afan	D	13.6.91	Sh Ch Dalati Sioni Sh Ch Dalati Sarian	Owners	Mr & Mrs N Hunton Morgans
Sh Ch Pennylock Beth	B	25.4.89	Wainfelin Golden Minstrel Pennylock Annabelle	Owner	Mrs E A Jones
Sh Ch Taimere's Tempest	D	7.10.90	Sh Ch Fiveacres Firecrest Sh Ch Firebrand Freesia from Taimere	Mr & Mrs G Tain	Mr M McGrath
Sh Ch Wainfelin Ace of Diamonds	D	8.3.91	Dalati Sgwier Sh Ch Wainfelin Pur Eirion	Mr & Mrs M Young	Mrs S A Bell & Mr R H Palmer
Sh Ch Taimere's Tiercel	B	26.11.91	Trealvi Tenacious Taimere's Total Surprise	Owners	Mr & Mrs G Tain
Sh Ch Wainfelin Super Trouper	D	12.8.92	Dalati Syniad Sh Ch Wainfelin Pur Eirion	Owners	Mr & Mrs M Young
Sh Ch Ferndel Sweet Charity at Mariemead	B	13.1.92	Weslave Weeping Willow Sh Ch Ferndel Vogue	Owner	Mr J S Thirlwell
Sh Ch Kazval Kamal On Nyrilam	B	2.5.91	Sh Ch Dalati Sioni Sh Ch Canisbay Captivation of Kazval	Mr F H Whyte	Mr T Graham
Sh Ch Dalati Heini	B	13.6.91	Sh Ch Dalati Sioni Sh Ch Sarian	Owners	Mr & Mrs N Hunton Morgans
Sh Ch Weslave Wood Tiger	D	28.9.90	Sh Ch Fiveacres Firecrest Weslave Polly Flinders	Owners	Mr & Mrs J W Hartley
Sh Ch Northoaks Sea Glympse of Menstonia	B	15.3.90	Sh Ch Dalati Sibrwd Menstonia Moonlight Mist	Mr C J Anderson	Mr M D Greenwood

Champion	Sex	DOB	Sire and Dam	Breeder	Owner
Sh Ch Blorenge Morfydd	B	8.2.88	Blorenge Morgan Sh Ch Blorenge Megan	Owner	Mrs M Powell
Sh Ch Wainfelin Casey Jones	D	12.5.93	Sh Ch Russethill Royal Salute Over Nyrilam Sh Ch Wainfelin Gelli Fawr	Mr &Mrs M Young	Jones & Young
Sh Ch Menstonia Muscatel	B	19.8.91	Sh Ch Ferndel Stroller Menstonia Martinique	Owner	Mrs C Knowles
Sh Ch Kazval Rival Bid	D	25.7.92	Ferndel Freshman Sh Ch Canisbay Captivation of Kazval	Mr F Whyte	Fox & Grindle
Sh Ch Melladomina Red Tulip	B	6.6.87	Sh Ch Wainfelin Barley Mo Melladomina Red Rose	Owner	Ms P A G Lazenby
Sh Ch Taimere's Tempra	B	14.5.93	Trealvi Thorn Taimere's Total Surprise	Owners	Mr & Mrs C G Tain
Sh Ch Wainfelin Gwir Trysor	D	7.6.90	Sh Ch Dalati Sioni Sh Ch Wainfelin Pur Eirion	Mr & Mrs M Young	Mr & Mrs D R Price
Sh Ch Northey Scarlet Lady at Trimere	B	20.9.90	Sh C Northey Wish Me Luck Highclare Temptress of Northey	Mrs C McDonald	Mrs A Corbett
Sh Ch Mynyddmaen Graig Coch	D	17.7.94	Sh Ch Wainfelin Casey Jones Mynyddmaen Catrin	Owners	Mr & Mrs J & Miss C Derrick
Sh Ch Wainfelin Crescent Moon	B	14.1.94	Sion of Pontymister Wainfelin Carousel	Owners	Mr & Mrs M Young
Sh Ch Northey Cameo from Zamberlan	B	25.5.94	Northey Jack Frost Northey Silver Lining	Mrs C McDonald	Mrs J E Hopkins
Sh Ch Cwrt Afon Llion	D	29.12.92	Sh Ch Russethill Royal Tan Sh Ch Cwrt Afon Lowri	Owners	Mr & Mrs L & Miss Morgan

Sh Ch Highclare Search For A Star	B	27.5.92	Weslave Travelling Man Ch Highclare Strands of Gold	Miss G A Tully	Mrs P Lucking
Sh Ch Northoaks Sea Breeze	B	15.3.90	Sh Ch Dalati Sibrwd Menstonia Moonlight Mist	Owner	Mr C J Anderson
Sh Ch Solva Turandot	B	10.4.91	Sh Ch Ferndel Farmers Boy Solva Rosina	Owner	Mrs J M Luckett-Roynon
Sh Ch Sweet Toffee Apple	B	28.8.91	Delkens Yankee Doodle Delkens Tivian	Mr K T Turner	Mrs P Catling
Sh Ch Dalville Dancing Water	D	19.7.93	Ferndel Dancing Brave Dalville Tropical Tango	Mr & Mrs G Dalrymple	Thirlwell & Dalrymple
Sh Ch Melladomina Molly Mu	B	12.4.94	Weslave Weeping Willow Sh Ch Melladomina Red Tulip	Owner	Ms P A G Lazenby
Sh Ch Solva Troilus	D	23.9.92	Sh Ch Dalati Sioni Sh Ch/Ir Ch Solva Arabella	Mrs J M Luckett-Roynon	Mr & Mrs S J Browne
Sh Ch Heronsmere Damask Rose	B	1.7.91	Sh Ch Fiveacres Firecrest Sh Ch Russethill Rose Garland at Heronsmere	Owner	Mrs B Simpson
Sh Ch Weslave Back to the Future	D	23.10.93	Sh Ch Weslave Will O' The Wisp Weslave Ruby Tiger	Owner	Mr & Mrs J Hartley

Appendix G
Classification

Annex A to F Regulations
Definitions of Classes at Championship, Open, Limited, Sanction and Primary Shows

Printed with kind permission of The Kennel Club.

1. For the purposes of Kennel Club Show Regulations, the term 'Variety Class' also applies to 'Stakes Classes'.
A Variety Class is one in which more than one breed or variety of a breed can compete. There must be no stipulation that exhibits must be entered for Variety Classes as well as Breed Classes and no minimum number of classes in which a dog must be entered may be fixed.

2. Wins at Championship Shows in breed classes where Challenge Certificates are not on offer shall be counted as wins at Open Shows.

3. Show awards issued by the Irish Kennel Club which count towards the title of Champion, shall be five point Green Stars or more.

4. In the following Definitions, a Challenge Certificate includes any Show award that counts towards the title of Champion under the rules of any governing body recognised by The Kennel Club.

5. No class may be provided unless a definition of the class is given in the Schedule. Where a breed is separately classed an Open class for the breed must be provided at Championship, Open and Limited Shows and a Post Graduate class must be provided at Sanction Shows and a Best of Breed declared in accordance with the provisions of Regulation F(1)7.b.
Championship, Open and Limited Shows – judged on the Group system must schedule at least one Any Variety Not Separately Classified class, unless a class for every breed eligible for classification is provided.

6. No class higher than Post Graduate may be offered at a Sanction Show.

7. No class higher than Maiden may be offered at a Primary Show.

8. No dog is eligible for exhibition at a Limited, Sanction or Primary Show which has won a Challenge Certificate or obtained any Show award that counts towards the title of Champion under the rules of any governing body recognised by The Kennel Club.

9. Subject to the following and to any individual Show Regulations, Show Committees may offer such prizes and make such classification and definitions thereof as they think fit except that:

(a) All classes advertised in the Schedule of the Show must be clearly defined in the Schedule, in accordance with The Kennel Club Show Regulations.

(b) If any class be provided with a definition other than those defined below, the word 'Special' must precede the name of such class.

(c) The words Grand or Challenge must not be used in the designation of any class of Prize for which an entrance fee is charged and for which entry has to be made prior to the day of the Show.

The word 'Champion' can only be used in the designation of the Champion Variety class as previously defined, and further explained in the Champion class definition in these Regulations.

(d) Sweepstake classes may only be scheduled in respect of Brace, Team, Stud Dog, Brood Bitch ,Veteran and Breeders classes only; entry fees may be given as prize money in such proportion as the Committee of the Show may determine.

In the following definitions:
* applies to Championship and Open Shows only.
** applies to Limited, Sanction and Primary Shows only.

Where there is no qualification, the Definition applies to all types of Shows.

In estimating the number of awards won, all wins up to and including the seventh day before the day of closing of entries shall be counted when entering for any class. Wins in Variety Classes do not count for entry in Breed Classes, but when entering for Variety Classes, wins in both Breed and Variety Classes must be counted. A First Prize does not include a Special Prize of whatever value.

Minor Puppy For dogs of 6 and not exceeding 9 calendar months of age on the first day of the Show.

Puppy For dogs of 6 and not exceeding 12 calendar months of age on the first day of the Show.

Junior For dogs of 6 and not exceeding 18 calendar months of age on the first day of the Show.

Beginners *For owner, handler or exhibit not having won a first prize at any Show.

**For owner, handler or exhibit not having won a first prize at any Show.

Maiden *For dogs which have not won a Challenge Certificate or a First Prize at an Open or Championship Show (Minor Puppy, Special Minor Puppy, Puppy and Special Puppy classes excepted, whether restricted or not.
**For dogs which have not won a First Prize at any Show (Minor Puppy, Special Minor Puppy, Puppy and Special Puppy classes excepted whether restricted or not).

Novice *For dogs which have not won a Challenge Certificate or 3 or more First Prizes at Open and Championship Show (Minor Puppy, Special Minor Puppy, Puppy and Special Puppy classes excepted, whether restricted or not).
**For dogs which have not won 3 or more First Prizes at any Show (Minor Puppy, Special Minor Puppy, Puppy and Special Puppy classes excepted, whether restricted or not).
Tyro *For dogs which have not won a Challenge Certificate or 5 or more First Prizes at Open and Championship Shows (Minor classes excepted, whether restricted or not).
**For dogs which have not won 5 or more First Prizes at any Show (Minor Puppy, Special Minor Puppy, Puppy and Special Puppy classes excepted, whether restricted or not).

Debutante *For dogs which have not won a Challenge Certificate or a First Prize at a Championship Show (Minor Puppy, Special Minor Puppy, Puppy and Special Puppy classes excepted, whether restricted or not).
**For dogs which have not won a First Prize at an Open or Championship Show (Minor Puppy, Special Minor Puppy, Puppy and Special Puppy classes excepted, whether restricted or not).

Undergraduate *For dogs which have not won a Challenge Certificate or 3 or more First Prizes at Championship Shows (Minor Puppy, Special Minor Puppy, Puppy and Special Puppy classes excepted, whether restricted or not).
**For dogs which have not won 3 or more First Prizes at Championship Shows (Minor Puppy, Special Minor Puppy, Puppy and Special Puppy classes excepted, whether restricted or not).

Graduate *For dogs which have not won a Challenge Certificate or 4 or more First Prizes at Championship Shows in Graduate, Post Graduate, Minor Limit, Mid Limit, Limit and Open classes, whether restricted or not.
**For dogs which have not won 4 or more First Prizes at Championship Shows in Graduate, Post Graduate, Minor Limit, Mid Limit, Limit and Open classes, whether restricted or not.

Post Graduate *For dogs which have not won a Challenge Certificate or 5 or more First Prizes at Championship Shows in Graduate, Post Graduate, Minor Limit, Mid Limit, Limit and Open classes, whether restricted or not.
**For dogs which have not won 5 or more First Prizes at Championship Shows in Graduate, Post Graduate, Minor Limit, Mid Limit, Limit and Open classes, whether restricted or not.

Minor Limit *For dogs which have not won 2 Challenge Certificates or three or more First Prizes in all at Championship Shows in Minor Limit, Mid Limit, Limit and Open classes, confined to the breed, whether restricted or not at Shows where Challenge Certificates were offered for the breed.
**For dogs which have not won 3 or more First Prizes in all at Open and Championship Shows in Minor Limit, Mid Limit, Limit and Open classes, confined to the breed, whether restricted or not.

Mid Limit *For dogs which have not won 3 Challenge Certificates or five or more First Prizes in all at Championship Shows in Mid Limit, Limit and Open classes, confined to the breed, whether restricted or not at Shows where Challenge Certificates were offered for the breed.
**For dogs which have not won 5 or more First Prizes in all at Open and Championship Shows in Mid Limit, Limit and Open classes, confined to the breed, whether restricted or not.

Limit *For dogs which have not won 3 Challenge Certificates under 3 different judges or 7 or more First Prizes in all, at Championship Shows in Limit and Open Classes, confined to the breed, whether restricted or not, at Shows where Challenge Certificates were offered to the breed.
**For dogs which have not won 7 or more First Prizes in all at Open and Championship Shows in Limit and Open classes, confined to the breed, whether restricted or not.
Open: *For all dogs of the breed for which the class is provided and eligible for entry at the Show.

Veteran For dogs of not less than 7 years of age on the first day of the show.

Champion For dogs which have been confirmed a Champion, Show Champion or Field Trial Champion. Champion classes may not be scheduled for individual breeds or varieties of breed.

Rare Breeds Confined to those breeds not granted Challenge Certificates in the current year, with the exception of those breeds whose registration is confined to the Imported Register.

Field Trial For dogs which have won prizes, Diplomas or Merit or Certificates of Merit in actual competition at a Field Trial held under Kennel Club or Irish Kennel Club Field Trial Regulations.

Working Trial For dogs which have won prizes in competition at a Bloodhound Working Trial and Kennel Club licensed Working Trials, held under Kennel Club Regulations.

Stud Dog For stud dogs and at least two progeny of which only the progeny must be entered and exhibited in a breed class at the Show.

Brood Bitch For brood bitches and at least two progeny of which only the progeny must be entered and exhibited in a breed class at the Show.

Progeny For a dog or bitch, accompanied by at least three of its registered progeny. The dog or bitch not necessarily entered in another class however, all progeny having been entered and exhibited in another class. The dog or bitch and the progeny need not be registered in the same ownership.

Brace For 2 exhibits (either sex or mixed) or one breed belonging to the same exhibitor, each exhibit having been entered in some class other than Brace or Team.

Team For 3 or more exhibits (either sex or mixed) of one breed belonging to the same exhibitor, each exhibit having been entered in some class other than Brace or Team.

Breeders For dogs bred by the exhibitor.

Imported Register When an Interim Breed Standard has been approved by The Kennel Club, breeds whose registration is confined to the Imported Register may be exhibited in this class only, and are ineligible for any other competition whatsoever.

Any Variety Not Separately Classified For breeds of dog for which no separate breed classes are scheduled.

Classified Kennel Club Junior Organisation Stakes For Any Variety dog or bitch exhibited and handled by a member of the Kennel Club Junior Organisation and registered, either solely or jointly, in the member's name or in the name of a member of the family, resident at the member's address.

Not for Competition Societies may at their discretion, accept Not for Competition entries. Societies may accept such entries from breeds of dog not included within the title of the Society and at Shows held over more than one day, such entries may be accepted on any day from any breed.

Useful Addresses

The Kennel Club
1–5 Clarges Street
Piccadilly
London W1Y 8AB
Tel: 0171 493 6651

The American Kennel Club
51 Maddison Avenue
New York
NY 10010
USA
Tel: 001 212 696 8200
Fax: 001 212 696 8329

Australian National Kennel Council
PO Box 285
Red Hill South
Victoria 3937
Australia
Tel 00 61 015 304 338
Fax 00 61 059 89 6343

Canadian Kennel Club
89 Skyway Avenue
Etobicoke
Ontario
Canada M9W 6R4
Tel: 001 416 675 5511
Fax: 001 416 675 6506

Danish Kennel Club
Jersie Strand
DK 2680
Solrod Strand
Denmark
Tel: 0045 56 14 74 00
Fax: 0045 53/14 30 03

Dutch Kennel Club
Emmalaan 16
PO Box 75091
NL 1070 Ax
Amsterdam Z
Tel: 00 31 20 68 644 471
Fax: 00 31 31 20 67 10846

Finnish Kennel Club
Kamreerintie 8
SF 02770
Espoo
Finland
Tel: 00 358 0 805 7722
Fax 00 358/0805 46 03

French Kennel Club
155 Avenue Jean Jaures
F 93535
Paris-Aubervilliers Cedex
France
Tel: 00 33 1 49 37 54 00
Fax: 00 33 1 49 37 01 20

New Zealand Kennel Club
Prosser Street
Eldson
Private Bag 50903
Porirua
Wellington
New Zealand
Tel: 00 64 4 237 4489
Fax: 00 64 4237 0721

Swedish Kennel Club
S-163 85 Spanga
Sweden
Tel: 00 46 08 795 30 00
Fax: 00 46 08 795 3040

British Veterinary Association
7 Mansfield Street
London W1M 0AT
Tel: 0171 636 6541

Council of Docked Breeds
Secretary: Ginette Elliott
Marsburg Kennels
Whitehall Lane
Thorpe-le-Soken
Essex CO16 0AF

Dog World
Somerfield House
Wotton Road
Ashford Kent TN23 6LW
Tel: 01233 621877
Fax: 01233 645699

Our Dogs
5 Oxford Road
Station Approach
Manchester M60 1SX
Tel: 0161 228 1984
Fax: 0161 236 0892

Photo: John Curtis

Index

q

r

s

t